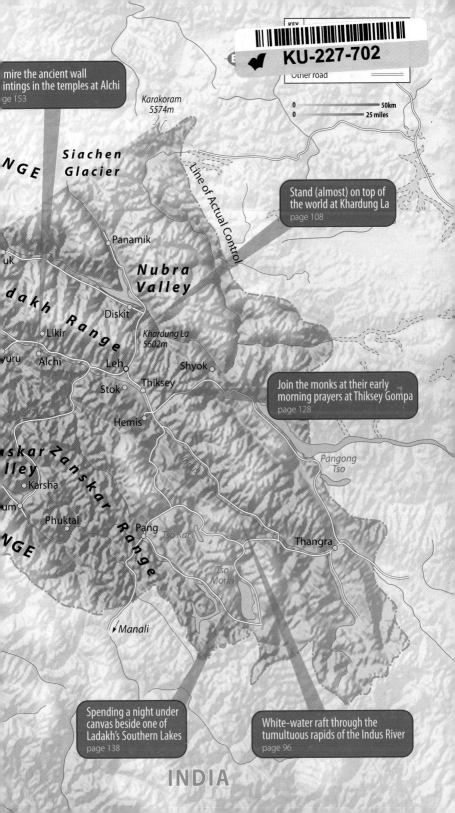

mire the ancient wall
intings in the temples at Alchi
ge 153

Karakoram
5574m

Siachen
Glacier

NGE

Line of Actual Control

Other road

0   50km
0   25 miles

Stand (almost) on top of
the world at Khardung La
page 108

Panamik

Nubra
Valley

uk

dakh *Range*

Diskit

Likir

Khardung La
5602m

yuru

Alchi

Leh

Shyok

Stok

Thiksey

Join the monks at their early
morning prayers at Thiksey Gompa
page 128

Hemis

Indus

Pangong
Tso

skar *Zanskar*

lley

Karsha

Range

um

Phuktal

Pang

Tso Kar

Thangra

NGE

Tso
Moriri

Manali

Spending a night under
canvas beside one of
Ladakh's Southern Lakes
page 138

White-water raft through the
tumultuous rapids of the Indus River
page 96

INDIA

Kashmir
Don't
miss...

**Houseboats of
Srinagar**
Relax for hours in one of
India's floating palaces on
Dal or Nagin lakes (JP/SH)
page 199

Thiksey Gompa
Join the monks in their early
morning prayers at this monastery
in Ladakh (MEP) pages 128–30

Kashmir
Jammu • Kashmir Valley
Ladakh • Zanskar

the Bradt Travel Guide

Sophie and Max Lovell-Hoare

edition

|

www.bradtguides.com

Bradt Travel Guides Ltd, UK
The Globe Pequot Press Inc, USA

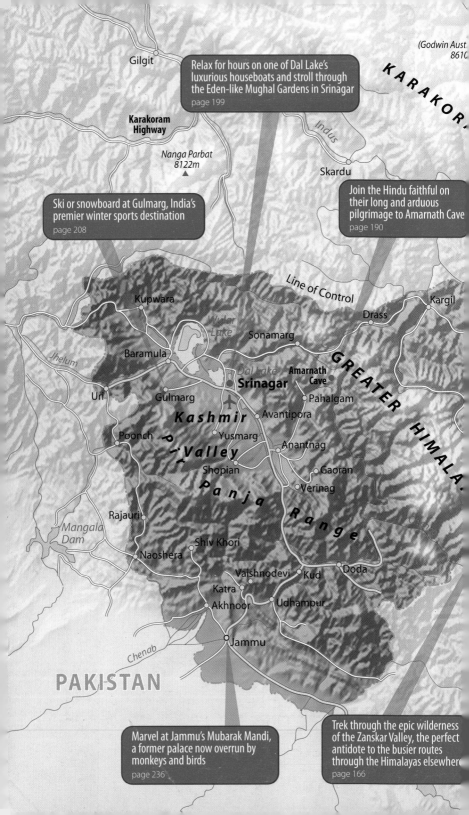

Relax for hours on one of Dal Lake's luxurious houseboats and stroll through the Eden-like Mughal Gardens in Srinagar
page 199

Join the Hindu faithful on their long and arduous pilgrimage to Amarnath Cave
page 190

Ski or snowboard at Gulmarg, India's premier winter sports destination
page 208

Marvel at Jammu's Mubarak Mandi, a former palace now overrun by monkeys and birds
page 236

Trek through the epic wilderness of the Zanskar Valley, the perfect antidote to the busier routes through the Himalayas elsewhere
page 166

Gilgit

(Godwin Aust. 8610

KARAKOR

Karakoram Highway

Indus

Nanga Parbat 8122m

Skardu

Line of Control

Kargil

Kupwara

Wular Lake

Drass

Sonamarg

GREATER HIMALA.

Baramula

Jhelum

Dal Lake

Srinagar

Amarnath Cave

Uri

Gulmarg

Pahalgam

Kashmir

Avantipora

Valley

Yusmarg

Anantnag

Poonch

Pir

Shopian

Gaoran

Verinag

Panjal

Rajauri

Range

Mangala Dam

Shiv Khori

Naoshera

Vaishnodevi

Kud

Doda

Katra

Akhnoor

Udhampur

Jammu

Chenab

PAKISTAN

Chadar winter trek
This six-day hike along a frozen river is the ultimate challenge for visitors to Zanskar (F/DT) pages 176–7

Amarnath Yatra
Join Hindu pilgrims making the annual journey to the Amarnath Cave, one of their religion's most sacred shrines (AZ/A) page 190

Khardung La
Stand (almost) on top of the world at this pass along the earth's highest motorable road (AS/DT) pages 108–9

Kashmir in colour

top — Kayaking, sailing and windsurfing are all popular at Srinigar's Dal Lake in summer (J&KT) page 202

above left — Gulmarg is India's winter sports capital; its gondola transports skiers and snowboarders up to a height of 4,267m (J&KT) pages 208–11

above right — The ever-changing colours of Pangong Tso entrance visitors, and its beautiful scenery has provided the backdrop to many a Bollywood movie (KM) pages 138–9

above Built in memory of Indira Gandhi, Srinagar's stunning Tulip Garden is ablaze with colour in the springtime (J&KT) page 203

right The mighty Indus River snakes through Ladakh; its rapids are ideal for white-water rafting (ST/SH) page 28

below The Zabarwan mountain range is home to the Dachigam National Park and harbours wildlife including leopard cats and the endangered hangul (J&KT) page 9

Sophie and Max Lovell-Hoare first met at the Royal Society for Asian Affairs, two months before Sophie went up to Cambridge to read Hindi and Urdu. India remained central to their relationship: they lived in Rajasthan in 2006–07, and have subsequently undertaken projects in Delhi, Jammu and Kashmir (J&K) and West Bengal with their company, Maximum Exposure Productions. The company works in economic development and investment promotion, particularly in the fields of tourism, mining, infrastructure and energy.

Sophie and Max have also written Bradt guides to South Sudan, Sudan, Tajikistan and Uzbekistan, and updated the guides to Kazakhstan and Kyrgyzstan.

AUTHORS' STORY

The crowds were biblical in proportion, and the scene could well have been described in the Gospels. Unable to reach the assembly grounds by vehicle, we left the road and followed on foot the thousands of families picking their way first across the dusty plain and then through the higgledy-piggledy, low-rise alleyways of Choglamsar. Fathers carried children upon their shoulders; mothers guided elderly relatives by the hand, while balancing their picnics, umbrellas and rugs on their backs or under an arm. Huge numbers of people were moving across the landscapes, striding out with a feeling of purpose, of expectation and excitement.

When we arrived, the grounds were already full, the grass invisible beneath a sea of picnic blankets, people and their parasols. The sun beat down, and we found the corner of a blanket to share, the good-natured hubbub of voices all around.

And then he began to speak. You could have heard a pin drop. Tens of thousands of faces all turned to the lectern where the Dalai Lama stood, hanging on his every word. Loudspeakers relayed his message in Ladakhi, in Tibetan and in English, and for the next two hours, he preached. We were utterly transfixed.

Before coming to J&K we'd had little exposure to Buddhism, at least not in its living sense. The statuary and the gompas are undoubtedly striking, but it was the gentle spirituality of the people that made the greatest impression. Religion here is a central component of life: Buddhism, Hinduism and Islam each has had a profound impact on the way of life in different parts of the state. Faith permeates everyday actions here, and it prompted us to look at ourselves and reflect on our own values in a way that was quite unexpected.

PUBLISHER'S FOREWORD
Adrian Phillips, Publishing Director

In their introduction to this book, Sophie and Max observe that the landscapes and people of Kashmir linger on your mind long after you leave. I couldn't agree more. I visited a few years ago (trekking into the Ladakh range to write a newspaper piece on efforts to protect the snow leopard) and it's a trip I still think about often. The shifting colours of the mountains are extraordinary, as is the sight of golden eagles spread against the sky and blue sheep leaping among rocks high on the slopes. I remember staying a night with a local family in a remote village; they spoke no English, but we spent a happy evening together sitting on the floor, drinking butter tea and making pasta for our dinner. The region's pleasures might be simple, but they are vivid and life-enhancing. Sophie and Max's guide will help you bank a treasure of memories.

First edition published July 2014
Bradt Travel Guides Ltd, IDC House, The Vale, Chalfont St Peter, Bucks SL9 9RZ, England
www.bradtguides.com
Print edition published in the USA by The Globe Pequot Press Inc,
PO Box 480, Guilford, Connecticut 06437-0480

Text copyright © 2014 Sophie and Max Lovell-Hoare
Maps copyright © 2014 Bradt Travel Guides Ltd
Photographs copyright © 2014 individual photographers (see below)
Project Manager: Maisie Fitzpatrick
Cover research: Pepi Bluck, Perfect Picture

ISBN: 978 1 84162 396 2 (print)
e-ISBN: 978 1 84162 878 3 (e-pub)
e-ISBN: 978 1 84162 879 0 (mobi)

British Library Cataloguing in Publication Data
A catalogue record for this book is available from the British Library

Photographers
Age Fotostock: Franch Bienewaldimage (FB/AF); Alamy: Altaf Zargar/Zuma Press (AZ/A); FLPA: Theo Allofs/Minden Pictures (TA/FLPA), John Holmes (JH/FLPA), David Hosking (DH/FLPA), Imagebroker (I/FLPA), Imagebroker/Olaf Kräger (I/OK/FLPA), Konrad Wothe/Minden Pictures (KW/FLPA); Jammu & Kashmir Tourism (J&KT); Keith Mackintosh (KM); Maximum Exposure Productions (MEP); Shutterstock: Curioso (C/SH), Natalia Davidovich (ND/SH), f9photo (f9/SH), filmlandscape (f/SH), Attila JANDI (AJ/SH), Pius Lee (PL/SH), Jittapat Prompong (JP/SH), Seree Tansrisawat (ST/SH), Zzvet (Z/SH)

Front cover Shikara on Dal Lake, Srinagar (FB/AF)
Back cover Pangong Tso (KM)
Title page Dal Lake, Srinagar (f/SH); Thagthog Gompa (MEP); steep rockface, Ladakh (C/SH)

Maps David McCutcheon FBCart.S

Typeset from the authors' disc by Ian Spick, Bradt Travel Guides
Production managed by Jellyfish Print Solutions; printed in Malta
Digital conversion by the Firsty Group

Acknowledgements

Researching and writing *Kashmir* has taken almost a year and involved the input of quite literally hundreds of people, many consciously offering assistance and advice, and others quite unaware of their contribution. We are hugely grateful to everyone who has helped us along the way, but want to express our particular thanks to the following.

For their wonderful tint boxes, which have certainly enhanced our understanding of Kashmir and its culture, and given you additional, well-informed perspectives, we're grateful to Keith Mackintosh (*www.nomadical.co.uk*), Bryn Kewley, Steve Dew-Jones, Ben Tavener (*www.bentavener.com*), Tanzin Norbu (*www. mountaintribalvision.com*), Hilary Stock and Nicole Hydrick.

In the UK, and going back a little in time, Aishu Kumar, Sudeshna Guha and Katie Commons showed great patience and good humour in the South Asian Studies department, and it's thanks to them that at least some of the Urdu and Mughal history stuck. Sudeshna, you can give us all the corrections over coffee!

Maisie Fitzpatrick and Rachel Fielding at Bradt have been hugely patient and diligent from the start to finish of the guide's production. Thank you both. Sam Kirton at Keene Communications arranged our flights with Jet Airways, and has certainly given us a taste for travelling business class. It was great to travel in style.

Before, during and after our research trip, in the UK and in Leh, Tanzin Norbu and Tansy Troy gave us invaluable advice and warm hospitality, as did their wonderful extended family in Zanskar. In Leh we also benefited hugely from the time, thought, expertise and consideration of G M Kakpori (*www.hotelcaravancentre.com*), Dorje and Konchok (*www.dorjeguesthouse.com*) and Javeed Iqbal (*www.dreamladakh.com*).

In Kargil, we were able to truly appreciate the area's long and distinguished history thanks to the sterling efforts of Mohd Hamza and Mohd Ali of the Sewak Travel Company, and also Aziz and Muzammil Hussain at the Central Asian Museum.

In Srinagar we were inspired by the vision and pragmatism of Talat Parvez at J&K Tourism, and hugely appreciate the time he took to show and explain to us how tourism in the state is developing. The Wangnoos (*www.wangnoohouseboats. com*) on Nagin Lake treated us like family and it was a fascinating experience to share with them a traditional Kashmiri wedding and the delicious *waazwaan*. On Dal Lake, Ajaz Khar (*www.chicagohouseboats.com*) humbled us both with his warmth, generosity and eloquence. We truly value your friendship.

And last but certainly not least, our profound thanks and plenty of hugs to Mum and Dad, Ash and Carolyn, Grandma and Pa, Bijan and Sam, and Martha. India has left its mark on most of us: the desire to return, particularly to while away the hours on a houseboat on the lake, is something we all can share.

Contents

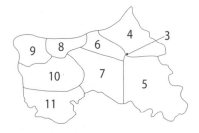

LIST OF MAPS

NOTE ABOUT MAPS

KEYS AND SYMBOLS

Maps include alphabetical keys covering the locations of those places to stay, eat or drink that are featured in the book. Note that regional maps may not show all hotels and restaurants in the area: other establishments may be located in towns shown on the map.

GRIDS AND GRID REFERENCES

Several maps use gridlines to allow easy location of sites. Map grid references are listed in square brackets after the name of the place or site of interest in the text, with page number followed by grid number, eg: [88 B3].

Introduction

Gar firdaus ae baruhe zamin ast
Hamin astu hamin astu hamin ast.

If there is heaven on earth,
It is here, it is here, it is here.

Emperor Jahangir, 17th century

Whether you were fortunate enough in times gone by to be a Mughal emperor, a civil servant of the Raj, a hippie on the hippie trail, or are a modern visitor discovering Kashmir now for the very first time, you cannot fail to be impressed: the incredible beauty of the natural landscapes, the richness of the history and the warmth and diversity of the people get deep under your skin and linger on your mind long after you have had to leave. Standing on the veranda of the Vivanta by Taj, looking down across Dal and Nagin lakes with Hari Parbat peaking up through the mist, the sunlight glinting on the water as a solitary *shikara* paddles by, brings a lump to your throat. If there is heaven on earth, can it be anywhere else but here?

The geographical scope of this guide is the Indian state of Jammu and Kashmir (J&K), a vast stretch of northern India encompassing lands from the plains of Jammu, up through the Kashmir Valley to Srinagar, and east through the mountainous landscapes of Ladakh. Although a successor to the princely state of the same name, this earlier, far larger territory has been divided as a result of 20th century conflicts, and has only recently emerged from a period of extreme trauma: the damage to the land, the economy and, most importantly, the people, has been severe. But, like a phoenix rising from the ashes, there is justifiable optimism for a far brighter future.

Ladakh and Zanskar, virtually unknown to visitors in the 1980s, benefited from the troubles in the Kashmir Valley as tourists looked for new areas to explore. The much-improved road infrastructure would not have materialised if it weren't for military demand, and now that the army presence is decreasing, this physical legacy is proving a great boon for tourists eager to explore the likes of the Nubra Valley, the Dardic villages around Dha-Hanu, and the breathtaking turquoise southern lakes.

The fall-off of foreign visitor numbers also encouraged J&K's travel agents and hoteliers to work hard to appeal to India's domestic tourist market. Family-friendly resort hotels have already popped up in the hill stations along the Kashmir Valley; the railway network is being extended and will ultimately reach as far as Srinagar; and better transport links and hotel accommodation have already been built around key Hindu and Muslim pilgrimage sites. The state's director of tourism, Talat Parvez, is taking a proactive approach to both development and promotion, ensuring there is a new generation of activities and attractions, from urban cable cars to boat clubs, visitor centres to eco-reserves, to widen the state's appeal and reinforce the message that J&K is once again fully open for business.

Ajaz Khar, our friend at Chicago Houseboats in Srinagar, has a clear vision for what he would like to see happening in his homeland. 'We want peace to continue in Kashmir, so that travellers will come again to appreciate the wonders of our gorgeous mountains and valleys, and so that our indigenous crafts can continue, and our business can thrive,' he says. 'We look forward to sharing with others our easy-going spirituality, our joy in musical and poetic evenings, our love of good food and good company. Mostly, like others in the world, we want our families to remain stable, our children to be educated, happy and properly fed, and our land to be respected again for its tremendous beauty.'

Though Ajaz expresses this unusually eloquently, it is a view shared by ordinary people across J&K, and most fervently in the valley itself. The war is over, and the people and their culture have survived. Now is the time for them to again celebrate what they have, to share it with others, and to do so with justified pride. Any guests fortunate enough to be on the receiving end of such hospitality will realise, like generations before them, that Kashmir is indeed a slice of heaven on earth.

FEEDBACK REQUEST AND UPDATES WEBSITE

At Bradt Travel Guides we're aware that guidebooks start to go out of date on the day they're published – and that you, our readers, are out there in the field doing research of your own. You'll find out before us when a fine new family-run hotel opens or a favourite restaurant changes hands and goes downhill. So why not write and tell us about your experiences? Contact us on ☎ 01753 893444 or e info@bradtguides.com. We will forward emails to the author who may post updates on the Bradt website at www.bradtupdates.com/kashmir. Alternatively you can add a review of the book to www.bradtguides.com or Amazon.

FOLLOW BRADT

For the latest news, special offers and competitions, subscribe to the Bradt newsletter via the website www.bradtguides.com and follow Bradt on:

f www.facebook.com/BradtTravelGuides
🐦 @BradtGuides
📷 @bradtguides
ⓟ pinterest.com/bradtguides

Part One

GENERAL INFORMATION

JAMMU AND KASHMIR AT A GLANCE

Location A state of India located mostly in the Himalayan mountains. International border with China in the north and east; the Line of Control separates it from Pakistani-controlled territories in the west and northwest.

Area 222,236km² (85,806 square miles)

Climate Varies from subtropical to mountain desert depending on altitude

Population est. 13m (2013)

Life expectancy 65.8 (male), 68.1 (female)

Capital Jammu (winter), Srinagar (summer)

Other main towns Kargil, Leh

Main exports Agricultural produce, handicrafts

GDP US$12.6 billion (2012–13)

Official language Urdu. English, Hindi, Ladakhi and Kashmiri are also widely spoken.

Religions Islam, Hinduism, Buddhism

Currency Indian rupee (Rs)

Exchange rate £1=Rs99, €1=Rs81, US$1=Rs59 (May 2014)

National airline Air India

International dialling code +91

Time GMT + 5½ hours

Electric voltage 240v

Weights and measures Metric

Flag Orange, white and green horizontal stripes with a *chakra* in the centre

National anthem 'Jana Gana Mana'

Major sports Hockey and ice hockey, polo, water sports, skiing

Public holidays* 26 January (Republic Day), 27 February (Maha Shivaratri), 17 March (Holi), 1 April (Bank Holiday), 14 April (Dr Ambedkar Jayanti), 14 May (Buddha Purnima), 25 July (Jumat-ul-Wida), 29 July (Eid al Fitr), 15 August (Independence Day), 18 August (Janmashtami), 30 September (Bank Holiday), 2 October (Mahatma Gandhi's Birthday), 4 October (Dussehra), 6 October (Eid al Zuha), 23 October (Diwali), 4 November (Muharram), 6 November (Guru Nanak Jayanti), 25 December (Christmas Day)

* These dates are correct for 2014. As some of the religious festivals are calculated according to the lunar calendar, dates will change from year to year. See page 64 for festival dates up to 2016.

1

Background Information

GEOGRAPHY

When talking about the political geography of Kashmir, there are two things to consider: the geography of greater Kashmir, and the more limited geography of J&K state.

Greater Kashmir (also known as the Princely State of Kashmir and Jammu) includes territories administered by India, Pakistan and China. In the west are the provinces of Azad Kashmir and Gilgit-Baltistan; to the north and east are Aksai Chin and the Trans-Karakoram Tract; and the south and central parts are the regions of Jammu, the Kashmir Valley and Ladakh. Historically nomads, traders and the population at large could move back and forth across Kashmir (and beyond) at will. This mobility ended with the solidification of borders following conflicts between India and Pakistan, and India and China, in the 20th century (see *History*, page 14), and Kashmir has been fractured ever since.

Jammu and Kashmir (referred to in this book as J&K), however, is a state of the Republic of India. The United Nations refers to it as Indian-administered Kashmir, while the government of Pakistan calls it Indian-occupied Kashmir. The semantics are politically charged.

J&K is made up of three divisions – Jammu, the Kashmir Valley and Ladakh – and is further divided into 22 districts, most of which take their name from their major town. The state has two principal cities, Jammu and Srinagar, and a number of smaller towns including Kargil and Leh.

The state's physical geography is diverse due to its varied elevations: the biogeography varies from barren deserts to subtropical pine forests, alpine meadows to scrub and steppe. The 70km-long Siachen Glacier is the longest in the Himalayas, and the waters of the Chenab, Indus, Jhelum, Ravi and Tawi rivers have cut valleys through the rock and continue to irrigate the land. Much of the landscape is mountainous thanks to the Himalayan, Hindu Kush, Karakoram, Ladakh and Pir Panjal ranges; the highest peaks in the state are the 7,135m Nun and the only slightly shorter Kun at 7,077m, both of which lie in the Suru Valley south of Kargil.

GEOLOGY The Indian Himalayas, which cover the vast part of J&K state, were created by the collision of the Indo-Australian and European tectonic plates, a process which has been ongoing for the past 50 million years. The edge of both of these plates is low-density crust, which is why they have thrust up and folded into the mountain range we see today. The Himalayas continue to grow at a rate of around 5mm per year, leading to intense seismic activity in the area.

Earthquakes Earthquakes are an ongoing concern in J&K as a result of the fact that the state straddles this tectonic fault line. Though most of the tremors are small

1

3

J&K has no oil, but there are small reserves of natural gas and semi-bituminous coal near to Jammu. Seams of low-grade coal are also found further north in the Kashmir Valley.

More interesting than its fossil fuels, however, are the mineral resources. There are significant bauxite and gypsum deposits around Udhampur, substantial quantities of thorium and uranium in Ladakh, and small amounts of copper, granite, halite, iron, marble, sulphur and zinc elsewhere in the state. It is also possible to find gemstones, including precious stones such as sapphires and rubies.

J&K's greatest natural resource is undoubtedly water. The Himalayan glaciers and meltwater feed the rivers of the subcontinent, providing water for more than a billion people, and not only irrigate the crops but can also be harnessed for hydro-power.

and cause only relatively minor rockfalls, there are eight to ten quakes each year measuring 4.0 magnitude or more on the Richter scale. Major earthquakes of 7.6 and 7.2 magnitude shook the state in 2005 and 2008 respectively, the former causing an estimated 100,000 deaths (mostly in Azad Kashmir) and displacing more than 3.5 million people.

CLIMATE

J&K has a varied climate due to the state's size and its variation in altitude and topography. Jammu has a humid, subtropical climate with summer temperatures well into the 40s (°C); a substantial drop in winter sees lows just above freezing. The area receives monsoon rains between June and September, and annual rainfall averages 1,100mm.

Srinagar is also subtropical and humid, though due to its increased altitude, temperatures are generally lower. Summer days touch a pleasant 30°C, but in winter there can be deep snow and temperatures hover around freezing during January and February. There is less rainfall here than in Jammu, though the spring can still be wet and we've been caught in storms and hail in September.

The climate up in Leh is dramatically different: it's a desert. Winters are long and harsh with months of deep snowfall and bitter temperatures: it can get as low as −28°C. There's little rainfall here – just a few millimetres each month – and for much of the year the days are warm and bright, albeit cooler at night.

In the last three to five years, however, Ladakh has experienced a marked shift in its weather, most likely due to climate change. Much less snow is falling, leading to concerns about the availability of water. In the same timeframe, however, there have also been huge and unanticipated cloudbursts: in August 2010 four inches of rain fell in just 30 minutes. Floods washed away villages, as well as homes in Leh, and more than 250 people were killed.

NATURAL HISTORY AND CONSERVATION

PALAEONTOLOGY J&K is rich in fossils on account of once having been at the bottom of the sea (see *Geology*, page 3). One of the oldest fossil beds, discovered by a British palaeontologist in 1886, is the Permian-period (approximately 260 million years old) Guryul Ravine to the south of Srinagar. The fossils found here, which are the remains of creatures that were wiped out during a period of mass extinction between the Permian and Triassic periods, are those of therapsids (large, reptilian land animals), small invertebrates, and primordial corals and plants. Though theoretically a protected site, the Guryul Ravine is allegedly mined for limestone and stone chips used in local cement factories.

Not far away, in the saffron fields of Pampore, Indian geologists have excavated one of the largest elephant fossils in the world: the skull alone measures 1.2m by 1.5m. Carbon dating has shown the fossil to be some 50,000 years old, revealing Kashmir must at that time have had a significantly different climate from the present day, as elephants are no longer found in the mountainous foothills.

The fossil record of Ladakh is particularly well preserved due to the dry climate and limited impact of humans. Ostracods and avian fossils have been found in large numbers around the southern lakes and Nubra Valley; palm leaf fossils in the Nidar Valley show there was once a tropical climate here; and fossilised woods have been found on both sides of the Indus River.

The Palaeontological Society of India (*http://palaeontologicalsociety.in*) publishes detailed reports on fossil sites in the country, as well as field guides, and occasionally delivers public lectures.

FLORA Partly due to the low population density, but also the diversity of climates, altitudes and eco-systems, J&K has the greatest biodiversity of any state in India. The varied natural environments are known to support 3,054 species of plant, of which 880 are found in Ladakh, though this does not include species of fungi and algae.

J&K's flora can be roughly split into three categories, reflecting the principal phyto-geographic regions. **Alpine desert vegetation** is found in Ladakh, typically at heights above 4,000m where there is little soil, little water and extremes of temperature. Trees are exceedingly scarce (and hence such areas are often referred to as being 'above the tree line'), and much of the flora you do see is either in small oases on river banks and surrounding springs, or is artificially irrigated and cultivated by man. Ladakh is known for its medicinal plants, however, and practitioners of *sowa rigpa* (traditional Tibetan medicine) will travel for days on foot to pick plants such as Himalayan larkspur (*Delphinium cashmerianum*), Himalayan mayapple (*Podophyllum hexandrum*), Himalayan rhubarb (*Rheum spiciformae*), tarragon (*Artemisia dracunculus*), atis (*Aconitum heterohyllum*) and manjistha (*Rubia cordifoliam*). WWF India produces a detailed field guide to Ladakhi flora, which can be downloaded for free from http://awsassets.wwfindia. org/downloads/field_guide_floral_diversity_of_ladakh.pdf.

In the Kashmir Valley, where temperatures are less extreme but rainfall is more frequent, there is **temperate vegetation** that abounds around the lakes and lagoons, and also in the Pir Panjal forests. Here there are plentiful fruit and nut trees, including pomegranate (*Punica granatum*), walnut (*Juglans regia*) and almond (*Prunus dulcis*). The trees are not only more numerous but taller and with thicker trunks. Many of the varieties found in this region are broad-leafed. There are both coniferous and deciduous forests, though the cedar forests (*Cedrus deodara*) in particular have been over-cut, a problem that dates back to at least the 1500s. Reforestation programmes are important for the state's future, and consequently sites such as the hill beneath Hari Parbat are being replanted and protected by the Department of Forestry.

In this temperate zone you will also find numerous aquatic plants, such as those that comprise the floating gardens in Srinagar (known as *Rad* in Kashmiri; see page 203). In addition to the many beautiful varieties of water lilies (*Nymphaeaceae*) and lotuses (*Nelumbo nucifera*), cucumbers (*Cucumis sativus*), tomatoes (*Solanum lycopersicum*) and members of the melon family (*Cucurbitaceae*, which includes gourds as well as the sweet melon fruit) grow particularly well in the nutrient-rich gardens. You will see the finest examples of these crops for sale at the floating vegetable market.

Saffron (*Crocus sativus*) grows particularly well in the fertile soil around Pampore and is an important export for the state (see box, page 215).

Further south around Jammu, where year-round temperatures are much warmer, **sub-tropical vegetation** is to be found. Trees and plants here are typically deciduous and require little water, though in higher areas (such as around Patnitop) you will again find evergreen forests of deodar (*Cedrus deodara*), and also types of *chir*, or pine (*Pinus*). At slightly lower altitude, in the foothills, the forests are of fir (*Abies pindrow*); there are pockets of oak trees (*Quercus*) east of Batote; and large, mixed forests to the south-west of Udhampur.

FAUNA J&K is home to a vast range of animals, and as Ladakh lies at the confluence of three zoogeographic zones, it is a superb place for spotting wildlife.

Mammals One of the most ubiquitous creatures in the mountains is the fat and fluffy **Himalayan marmot** (*Marmota caudate*), a close relative of the steppe marmots of Mongolia which, at least according to Stephen Fry on QI, have killed more people than any other mammal, as it is from marmots that the bubonic plague first made the leap to humans. Equally cute (but rather less lethal) are the **flying squirrels** (*Eoglaucomys fimbriatus*), which are relatively common in the west of J&K towards the Line of Control (LoC).

In all parts of the state you will see large numbers of herbivores, in particular domesticated sheep, goats, yak and dzo (a cross between a cow and a yak). The nomads' flocks are nothing unusual – most of them will be slaughtered at Eid and eaten – but now and then you'll come across a changthangi, or Pashmina goat, with its highly sought-after fleece that is used to make pashmina shawls.

The rarest of the wild herbivores is the critically endangered but stunningly beautiful **hangul** (*Cervus elaphus hanglu*). It is a subspecies of European red deer but has been hunted almost to extinction on account of its impressive antlers. The exact number of animals surviving in the wild is unknown, but there are thought to be between 400 and 500 in the Dachigam National Park (see page 207). With a good guide, patience and a little luck, you may also be fortunate enough to see Tibetan antelopes (*Pantholops hodgsonii*), Tibetan gazelles or goas (*Procapra picticaudata*), markhor (*capra falconeri*), Himalayan musk deer (*Moschus crysogater*) and wild yaks (*Bos grunniens*).

Easier to spot on account of their larger populations and frequent apathy towards the presence of humans are J&K's primates. The Rhesus macaque (*Macaca mulatta*) is an urban pest and steals much of its food from humans living nearby. They can occasionally be aggressive, especially if they think they're being challenged, so don't try to get too close. Far rarer is the tree-dwelling **Kashmir grey langur** (*Semnopithecus ajax*) which lives in alpine forests above 2,200m. Urban development has encroached on much of its natural habitat and populations have consequently fallen to the point that this langur is sadly now considered an endangered species.

J&K is home to a number of species of large carnivores, and if you are fortunate enough to see one it will be a highlight of your trip. In Ladakh, particularly in the Hemis National Park (see page 9), there are majestic **snow leopards** (*Uncia uncia*) and you can increase your chances of spotting one, albeit at a distance, by taking a winter trek to Zanskar with Tanzin Norbu (see page 30). They are painfully shy of people (and rightly so, given that they're attractive to illegal hunters), so be sure to carry binoculars. Here too you might see the strange-looking Pallas' cats (*Otocolobus manul*) with their distinctive markings. They are indigenous to the area but more often seen in central Asia.

There's a greater variety, and larger numbers, of **large carnivores** in the quieter parts of the Kashmir Valley, especially in mountainous areas towards the Line of Control where food is plentiful but the human population is still relatively small. Here you can hope to see Himalayan brown bear (*Ursus artos*), Himalayan black bear (*Ursus thibetanus*), Indian wild boar (*Sus scrofa cristatus*), leopards (*Panthera pardus*), jackals (*Canis aureus*), jungle cats (*Felis chaus*) and Indian wild dogs (Cuon alpinus). If you are travelling by car you're unlikely to see a thing, so be sure to plan at least a short trek on foot to get away from the roads and out to quieter locations where the wildlife will be more at ease.

The J&K Wildlife Protection Department (*www.jkwildlife.com*) produces an informative brochure on the state's endangered species, which includes close-up photos and advice on where and when the animals might be spotted. It can be downloaded for free from www.jkwildlife.com/pdf/wild_species.pdf. An equally useful resource, this time produced by WWF India and focused on Ladakh's mammals, can be downloaded from http://awsassets.wwfindia.org/downloads/field_guide_mammals_of_ladakh.pdf.

Birds   Around 150 species of avifauna have been spotted in J&K. Some of them are resident year round, and many more are seasonal visitors as the state lies beneath migration paths. The official state bird is the **black-necked crane** (*Grus nigricollis*); there are just 5,000 of these birds worldwide and its only breeding ground outside of China is Tso Moriri in Ladakh.

Nearly a quarter of the birds in J&K are aquatic, favouring either the muddy river banks or the pristine waters of the high-altitude lakes. Very common local residents include the little grebe (*Tachybaptus ruficollis*), the red-wattled lapwing (*Vanellus indicus*) and the common moorhen (*Gallinula chloropus*), which in Kashmiri is called the *tech*. The pheasant-tailed jacana (*Hydrophasianus chirurgus*) is a common summertime visitor, as is the whiskered tern (*Chlidonias hybridus*), while in the winter months you can expect to see common teals (*Anas crecca*) and northern pintails (*Anas acuta*) with their attractive, if rather unusual, bright blue beaks.

In the mountainous areas you will find J&K's **birds of prey**. Common kestrels (*Falco tinnunculus*) reside year-round near Gulmarg, and the Eurasian hobby (*Falco subbuteo*), a kind of falcon that migrates vast distances, spends its summers in the mountains around Pahalgam, where it is also possible to see Himalayan griffons (*Gyps himalayensis*). The state is also home to black kites (*Milvus migrans*), bearded vultures or lammergeiers (*Gypaetus barbatus*) and, occasionally, long-legged buzzards (*Buteo rufinus*).

J&K also has birds in glorious, bright colours that are a pleasure to spot for amateur and aficionado bird spotters alike. The Eurasian golden oriole (*Oriolus oriolus*), or *posh nool* as it is called in Kashmiri, is canary-yellow with a fetching black stripe; there's no prize for guessing the striking colouring on the blue throat (*Luscinia svecica*); the long-tailed minivet (*Pericrocotus ethologus*) is flame red and black; and the slaty-headed parakeet (*Psittacula himalayana*) has a plumage predominantly in gorgeous, pistachio green.

Reptiles and amphibians   Living in India you become quickly friendly with **geckos**, and visiting J&K is no different. The Ladakhian, or bow-fingered frontier gecko (*Cyrtodactylus stoliczkai*), is a small, stripy creature with a disproportionately

With thanks to Ben Tavener (www.bentavener.com)
Although the overall fauna of the Kashmir region has much in common with that of central Asia and the Tibetan Plateau, the birdlife of the region includes species from an even wider area, both due to migration routes, for example from warmer parts of India to Ladakh, and the fact that the area bridges both Oriental and Palaearctic avifauna regions, even incorporating species from the Mediterranean. All this gives the chance for highly rewarding birding.

Some regional specialities to look out for include Kashmir flycatcher, Kashmir nuthatch, Tibetan snowcock, Tibetan sandgrouse, Tibetan blackbird, Himalayan jungle-crow, Himalayan (white-tailed) rubythroat and Himalayan woodpecker, as well as the stunning iridescent Himalayan monal.

Other birder favourites include the red-fronted serin, black francolin, brahminy (ruddy) shelduck, long-tailed shrike, blue rock thrush, blue-cheeked bee-eater, and fire-capped and rufous-naped tits, while summer visitors include the hoopoe and the charismatic black-necked crane, which breeds in parts of Ladakh. Two other species of crane – demoiselle and Siberian – can also be found here. Brown-flanked bush warbler, Tickell's leaf warbler and variegated laughingthrush will likely be on keener birders' target lists.

Globally important populations of raptors, including Indian peregrine falcon, lammergeier, Himalayan griffon, white-eyed buzzard, crested honey-buzzard and steppe and golden eagles, are resident here.

Multiple species of finch (including plain mountain-finch, spectacled finch, pink-browed rosefinch), accentor (including robin accentor), bunting (such as white-capped bunting), redstart and wheatear reside here, helping birders to healthy list totals and a flurry of lifers. Take time to record all European species you have seen before, as some of the region's subspecies will likely be candidates for future splits.

For an up-to-date list of birds in Kashmir, see www.kashmirnetwork.com/birds. The site is curated by amateur naturalist Dr Bakshi Jehangir.

large head. It comes from the area around Dras. There are also four different species of **iguana**, including Theobald's toad-headed agama (*Phrynocephalus theobaldi*) and the indigenous Kashmir rock agama (*Laudakia tuberculata*).

A variety of **snakes**, both venomous and non-venomous, are found across J&K, though fortunately they avoid people as much as they can. The poisonous ones (and so the ones you really should try not to step on) include the Indian cobra (*Naja naja*), which is considered sacred in Hindu mythology and, despite protection under the 1972 Indian Wildlife Protection Act, is still sometimes used by snake charmers; the rat snake (*Zamenis longissimus*), a very long constrictor that feeds principally on rodents and birds; and the pit viper (*Hypnale hypnale*), a species endemic to India and Sri Lanka.

Drawing a deep breath and trying not to think too much about snakes, we move on to J&K's amphibian population: there are lots of **frogs and toads**. Ladakh has its own high-altitude toad (*Scutiger occidentalis*) and plateau frog (*Nomorana pleskei*), while lower down you'll find the Himalayan toad (*Bufo himalayanus*), green toad (*Bufo viridis*), the Indian skipper frog (*Euphlyctis cyanophlyctis*) and the ornate narrow-mouthed frog (*Microhyla ornata*).

Fish With its many rivers, lakes and reservoirs, numerous species of fish are found in J&K, though not all of them are indigenous; brown trout (*Salmo trutta*), for example, was introduced by the British, who thought it would be good for fishing. The brown trout flourished in its new environment, as did the rainbow trout (*Oncorynchus mykiss*), introduced at the same time, and we're still eating their descendants today.

For those who understand the categorisation of fish, four orders are represented in J&K: *Cypriniformes, Siluriformes, Salmoniformes* and *Cyprinidontiformes*. Unique to the area is the algaad (*Schzothorax niger*), though its survival is threatened by pollution caused by the dumping of fertilisers and pesticides in the water courses. Other species of fish that are similarly endangered include the rama gurun (*Botia birdi*), chhurn (*S. esocinus*), chosh (*S. labiatus*), khont (*S. plagiostomus*) and sater gaad (*S. curvifrons*).

Information on angling in J&K is available from the Department of Fisheries (*www.jkfisheries.in*).

NATIONAL PARKS There are currently three national parks in J&K with a combined area of nearly 5,000km². A remarkable 90% of this land is within the confines of a single reserve, the **Hemis National Park** (see page 136), which was established in 1981 and at 4,400km² is the largest national park in India. Bounded to the north by the Indus River, Hemis is on the Karakoram-West Tibetan Plateau and so has an alpine steppe eco-system with a varied landscape of pine forest, alpine shrub and tundra, and meadow. The park is home to a recorded 16 species of mammal (including an estimated population of 200 snow leopards, the Tibetan wolf, Eurasian brown bear and small numbers of shapu and ibex) and 73 types of birds, including birds of prey. It is a prime location to spot golden eagles and the Himalayan griffon vulture.

J&K's other two national parks are the small **Dachigam National Park** (141km²; see page 207) near Srinagar, and the larger **Kishtwar National Park** (400km²) in Kishtwar district. There used to be a fourth park, the tiny Salim Ali National Park, in Srinagar, but this was converted into the Royal Springs golf course in the late 1990s. The name Dachigam means 'ten villages' and is said to refer to the ten villages that were relocated when it was formed. Located in the Zabarwan mountain range, the park is set on the mountain slopes with terrain varying from bare, rocky cliffs to much lusher grassland. Leopards and leopard cats, Himalayan black and brown bears, musk deer, jackals, jungle cats and otters all live here in sizeable numbers, as well as the critically endangered hangul, or Kashmir stag, J&K's state animal. Kishtwar National Park is criss-crossed with rivers that cut narrow valleys through the landscape and are fed by the glaciers above. The extensive forests include silver fir, cedar, blue pine and spruce, and they provide an ideal habitat for Himalayan brown bears, hangul, markhor, langur, leopards and Himalayan snowcocks (a type of pheasant).

Thought not technically a national park, the **Gulmarg Biosphere** (180km²) is also a haven for wildlife. Snow covered in winter but lush and green by late spring, conifer forests spread across almost 90% of the reserve and support populations of musk deer, brown and black bears, leopards, red foxes and hangul.

HISTORY

The history of Kashmir, and in particular its history since 1947, is a deeply sensitive subject about which many different deep and often mutually incompatible views are

The protection of snow leopards in Ladakh is spearheaded by the **Snow Leopard Conservancy India Trust** (SLC-IT), a local NGO founded in 2000. The SLC-IT believes that community participation, combined with ecotourism, is the best way to protect snow leopards' habitats and ensure their future.

The core components of the conservation programme are scientific research (including surveys); initiatives such as building predator-proof enclosures to reduce the impact of snow leopards on local communities and their livestock; and training local guides so that the presence of wildlife can be beneficial to the local economy.

Equally important for the long-term success of the project is education and outreach: workshops in schools instil in children an appreciation of the importance of biodiversity and how people and wildlife can live together. The SLC-IT works in government schools and encourages field trips to Hemis National Park and other areas of ecological importance.

More information on the SLC-IT, its work and how to get involved can be found at www.snowleopardhimalayas.in.

held. No account, however bland, is going to satisfy everyone, and so our approach in this section is to present our own, personal understanding of, and opinion on, the region's past. It is reflective of our own experiences, readings and conversations and is not aligned with any particular school of thought.

The history of Ladakh and Zanskar is, at least until the 19th century, quite separate from that of Kashmir and so we have dealt with it separately in the box on page 15.

EARLY HISTORY Origin myths are one of the earliest forms of oral history; they're the stories passed down from one generation to the next about who people are, and where they come from. Though they do not always tally with geological and archaeological records, they give us insight into the beliefs of early peoples.

In **Hindu legend**, Kashmir was once a lake (which does in fact agree with the geological record) that was drained when the *rishi* (sage) Kashyapa, a son of the god Brahma, cut the hills at Baramulla in two, allowing the water to flow out.

There has been human habitation in the Kashmir Valley since at least 3,000 BC, and archaeologists have found the remains of mud houses and stone tools dating from this earliest period in the Neolithic site at Burzahom, a little to the north of the Shalimar Gardens. These early people would principally have been hunter-gatherers, though there is some suggestion they may also have grown wheat and lentils. They produced primitive pottery and also expressed themselves artistically: in the 1960s archaeologists working here uncovered a stone slab depicting a hunting scene.

It is not until the Classical period that we have written sources to supplement the archaeological record: we start to get a clearer picture of the area from the 4th century BC onwards when the Greeks and other chroniclers make mention of Kashmir's rulers and their battles. The kings of Kashmir and Paurava (now in Pakistan) fought together against Alexander the Great at the **Battle of Hydaspes** (the Hydaspes River is now known as the Jhelum and flows through the Punjab) in 326 BC, and when they were defeated, the Kashmiris sent Alexander tribute. The Paurava king Porus became a Macedonian *satrap* (provincial governor).

Shortly after this, Kashmir became incorporated into the mighty **Mauryan Empire** (322–185BC), an empire which grew up in the vacuum left by the retreat of Alexander's forces. It is during this period that Buddhism spread from its homeland in what is now the state of Bihar to Kashmir, first introduced under the auspices of the Emperor Asoka (304–232BC), a man still greatly respected for his military prowess, skill as an administrator, and Buddhist teachings. The Asokan column, with its finial of three, realistically carved lions, is the national emblem of India and appears on all of the bank notes. Kashmir remained a centre of learning for both Hindus and Buddhists until the early 6th century AD.

The quiet and cultured civilisation that had emerged in Kashmir came to an abrupt end with the **Hephthalite invasion** in the late 5th century AD. Known also as the White Huns, the Hephthalites were central Asian warriors who led an aggressive campaign across the Sogdian Empire, western China and then in northern India. When the Hephthalite Emperor Mihirakula (r515–30) was eventually driven back from Malwa (in what is now Madhya Pradesh), he fled to Kashmir, where he was at first welcomed by the local king but then led an armed revolt, overthrowing his host and generally leaving destruction in his wake. Buddhist shrines were particularly vulnerable to his wrath, and he caused untold damage to religious structures both in Kashmir and, further west, in Gandhara.

Kashmir did recover, fortunately, and in the following centuries the region became known once again for its religious scholars, philosophers, artists and poets. The 8th century Karkota emperor Lalitãditya Muktapida (r724–60) oversaw a Kashmir-centred empire that stretched from Iran in the west to Tibet in the east and reached well up into Turkestan. He was able to defeat incursions from the Turks, Tibetans and Dards, and even to resist the Arabs. He was a noted patron of the arts, and actively encouraged trade. The Karkotas' regional dominance was not to last, however: by the 10th century the kingdom was increasingly unstable politically and hence vulnerable to attack.

MUSLIM RULE The invaders came from the west and took their name, the Shah Miri (King of Commanders), from their leader, Shams-ud-Din Shah Mir (r1339–42). Also known as the **Sayyid dynasty**, these possibly Afghan kings claimed descent from the Prophet Muhammad and their invasion was motivated by religious zeal as much as by the possibility of territorial acquisition. They would rule Kashmir from 1339 right up until 1561.

The Shah Miri dynasty brought with them relative stability, and political, trade and cultural connections that spread across central Asia and Persia. They also oversaw the conversion of many of Kashmir's Hindus, though more through the work of missionaries than by the sword. There were a number of revered Islamic preachers in Kashmir during this period, most notably Sheikh Nooruddin Noorani, who combined Shaivism with Sufi mysticism in his discourse, making his teachings accessible to local people through their familiarity. The rulers were generally tolerant of non-Muslims (with the exception of Sultan Sikander, an iconoclast who encouraged forced conversions) and the transition to Islam in the valley was evolutionary rather than revolutionary.

It could rightly be argued that this medieval period was a golden age for Kashmir: it was a wealthy, cosmopolitan place and people travelled vast distances to appreciate its beauty. Persian replaced Sanskrit as the court language, introducing a rich new literary canon; artisans were invited from across central Asia and Persia to come to the court and practise their crafts, including papier mâché, wood carving and weaving; and many of the architectural masterpieces we admire today, such as the Jamia Masjid and Makdoom Sahib shrine in Srinagar, date from this period too.

1

Having such a jewel on his northern borders inevitably captured the attention of the **Mughal emperor Humayun** (1508–56), who sent his general, Mirza Muhammad Haidar Dughlat, to seize the kingdom in 1540. The Mughals were central Asians, claiming descent from the infamous Timur (known in the west as Tamerlane), and had come to India under Humayun's father, Babur (1483–1530). Babur considered the country uncivilized and a mere shadow of what he had left behind, and as Humayun too had spent significant periods in exile at the Safavid Court in Iran, it is likely that he too would have felt a certain nostalgia for high Persian culture. In many ways closer in its natural and cultural environments to the Timurid world than to other parts of India, Kashmir would have felt wonderfully familiar. Possessing it was the next best thing to going home.

Though Humayun never came to Kashmir in person, his son, **Akbar the Great** (1542–1605), arrived in1589 and it was only then that Kashmir came under direct Mughal rule. Akbar was responsible for the construction of the heavily fortified wall that surrounds the Hari Parbat Fort in Srinagar, and it is for this reason that it is often referred to as a Mughal Fort even though the actual fort is far later in date. Akbar and his descendants also built the stunning series of Persian-style gardens, the so-called Mughal Gardens, taming the natural landscape and re-shaping it in the style of gardens in Kabul, Lahore, Samarkand and beyond. The gardens they created must have been fairly close to perfect as Akbar's grandson, the emperor Jahangir (1592–1666), saw Kashmir and proclaimed, 'If there is a heaven on earth, it is here, it is here, it is here.' Emperor Jahangir certainly knew a few things about beauty: he himself was responsible for the building of the Taj Mahal.

The Mughals were strong administrators as well as able military commanders, and Akbar in particular was renowned for his religious tolerance, inviting the leaders of all faiths to debate with him in the Ibadat Khana (Debating Hall) at his palace at Fatehpur Sikri. Major restriction on religious freedom, including iconoclasm and an excessively heavy tax burden for non-Muslims, did not return until the last of the Great Mughals, Emperor Aurangzeb (1618–1707), murdered his brothers and seized the throne with support from the Islamic orthodoxy in 1658.

Though the influence of the Mughals declined in Kashmir after Aurangzeb's death, Islam was here to stay. The Mo-i Muqqadas (the hair of the Prophet) was brought to Srinagar in 1700 and housed at the Hazratbal Shrine (see page 205), making Srinagar a major place of pilgrimage for Muslims from across the Indian subcontinent.

When the Persian Nadir Shah invaded India in 1738–9, he fractured what was left of the Mughal Empire and Kashmir once again was seized by Afghans. Ahmad Shah Durrani (1722–72), founder of the Durrani Empire and often regarded as the father of modern Afghanistan, took control of Kashmir in the mid-1700s, adding it to an empire that already stretched north to the Bukharan Khanate (now in Uzbekistan) and to the Arabian Sea in the south. Ahmad Shah's son, Timur Shah Durrani (1748–93), was not a statesman of the same calibre as his father, however, and so by the end of the 19th century the Durrani Empire was already starting to disintegrate.

SIKHS AND DOGRAS Maharaja Ranjit Singh (1780–1839), founder of the Sikh Empire, wrested control of Kashmir from the Afghan Durranis in 1819. His army was generally less destructive than those that had come before him, and the Sikhs were relatively tolerant of other faiths, though their blanket ban on cow slaughter did not go down well with Kashmir's meat-loving Muslims. A state-wide famine in 1832 shook Kashmir severely, but the Sikh rulers cut taxes and made available loans to enable a swift recovery. Jammu, though still with its own ruler, was vassal state to the Sikh Empire, and Ladakh and Baltistan were annexed by General Zorawar Singh in the 1830s and early 40s.

The **First Anglo-Sikh War** broke out in 1845: the British were terrified that the Sikh Empire, which by this time was seen in turn as corrupt and unstable, was still a military threat to British territory. Diplomatic relations between the Sikh court and the East India Company (the principal British entity in India prior to the start of direct rule in 1857) broke down. An East India Company force (comprised of Bengali and British units) began marching on Ferozepore, and Sikh forces crossed the Sutlej River to meet them. The British interpreted this move as an act of war.

The war was to last just three months but included the **Battle of Mudki** and the **Battle of Aliway** (both in the Punjab), as well as smaller encounters. The Sikhs were finally defeated after British artillery fire destroyed bridges behind their lines, preventing troops from retreating. Refusing to surrender, they were slaughtered.

The **Treaty of Lahore**, the peace treaty, was signed in March 1846. It required the Sikhs to surrender the Jullunder Doab (the land between the Beas and Sutlej rivers) and pay an indemnity of Rs15m. When the Sikhs were unable to raise this sum, they forfeited Kashmir and the Hazara region on the borders of what are now Pakistan and Afghanistan.

The British promptly sold Kashmir to the Raja of Jammu, Gulab Singh (1792–1857), for Rs7.5m, and the **Princely State of Jammu and Kashmir** was born. Thanks to Zorawar Singh, it already included Ladakh and Baltistan, as well as Jammu and the Kashmir Valley.

Gulab Singh's son and successor, Ranbir Singh (1830–85), had remained loyal to the British in the 1857 Indian Mutiny (also known as the Rebellion or the First War of Independence) and so was able to maintain a good relationship with the British Government, which was by now the dominant political and military power in India. He added to the Princely State's territory the fort at Gilgit, and his own son, Pratap Singh (1848–1925), incorporated the kingdoms of Chitral, Hunza and Nagar, all of which now lie on the Pakistani side of the Line of Control (LoC).

POST-INDEPENDENCE British India gained independence on 15 August 1947 and was divided into two new countries: India and Pakistan. The Maharaja of Kashmir, Hari Singh (1895–1961), like other princely rulers, was given the option of acceding to either country or, at least in theory, heading an independent kingdom. The expectation was that those states with Muslim-majority populations would join Pakistan, and those with a Hindu majority would accede to India.

Kashmir had a Muslim-majority population but was ruled by a Hindu king. The local working party took the decision to support accession to India, but Maharaja Hari Singh preferred for Kashmir to remain independent and so offered a **standstill agreement** to both countries to retain the status quo. Pakistan accepted the suggestion, but India declined it.

Following an **uprising** in Poonch and Mirpur, backed by Pashtun tribesmen who then started advancing on Srinagar, Hari Singh called for support from the Indian army. The Indian government agreed to support him, but only if he acceded to India. Hari Singh agreed, signed the **Instrument of Accession** on 26 October 1947, and volunteers from the Jammu and Kashmir National Conference supported the Indian army to drive back the incursion.

Pakistan believed Hari Singh had no right to call in the Indian army, but in spite of receiving orders to send troops to the front, General Sir Douglas Gracey, commander-in-chief of the Pakistani army, initially refused to do so. By the time Pakistani troops were finally dispatched, Indian forces had occupied the eastern

1

two-thirds of Kashmir, though Gilgit and Baltistan were secured for Pakistan by the Gilgit Scouts. This was the start of the **First Kashmir War**, in which both sides grabbed territory in Kashmir, and the conflict ended with a UN-negotiated ceasefire in 1948 that required Pakistan to withdraw its forces but retain around 40% of the territory, India occupying the remaining 60%. The UN resolution also required a plebiscite to be held to determine the future of Kashmir (as of 2014, the referendum has still not taken place).

It is from this point on that we can discuss J&K as a state of the Republic of India, and Pakistan was by no means the only regional power pressing at its borders. Indian and Chinese troops clashed in the 1962 Sino-Indian War, leading to the swift annexation by the Chinese of Aksai Chin, and the demarcation of the Line of Actual Control (not to be confused with the Line of Control, see page 59) between Pakistan, India and the Trans-Karakoram tract, now also claimed by China.

Two further conflicts broke out between India and Pakistan in 1965 and 1971. The first of these, the Second Kashmir War, erupted after the discovery of Operation Gibraltar, in which Pakistani insurgents were infiltrating J&K to destabilise the state from within. Some 30,000 Pakistani troops crossed the LoC on 5 August 1965 and the war began in earnest. Pakistan's principal attack, code-named Operation Grand Slam, aimed to capture Akhnoor in Jammu, breaking India's supply lines, and for the next five months both sides tore into each other with air strikes, tank battles and, albeit on a far smaller scale, naval hostilities. Independent sources estimate 6,800 soldiers died (3,000 of them Indian), and both the US and the USSR brought diplomatic pressure to bear to end the conflict and negotiate a ceasefire.

The 1971 **Indo-Pakistan War** began when Pakistan launched pre-emptive strikes on 11 Indian air bases during Operation Chengiz Khan, prompting India to join forces with nationalists in East Pakistan fighting for their independence. Although the focus of the conflict was principally East Pakistan, Kashmir was drawn into the conflict too. The war ended with Pakistan's defeat and the creation of the new sovereign state of Bangladesh. The **Simla Agreement** was signed by both India and Pakistan in July 1972. It committed both sides to settling future disputes, including those in Kashmir, by bilateral negotiations and effectively solidified the LoC that divided the Indian- and Pakistani-administered areas of Kashmir into a de facto border.

MILITANCY PERIOD State Assembly elections took place in J&K in 1987. There were widespread allegations of election fraud, and this gave impetus to a pro-independence insurgency spearheaded by the militant Jammu and Kashmir Liberation Front (JKLF). The JKLF stated that theirs was a nationalist, not Islamist, cause but the Indian government believed the unrest was being fomented by Pakistan. The Indian army killed 100 demonstrators at Gawakadal Bridge in 1990, after which the insurgency escalated.

Several additional militant factions emerged, including the **Hizbul Mujahideen**, which allied itself closely with Pakistan and projected the conflict as a holy war. Mujahideen fighters who had been battling the Soviets in Afghanistan turned their attentions on Kashmir, and their existing training camps produced a new generation of militants, this time to fight the Indian army. Both sides deployed hundreds of thousands of troops, mostly in the Kashmir Valley, and the civilian population bore the brunt of the pain: ethnic cleansing caused Hindu pandits to flee; those who remained (both Hindu and Muslim) suffered mass killings, disappearances, arbitrary imprisonment, torture and rape. Both the Indian army and the militants were responsible for these crimes.

Militants crossed into Kargil district in 1999. India believed the Pakistani government was behind this incursion, and this sparked the Kargil War (see box, page 187). There was serious concern that the conflict would escalate into nuclear war as the previous year Pakistan had carried out successful atomic tests and India had been testing its nuclear weapons since 1974. Both countries were therefore nuclear powers. The war lasted three months and included heavy shelling and air strikes. A memorial stands near Kargil to those who died in the war.

THE HISTORY OF LADAKH AND ZANSKAR

Petroglyph rock carvings show that Ladakh has been inhabited since **Neolithic** times. The area's population has always been sparse, however, and the majority of inhabitants were either nomadic or passing through *en route* to elsewhere, so little else from this early period remains.

Like with Kashmir, our earliest historic records about Ladakh come from the pens of outsiders: the Mons and Dards, the two principal tribes of Ladakh at the time, are referenced in the writings of Herodotus, Megasthenes and Ptolemy, among others.

In the 1st century AD Ladakh was part of the **Kushan Empire**, which spread from Bactria (around the Oxus River in central Asia), south to what is now Karachi on the Arabian Sea, across northern India and as far north as Turfan in Xinjiang, China. It was during this period that Buddhism arrived here from elsewhere in India, though the local people were mostly still followers of Bon (see box, page 104).

China and Tibet were both expanding their influences in the 8th century, and Ladakh was consequently hotly contested territory. When the Tibetan Empire broke up in 842, a court official called Nyima-Gon was able to take control of Ladakh and establish for himself the first **Ladakhi dynasty**. The local population was by now predominantly Tibetan, and the dynasty spread Buddhism widely.

As the Islamic conquests sped through south Asia in the 1300s, Ladakh aligned itself closely with Tibet, helping it preserve its Buddhist identity. Some Ladakhis did convert to Noorbakshi Islam, but they were the minority.

Ladakh's most famous royal lineage, the **Namgyal dynasty**, emerged in the late 15th century. Lhachen Bhagal Namgyal (the Namgyal suffix meaning 'victorious') of Basgo overthrew the King of Leh to unite Ladakh under his rule, and his successors built numerous fortifications to expel central Asian raiders and expand their territory into Zanskar, Spiti and, albeit briefly, Nepal. The dominance of the Mughals prevented expansion further west into Kashmir.

The Namgyals were doing well until they decided to side with Bhutan in a war against Tibet. When the Tibetans then invaded Ladakh, they were forced to ask the Mughals for assistance in repelling the invaders. Help was granted, but the 1684 **Treaty of Tingmosgang** severely restricted Ladakh's independence and required the king to convert to Islam, as well as to build Leh's first mosque.

In 1834, the Dogra general Zorawar Singh annexed Ladakh on behalf of Gulab Singh and, despite a rebellion in 1842, Ladakh was incorporated into the **Princely State of Jammu and Kashmir**. The Namgyal family were awarded the *jagir* (a feudal land grant) of Stok, but otherwise stripped of their power.

The early 2000s were marked with a number of terror attacks in J&K, including an assault on the state legislature in Srinagar in 2001 that killed 38 people, and the killing of 30 people, mostly the families of Indian servicemen, in an attack in May 2002. The latter caused tensions to escalate, with Pakistan implying it might use nuclear weapons to counteract any Indian attack. The situation was defused, in part, by the intervention of US diplomats.

In general security improved in J&K in the late 2000s, though there were still several incidents of concern: major protests took place in 2010 after a demonstrator was killed by the Indian Army, and the following year the Indian State Human Rights Commission (ISHRC) confirmed the discovery of 2,000 bodies in an unmarked grave near to the LoC. Many of the victims are thought to have been Kashmiris who disappeared having been arrested by security forces. In a positive step that bodes well for the future, however, the prime ministers of both India and Pakistan did meet in September 2013, agreeing to try to reduce the number of violent incidents along the LoC.

GOVERNMENT AND POLITICS

J&K has special status within India: **Article 370** of the Indian Constitution grants the state special autonomy. With the exception of legislation relating to defence, foreign affairs, finance and communications, which is drafted and voted on in Delhi, the Indian parliament requires the agreement of J&K's state government to implement all other laws. J&K has its own flag and constitution, and laws regarding citizenship and property rights (see *Buying property*, page 71) differ from elsewhere in India.

At a basic level, J&K has a multi-party, democratic system of governance. Representatives are elected to the **J&K Legislative Assembly** on six-year terms, one year longer than in other state assemblies in India. The last assembly elections took place in November 2008, after which a coalition government was formed by members of the J&K National Conference (NC) and Congress. Turn-out was a little over 60%, significantly higher than in previous elections. Interestingly, although there are 111 seats in the assembly, only 87 are currently filled: the balance remain officially vacant for the constituencies on the other side of the LoC.

The state's current chief minister is **Omar Abdullah**, leader of the Jammu and Kashmir National Conference (JKN) party. He is a young and charismatic individual who came to power in January 2009 at the age of just 38. Born in London, his mother is English and he is the son and grandson of men who have also been J&K's prime and chief ministers. He first entered politics in the late 1990s, as an MP at the Lok Sabha, and he has been both Union Minister of State for External Affairs and President of the National Conference party.

The UN Refugee Agency UNHCR's 2009 report *Freedom in the World*, a survey of democracy and political freedom, rated J&K as partly free.

HUMAN RIGHTS Since the start of the militancy in 1989, numerous and well-founded allegations of severe human rights abuses have been made, including – as mentioned above – ethnic cleansing, disappearances, extra-judicial killings by security forces, and the massacre and rape of large numbers of civilians. Atrocities have been committed both by militants belonging to the Jammu Kashmir Liberation Front (JKLF) and by the Indian Armed Forces and police.

Amnesty International, Human Rights Watch and the UN have all raised serious objections to the Indian government in the past, and it is generally considered that troops and police continue to commit such crimes with the tacit acceptance of their superiors. They are able to do so thanks to the 1958 **Armed Forces (Special Powers) Act** (AFSPA) which permits, among other things, firing on civilians for the maintenance of public order, arresting without warrant those who are suspected of an offence, and legal immunity for army officers.

ECONOMY

Since the end of the militancy in the early to mid 2000s, J&K's economy has been expanding rapidly: the state's GDP in 2012–13 (the last financial year for which complete data is available) stood at US$12.6 billion and the economy has grown by at least 13% year on year for the past five years. Poverty levels have been falling steadily since the early 1990s (the poverty rate currently stands at around 10%, as opposed to 32.7% in India as a whole), with the vast majority of those falling below the poverty line living in rural areas.

Tourism was the staple of J&K's economy for much of the 20th century, and in the last few years the partial recovery of the tourism industry has been a major contributor to the growth in GDP. Some 1.4 million tourists came to the state in 2012, most of them domestic tourists from other parts of India. Hindu pilgrims visiting the Vaisno Devi shrine alone contribute more than US$75 million to the local economy each year.

The other significant economic sector is **agriculture**. Kashmir is known for its high-grade timber, especially cedar and willow (used in cricket bats), its fruits, grain, nuts and, of course, its saffron. Sericulture, handicrafts production and the manufacturing of consumer goods are also important.

Improvements to **infrastructure** and, in particular, the transport infrastructure, are key for enabling economic development in the state. As it stands, moving goods and passengers by road is expensive and time-consuming, and many areas are completely inaccessible in the winter months. The completion of the Kashmir Railway project, which will ultimately connect Srinagar to the rest of the Indian Railways network, will be hugely beneficial, as will an increased number of road tunnels and, at some stage hopefully in the not too distant future, the landing of commercial flights at Kargil's airport.

The state may also look at harnessing its **natural resources**, specifically its rivers, to generate power that could both be used locally and exported to other parts of India.

PEOPLE

According to 2011 census data, the population of J&K state is around 12.5 million, just over 1% of India's total. The population density is 56 people per square kilometre, which is about one sixth of the national average and there are 889 women for every 1,000 men, a nationwide problem that results from a preference for, and preferential treatment of, male children. The population of J&K has increased by just over 23% in the past decade, which can be attributed to the returning home of refugees as well as a greater life expectancy for residents.

Given its location, Kashmir's history is one of human migration, in some cases from places as far away as Iran, Iraq and the Caucasus. Some people just passed through; others chose to stay. Many of them left their genetic mark. The largest ethnic groups you are likely to encounter are mentioned here, though their genetic identities are by no means separate due to centuries of inter-marriage with other communities.

DARDS The Dards have been known in the West since at least the time of Ptolemy, who refers to the community as the *daradrai* in his 2nd-century treatise the *Almagest*. Most Dards live in Dardistan in the northern part of the Kashmir Valley, as well as in Gilgit and Chittral in Pakistan-administered Kashmir, and they are thought to be descended from Aryan-speaking tribes. They were historically followers of Buddhism and animism, and this is still evident in the practices of Dards in Dha-Hanu (known as the Brokpa), though now many Dards are Muslim.

The Dards are one of India's Scheduled Tribes and therefore benefit from positive discrimination when applying for higher education and government jobs.

DOGRAS The Dogras are mostly Hindus who inhabit Jammu region and also parts of Punjab. A dynasty of Dogra kings ruled Kashmir from 1846–47, and they continue to hold prominent positions in politics, business and as military officers. The British categorised the Dogras as a martial race, and hence they are still well represented and respected in the armed forces.

Social anthropologists are unsure as to the origins of the Dogra people: the *Imperial Gazetteer of India* suggests, however, that the word is a corruption of *dwigart desh* and refers to the land between the two lakes of Mansar and Sruinsar, the Dogra's traditional territory. Clan identity remains strong, and many families take Dogra as a surname.

GUJJARS The nomads that you see driving their flocks of sheep, goats and cattle in the southwestern parts of J&K are the Gujjars. Again, their origins are unclear: there is some evidence that they came from the Caucasus and Iran, though many Gujjars believe that their forefathers migrated here from Gujarat and Rajasthan. In any case, it seems they have been present in Kashmir since the 5th or 6th century AD.

The community is loosely divided into two: those who practise settled agriculture, and those who are transhumant. In traditional mud-brick houses families share their living quarters with the cattle, which keeps them warm in winter. Their language has no written form, and so stories and information are instead passed down through song.

HANJIS The Hanjis are the boatmen you see on the lakes around Srinagar. Some Hanjis claim descent from the Prophet Noah (and hence, one would hazard, a strong desire to keep their feet dry); others believe them to have come originally from Sri Lanka. Though most of the Hanji population are Muslim, prior to this they were probably *ksatriya* Hindus.

Most Hanjis make their living from trades connected to the lakes: they are the vegetable growers and sellers, the fishermen and the men who punt the *shikaras*. Incomes and literacy rates are low by local standards, and the return of tourism will be of great benefit to the community.

KASHMIRIS Kashmiris are widespread in the state but concentrated in the Kashmir Valley. The community, which is thought to include ancient immigrants from Afghanistan, central Asia, Iran and Turkey, is predominantly Muslim, having converted to the faith from the 14th century onwards. A sizeable population of Kashmiri Hindus does, however, survive.

The majority of Kashmiris belong to familial clans, and the clan name denotes their place of origin and business: the Wain or Wani are thought to have come from the Persian Gulf and are traditionally traders; the Lone are an agricultural clan whose members are concentrated in the north of the Kashmir Valley; and the Maliks are descendants of Hindu Rajput clans that have long since converted to Islam.

The modern Kashmiris are a settled population: those in the villages depend on agriculture (in particular orchards and saffron fields) for their living while the urban population makes its money from handicraft production and business activities. Kashmiri families are active players in the tourism industry, often running hotels, restaurants and shops. For information on the Kashmiri language, see below.

LADAKHIS The Ladakhis are not actually a single ethnic group: it's a catch-all term used to describe the various ethnic groups (including Tibetans, Monpas and some Dards) that inhabit Leh and Zanskar districts. Many of them are descended from Mongoloid tribes from the Tibetan Plateau (including more recent Tibetan refugees who left at the same time as the Dalai Lama), and they are predominantly followers of Buddhism.

The total population of Ladakh is tiny: just over 250,000 people. Many of the inhabitants live in remote villages, growing the few crops that can survive at such high altitude and herding sheep and goats. Although Ladakhis do work in the tourism industry, particularly as trekking guides, many of the people you see around Leh in the summer are in fact migrant labourers who have come for the tourist season.

LANGUAGE

The official language of J&K is **Urdu**, an Indo-Iranian language mutually intelligible with Hindi but that is written from right to left in the Perso-Arabic script (Hindi is written from left to right and in the Devnagri script, showing its Sanskritic roots). Urdu is closely related to Persian, and indeed many of the canonical works of literature are shared, and it also includes many loanwords from Arabic.

There are over five million speakers of **Kashmiri** in India, and most of them live in the Kashmir Valley. Another Indo-Aryan language, but in this case in the Dardic sub-group, it is a compulsory subject in local schools for primary age children. It has been written at different times in the Sharada, Devnagri and Perso-Arabic scripts, but still it preserves many grammatical features that are present in Sanskrit but have been lost in Hindi and Urdu.

Ladakhi is a Tibetan language, though not mutually intelligible with Standard Tibetan. It can be further broken down into four regional dialects; those dialects spoken in northern Ladakh and in Zanskar are similar to those from central Tibet. Ladakhi is written using the *uchen*, or Tibetan, script, and pronunciation is similar to that of Classical Tibetan.

In Ladakh, the principal language of instruction in government schools is Urdu, followed by English. Ladakhi and Tibetan are only taught as additional subjects, though they are understandably given greater priority in monastery schools.

For helpful phrases and a guide to pronunciation, see pages 239–41.

RELIGION

Though J&K is home to followers of all manner of faiths, including Zoroastrianism, Sikhism and Christianity, the majority of people follow Islam, Hinduism and Buddhism (listed in order of number of adherents).

ISLAM J&K is a Muslim majority state: somewhere in the region of 67% of the total population is Muslim, although most of them reside in the Kashmir Valley. In Jammu and in Ladakh, they are a minority.

Though Islam first came to Kashmir sometime in the 8th century, it was not widely adopted for the next 500 years. The end of Hindu rule in 1346 gave way to a succession of Muslim sultans, some of whom were tolerant of other faiths and others less so, and Kashmir's trading prowess meant that the valley was a melting pot of mostly Muslim traders from Afghanistan, central Asia and Iran, as well as from elsewhere in India.

The majority of Muslims in J&K are **Sunnis**, after Muslims who followed Muhammad's companion, Ali Bakr, and not his son-in-law Ali, following the Prophet's death. Many Kashmiri Muslims are **Sufis**, a mystical branch of Sunni Islam that teaches its followers that they can grow close to God in this life, as well as in the next. They believe that by purifying themselves (and in particular their spirit), they will be rewarded with an esoteric knowledge of God.

BUDDHISM IN LADAKH AND ZANSKAR

With thanks to Tanzin Norbu (www.mountaintribalvision.com)
The early religion of Ladakh and Zanskar was the animistic **Bon**, worshipping spirits and mountains. Even these days at New Year, people give recognition to these spirits as Protector deities, and in the Dard regions, people still celebrate Bono-Na festival every two in three years.

It is believed that Buddhism was introduced to Ladakh before it arrived in Tibet, during the **Third Buddhist Council** in Kashmir (272–232BC) when Emperor Asoka sent a Buddhist missionary to Ladakh. Evidence for this includes an early Kushan-period stone cave in Sani, Zanskar, which dates from somewhere between 100BC and AD500. Contemporary rock carving can be seen at Khalatse and Mulbekh, and also in the giant Buddha at Kartse Khar.

Conversely, early Mahayana stone carvings may in fact have travelled here from Tibet: statues of Buddhas and bodhisattvas from these periods can be seen in the Zanskari villages of Karsha, Padum, Tong-de and Mune.

During this period however, though the Tibetan emperors were at their height, Tibet still had a somewhat limited knowledge of Buddhism. Around 600–800, **Tibetan Buddhism** started to travel from India towards Zhang-Zhung in western Tibet. Around 842, after the assassination of the Lang-dharma, the last emperor of Tibet, his descendants moved further west to establish a new kingdom which included the provinces of Rudok, Purang and Guge.

As Buddhism started to find its niche, one of the kings of Guge, Ye-shey-Od, became a monk. In order to improve the quality of Buddhism and to propagate the new religion, he invited Atisa, a scholar and a professor of Nalanda University, to be his teacher. He also sent a group of young students to study Buddhism in India so they could return as learned men and help to spread Buddhism in Tibet. Only two students returned, one of whom was **Rinchen Zangpo**, a great translator and artist. He established the monastery at Alchi and, later, Sumda and Mangyu monasteries, which were built with the help of Kashmiri artists. These are some of the oldest monasteries in Ladakh.

Although Buddhism may have taken root in Ladakh and Zanskar earlier, Tibet was the country that introduced the Mahayana form of Buddhism here. Travelling Buddhist hermits, scholars and teachers influenced and gave shape to Ladakhi and Zanskari Buddhism. Padmasambava, known as '**the Second Buddha**', visited Baltistan, Kargil, Phokar-Zong and Sani, meditating in caves along the way. In Sakti village, the U-rgyan rock bears imprints of his body, and the Thagthog Gompa was

HINDUISM   A little under 30% of J&K's population is Hindu. Kashmir traditionally had two main Hindu populations: those around Jammu; and the Kashmiri Pandits, Brahmins of the Kashmir Valley. Most Kashmiri Pandits fled during the militancy (see page 14), either to refugee camps around Jammu, or elsewhere in India.

Jammu is known as the City of Temples and here Hindus are in the majority at around 65% of the total population. The city's population swells during important festivals, however, with Hindus from other parts of India visiting Jammu's shrines and also passing through *en route* to the Amarnath and Vaisno Devi shrines.

Hinduism is a polytheistic religion, the amalgamation of numerous and diverse regional belief systems. The word Hindu was not historically used by followers but entered into European languages from the Arabic *al Hind* (the land beyond the Indus) and then into Indian languages also. The three principal strands of

built in a cave where he meditated. This monastery still follows the Nying-ma-pa school of Buddhist thought, founded by Padmasambava and Santaraksita, and it is the only one to do so in Ladakh.

Around 935–1045, the great yogi and pandit **Naropa** meditated in Dzongkhul cave in Zanskar (the site of the Dzongkhul Gompa). His teachings were based on oral traditions, and he passed on his wisdom to disciple Lama Marpa, who in turn passed it on to Milarepa. This lineage later became known as the Kagyu (or Kagyupa) tradition. Similarly, Stongdey Gompa was founded by Lama Marpa (it is also known as the Marpa Ling).

Roughly at the time of Rinchen Zangpo, a famous Zanskari translator called **Phagspa Sherab** (also known as Zanskar Lotsawa) translated parts of the 200-volume *Bstan-gyur*. It is said that he founded Karsha and Phugthar gompas in Zanskar, monasteries that now follow the Gelugpa school (see below).

After Rinchen Zangpo, the school of Bka-dam-pa founded by Atisha and Brom-ton flourished in Ladakh. In the 13th century, however, Je Tsongkhapa founded the somewhat more austere and scholarly **Gelugpa** (Yellow Hat) school of Tibetan Buddhism. It is said that one of Tsongkhapa's main disciples, Sharap Zangpo, founded the monastery of Diskit in the Nubra Valley and Stagmo Lakhang in Stagmo, travelling to Zanskar to set up the Gelugpa lineage at Karsha and Phugthar gompas. He died in Phugthar, where a stupa containing his relics remains, and is known as Sharap Zangpo's Stupa. Later on, his nephew Paldan Shera founded the monastery of Thiksey.

King Singay Namgyal, the Lion King, ruled Ladakh between 1590 and 1620, and during this period Ladakh enjoyed an excellent relationship with Bhutan. The Lion King sent his son to Bhutan to become a disciple of Lama Stag-tsang-ras pa, a renowned Tibetan monk known as the Tiger Lama. The lama became teacher to both father and son, and together they founded the gompas at Hemis, Chamre and Hanley.

While the mountains of Ladakh and Zanskar connect earth and sky quite literally, the ancient monasteries provide a spiritual bridge between worlds past and present. The culture and tradition of Ladakh and Zanskar promote the notion of interdependence and sustainability: two reasons why people have thrived for thousands of years in such a harsh environment. Ladakh, which is also known as Little Tibet because of its religious, cultural and architectural resemblance to Tibet, has prompted the Dalai Lama to state that Ladakh and Zanskar are two places beyond the borders of Tibet where the future of Tibetan Buddhism may thrive.

1

Hinduism are Shaivism (followers of the god Shiva), Vaisnavism (followers of the god Vishnu) and Shaktism (those who worship the goddess Shakti).

EDUCATION

State-wide, **literacy** in J&K stands at 65.57%, an increase of more than 10% in the past decade. Access to basic education is unequal, however, with a gender gap of more than 16% and children in urban areas far more likely to be in school than their rural counterparts. Though this is in part due to cultural and economic reasons, corruption also plays a part: state schools in remoter areas are frequently underfunded and understaffed, with teacher truancy high. Many teachers have had no formal training. The militancy period seriously disrupted the education of many in the Kashmir Valley with schools closed and many children sent away for their safety.

State education in J&K is provided by the Jammu and Kashmir State Board of School Education (JKBOSE). There are ten years of compulsory schooling in primary, middle and high schools, and a minority of students continue on to college or university education.

There are a number of well-regarded **universities** in the state, including the University of Jammu, the University of Kashmir and the Islamic University of Science and Technology.

CULTURE

The rich and diverse cultures of J&K are one of the principal reasons for coming here: whether you want to immerse yourself in meditation at a Buddhist monastery in Ladakh, watch carpet making and woodwork in Srinagar, or sing and dance on the set of a Bollywood movie on an alpine pasture, J&K has it all.

MUSIC Each of J&K's regions has its own distinctive style of music, which reflects their diverse cultures and historical influences: Jammu's music is closely related to other classical styles of northern India; the Kashmir Valley takes inspiration from Persia and central Asia; and Ladakh's music is similar to that of Tibet's. Your best opportunities to hear traditional music are at weddings and during festivals.

Indian classical music is well represented in J&K and two of India's most famous *santoor* (a trapezoid hammered dulcimer) players hail from the state: Shivkumar Sharma of Jammu has recorded three platinum-selling albums, and Srinagar's multi award-winning *Bhajan Sopori*. The santoor has its roots in Persia, but the version played in India today was developed in Kashmir. It is used along with harmonium, *saz* (a long-necked lute), *setar* (a four-stringed lute with moveable frets) and *tabala* (a goblet drum) to perform **Sufiana Kalam**, the music of Kashmir's Sufi mystics, which arrived here from Persia sometime in the 15th century.

There are many varieties of **folk music**, often based on songs that tell stories or are linked to specific events such as a wedding or the harvest. **Chakri** – played with the harmonium, *rubab* (a short-necked lute originating in Afghanistan) and *sarangi* (a short, stringed instrument played with a bow) – is used to accompany epic love songs and may also feature **rouf**, traditional dancing at a wedding.

Also fitting into the folk category is **ladishah**, humorous and sometimes rude songs performed by travelling musicians. The lyrics of each song are tailored to the village in which they are being sung.

Ladakhi music is, not surprisingly, influenced by that of Tibet, though it does have some unique characteristics. Here the music is frequently linked to religious events, drum beats and rhythmic chanting an ancient way of reciting holy texts. This music often accompanies dances by masked and costumed figures. The dances symbolise the triumph of good over evil and are given as offerings to the monastery's protective deity. The main instruments that you will see in the orchestra are the *nga* and *damaru* (two types of drum), *drilbu* (bells), *dungchen* (long horn), *dung* (conch shell) and *silnyen* (cymbals).

LITERATURE Kashmir has a rich literary canon with fine works of poetry and prose in Sanskrit, Persian, Urdu, Hindi, English and Kashmiri.

Kashmir was a centre of Shaivism in the early medieval period, and so the earliest surviving works are on religious topics. **Vasugupta**'s *Shiva Sutras* date from the 9th century; the 10th-century philosopher and mystic **Abhinavagupta** wrote more than 30 works, including *Tantrāloka* and *Abhinavabharati*; and his disciple, **Rajanaka Kṣemarāja**, compiled the Pratyabhijna *Hridayam*. These works were in Sanskrit, a more-or-less dead language comparable to Latin and Greek in which many canonical texts of Hinduism and Buddhism were written.

The use of the Kashmiri language in literature began in the middle of the 13th century with **Shitikantha**'s writing of the *Mahanayakaprakash* (Light of the Supreme Lord), a text that popularised the esoterics of Shaiva Tantra. The Kashmiri language was well suited to producing religious poetry, and so some of the finest literary works of this period are poems: the *Vakhs* of the poetess **Lal Ded** are particularly revered, as are those of the poet-saint **Sheikh Noor-ud-din Wali**.

The 16th to 19th centuries were particularly fruitful for Kashmir's writers and poets. The beautiful **Habba Khatoon**, 'the Nightingale of Kashmir', wrote melodious love songs that twist between joy and the sorrow of separation. Her songs remain popular today. Other prominent mystic poets, many of them female, include **Rupa Bhawani**, **Arnimal**, **Mahmud Gami** and **Rasool Mir**.

Since independence, J&K has also produced notable poets, writers and playwrights. The contemporary playwright **Moti Lal Kemmu**, recipient of the Padma Shri award (an Indian honour similar to the OBE), writes in both Kashmiri and Hindi; **Amin Kamil** is known for his poetry, short stories, novels and literary criticism; and **Ghulam Nabi Firaq** has published dozens of works, including his own poems in various styles, and translations of great English poems into Kashmiri.

FILM Bollywood loves Kashmir. Though there is not a major indigenous film industry, the romantic lakes of Srinagar and the spectacular surrounding hills, not to mention the ski resort at Gulmarg, are familiar to any devotees of Indian films. Two of Shammi Kapoor's classics, *Jaanwar* (Animal) and *Junglee* (Wild) were shot partly in Kashmir, as was one of our personal favourites, the artistically shot but terribly sad *Pakeezah* (Pure), in which the heroine floats one night on a houseboat.

The troubles in Kashmir have also provided plenty of fodder for Bollywood's scriptwriters, sometimes with great success. If you're new to Bollywood and can't stand the thought of too many syrupy song and dance numbers (though you can't avoid them entirely), you might want to watch the 2006 tear-jerker *Fanaa* (Destroyed in Love, or Annihilation), the tale of a Kashmiri girl who falls in love with a terrorist and in which both lovers must choose between their love for each other and what they believe to be right. Roles are reversed in *Dil Se* (From the Heart), and this time it's the hero who falls for a female terrorist. Having pursued her unsuccessfully throughout the film, they die when they finally embrace as the bomb she has set explodes.

ARTS AND CRAFTS J&K is famed for its handicraft production, and especially for its fine silk carpets and valuable pashmina shawls. In addition to some superb

1

shopping opportunities, you can also see artisans following traditional production methods. You'll learn most about these crafts and the families who produce them by taking a Heritage Walk in Srinagar (see page 196).

Kashmir's jewel-like **carpets** are rightly famous around the world and, if you have the budget, are one of the most beautiful souvenirs you can take home from your trip. This kind of carpet making was introduced from Persia, and the finest examples are made from pure wool or a mixture of wool and silk. Synthetic materials feature only in the 'lower-grade' carpets. Kashmiri carpets are hand-knotted on a loom. Production typically takes place in people's homes rather than a factory, and even a small carpet takes months to complete. Many members of the same family may contribute to the process, and the skills required are passed down from one generation to the next. Popular patterns include the 'paisley' motif (inspired by the shape of an almond or mango stone), the Chinar tree and the tree of life.

Far more portable and accessible on a greater range of budgets is locally made **jewellery**. Sapphires and rubies are both mined in J&K, but they're usually cut, polished and set in Rajasthan before being shipped back to the shops in Jammu and Srinagar. Arguably more striking, and certainly more affordable, are pieces of Ladakhi jewellery with coral, turquoise and lapis lazuli set into silver or made into hundreds of beads. Although antique pieces are available, and attract a premium price, modern replicas are often just as attractive and the craftsmanship, in many cases, is fine.

Kashmir has always been renowned for its artists, and they paint in a variety of styles. Largest in scale are the **mural paintings** that decorate many of the Buddhist monasteries in Ladakh. Frequently depicting scenes from the life of the Buddha, or of guardian figures and demons, the conservation of these ancient works and, in some cases, production of new paintings, is keeping yet another generation of artists in business.

Far smaller but produced with no less skill are the *thangka*, paintings on silk that are frequently surrounded by a rich brocade border. These lustrous wall hangings were originally teaching tools and so depict scenes such as the Wheel of Life (the explanation of Buddhist cosmology). Originally a Nepalese art form, *thangkas* were exported to monasteries in Tibet from the 11th century onwards. They could be easily rolled up and carried and hence became quickly popular.

Kashmir also has its own schools of **miniature painting**. Though often small in size, the word miniature actually comes from *minium*, the Latin for red lead. These paintings were produced to illustrate valuable manuscripts, both secular and religious, and became particularly popular from the 15th century onwards. Often removed from their original bindings for display, you can see a large collection at the Dogra Art Museum in Jammu (see page 236–7).

Papier mâché is thought to have been introduced to Kashmir from Seljuk Iran, whence it spread across central Asia and into Kashmir. It was produced in and around Srinagar from the 14th century onwards, and although no examples from this period survive, we do have manuscript descriptions of its existence.

The interest in papier mâché was revived in the 19th century, as French merchants wanted their pashmina shawls wrapped and shipped in papier mâché boxes. Though costing almost nothing in Srinagar, the boxes fetched a high price in Paris and so a separate trade in the boxes developed, with production being targeted towards European tastes. Papier mâché items produced in Srinagar today can be made of either pulped paper or, more frequently, paperboard sheet or another substructure that has been painted and covered with lacquer.

Kashmir is also known for its exquisite **woodcarving** and a number of carpentry workshops survive in Srinagar in particular. These artisans once produced the intricate cedar wood panels for the houseboats, and indeed they continue to restore them and produce replacements, but now most of their output is carved furniture, screens and decorative items for the home.

SPORT

The national sport of J&K is undoubtedly **polo**, and games draw vast crowds of spectators. Although variants such as running polo and even elephant polo can be seen elsewhere in India, here the original, horse variety is king. This is a particularly apt phrase as given the royal lineage of many of the top players, polo is still often referred to as the sport of kings.

The best place to watch professional polo matches is at Drass (see page 187) where families are proud of producing generations of polo players and see the game as a key part of their heritage. At around 3,350m, the polo field at Gulmarg is the highest in India and you'll occasionally catch games there too.

Due to the mountainous terrain, J&K is a hub for **adventure sports**. The state offers the best **trekking** opportunities in the Himalayas, and routes are far less crowded than those in neighbouring Nepal. **Mountaineers** will find peaks for all levels of ability, and there are numerous pleasant **walks** for those with less energy. **Mountain biking** and **climbing** are perennially popular among visiting tourists, as is **motorcycling**.

Various **watersports** are already on offer, and more activities are being added each season. **White-water rafting** is well developed across Ladakh in particular, a new boat club is under construction in Srinagar to teach **sailing** and rent out boats, and you can also hire **jet-skis**, **kayaks** and **windsurfs**. In the summer months **swimming** is an attractive option in some of the crystal-clear high-altitude lakes, as is **fishing** for brown trout.

India's premier ski resort is at Gulmarg, so in the winter months you can **ski** and **snowboard** at a fraction of the cost of European and American resorts. It's also possible to **snow shoe**, **heli-ski** and **ice skate**. There's even a growing interest in **ice hockey**, with popular teams in Leh and Kargil and players drawn from several army regiments and police forces.

2

Practical Information

WHEN TO VISIT

The state of J&K is a year-round destination: there are major attractions in every season, though if you want to visit a specific place or undertake a particular activity you will need to take the extremes of weather into consideration.

In winter Ladakh is only accessible by air, as the roads are closed by snow. This is the best time to spot snow leopards and to undertake the Chadar Winter Trek along the frozen Zanskar River, accompanying local teachers returning to Zanskar's remote villages after their winter break. Ladakhi Losar, the New Year, is celebrated in late December or early January, the exact date set by the lunar calendar.

Srinagar in the snow is a postcard-perfect scene. You can keep warm with a *kanger* beneath your *phiren*, tucked up toasty warm on a houseboat, or use the city as a springboard for Gulmarg. The most developed ski resort in the Himalayas, ski passes, kit hire and lessons are exceptionally cheap and you can even try your hand at heli-skiing.

The spring is when the snows begin to melt and the alpine meadows erupt into rainbows, with wild flowers everywhere you look. In Srinagar the magnificent tulip fields also come into bloom, and though the domestic tourists have begun to arrive, there are relatively few foreigners to be seen. Everything is lush, green and fresh, and the lower trekking routes start to beckon.

In the summer months, it's time for trekking. The snow has retreated to the uppermost peaks, and the roads are clear enough to drive to Leh and even down to Zanskar. While Leh itself is busy, there are plenty of quiet retreats in the surrounding valleys. You can walk, you can ride, and few things are more beautiful than sitting out around a campfire beneath the stars.

Even the rivers and lakes look enticing in July and August. There are plenty of opportunities for kayaking and white-water rafting on the rivers of Ladakh, while to the west the lakes of Kashmir offer a variety of watersports, leisurely boat trips and trout fishing.

The greatest draw in autumn is the Ladakh Festival, which runs for two weeks at the start of September. It's a wonderful celebration of Ladakhi culture and a prime opportunity to see traditional costumes and masked dance, archery competitions and polo. Come November the saffron fields of Kashmir are riotous purple; the crocuses are harvested and the saffron dried.

HIGHLIGHTS

It is often said that a place has something for everyone, but in the case of J&K that is actually true. Thousands of years of history sit side by side with vibrant modern communities; spectacular natural landscapes ripe for exploration are dotted with all manner of architectural curiosities. Whether your idea of heaven is heli-skiing in Gulmarg or joining the monks for their early morning meditation, trekking along the frozen Zanskar River, white-water rafting on the Indus or simply lazing on a houseboat with a good book, you won't be disappointed.

BUDDHAS OF KARGIL Far less famous but no less impressive than the ill-fated Buddhas of Bamiyan in Afghanistan, which were destroyed by the Taliban in 2001, is the 7m-tall rock-cut Buddha at Kartse Khar. Dating back to the 7th/8th century AD, this statue was carved by early missionaries and the depiction of the body, jewellery and hair are typical of the Kashmiri style. Four other Buddha carvings, including the standing Buddha at Mulbekh, are also found within the district.

THE MUGHAL ROAD When the Mughal emperors travelled to their Kashmiri paradise in the 1600s, the road they took was far west of the current National Highway. Their route has recently been paved and now hosts the annual Mughal Road Car Rally, as well as giving other motorists the opportunity to pass through the spectacularly beautiful Hirpora Wildlife Sanctuary.

MUBARAK MANDI At first glance Jammu's Mubarak Mandi is a crumbling wreck, a pitiful place of neglect. Look closer, however, and this 19th-century palace complex has remarkable, wedding-cake architecture and is overrun with monkeys. Some restoration work has already been done and shows the possibility that the buildings may yet return to their former glory.

TREKKING IN ZANSKAR The vast majority of trekkers head to Ladakh as the routes are more easily accessible from Leh, but it's well worth the effort of travelling further afield to Zanskar. The landscapes are more striking, there are fewer people on the trails and there are fantastic opportunities for spotting flora and fauna, including the elusive snow leopards. Even in winter you can join local teachers on the Chadar trek as they brave the snow and ice to return to their rural schools after the winter break.

MEDITATING AT THIKSEY MONASTERY Joining the monks in their early morning prayers sends shivers down your spine. The room, dark save for candlelight, resonates with sonorous chanting and we sat completely spellbound. Though other monasteries such as Hemis are better advertised, we prefer the laid-back atmosphere of Thiksey where you feel more a part of the community than simply a spectator.

MUGHAL GARDENS We grew up with the idea of the Shalimar Gardens as an Eden-like place, never guessing once that they were real. The discovery that they did exist, and indeed survive to the present day, was a cause for great excitement. Come early in the morning to Shalimar, or to the equally beautiful Chashma Shahi, and you'll not only be able to explore the gardens before the crowds but also see the mist rising eerily off the lawns and water channels.

HOUSEBOATS OF SRINAGAR If you take home one image of Srinagar, it'll be of India's floating palaces, the houseboats of Dal and Nagin lakes. Stay just one night afloat and you'll see why the colonial British hired boats for months on end; take a *shikara* ride among the lotus gardens and you'll probably never want to leave.

KHARDUNG LA There's a certain draw to visiting places with superlatives attached to them, and the (probably) highest motorable road on earth is no exception. Yes it's

- Run the Ladakh Ultra Marathon and prove your endurance at altitude (see page 95)
- Mountain bike from Khardung La down the world's highest motorable road to Leh
- Rock climb in the sandstone cliffs around Sonamarg
- White-water raft through the rapids of the Indus River
- Fish for trout in high-altitude lakes around Srinagar
- Complete the Chadar Winter Trek across frozen rivers to Zanskar
- Ski off-piste at Gulmarg, India's top winter sports resort
- Horse trek to the Thajiwas Glacier
- Paraglide above the lush, green landscapes of the Vale of Kashmir
- Try heli-skiing at a price you can afford

touristy, yes it gets crowded, but without climbing Everest it's probably the closest you'll get to standing on the roof of the world, and that makes it worth the effort.

SUGGESTED ITINERARIES

Your itinerary is inevitably going to depend on a variety of factors: the time you have available, how far you want to travel, the time of year and, if time is short, whether you're going to focus on Srinagar or Leh. We've therefore suggested a mixture of options in the hope that there's something here for you, wherever and whenever you're going.

A WEEKEND With just two days based in Srinagar, book yourself on to Chicago Houseboat to see what it's like to live aboard. On the first day take a ride on the new gondola to the shrine of Makhdoom Sahib, then continue up the hill to Hari Parbat Fort and have a picnic in the surrounding eco-reserve, looking out across the city. After lunch pay a visit to the Hazratbal Shrine with its sacred hair of the Prophet, then return to Dal Lake via the Jamma Masjid, making sure you're back on the boat in time to watch the sunset across the water.

Rise at dawn and take a *shikara* ride to the floating vegetable market, admiring the patchwork of floating islands as you go. Buy some honey macaroons to keep hunger pangs at bay, and then return to land for a tour of the Mughal Gardens. Chashma Shahi and the Shalimar Gardens are a must, as are the tulip gardens if you're visiting in April. Finish up your day with a drink at the Vivanta by Taj hotel, the entirety of Srinagar laid out at your feet.

If your two days are in Leh, prepare yourself for immersion in Ladakh's Buddhist culture. Start your visit with a walk in the Old Town, climbing up the narrow streets from Main Bazaar to the LAMO centre for an introduction to Leh's history. Have a cup of tea at the atmospheric Lonpo House before continuing up to Leh Palace and then Tsemo Fort. If you're feeling less than fit, or haven't yet acclimatised to the altitude, you might need to take a taxi between the two.

On day two go to the Shanti Stupa before breakfast so you can explore it before the crowds. Drive back into town via the far older Tisseru Stupa, and have a bite to eat at one of the many cafés in Changspa. If you're an adrenaline junkie you now have time to do the descent from Khardung La by mountain bike, or spend a more leisurely few hours taking a meditation class at the Mahabodhi International Meditation Centre.

A WEEK With a week in Ladakh, use Leh as your hub for exploring the district. Travel first to the south of Ladakh, visiting the monasteries of Thiksey and Hemis *en route* to Tsomoriri and Tso Kar lakes. Stay in a tented camp and take the opportunity to do some walking in the surrounding hills, being careful to keep back from the Chinese frontier.

Pass through Leh again as you drive back north, continuing on to visit Phyang and Likir, where you can spend the night with the boy monks at their school and admire the impressive, gilded Maitreya Buddha. There are finely preserved wall paintings at Alchi and, if you have time, the lunar landscapes just before Lamayuru are a fascinating geological feature. If at any stage during your trip the Dalai Lama is preaching, drop everything else and join the devotees hanging on his every word.

In a week you also have time to drive the length of the Vale of Kashmir from Srinagar to Jammu. Having explored Srinagar itself, travel to the relaxing hill resort of Pahalgam via the saffron fields at Pamore and the two remarkable temples at Avantipore. If it's winter and Pahalgam is inaccessible, go to Gulmarg instead for a rewarding (and affordable) day on the slopes at the Himalayas' premier ski resort.

The drive southwards through the valley is spectacular: the hairpin bends clinging to the mountainside are an attraction in their own right, if a little hair raising. Take time to visit the stunning Sun Temple at Martand and, if you've not yet had your fill of horticulture, the Mughal Garden at Verinag.

Approaching Jammu, the Hindu shrine at Katra is an important pilgrimage site, and quite a contrast from the Muslim pilgrimage places further north. End your trip staying at Hari Niwas, the former palace of Maharaja Hari Singh, sipping gin and tonics on the lawn overlooking the Tawi River.

If Kargil's airport reopens to commercial flights during the lifespan of this edition, a week will also enable you to visit the Central Asia Museum in Kargil town, the finest museum in the state, and some if not all of the five stone Buddhas. You'll be able to get up to Dha-Hanu or, alternatively, down into the stunning Suru Valley with its unique Dard culture and the twin peaks of Nun and Kun. If you're determined, it'd also be possible to reach the northern part of Zanskar, stopping for the night in the tent camp at the foot of Rangdum Gompa.

TWO OR MORE WEEKS A fortnight or longer is sufficient to travel across larger parts of the state and/or to do an extended trek. If your interest is primarily in Ladakh, start in Leh exploring the town and the monasteries between Leh and Lamayuru. Take the short (two day) trek from Lamayuru through the mountains to Rangdum and then allow yourself seven to ten days in Zanskar. Don't miss Karsha Gompa or the 12th-century rock-cut monastery at Phuktal, the latter of which is only accessible on foot. In Padum there are superb Buddha carvings down by the river, which are unfortunately often overlooked.

Coming back, drive through the Suru Valley, making sure you see the Buddha at Kartse Khar. Attempts on Mount Nun are best undertaken from the base camp at Tanyol, 6km from Panikhar, but more leisurely walks along the valley are also a pleasure, especially in spring when the slopes are covered in wild flowers.

The trekking opportunities in Kashmir are also under-appreciated, and two weeks is ample time to get up into the mountains and away from other foreigners. From Pahalgam to Sonamarg it's a four-day trek via the Amarnath Cave, and your companions will be Hindu devotees visiting the cave's Shiva ice lingam. You can then trek the further seven days from Sonamarg to Naranag (base camp for Mount Haramukh and Gangabal Lake), where there are some notable 8th-century Hindu temples (now in ruins), and then to Srinagar.

TOUR OPERATORS

International tour operators, many of which cover destinations across India and further afield, are listed below. For local tour operators, see individual chapters.

UK

Exodus   Grange Mills, Weir Rd, London SW12 0NE; 0845 863 9600; e sales@exodus.co.uk; www. exodus.co.uk. Multiple escorted tours to Ladakh, including adventurous options such as an ascent of Stok Kangri & a trek across the Changtang Plateau.

Expert Tours   PO Box 68518, London SW15 9EH; m 07854258321; e contactexperttours@ gmail.com. Small-group, luxury tours to unusual destinations led by authors, diplomats & academics with in-depth knowledge of their areas. We will be leading the 21-day Heaven on Earth tour in 2015, sharing our favourite corners of J&K & delivering lectures on aspects of the state's history & culture.

Explore   Nelson Hse, 55–59 Victoria Rd, Farnborough, Surrey GU14 7PA; 0845 291 4541; e res@explore.co.uk; www.explore.co.uk. We bumped into the Explore group in Thiksey. Their escorted 16-day Little Tibet tour takes in all the major monasteries in Ladakh then returns to the plains overland via Dharmsala & Amritsar.

Going Solo   PO Box 68518, London SW15 9EH; m 07977637576; e goingsolotravel@gmail.com; www.facebook.com/GoingSoloTravel. Expert Tours' sister company arranges group tours for single travellers who'd rather not be surrounded by couples or pay a singles' supplement. In J&K they offer a 7-day gardens & architecture tour based in Srinagar, & more strenuous women-only treks in Ladakh.

Indus Experiences   (See ad, 2nd colour section) KCB Harrow Exchange, 2 Gayton Rd, Harrow, London HA1 2XU; 020 8901 7320; e holidays@ indusexperiences.co.uk; www.industours.co.uk. Tailor-made & luxury tours to the Indian subcontinent & Indochina. The 9-day Kashmir: The Secret Garden tour includes cultural interaction with local communities & sightseeing in Srinagar & Gulmarg.

Mountain Tribal Vision   (See ad, page 179) 65 Blenheim Terrace, London NW8 0EJ; 020 7625 1520; m 07950 517 068; e tanzin.norbu@gmail. com; www.mountaintribalvision.com. If you want to travel with a Ladakh & Zanskar specialist, look no further than Mountain Tribal Vision. Owner Tanzin Norbu, a fellow of the RGS, was born in Zanskar & studied in India & the UK. His organised treks focus on snow leopards & other fauna in the winter, & wild flowers, photography & local culture in the summer. Tanzin is also an expert on Buddhism. His passion for his homeland is infectious.

Native Eye   (See ad, page 120) 22 Milton Rd, Lawford, Essex CO11 2EG; 020 3286 5995; e info@nativeeyetravel.com; www. nativeeyetravel.com. Small adventure travel company with a personal touch; specialises in unusual destinations. Offers tours taking in Leh, Shey, Thiksey, Hemis, the Nubra Valley, Diskit, Kargil, Zanskar & Srinagar & elsewhere in the wider region.

On the Go Tours   68 North End Rd, London W14 9EP; 020 7371 1113; e info@onthegotours.com; www.onthegotours.com. Private & group tours of both Kashmir & Ladakh, including mini breaks (4 days) in Srinagar & Gulmarg. Trips to Kashmir can also be combined with the Golden Triangle.

Steppes Travel   Travel Hse, 51 Castle St, Cirencester, Glos GL7 1QD; 01285 880 980; e enquiry@steppestravel.co.uk; www. steppestravel.co.uk. Offers a 10-day tour of Kashmir & Ladakh from £2,995 pp. Includes a domestic flight from Srinagar to Leh, but doesn't afford the chance opportunity to travel outside these 2 towns.

TransIndus   75 St Mary's Rd & The Old Fire Station, Ealing, London W5 5RH; 020 8566 3739; www.transindus.co.uk. Asia specialist TransIndus has a 12-day Ladakh tour with optional extension to Kashmir. Alternatively, the 12-day Vale of Kashmir tour focuses on sites in the valley itself. Accommodation options are luxurious & include Sukoon Houseboat on Dal Lake, Srinagar.

Wild Frontiers   Unit 6, Hurlingham Business Pk, 55 Sulivan Rd, London SW6 3DU; 020 7736 3968; e info@wildfrontiers.co.uk; www.wildfrontiers. co.uk. Well-run group & tailor-made tours to both Kashmir & Ladakh. Choose from wild walking, extended boat trips & mountain camping.

USA AND CANADA

Absolute Travel   15 Watts St, 5th Flr, New York, NY 10013, USA; +1 212 627 1950; e info@ absolutetravel.com; www.absolutetravel.com. Luxury tour operator offering tailored packages to Ladakh.

Adventure Center 579 Richmond St West, 4th Flr, Toronto, ON, Canada M5V 1Y6; +1 416 922 8136; e toronto@adventurecenter.com; www. adventurecenter.com. Adventurous, organised tours of Ladakh including trekking in the Markha Valley & family-friendly holidays combining shorter treks & cultural sites. Branch also in Vancouver (2227 Granville St, Vancouver, BC, Canada V6H 3G1; +1 604 737 8854; e vancouver@adventurecenter.com).

OTHER INTERNATIONAL TOUR OPERATORS

Kamzang PO Box No 12492, Kathmandu, Chabahil 44602 APO, Nepal; m +977 980 341 4745; e kamzang@kamzang.com; www.kamzang. com. American Kim Bannister runs exclusive treks across the Himalayas from her base in Kathmandu. 2–3 Ladakh & Zanskar treks take place each summer & they sometimes include previously untested routes. Kim brings her own team on every trek, ensuring the standard of catering, portering & customer service is 2nd to none.

On the Go Tours 3/690 Brunswick St, New Farm, QLD 4005, Australia; +61 7 3358 3385; e info@onthegotours.com; www.onthegotours. com. Australian office of UK company (see opposite).

Sawadee Sarphatistraat 650, 1018 AV Amsterdam, Netherlands; +31 20 420 2220; e info@sawadee.nl; www.sawadee.nl. Renowned Dutch tour operator offering a comprehensive, 22-day tour of Ladakh from €1,998 including KLM flights. The itinerary includes trekking from Lamayuru & returns to Delhi overland via Manali & Dharamsala.

RED TAPE

The Indian government loves red tape. Some claim this is a legacy of the British, but the bureaucrats have taken it one stage further. Photocopies, permits and triplicates rule the roost; computerised systems are still a decade away.

VISAS All foreign nationals (excluding Nepalese and Bhutanese) need a visa for entering India, and the vast majority of visitors come on a 180-day tourist visa, details of which are given here. For information on other types of visa, including business and residency visas, see http://in.vfsglobal.co.uk/aboutyourvisas.html.

Visas on arrival are currently available for those from Cambodia, Finland, Indonesia, Japan, Laos, Luxembourg, Myanmar, New Zealand, Philippines, Singapore and Vietnam. These visas are valid for 30 days only and cost US$60. In order to qualify, you must have purchased a return ticket, be travelling for tourism purposes only, and have at least six months left to run on your passport. If you, your parents or grandparents were born in Pakistan, even if you now have a passport from one of the qualifying countries, you will not be allowed a visa on arrival.

All other nationals must apply for a visa before travelling to India. The price of the visa depends on both your nationality and where you apply: UK passport holders applying in London currently pay £92.20 (which includes a £10.20 processing fee) while, for comparison purposes, other EU nationals applying in London pay just US$42.20. Visa fees are payable at the time of submitting your application and are non-refundable, even if your visa is refused.

In the UK, Indian visa applications are handled by a private contractor, VFS Global (*http://in.vfsglobal.co.uk*). You should download the application form from the VFS website and then either submit it by post or in person at one of the visa centres, for which you can book a timed appointment. There are VFS visa centres in London, Birmingham, Cardiff, Edinburgh, Glasgow and Manchester. Take a good book to read as they are frequently running late.

In addition to your printed and signed application form, you must submit two recent 50 x 50mm passport photos (NB: this is not the same size as a standard UK passport photo), your passport, any supporting paperwork and a self-addressed Special Delivery Envelope (SDE; this applies to postal applications only).

If you apply in person, it typically takes five working days to process your visa, though Pakistani, Sri Lankan and Bangladeshi nationals should allow significantly longer. Those applying by post should allow a minimum of ten working days and send their documents by recorded delivery.

REGISTRATION If you are travelling on a tourist visa, you do not usually need to register in India: this is a requirement for long-term visa holders only. However, special requirements are in place for Jammu and Kashmir due to the security concerns. If you arrive by air, you will be registered at the airport on arrival. Coming by road, you will need to fill in a registration form at a police checkpoint. There are no charges for this kind of registration and you do not need to show any documents other than your valid passport and visa.

PERMITS Non-Ladakhis wishing to travel close to the border with China must have an Inner Line Permit (see box, page 107). This is available only in Leh, can be processed in one day, and costs Rs20 with an additional Rs10 donation to the Red Cross. The permit is valid for seven days.

Mountaineering permits are required for some ascents. If the peak is under 7,000m you can apply yourself via the Indian Mountaineering Foundation's office in Leh (see page 99). Permits for higher peaks require prior authorisation from Delhi. Full information is available on the IMF website (*www.indmount.org*).

EMBASSIES

INDIAN EMBASSIES ABROAD India has a good network of overseas embassies, partly due to the large Indian diaspora. In some cases visas are not issued at the consulate but by a third-party agent, such as VFS Global in the UK, so check on the relevant embassy's website before turning up for a visa. A full list of India's overseas missions is on the Ministry of External Affairs' website (*www.mea.gov.in/indian-missions-abroad.htm*).

Afghanistan Malalaiwat, Shar-e-Naw, Kabul; +93 20 220 0185; e embassy@indembassy-kabul.com; www.meakabul.nic.in. India also has consulates at Mazar-e Sharif, Jalalabad & Kandahar.

Australia 3 Moonah Pl, Yarralumla, Canberra 2600; +61 2 6273 3999; e consular1@hcindia-au.org; www.hcindia-au.org. Visa & consular services are provided by VFS Global (www.vfs-au-in.com) at their centres in Adelaide, Brisbane, Canberra, Melbourne, Perth & Sydney.

Bangladesh House No 2, Rd No 142, Gulshan-1, Dhaka; +880 2 988 9339; e visahelp@hcidhaka.gov.in; www.hcidhaka.gov.in. There are Indian Visa Application Centres (IVACs) in Dhaka, Chittagong, Khulna, Rajshahi & Sylhet.

Bhutan India Hse Estate, Jungshina, Thimphu; +975 2 322 162; e amb.thimphu@mea.gov.in; www.indianembassythimphu.bt

Canada 10 Springfield Rd, Ottawa, Ontario K1M 1C9; +1 613 744 3751; e hicomind@hciottawa.ca; www.hciottawa.ca. Additional consulates in Toronto & Vancouver.

China 5 Liang Ma Qiao Bei Jie, Chaoyang District, Beijing; +86 10 8531 2500; e hoc.beijing@mea.gov.in; www.indianembassy.org.cn. Additional consulates in Guangzhou, Hong Kong & Shanghai.

France 15 Rue Alfred Dehodencq, Paris 75016; +33 1 4050 7070; e dcm.paris@mea.gov.in; www.ambinde.fr. Note that the consular department is situated separately from the embassy (20–22 Rue Alberic Magnard, Paris 75016; +33 1 4050 7171; e cons.paris@mea.gov.in) & that visa applications are handled by VFS Global (www.vfs-in-fr.com).

Germany Tiergartenstrasse 17, Berlin 10785; +49 30 257 950; e consular@indianembassy.de; www.indianembassy.de. Cox & Kings (*www.in.de.coxandkings.com*) handles visas in Berlin & Munich; Indo-German Consultancy Services (*www.igcsvisa.de*) processes applications in Hamburg & Frankfurt.

Italy   Via XX Settembre 5, Rome 00187;
+39 6 488 4642; e gen.email@indianembassy.
it; www.indianembassy.it

Japan   2-2-11 Kudan-Minami, Chiyoda-ku,
Tokyo 102 0074; +81 3 3262 2391; e embassy@
indembassy-tokyo.gov.in; www.indembassy-
tokyo.gov.in.

Nepal   PO Box No 292, 336 Kapurdhara Marg,
Kathmandu; +977 1 441 0900; e hoc@eoiktm.
org; www.indianembassy.org.np

Netherlands   Buitenrustweg 2, The Hague
2517 KD; +31 70 346 9771; ww.indianembassy.
nl. Visa applications are accepted Consular Services
Centres in The Hague, Amsterdam & Rotterdam.

New Zealand   180 Molesworth St,
Wellington; +64 4 474 6390; e hicomind@
hicomind.org.nz; www.hicomind.org.nz

Pakistan   G-5, Diplomatic Enclave, Islamabad;
+92 51 220 6950; e hc.islamabad@mea.gov.
in; www.india.org.pk. Visas issued to Pakistani
nationals are place-specific: you must list the cities
that you intend to visit & are likely to be called to
interview at the High Commission in Islamabad.

Russia   6–8 Ulitsa Vorontsovo Polye, Moscow;
+7 495 783 7535; e admin@indianembassy.ru;
www.indianembassy.ru. BLS (*www.blsindia-russia.*

com) runs centres in Moscow & St Petersburg.

South Africa   852 Schoeman St, Pretoria;
+27 1 2342 5392; e indiahc@hicomind.co.za;
www.indiainsouthafrica.com. India has additional
consulates in Cape Town, Durban & Johannesburg.

Sri Lanka   36–8, Galle Rd, Colombo;
+94 11 232 7587; e cons.colombo@mea.gov.in;
www.hcicolombo.org. IVS Global Services (www.
ivsvisalanka.com) accepts visa applications in
Colombo, Jaffna & Kandy.

UAE   Plot No 10, Sector W-59/02, Diplomatic
Area, off Airport Rd, PO Box 4090, Abu Dhabi;
+971 2 449 2700; e consular@indembassyuae.
org; www.indianembassyuae.org. BLS International
Services Ltd (www.blsindiavisa-uae.com) accepts
visa applications in Abu Dhabi & Dubai.

UK   India Hse, Aldwych, London WC2B 4NA;
+44 207 836 8484; e hoc.london@mea.gov.in;
www.hcilondon.in. See *Visas*, page 31.

USA   2107 Massachusetts Av, NW Washington,
DC 20008; +1 202 939 7000; e hoc.washington@
mea.gov.in; www.indianembassy.org. BLS
International Services Ltd (www.visa.blsindia-usa.
com) accepts visa applications in Washington,
Atlanta, Chicago, Houston, New York & San Francisco.

FOREIGN EMBASSIES   There are no foreign embassies in Kashmir itself, and foreign
governments typically warn that they can provide little consular support here. You
should apply for visas for onward travel and refer consular enquiries to the appropriate
embassy in New Delhi. The embassies below have the +91 international dialling code.

Afghanistan   5/50F, Shantipath,
Chanakyapuri, New Delhi 110021 011 2410
0412; www.afghanembassy.in

Australia   1/50 G Shantipath, Chanakyapuri,
New Delhi 110021; 011 4139 9900; e ahc.
newdelhi@dfat.gov.au; www.india.embassy.gov.au

Bangladesh   EP39, Dr S Radha Krishnan Marg,
Chanakyapuri, New Delhi 110021; 011 2412 1389;
e email@bdhcdelhi.org; www.bdhcdelhi.org

Bhutan   Chandragupta Marg, Chanakyapuri,
New Delhi 110021; 011 2688 9230; e bhutan@
vsnl.com; www.mfa.gov.bt

Canada   7/8 Shantipath, Chanakyapuri
New Delhi 110 021; 011 4178 2000; e delhi@
international.gc.ca; www.india.gc.ca

China   50D, Shantipath, Chanakyapuri, New
Delhi 110 021; 011 2611 2345; e chinaemb_
in@mfa.gov.cn; http://in.chineseembassy.org/
eng

France   2/50E Shantipath, Chanakyapuri,
New Delhi 110021; 011 2419 6100; www.
ambafrance-in.org

Germany   6/50G, Shantipath, Chanakyapuri,
New Delhi 110021; 011 4419 9199; e www.
new-delhi.diplo.de.

Italy   50E Chandragupta Marg,
Chanakyapuri, New Delhi 110021; 011 2611
4355; e ambasciata.newdelhi@esteri.it; www.
ambnewdelhi.esteri.it

Japan   4–5/50G Shantipath, Chanakyapuri,
New Delhi 110 021; 011 2687 6581; e jpembjic@
nd.mofa.go.jp; www.in.emb-japan.go.jp

Nepal   Barakhamba Rd, Connaught Pl, New
Delhi 110 001; 011 2332 8066; e consular@
nepalembassy.in; www.nepalembassy.in

Netherlands   6/50 F, Shantipath,
Chanakyapuri, New Delhi 110 021; 011 2419 7600;
e nde@minbuza.nl; http://india.nlembassy.org

E New Zealand Sir Edmund Hillary Marg, Chanakyapuri, New Delhi 110 021; ✆ 011 4688 3170; e nzhcindia@gmail.com; www.nzembassy.com/india

E Pakistan 2/50-G, Shantipath, Chanakyapuri, New Delhi 110 021; ✆ 011 2611 0601; e pahicnewdelhi@mofa.gov.pk; www.mofa.gov.pk

E Russia Shantipath, Chanakyapuri, New Delhi 110 021; ✆ 011 2611 0640; e emb@rusembassy.in; www.rusembassy.in

E South Africa B 18, Vasant Vihar, New Delhi 110 057; ✆ 011 2614 9411; e dtidelhi@thedti.gov.za; http://southafricainindia.wordpress.com

E Sri Lanka 27 Kautilya Marg, Chanakyapuri,

DELHI: A SHORT PRACTICAL GUIDE   *Telephone code: 011*

India's chaotic capital is a Marmite city: you'll either love it or hate it. What is certain is that if you can't tick a monkey, a naked holy man and a cross-dressing *hijra* off your eye-spy list before lunchtime, you're probably not making the most of Delhi.

GETTING AROUND Delhi is a mega-city, with all the transport problems that moniker infers. The best way to get around is by **metro**. Six lines cover central Delhi, and extensions are under way to reach out into suburbia. Trains are efficient, air conditioned and clean, and fares are just Rs8–12 depending on distance.

Alternatively you can take a **taxi** or **auto-rickshaw**. These are supposed to charge by the meter, but you may prefer to agree a price before you set off. Auto-rickshaws are about half the price of taxis (expect to pay Rs80–100 for a 20-minute journey as opposed to Rs200). Taxis with air conditioning charge more.

TRAVEL AGENTS

Abyss Tours 15A/56, B1 Lower Ground Flr, WEA Saraswati Marg, Karol Bagh; ✆ 4506 4008; e sales@abysstours.com; www.abysstours.com. Delhi-based firm arranging packages across India, including to J&K. Also offers car rental & hotel bookings.

Sea and Sky Travel 90/60 Malviya Nagar; m 98 6827 0378; e hamza@seaandskytravel.com; www.seaandskytravel.com. Established in 1974, Sea & Sky has offices across India & arranges adventure & cultural packages, transport & hotels.

SnowLion Expeditions (see ad, page 238) Suite 402, DDA Bldg 5, District Centre, Janak Puri, New Delhi; ✆ 2252 4389; e ashoak@snowlion-india.com; www.snowlion-india.com. Inbound operator with over 30 years' experience, in adventure tours across India. Also offers leisure & cultural tours. Trekking in Ladakh & Kashmir; mountain & motorbiking; jeep, camel & wildlife safaris; wellness & beach tours. Recognised by the Ministry of Tourism.

WHERE TO STAY By Indian standards, Delhi is an expensive city and this is reflected in the room rates.

Hotel Imperial (192 rooms) Janpath; ✆ 2334 1234; e luxury@theimperialindia.com; www.theimperialindia.com. India's 'Best Boutique Hotel 2013' is the place to stay if money is no object. Built in 1931 in a striking colonial style; previous guests have included Gandhi & Mountbatten. There's a world-class art collection. The service is impeccable. **$$$$$**

Hyatt Regency (See ad, page 76) (507 rooms) Bhikaiji Cama Place, Ring Rd; ✆ 2679 1234; e delhi.regency@hyatt.com; www.delhi.regency.hyatt.com. Delhi's premier business hotel. Staff are highly professional, every need is catered for, & the hotel has some of the best restaurants in the city. **$$$$$**

Hotel Alka Block P-16, Connaught Circus; ✆ 2334 4328; e info@hotelalka.com; www.hotelalka.com. Mid-sized hotel with clean, comfortable rooms in central Delhi. There's a restaurant, bar & café within the complex. **$$$$**

De Holiday Inn (39 rooms) 22/18 Raj Guru Rd, Chuna Mandi, Paharganj; ✆ 2356

New Delhi 110 021; ☎ 011 23010201;
e lankacomnd@mea.gov.lk; www.slhcindia.org
Ⓔ UAE EP-12, Chander Gupta Marg,
Chanakyapuri, New Delhi 110 021; ☎ 011 2687
2937; e info.newdelhi@mofa.gov.ae; www.
uaeembassy-newdelhi.com

Ⓔ UK Shantipath, Chanakyapuri, New Delhi 110
021; ☎ 011 2419 2100; e web.newdelhi@fco.gov.
uk; www.ukinindia.fco.gov.uk
Ⓔ USA Shantipath, Chanakyapuri, New Delhi
110 021; ☎ 011 2419 8000; e ndwebmail@state.
gov; www.newdelhi.usembassy.gov

2690; e deholidayint@hotmail.com; www.
deholidayinternational.com. As students we
spent many happy months at De Holiday
Inn, & still go back when we want a lemon
pancake. Staff are warm & helpful & it's by far
the cleanest option in the backpackers' area of
Paharganj. **$$$**

🏠 **International Youth Hostel** 5 Nyaya
Marg, Chanakyapuri; ☎ 2611 6285;
e hostelbooking@yhaindia.org. Part of India's
Youth Hostel Association & 1 of the few low-
priced options in Delhi. A room in a non-AC
dorm starts at Rs275 inc b/fast. Twin rooms also
available. Institutional feel but clean. **$–$$**

✖ **WHERE TO EAT** Delhi has probably the best restaurants in India, and whether
you're craving doughnuts or *dosas*, samosas or sushi, you won't be disappointed.
For international food, **La Piazza** and **TK's Oriental Grill** (*both at the Hyatt, see
opposite; $$$$$*) are expensive but worth the effort if you're looking to impress.
Lodhi, The Garden Restaurant (*Lodhi Rd;* ☎ *2649 4531; $$$$$*) has both indoor
and outdoor tables in a romantic setting and, for something more laid-back, you
can't beat **Turtle Café** (*Shop 23, 2nd Flr, Middle Lane, Khan Market;* ☎ *2465 5641;
$$$–$$$$*) and **The Big Chill** (*A-68, Prithviraj La, Khan Market;* ☎ *4175 7588; $$$–
$$$$*). The latter two also do excellent coffee and cakes.

For north Indian cuisine, we like opulent **Veda** (*H-27, Connaught Circus;*
☎ *4151 3535; $$$$$*) or, for traditional Mughlai dishes in more rough and ready
surroundings, the Old Delhi institution that is **Karim's** (*Nr Jama Masjid, Gali
Kababian;* ☎ *2326 4981; $$$*). The best parathas (*$–$$*) are from the stalls in Old
Delhi's **Paratha Gali** (Paratha Alley), a stone's throw from Karim's.

WHAT TO SEE Delhi has some 1,200 heritage buildings and more than 200
monuments of national importance. Standard tourist itineraries include
the **Qutb Minar** (*Mehrauli;* ⊕ *dawn–dusk daily; entrance fee Rs10/250 local/
foreigner*), the world's tallest brick-built minaret; **Humayun's Tomb** (*Mathura Rd;*
⊕ *dawn–dusk daily; entrance fee Rs10/250 local/foreigner*), one of the architectural
models for the Taj Mahal; the impressive **Red Fort** (*Netaji Subhash Marg;* ⊕ *dawn–
dusk Tue–Sun; entrance fee Rs10/250 local/foreigner*); and the **Jama Masjid** (*Off Netaji
Subhash Marg;* ⊕ *07.00–12.00 & 13.30–18.30 daily, closed to tourists during prayers;
free entry*). All of these are worth a visit, though often they're frustratingly crowded.

If you like archaeological sites marginally quieter, the crumbling **Purana Qila**
(*Mathura Rd;* ⊕ *dawn–dusk daily; entrance fee Rs5/100 local/foreigner*) is a large and
wild site with thick ramparts, impenetrable gateways and the library from the roof of
which Emperor Humayun fell to his death, probably in an opiate-induced haze. **Lodhi
Gardens** (*Lodhi Rd;* ⊕ *dawn–dusk daily; free entry*) contains a large number of tombs
from the Lodhi and Sayyid periods, including the octagonal tomb of Sikander Lodhi;
and the **Jantar Mantar** (*Connaught Pl;* ⊕ *dawn–dusk daily; entrance fee Rs5/100 local/
foreigner*), the 18th century astronomical observatory of Maharaja Jai Singh, is worth
an hour of your time if you're not going to see its larger sister observatory in Jaipur.

India is well connected to the rest of the world, particularly in terms of flights, and onward transport connections from the main hubs to Jammu, Srinagar and Leh are affordable. Bear in mind, however, that in the winter months Leh is only accessible by air, and that Jammu is currently the only major city in the state to have a rail connection to the rest of India.

As there are no international connections to J&K, this section is arranged as follows: international flights to Delhi and travel information on that city; domestic flights connecting J&K to other parts of India; train connections to Jammu (currently the only major city in J&K with an operational railway line); and road connections to J&K via Himachal Pradesh and the Punjab.

BY AIR India has superb flight connections around the world, and you'll generally be able to choose from a range of departures from your place of origin. If the primary focus of your trip is J&K, opt to fly into Delhi to maximise your onward travel options. Other major international airports in the country include Bangalore, Kolkata and Mumbai.

International flights via Delhi
Indira Gandhi International Airport (DEL) is the busiest airport in India and handles around 40 million passengers every year. The international terminal is brand new, making for a significantly more pleasant experience on landing.

The following airlines operate international flights to Delhi. Where they have an office in Delhi, local contact details have been given.

✈ **Aeroflot** Tolstoy Hse, 15–17 Tolstoy Marg; New Delhi 110 001; ☎011 2331 0426; e delmngr@ aeroflot.ru; www.aeroflot.com. Daily from Moscow.

✈ **Air China** Ground Flr, E9 Connaught Hse, Connaught Place, New Delhi 110 001; ☎011 4350 8888; e res@airchina.co.in; www.airchina.com. Regular departures from Beijing.

✈ **Air France** www.airfrance.com. Daily departures from Paris.

✈ **Air India** Terminal 3, Indira Gandhi International Airport, New Delhi 110 037; ☎011 4963 1097; e del.reservationmanager@airindia.in; www.airindia.com. The national airline has regular departures to Delhi from Europe, the Middle East & southeast Asia, plus flights to Chicago & New York.

✈ **British Airways** www.britishairways.com. 2 flights a day from London Heathrow.

✈ **Cathay Pacific** Terminal 3, Indira Gandhi International Airport, New Delhi 110 037; ☎022 6657 2222; e india_res@cathaypacific.com; www. cathaypacific.com. Daily departures to Bangkok & Hong Kong.

✈ **China Airlines** www.china-airlines.com/ en. Daily flights from Taipei with good connections across China & southeast Asia.

✈ **Druk Air** www.drukair.com.bt. Bhutanese national carrier. Daily flights from Paro.

✈ **Emirates** www.emirates.com. 4 flights a day from Dubai with good connections worldwide.

✈ **Jet Airways** (See ad, page 76) G11/12, Outer Circle, G Block, Connaught Circus, Connaught Place, New Delhi 110 001; ☎011 3989 3333; www. jetairways.com. India's best airline has direct flights from Canada, Europe, the Middle East & SE Asia.

✈ **Lufthansa** 12th Flr, DLF Bldg No 10, Tower B DLF City, Phase II; ☎012 4488 8888; e delteamd@ dlh.de; www.lufthansa.com. Daily departures from Frankfurt & Munich.

✈ **Malaysia Airlines** 16th Flr, Dr Gopal Das Bhawan, 28 Barakhamba Rd, New Delhi 110 001; ☎011 4151 2101; www.malaysiaairlines.com. Daily departures from Kuala Lumpur.

✈ **Pakistan International Airlines** Room 519–20, 5th Flr, Narain Manzil, 23 Barakhamba Rd, New Delhi 110 001; ☎011 2373 7791; www.piac. com.pk. Pakistan's national carrier. Daily flights from Lahore. Frequently sold out so book early.

✈ **Qatar Airways** Dr Gopal Das Bhawan, 28 Barakhamba Rd, New Delhi 110 001; ☎079 3061 6000; www.qatarairways.com. 2 flights per day from Doha.

✈ **Singapore Airlines** Unit 514, A & B Time Tower, MG Rd, Gurgaon 122 002; ☎012 4431 0999; e del_feedback@singaporeair.com.sg; www. singaporeair.com. 3 daily departures from Singapore.
✈ **Swiss** www.swiss.com. Flies daily from Zürich.
✈ **Turkish Airlines** Unit 1001A, Time Tower, MG Rd, Gurgaon 122 001; ☎012 4419 3019;

e delreservation@thy.com; www.turkishairlines. com. Daily flights from Istanbul.
✈ **United Airlines** www.united.com. 2 daily flights from New York, 1 of which routes via Frankfurt.
✈ **Virgin Atlantic** www.virgin-atlantic.com. Daily flights from London.

Domestic flights

Jammu, Leh and Srinagar all have airports with regular commercial flights to other parts of India, and it is hoped that flights out of Kargil will commence during the lifespan of this edition. Flying into the state is certainly the easiest way to get here, though if you head straight to Leh you will need to allow several days to acclimatise to the altitude.

The flight-booking portal Yatra (*www.yatra.com*) is an Indian version of lastminute and has the latest schedules for Indian domestic airlines. It also lets you book online. Alternatively, flight tickets can be booked from the airlines' own offices, at the airport counters, or from a local travel agent. Details of local ticketing offices and the airport's contact details are given in the relevant city chapters.

The main domestic airlines serving airports in J&K are **Air India** (*www.airindia. com*), **Go Air** (*www.goair.in*), **IndiGo** (*www.goindigo.in*), **JetKonnect** (*www. jetkonnect.co.in*) and **Spice Jet** (*www.spicejet.com*).

To Jammu You can fly to Jammu airport (IXJ) from Delhi, Chennai and Mumbai, and there are also occasional connections from Jammu to Leh and Srinagar. Flights from Delhi cost around Rs5,000 each way, and all of the options leave Delhi early in the morning. The flight takes 1 hour 20 minutes. Flights from Leh to Jammu also take 1 hour 20 minutes and cost Rs5,000.

To Leh There are regular flights to Leh airport (IXL) from Delhi, Chandigarh, Jammu and Srinagar. The flight from Delhi takes 1 hour 15 minutes and costs around Rs4,500 in the winter months but up to twice as much in summer. Tickets in high season can be in short supply, so book ahead to ensure you get the date you want and be aware that even in August bad weather can still cause flight delays and cancellations.

To Srinagar Srinagar (SXR) is the best connected of the state's airports thanks to the constant flow of domestic tourists holidaying on the lake. It's possible to fly here from Delhi, Mumbai, Amritsar, Bangalore, Chandigarh, Indore and Nagpur. The direct flight from Delhi takes 1 hour 10 minutes and tickets start at Rs4,500. Before booking check that you are looking at a direct flight, as some of the options route via Jammu.

Note that due to concerns that J&K flights might be targeted by terrorists, security on flights to and from destinations in the state is particularly tight. Additional baggage checks are common and you may not be able to carry hand luggage on the plane. Please check with your airline prior to flying for its latest baggage requirements.

BY TRAIN

The only major city in J&K to have a railway station is Jammu, and though the line is being extended to Srinagar, this part of the route is unlikely to be operational before 2017.

Travelling by train in India is a memorable experience, and if you buy a first- or second-class ticket it's a pleasurable one. Don't underestimate the value of travelling in an air-conditioned compartment. Trains run more or less on time and when you buy a ticket (which must be done in advance), you automatically get a seat reservation.

Practical Information GETTING THERE AND AWAY

2

37

Train timetables and fares are available from the Indian Rail website (*www.indianrail. gov.in*), though you might find private sites such as http://erail.in easier to use. It is possible to buy tickets online if you have an Indian SIM in your phone, otherwise it's easier to book through a local agent and you'll only pay a small commission. You can either buy a ticket for a single journey, or buy an IndRail Pass, which is valid for up to 90 days. The latter is only available to foreigners and must be paid for in foreign currency: more details are available at www.indianrail.gov.in/international_Tourist.html.

MANALI   *Telephone code: 01902*

The town of Manali lies in the Himalayan foothills of Himachal Pradesh, close to the northern end of the Kullu Valley. The River Beas is the local focal point, and domestic tourists flock here throughout the year to explore the surrounding countryside.

GETTING THERE AND AROUND   The **airport** serving Manali is 50km away at Bhuntar (KUU). Air India operates a daily flight here from Delhi. The flight takes 1 hour 20 minutes and costs from Rs5,900 one-way.

The majority of visitors to Manali come by **road**. NH1 goes as far as Chandigarh, after which the Kullu Highway (NH21) continues on to Manali. The drive from Delhi to Manali is 851km (528 miles) and takes at least 12 hours.

Volvo coaches leave Delhi's Kashmiri Gate bus stand for Manali each evening between 20.00 and 21.00, reaching Manali 14 hours later. Tickets cost Rs1,353 per person and can be booked via the Himachal Road Transport Company's website (*www.hrtc.gov.in*). Ordinary buses depart regularly throughout the day and cost Rs637.

Buses shuttle between Manali and Kullu every 15 minutes and cost Rs40 per person. **Motorbike hire** (*try Manali Bike Rental;* m *98 1662 2344;* e *info@ manalibijerental.com; www.manalibikerental.com*) is popular and a day's hire will set you back around Rs600 for a Bullet or Honda bike.

Car and driver hire is available from Car Rental Manali (m *98 1605 1236; www. carrentalmanali.com*). Local sightseeing in an Indica starts from Rs550.

TRAVEL AGENTS
Anrek Tours and Travels   1 The Mall, Circuit Hse Rd; ☎ 252 292; e info@antrek.co.in; www. antrek.co.in. Trekking & adventure sports packages, including paragliding, rafting & skiing.
Himalayan Adventurers   Opp Tourist Information Centre, 44 The Mall; ☎ 252 750; e info@himalayanadveturers.com; www. himalayanadventurers.com. Winter sports, birdwatching & cultural tours. Also books homestays in Manali town.
Jispa Journeys   Gompa Rd, Kullu District; m 94 1866 0225; e info@jispajourneys. com; www.jispajourneys.com. Arranges stays in tented camps, bike tours, jeep safaris & trekking. Pilgrimage tours a particular speciality.

🏠 **WHERE TO STAY**   Manali is a popular destination for domestic tourists, so book accommodation well in advance if you plan to stay here during holiday periods.

 Span Resorts   (20 rooms, 6 cottages) Kullu Manali Hwy; ☎ 240 138; e spanres@ airtelbroadband.in; www.spanresorts.com. Manali's only 5* property is 15km from the town centre beside the River Beas. Serving mainly domestic tourists on package tours, it has everything from a swimming pool to mini golf, & can arrange horseriding & paragliding. All rooms have AC & heating; if your budget allows, request 1 with a river view. $$$$$

Nine trains run daily from Delhi to Jammu (station code JAT). Delhi has several railway stations, so make sure you know which one you're leaving from. The **Malwa Express** (train 12919) leaves New Delhi railway station (station code NDLS) at 05.30 and arrives in Jammu at 16.05. Tickets cost Rs810/1,145 for class 3A/2A. There is no 1A class on this train. If you prefer to travel overnight, the **Jammu Mail** (train 14033) leaves Delhi Junction (station code DLI) at 20.10 and arrives the following morning at 09.15. Tickets cost Rs775/1,110/1,865 for class 1A/2A/3A.

🏠 **John Banons Hotel** (18 rooms) Manali Orchards; ☎ 252 335; e atbanon@sancharnet. in. Family-owned hotel in downtown location. Pleasant setting in orchard. Restaurant serves Indian & continental cuisine. **$$$$**

🏠 **Hotel Asia Sulphur Spring** (16 rooms) VPO Kalath; ☎ 258 801; e delhi@ asiahealthresorts.com. 6km outside Manali on National Hwy 21. The attraction of this hotel is the natural hot spring that gives it its name. Mountain views & restaurant on site. **$$$**

🏠 **Hotel New Adarsh** (12 rooms) The Mall; ☎ 253 693; e vimpy03@gmail.com; www.hotelnewadarsh.com. Behind Adarsh Restaurant, rooms here are simple & clean. It's a convenient location & staff are generally helpful. **$$–$$$**

🏠 **Sarthak Resorts** (54 rooms) VPO Khakhnal, Left Bank, Naggar Rd; ☎ 259 323; e sales@sarthakresorts.com; www. sarthakresorts.com. Well-maintained resort hotel with good views. Many rooms have balconies. Best rates are through online booking agents rather than the hotel directly. **$$**

✗ **WHERE TO EAT** The majority of Manali's hotels offer meal plans, as all-inclusive packages are preferred by Indian tourists. However, if you want to eat out, **Casa Bella Vista** (*Log Huts Rd;* m *98 1669 9663;* **$$$$$**) and **Ilforno** (*Dhungri Rd;* m *97 3684 0401;* **$$$$**) both serve authentic Italian food, and **Johnson's Bar & Restaurant** (*Circuit House Rd;* m *98 1604 5123;* **$$$**) does affordable Indian and continental cuisine with a great ambience and efficient service.

For a quick snack, **Manali Sweets** (*Off Mall Rd;* **$–$$**) serves divine *jalebis* and *rasgullas*, and excellent chickpea samosas.

WHAT TO SEE AND DO The attraction of Manali is its natural environment and, for many Indian visitors, their first opportunity to see snow. Trekking and picnicking within the **Van Vihat National Park** and the **Pin Valley National Park** are perennially popular, as is hiking to the **Jana** or **Rahala falls**. The **Rohtang Pass**, 50km north of Manali, will leave you literally and metaphorically breathless due to the altitude and is even more impressive when seen from the air: you can take a helicopter ride with **Heli Manali** (*Main Rd, Old Manali;* ☎ *252 365;* e *info@ helimanali.com; www.helimanali.com*) for Rs7,500 per person. Getting to the pass from Manali by taxi takes four to five hours and costs Rs1,500.

If you prefer something cultural, there are a number of attractive religious buildings: the **Hadimba Devi Mandir** (*off Circuit House Rd;* ⊕ *05.00–20.00; free entry*) is a striking 16th-century Hindu temple set on a hilltop and best reached on foot along a steep track through the peaceful surrounding woodland; the **Gadhan Thekchholking Gompa** (*off Mall Rd;* ⊕ *06.00–18.00; free entry*) gives you a small taste of what is to come if you're heading on to Ladakh; and the **Raghunath Temple** (*Kullu Town;* ⊕ *06.00–20.00; free entry*) has a striking façade, albeit in a poorly maintained setting. Although entry to these sites is free, you may be asked to make a donation. You should also observe any dress and behavioural requirements.

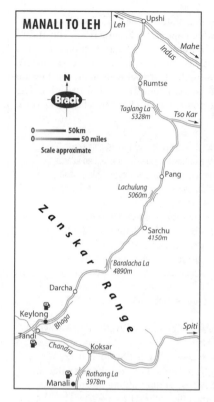

MANALI TO LEH

Three trains run daily between Amritsar (station code ASR) and Jammu. The **BTI JAT Express** (train 19225) runs overnight, departing from Amritsar at 01.10 and reaching Jammu at 06.15. It's much faster than the other two options: later in the day the **Tata JAT Express** (train 18101) and **Rou Muri JAT Express** (train 18109) both depart at 08.20 but do not reach Jammu until 05.50 the following morning. Prices are the same regardless of whether you take the fast or slow service: Rs470/665 for class 3A/2A.

If you are travelling to Kashmir from Rajasthan, the **All JAT Express** (train 12413) starts in Ajmer (station code AII) and stops in Jaipur (station code JP) before continuing on to Jammu. The journey takes 18 hours 5 minutes from Ajmer and 15 hours 40 minutes from Jaipur. Tickets cost Rs1,150/1,645/2,800 and Rs1,055/1,510/2,555 in classes 3A/2A/1A respectively.

There are longer and less frequent departures to Jammu from Mumbai (station code BDTS) on the **Swaraj Express** (Monday, Thursday, Friday and Sunday only; 30 hours 50 minutes; Rs1,695/2,470 for class 3A/2A), from Kolkata (station code HWH) on the **Himgiri Express** (Tuesday, Friday and Saturday only; 36 hours 35 minutes; Rs1,715/2,505/4,320 for class 3A/2A/1A).

BY ROAD

Via Himachal Pradesh Visitors heading to Ladakh by road from Delhi will probably come up from the plains via Himachal Pradesh. The long and arduous road that is closed in winter. The section from Delhi to Chandigarh and then the popular hill resort of Manali (see box, pages 38–9), the usual point at which travellers break their journey, is not too bad. The Manali–Leh Highway is the most challenging section of the route.

The **Manali–Leh Highway** runs 490km between the two towns and crosses a number of high passes: Rohtang (3,979m), Baralacha La (4,890m), Lachulung La (5,060m) and Taglang La (5,328m) among them. There is significant risk of altitude sickness at these points, and snowfall and ice frequently close the passes even in late spring. A tunnel is under construction beneath the Rohtang Pass but as less than half of the length had been excavated at the time of going to press, it is unlikely to open during the lifespan of this edition.

Travelling by road, you should allow two days to reach Leh from Manali: the going is very slow. The buses break the journey at Keylong or Sarchu, and those in private vehicles are advised to do likewise. The **Himachal Pradesh Tourism Development Corporation** (*www.hptdc.nic.in*) runs daily tourist coaches from 1 July to 15 September. One-way tickets cost Rs1,600/2,200 (with/without accommodation). HPTDC also runs an onward connection to Delhi from Manali (Rs1,220) in air-conditioned Volvo coaches. If you are hiring a taxi, Leh-based drivers charge from Rs16,355. Expect to complete the journey to Manali in around 18 hours, still split across two days.

Via Punjab If you are travelling to the western part of J&K (Jammu and Kashmir districts, as opposed to Ladakh and Zanskar), it is more appropriate to drive up from the Punjab. It's just 211km from Amritsar to Jammu and the journey takes around three hours. **J&K State Road Transport Corporation** (JKSRTC; *www.jksrtc.co.in*) operates a bus service between the two cities with more than a dozen departures every day, and tickets cost just Rs135. Hiring a **taxi** for the same journey will cost you Rs4,200.

Continuing on to Srinagar, the road is far slower and prone to landslides and closures during bad weather. The opening of the Chenani–Nashri Tunnel near Patnitop, scheduled for 2016, will significantly reduce the journey time, but until then the highway is closed around 40 days each year.

The main route between the two cities is the 289km National Highway 1A (NH1A). Driving this road takes eight to ten hours depending on the weather, though as there are plenty of interesting things to see on the way (see page 56) it'd be a pity to just drive straight up the valley without stopping. JKSRTC (see above) operates numerous **buses** along this route every day and fares start from Rs230. A **taxi** will cost you Rs4,500.

HEALTH

There's a reason everyone has heard of (and dreads) Delhi Belly. Unfortunately, it's not limited to the capital. Take your health seriously, prepare before you go and be careful what you eat, drink and do while you're on the road.

BEFORE YOU GO

Travel insurance Comprehensive travel insurance should be the first thing on your shopping list when you contemplate visiting Kashmir. Choose a policy that includes medical evacuation (MedEvac) and make sure that you explicitly state your destination when getting quotes: many policies will not cover you for travel to places about which the FCO advises against all, or all but essential, travel. Even if the insurance policy covers India in general, it may not include all of Kashmir.

Check the small print carefully for terms and conditions relating to claims resulting both from acts of terrorism and natural disasters (sometimes referred to as acts of God or *force majeure*). If you plan to mountaineer, trek at high altitude, ski, horseride or engage in any other activity that may be perceived to have additional risks attached, ensure you are fully covered. The moment you call the insurance company to report you've broken your leg skiing off-piste in Gulmarg is not the time you want to discover your policy does not include winter sports cover.

Leave a copy of the policy documents at home with someone you trust, email them to yourself as a PDF attachment, and keep a copy of your policy number and the emergency contact number on you at all times just in case you need them.

Vaccinations Your GP or a specialist travel clinic (see page 42) will be able to check your immunisation record and advise on any extra inoculations you might need for travelling to Kashmir. It is wise to be up to date on **tetanus**, **polio** and **diphtheria** (now given as an all-in-one vaccine, Revaxis, that lasts for ten years), typhoid and **hepatitis A**. Immunisations against rabies and hepatitis B may also be recommended depending on the duration of your stay and the sort of activities you will be undertaking.

Hepatitis A vaccine (Havrix Monodose or Avaxim) comprises two injections given about a year apart, though you will have cover from the time of the first injection. The course typically costs £100 and, once complete, gives you protection for 25 years. The vaccine is sometimes available on the NHS. **Hepatitis B** vaccination should be considered for longer trips (two months or more) and by those working in a medical setting or with children. The vaccine schedule comprises three doses taken over a six-month period, but for those aged 16 or over it can be given over a period of 21 days. The rapid course needs to be boosted after one year. For those aged 15 or younger, the course takes a minimum of eight weeks to do. A combined hepatitis A and B vaccine, 'Twinrix', is available, though at least three doses are needed for it to be fully effective. The schedules used are similar to those for hepatitis B vaccine alone.

The newer injectable **typhoid** vaccines (eg: Typhim Vi) last for three years and are about 85% effective. Oral capsules (such as Vivotif) may also be available for those aged six and over. Three capsules taken over five days last for approximately three years but may be less effective than the injectable version depending on how they are absorbed. Typhoid vaccines are particularly advised for those travelling in rural areas and when there may be difficulty in ensuring safe water supplies and food.

Rabies is present across India and vaccination is highly recommended for those travelling more than 24 hours from medical help or who will be coming into contact with animals. Street dogs are typically blamed as the carriers but monkeys do also get rabies and it is not uncommon for them to attack humans when they feel threatened. A pre-exposure course of rabies vaccine takes around 21 days to do and changes the treatment you need – see *Rabies*, page 48.

There is a small risk of **Japanese encephalitis**, a viral infection spread through the bites of infected mosquitoes. There is no treatment for the disease once you are infected, and about 30% of those who develop the disease will die. Approximately the same proportion will have permanent neurological damage. If you are planning to spend a lot of time in areas where infected mosquitoes may be present (rice paddies and piggeries are their favourite breeding grounds), have the inoculation and take the usual precautions against being bitten (see page 46). The highest risk of the disease is during the rainy season of May to November. The course of Japanese encephalitis vaccine (Ixiaro) is two doses a month apart. This vaccine can be used from two years and over.

Travel clinics and health information

A full list of current travel clinic websites worldwide is available on www.istm.org. For other journey preparation information, consult www.nathnac.org/ds/map_world.aspx (UK) or http://wwwnc.cdc.gov/travel/ (US). Information about various medications may be found on

ANTIMALARIALS

Jammu and Kashmir is categorised as an area with little or no malarial risk. The same categorisation applies to much of northern India, so even if you are routing via Amritsar or Delhi, you will not need to take antimalarial drugs.

That said, there is a risk of malaria in parts of central and northeastern India. If your itinerary includes these areas you should consult your GP as to which, if any, prophylaxis treatment is appropriate for you. To see whether the area you are travelling to has malaria go to www.fitfortravel.scot.nhs.uk. Malaria tablets have to be taken for a period of time before and after travel so go in plenty of time to discuss this with your health care professional.

While there are reasonably well-equipped pharmacies in towns across Kashmir, it is still highly advisable to prepare your own first-aid kit and to carry it with you wherever you travel. A minimal kit should contain:

- A good drying antiseptic, eg: iodine or potassium permanganate
- A few small dressings (Band-Aids)
- Suncream
- Insect repellent
- Aspirin or paracetamol
- Imodium and rehydration salts
- Ciprofloxacin or norfloxacin (for severe diarrhoea)
- A pair of fine-pointed tweezers (to remove thorns, splinters, ticks, etc)
- Alcohol-based hand sanitiser or bar of soap in plastic box
- Clingfilm or condoms for covering burns
- Tampons (highly absorbent and excellent for nose bleeds)
- Sterile needles, scalpel and surgical thread
- Water purification tablets (essential for trekkers)

www.netdoctor.co.uk/travel. All advice found online should be used in conjunction with expert advice received prior to or during travel.

COMMON MEDICAL PROBLEMS
Travellers' diarrhoea   Diarrhoeal diseases and other gastrointestinal infections are incredibly common in all parts of the Indian subcontinent. Travellers' diarrhoea and more serious conditions such as typhoid (of which there are not infrequent outbreaks in Kashmir) come from getting bacteria in your mouth. To minimise the risk, you should ensure that you observe good hygiene practices, such as regular hand washing, using bottled water (including for cleaning teeth), and avoiding foods of doubtful provenance. Many travellers use the following maxim to remind them what is safe:

PEEL IT, BOIL IT, COOK IT OR FORGET IT

This means that fruit you have washed and peeled yourself, and hot foods, should be safe but raw foods, cold cooked foods, salads, ice cream and ice are all risky, and foods kept lukewarm in hotel buffets often harbour numerous bugs. That said, plenty of travellers and expatriates enjoy fruit and vegetables, so do keep a sense of perspective: even street food, if deep fried in front of you and eaten then and there, can be perfectly safe.

If you are struck down with diarrhoea in spite of your precautions, remember that dehydration is your greatest concern. Drink lots of clear fluids. Sachets of oral rehydration salts give the perfect biochemical mix to replace all the fluids you are losing. If you don't have rehydration salts, or can't stand the taste, any dilute mixture of sugar and salt in water will do you good: try Coke or orange squash with a three-finger pinch of salt added to each glass (if you are salt-depleted you won't taste the salt). Alternatively you can add eight level teaspoons of sugar (18g) and one level teaspoon of salt (3g) to one litre (five cups) of safe water. A squeeze of lemon or orange juice improves the taste and adds potassium, which is also lost if you have diarrhoea. Drink two large glasses after every bowel action, and more if you are thirsty.

These solutions are still absorbed well even if you are vomiting, but you will need to take small sips at a time or you will bring it straight back up again. Even if you are not eating you need to drink three litres a day plus whatever is pouring into the toilet. If you are in any doubt, look at the colour of your urine. If it is anything other than clear and colourless, you need to drink more, and this is a helpful reminder even when you're feeling perfectly healthy.

If you feel like eating, take a bland, high carbohydrate diet. Plain rice, dry bread or digestive biscuits are ideal.

If the diarrhoea is bad, or you are passing blood or slime, or you have a fever, you will probably need antibiotics in addition to fluid replacement. Consult a doctor as soon as possible. A dose of norfloxacin or ciprofloxacin repeated twice a day until better may be appropriate and they can both be bought over the counter from pharmacies in Kashmir. If you are planning to take an antibiotic with you, note that both norfloxacin and ciprofloxacin are available only on prescription in the UK. Read the instructions carefully, follow them, and make sure you take the full course, even if you are feeling completely recovered. Failure to complete courses of antibiotics is the main reason for the rise in antibiotic-resistant strains of previously treatable diseases.

Prickly heat   All parts of Kashmir, including mountainous areas such as Ladakh, can become exceptionally hot in summer: temperatures well above 40°C are not unknown. A fine pimply rash on the chest or forearms is likely to be heat rash; it is caused by sweat becoming trapped beneath the skin and causing a histamine reaction. Cool showers, dabbing dry, and talcum powder (usually available in local pharmacies) will help. Treat the problem by wearing only loose, 100%-cotton clothes and, if it is at all possible, sleeping naked under a fan. An antihistamine tablet may help reduce the itching, as will hydrocortisone cream or Sudocrem.

Sunstroke and dehydration   The sun in Kashmir can be very harsh, even in the mountains where the lower temperatures may suggest otherwise. Sunstroke and dehydration are serious risks.

Wearing a hat, long loose sleeves and sunscreen helps to avoid sunburn. Prolonged unprotected exposure can result in heatstroke, which is potentially fatal. Try to stay out of the sun between noon and 15.00 when the rays are at their strongest.

In the heat you sweat more, so dehydration is likely. Don't rely on feeling thirsty to tell you to drink – if your urine is anything other than colourless and odourless then you aren't drinking enough. Carry bottled water with you at all times and make sure you stop to drink it. For advice on rehydration, see page 43.

Tetanus   Tetanus is caused by the *Clostridium tetani* bacterium and though it can accumulate on a variety of surfaces, it is most commonly associated with rusty objects such as nails. Cutting yourself or otherwise puncturing the skin brings the bacteria inside the body, where they will thrive. Clean any cuts thoroughly with a strong antiseptic.

Immunisation against tetanus gives good protection for ten years, and it is standard care practice in many places to give a booster injection to any patient with a puncture wound. Symptoms of tetanus may include lockjaw, spasms in any part of the body, excessive sweating, drooling and incontinence and the disease results in death if left untreated.

Mild cases of tetanus will be treated with the antibiotic metronidazole and tetanus immunoglobulin while more severe cases will require admission to intensive care, tetanus immunoglobulin injected into the spinal cord, a tracheotomy and mechanical ventilation, intravenous magnesium and diazepam.

Acute mountain sickness (AMS or altitude sickness) can occur at any altitude above 10,000ft, so visitors to almost any part of Ladakh and Zanskar, as well as the higher peaks in Kashmir, are at risk. Symptoms include headache, nausea and confusion and can herald the onset of high altitude cerebral eedema (HACE) and high altitude pulmonary oedema (HAPE), both of which can result in death.

SYMPTOMS OF AMS If you spend more than six hours at an altitude of 2,500m or more, you may start to experience headaches, nausea and vomiting, loss of appetite, fatigue, breathlessness and inability to sleep. Those with asthma, diabetes, epilepsy and existing heart and lung conditions, or who are pregnant, are at particular risk of developing these symptoms.

PREVENTION OF AMS The single most important piece of advice is take time to acclimatise. If you are travelling by land, increase your altitude steadily, and if you are flying straight to a high-altitude destination such as Leh, spend at least two to three days acclimatising there before going any higher. Get lots of rest, drink plenty of fluids (but avoid alcohol), eat lightly and do only gentle exercise while you are acclimatising. If gradual ascent is not possible, you may also consider taking acetazolamide (Diamox), which can be prescribed by your GP or at a travel clinic.

TREATMENT OF AMS If you are suffering the early symptoms of AMS (see above), stop and do not go any higher. Rest for 24 hours, take ibuprofen or paracetamol to treat your headaches and, if necessary, also an anti-nausea medication such as promethazine. Drink plenty of fluids and, if your symptoms have not improved, descend by at least 500m.

HACE AND HAPE Left untreated, AMS can develop into the far more serious HACE (gathering of fluid on the brain) and HAPE (gathering of fluid in the lungs). Both of these conditions are medical emergencies and can be fatal if not treated quickly. Sufferers would need to be rapidly evacuated to lower altitude by stretcher or helicopter, as continued physical exertion would worsen their condition.

Further information on AMS is available from the Academic Unit of Respiratory Medicine (*www.altitude.org*), the British Mountaineering Council (*www.thebmc.co.uk*) and Medex (*www.medex.org.uk*).

Practical Information   HEALTH

2

MEDICAL EMERGENCIES If you or someone you are travelling with has a major accident or injury, try not to panic. It would make things worse. Call for help (this could be phoning a hospital, your insurance company or even flagging down a passer-by) but don't wait for help to arrive before starting treatment if the injury is serious and you are some distance away from professional assistance. Given India's restrictions on the use of satellite phones (see box, page 70) and the limited availability of cellphone networks across the state, trekkers in particular may have to stabilise a casualty for a protracted period.

Whether you are waiting up a mountain for someone to fetch help, by the side of the road awaiting an ambulance, or riding in the back of a lorry to the hospital, keep note (written or mental) of what has happened, any changes in your patient's condition, and the type and quantity of any drugs you administer. The doctor will want this information.

Bleeding Applying pressure to a minor wound will stop it bleeding, as after a short time the blood will begin to clot naturally. If the wound is on a limb, raising it above the heart will also help as the blood will pump more slowly.

Large wounds require the application of pressure for longer. Pack the wound with a large, clear dressing and then apply pressure for ten minutes. This should slow or stop the bleeding. Wrap a bandage tightly around the original dressing to maintain the pressure and then, once the bleeding has stopped completely, apply a clean dressing. Stitches may be required. If the blood is pumping out fast and at high pressure, there may be damage to an artery. Put pressure on the wound and, if you know how, tie a tourniquet further up the limb. Seek medical help fast. Internal bleeding is difficult to diagnose but symptoms may include pain, external bruising, bloody discharge the ear, nose, mouth, anus or urethra. If this type of bleeding is suspected, get the casualty to hospital straight away and, in the meantime, treat them for shock (see page 48).

Burns Minor burns (first- and second-degree burns) can be superficial (such as sunburn) or slightly deeper, causing the skin to blister. Normally these will heal naturally if kept clean and dry, but if blisters cover more than 20% of the body (10% for children) they should be treated as per severe burns (see below), as the fluid loss from the blisters can cause fatal shock.

Severe or third-degree burns affect all layers of the skin and may burn nerve endings, preventing the casualty feeling pain. Electrical and chemical burns are also included in this category. Casualties with severe burns almost always suffer from shock (see page 48) due to fluid loss and need to be taken to hospital as soon as possible. There is also a significant risk of the burn becoming infected.

Cool the burn by running it under cold water for at least ten minutes. If anything is stuck to the burn (such as clothing), cut it as small as possible but do not pull it off. Do not burst any blisters or add any creams. Using clean plastic (ideally cling film but a plastic bag or condom will also do if there is none to hand), cover the burn to keep bacteria out. Tape the plastic in place, ensuring the tape is stuck only to the plastic and not to the skin.

To replace lost fluids, dissolve half a teaspoon of salt and a tablespoon of sugar in 500ml of water and give it to the casualty to drink. However, if the burn may have to be operated on shortly, give only small sips of this liquid.

Fractures If bones are broken a long way from help, you may need to set them temporarily to prevent further damage. Closed fractures (those where the skin is unbroken) may be diagnosed by the pain, almost immediate swelling of the limb and even the feeling of bones grating together (don't make the casualty move to see if this is the case!). If you expect help to arrive soon, immobilise the broken limb using a splint (anything from a stick to a rolled up newspaper will do). If help may be a while away, you may consider using traction (slowly pulling the limb until the ends of the bone fall back into the right place) before tying the splint.

LONG-HAUL FLIGHTS, CLOTS AND DVT   Dr Felicity Nicholson

Any prolonged immobility, including travel by land or air, can result in deep-vein thrombosis (DVT) with the risk of embolus to the lungs. Certain factors can increase the risk and these include:

- Previous clot or a close relative with a history
- Being over 40, with increased risk over 80 years old
- Recent major operation or varicose-veins surgery
- Cancer
- Stroke
- Heart disease
- Obesity
- Pregnancy
- Hormone therapy
- Heavy smoking
- Severe varicose veins
- Being very tall (over 6ft/1.8m) or short (under 5ft/1.5m)

A deep-vein thrombosis causes painful swelling and redness of the calf or sometimes the thigh. It is only dangerous if a clot travels to the lungs (pulmonary embolus). Symptoms of a pulmonary embolus (PE) – which commonly start three to ten days after a long flight – include chest pain, shortness of breath, and sometimes coughing up small amounts of blood. Anyone who thinks that they might have a DVT needs to see a doctor immediately.

PREVENTION OF DVT
- Keep mobile before and during the flight; move around every couple of hours
- Drink plenty of fluids during the flight
- Avoid taking sleeping pills and excessive tea, coffee and alcohol
- Consider wearing flight socks or support stockings (see *www.legshealth. com*)

If you think you are at increased risk of a clot, ask your doctor if it is safe to travel.

If the bone pierces the skin (an open fracture) it will need urgent medical help. Clean the wound with antiseptic and dress it to reduce the risk of infection. Straighten the limb immediately (ideally before it becomes swollen) and splint it. If the patient is unconscious, splint the wound before bringing them round as the pain will be excruciating.

Head injury Even a small bang to the head can cause brain injury but, that said, the amount of blood often makes head injuries look more severe than they actually are. If a casualty is unconscious or has signs of brain injury (closed eyes, blood or clear discharge from the facial orifices, failure to respond to questioning or making incoherent noises), call for help immediately. Dress the wound and put the casualty in the recovery position. Carefully monitor their breathing, circulation and responses until professional help arrives.

Heart attack A heart attack is usually caused by a clot or blockage that cuts off the blood supply to part of the heart. If the casualty has chest pain, a shooting pain in the arms, difficulty breathing, an irregular pulse, blue lips, dizziness and an impending sense of doom (a genuine, medically recognised symptom), get immediate medical attention.

If the casualty is conscious, make them sit or lie down to reduce strain on the heart. Give them aspirin (300mg) to thin the blood. Keep checking their pulse and breathing, beginning CPR if either of these vital signs fails.

Shock Shock is the inadequate circulation of blood and resultant deprivation of oxygen to the heart, kidneys, brain or other organs. It typically results from extreme fluid loss, heat problems, spinal cord injury, hypothermia, major infections, severe allergic reactions or low blood sugar. Shock can kill.

The initial symptoms of shock are a racing heartbeat, sweating and clamminess. The casualty may also start panting, feel dizzy and sick, and have a weak pulse as the condition worsens. If the shock is extreme, the person may become aggressive, gasp and yawn and then fall unconscious. The heart will ultimately stop.

If someone is suffering from shock, get professional help fast. In the meantime, you need to get blood to the brain and the heart. Get the casualty to lie down with their feet raised. Keep them warm with a blanket or your own body heat. Give them only sips of water and no food in case surgery is shortly required.

Rabies Rabies can be carried by any warm-blooded mammal and the disease is transmitted to humans through contact with an infected animal's saliva. If you are bitten, scratched or licked on broken skin, you must assume that the animal has rabies even if it looks healthy. Dogs and monkeys are particularly likely to be carriers of the disease. Scrub the wound with soap under a running tap or while pouring water from a bottle, then pour on a strong iodine or alcohol solution of gin, whisky or rum. This helps stop the rabies virus entering the body and will guard against wound infections, including tetanus.

Pre-exposure vaccinations for rabies are ideally advised for everyone, but is particularly important if you intend to have contact with animals and/or are likely to be more than 24 hours away from medical help. Three doses of vaccine should be taken over a minimum of 21 days to change the treatment needed. Contrary to popular belief these vaccinations are relatively painless.

If you are bitten, scratched or licked over an open wound by a sick animal, then post-exposure prophylaxis should be given as soon as possible, though it is never too late

SAFE SEX

It goes without saying that if you are having sex (gay or straight) with a new partner while travelling in India then you should use a condom. As many as 2.4 million people in the country are thought to be infected with AIDS and many of them do not know that they have it.

Condoms are widely available across India, though if you want to be sure of the quality, you should bring your own supplies with you. Sizing may also be different. Knowledge of how to prevent HIV transmission is still quite low in the country, especially among women, so you should act responsibly and teach by example.

to seek help, as the incubation period for rabies can be very long. Those who have not been immunised will need a full course of injections and will also need a blood product called Rabies Immunoglobulin (RIG) injected around the wound. RIG is very hard to come by as there is a worldwide shortage. If you have had all three doses of rabies vaccine before the exposure then you will no longer need the RIG and would only need to get two further doses of rabies vaccine, ideally given three days apart but can be up to seven days apart. Although the vaccine is moderately expensive the course of rabies vaccine provides long-term cover (unless you are a vet working abroad when regular boosts or blood tests are recommended). And remember that, if you do contract rabies, mortality is almost 100% and death from rabies is probably one of the worst ways to go.

SAFETY

Despite the highly visible military presence in the state, at the time of going to press, J&K was generally a safe place for foreigners and domestic tourists to travel. The Foreign and Commonwealth Office (*www.gov.uk/foreign-travel-advice/india*) has no travel restrictions for the cities of Jammu and Srinagar, travel on the National Highway between them, or for Ladakh and, as there has been a general decline in violence in the state in recent years, it is hoped that other areas of the state will soon have their FCO travel threat removed.

When violence does occur in the state it is not targeted at foreign tourists, though two British nationals were killed during a grenade attack on a minibus in Bijbehara, a village in Anantnag district, in July 2012.

The three greatest threats to the safety of tourists in J&K are **natural disasters**, being caught up in local protests, and road accidents. The area suffered a major earthquake in 2005 which measured 7.6 on the Richter scale and killed more than 76,000 people, 1,400 of them in J&K. Smaller earthquakes occur frequently (at least four in 2013), often causing loss of life due to collapsed buildings and landslides on mountain roads. Flooding, caused both by glacial meltwater and heavy rains, is equally commonplace. If you plan to travel in mountainous areas in particular you should pay attention to the weather forecast and avoid travelling during bad weather. The same applies whether you are driving or on foot: numerous pilgrims die each year trying to complete the Amarnath pilgrimage (see page 190) because they ignore weather warnings and are caught by the snow and ice.

Local protests and riots occur frequently, especially in Srinagar and the Kashmir Valley. Though they are frequently publicised in the media as clashes between the police and terrorists, local people often disagree, citing police brutality, corruption or communal issues as the real causes. In any case, such incidents can and do turn violent and so you should avoid getting too close to either protestors or uniformed officials. Avoid areas where there is a strike, and if there is a curfew imposed, remain in your hotel.

Last but not least are the **roads**. Driving in India instils fear in even the most seasoned travellers, and hence hiring a car and driver together is far more common than elsewhere in the world. Roads in J&K are frequently poorly maintained, especially in more remote areas, riddled with pot-holes and at risk of flooding and landslides. Street lights are a rarity and other people on the roads may not have lights on their vehicles (or herds of goats, which they seem to like moving after dark). Plan your journeys so that you can leave and arrive in the light. If you are hiring a taxi, check the vehicle yourself (see box, page 59) and make sure the driver is both competent and sober. If you are in any doubt, find another taxi, as you need all your wits about you to keep a car on the road even when the weather is fair.

WOMEN TRAVELLERS

Women usually travel in India trouble-free: people are typically conservative but are used to seeing both local and foreign women travelling independently, working in all occupations and taking prominent roles in both politics and the media. It is often possible for females to get a seat in women-only compartments on trains, join women-only queues and, where the latter are not available, queue-jump straight to the front to avoid waiting among unfamiliar men.

Privately, however, attitudes towards women are more old-fashioned: many families expect their daughters-in-law to give up working after marriage and to look after elderly relatives. Dowry payments are still often required when a girl gets married, despite the practice being illegal, and violence against women, particularly in the home, is high. Friendships between men and women are not encouraged and thanks to years of damaging stereotypes in the Indian media, foreign women who are open and friendly towards Indian men, even in a solely platonic way, are seen to be 'easy'.

Some foreign women do report verbal and occasionally physical harassment, particularly when wearing clothing that shows their shoulders or legs, or when visiting bars and clubs. This kind of abuse is more common in larger cities such as Delhi: I (Sophie) have never experienced it in J&K, though you do get quickly used to being stared at and photographed on camera phones wherever you travel in India.

In recent years there have been a number of more high-profile attacks on women in India, including a serious sexual attack on a Swiss tourist in Madhya Pradesh in March 2013. British women have been victims of sexual assault in Bangalore, Delhi, Goa and Rajasthan. If you are attacked, the police number to call is 100 (112 from mobile phones). You should also contact your embassy (see *Foreign embassies*, page 33) for consular assistance and support.

GAY TRAVELLERS

India decriminalised homosexuality in 2009 and Delhi's first Pride Parade (now an annual event) took place the same year. However, in December 2013 the Supreme Court overturned the legislation, re-criminalising gay sex, leading to protests around the world and a backlash in the Indian media. At the time of going to press it is unclear which case will stand.

There is a burgeoning gay scene in many of India's larger cities (Mumbai is the undisputed gay capital) and there are now a number of LGBT travel agents in India that are part of the International Gay & Lesbian Travel Association (*www.iglta.org*).

That said, regardless of the law, most of India's LGBT community continue to keep their sexuality very private. Most people remain deeply conservative on the issue and coming out is generally considered to bring shame on a family. While two men holding hands or sharing a room will not raise eyebrows, open displays of affection most certainly will. Verbal harassment is common (though more likely to be suffered by locals) and police harassment is also a possibility.

TRAVELLERS WITH DISABILITIES

While it is possible to travel in India if you are disabled, it certainly isn't easy. Poor infrastructure and health-care facilities pose difficulties for all visitors, and the challenges are undoubtedly magnified if you have a physical disability. Hotels, tourist sites and public places are rarely wheelchair accessible and little if any assistance is provided for those with hearing or sight problems. There is widespread discrimination against the disabled, with many people believing that a disability is the result of wrongdoing in a previous life. India has no welfare support for those with disabilities and consequently many disabled people resort to begging on the streets.

If you do travel to Kashmir, you will need to plan ahead and make sure all transport and accommodation providers are briefed about your needs well in advance. Airlines and upper-end hotels are generally helpful provided you give them time to prepare and are explicit about what you need. For tips about travelling with a wheelchair, and for details of wheelchair-accessible hotels, contact **Accessible Journeys** (*35 West Sellers Av, Ridley Pk, PA 19078, USA;* +1 800 846 4537; e *sales@ accessiblejourneys.com; www.accessiblejourneys.com*).

TRAVELLING WITH CHILDREN *With thanks to Hilary Stock*

Because of the dangers of altitude mountain sickness (AMS), this destination is not recommended for babies or children too young to communicate symptoms. For older children and teenagers, it is a dream place to travel.

There are abundant homestays, allowing families to gain unprecedented access to the local culture. Accommodation is cheap, the food is child-friendly and activities abound: cycling, river rafting, camping, trekking, sightseeing, shopping in markets.

There has been little research into the effects on children of the popular drug Diamox, which counters the effects of AMS. Better to do a gradual, drug-free ascent if possible, or if you fly in, be sure to block off at least three days on arrival to do nothing and acclimatise.

Teenagers are said to suffer more from AMS than younger children or adults. Try to be clear of any international jet lag before travelling to the region as it can muddle symptoms. AMS can sound frightening and should be taken seriously, but it's the only health hurdle you have to deal with in order to access one of the most beautiful and welcoming areas in the world. (And some children don't suffer at all.)

High altitude desert in summertime is a good climate for travelling with children as long as you're equipped properly. Travel light and efficiently, but be warned: appropriate clothing might not be a teenager's idea of fashion. The sun is extreme, so pack good sunglasses and wide-brimmed hats, and the very highest factor suncreams and lipsalve. Take any children's medicines with you. Dehydration is a challenge. Children are particularly vulnerable and need to be reminded constantly to drink water.

2

WHAT TO TAKE

You may wish to consider taking the following items, in addition to your usual packing.

- **Plug adaptors** Sockets across India are the twin round pin, continental European type. The voltage is 220v. Look for an adapter that fits close to the wall as sockets are often loose and the weight of plug plus adapter may frustratingly pull out of the wall.

TREKKING KIT

There are numerous online and high-street retailers selling hiking and winter sports wear, though some of it definitely veers more towards fashion than functionality. If you don't know exactly what you need, or simply want advice on how your boots, rucksack, etc should fit, the following companies have knowledgeable staff and will take the time to talk you through what's right for you and your trip.

Blacks (*www.blacks.co.uk*) High-street brand with enthusiastic staff. Wait for the sales when prices are heavily discounted.

Keela (See ad, page 76; *www.keela.co.uk*) Emerging brand with brightly coloured fleeces and affordable base layers and socks.

Mountain Warehouse (See ad, page 25; *www.mountainwarehouse.com*) Cheap and cheerful outdoor clothing and accessories.

Rohan (See ad, page 25; *www.rohan.co.uk*) High-quality outdoor clothing and footwear. Ideal for trekking. UK supplier of Eagle Creek products.

In our experience, the two items that make the biggest difference to your trekking experience are your boots and socks. Boots need to be strong and give support to your ankles but still flexible enough to be comfortable as you move. Choose a pair with good grip and ideally with a fully waterproof upper, as tromping around with sodden feet is miserable. Pick socks with a high percentage of natural fibres so that your feet can breath. Specialist hiking socks (as opposed to general sports socks) are reinforced in just the right places and so reduce the chance of blisters. You should also pack:

- Breathable base layers
- A fleece
- A waterproof (and ideally windproof) outer layer
- Sunscreen and sunglasses
- A durable water bottle with internal filter and/or purification tablets
- High energy snacks such as dried fruits, nuts and energy bars
- A map, compass and GPS unit
- First-aid kit (see box, page 43)

However long or short your intended trek, always tell someone where you are going, the route you plan to take, and how long you expect it to take.

- **A torch** Many parts of Kashmir, including city streets, are unlit at night, and pavements may conceal dangers such as uncovered manholes and other trip hazards. Power cuts are commonplace too. If you are planning to camp, or stay in rural areas, you'll need a torch to navigate to the latrine at night. A head torch is especially useful as it leaves your hands free.
- **Mosquito repellent** Kashmir may not be a malarial area, but the swarms of mosquitoes you may encounter in summer among its lakes and forests can still damage enjoyment of your holiday. Make sure you pack long-sleeved shirts (you'll also need these for visiting conservative areas and religious places).
- **Warm clothing** If you are going anywhere other than Jammu, pack plenty of warm layers, whatever time of year you are travelling. The weather can turn quite unexpectedly in the mountains, temperatures often plummet at night, and even in Srinagar September rains can turn to biting hail. Several thinner layers are better than one thick layer.
- **Good footwear** In winter, wear rubber-soled boots, preferably lined with fleece. If you are trekking, good hiking boots are essential (see *Trekking kit*, page 000, for more detailed kit advice).
- **Flip-flops** You'll need these if you're planning to visit temples and mosques, as unlacing and removing boots every time you want to step across the threshold is a faff. They also come in useful in less than savoury bathrooms, which are numerous.

If you will be staying in bottom-range accommodation, a **sheet sleeping bag**, of the kind used by youth hostellers, can help save you from grubby bedding. A **universal sink plug** is also worth packing.

Good **suncream**, **lipsalve** and **sunglasses** are essential in the mountains: the glare of the sun is harsh and you will burn quickly. **Toilet paper**, **wet wipes** and **hand sanitiser gel** are highly advisable and will make staying clean infinitely easier. **Dental floss** and a **needle**, a roll of **gaffer tape** and a packet of **cable ties** will enable you to fix almost anything while you're on the go. A small **penknife** or **multi-tool** also comes in handy, but don't forget to pack it in your hold luggage before flying.

Small **gift items** related to your home country make ideal presents for hosts: consider taking tea towels featuring cathedrals, boxes of fudge, snow globes with castles, and a few snapshots of your family and home.

What you pack your gear into will depend in large part on the sort of activities you'll be undertaking. If you're taking a leisurely trip with hotel accommodation and a car and driver, a standard suitcase will be fine. If you're travelling more by public transport, a strong duffle bag (with or without wheels) or rucksack will be easier to manhandle on and off buses and jeeps, and will squish under seats or lie across laps more comfortably. For reference, we took rolling 110 litre Eagle Creek duffles for our everyday gear, and a Traveller 80 rucksack for trekking: the latter has the advantage of having a zip-on daypack that can be used separately from the main bag, enabling you to carry only your valuables and leave everything else in the hotel if you want to pop out unencumbered.

MONEY

India's currency is the rupee (Rs). Each rupee is made up of 100 paisa. Paper notes come in denominations of 5, 10, 20, 50, 100, 500 and 1,000, and the standard issue (ie: non-commemorative) coins are Rs1, 2 and 5. These days it is very rare to actually see coins of less than Rs1 in face value as they are virtually worthless, and only the 50 paisa coin remains legal tender. On the rare occasions that your shopping does not come to an exact number of rupees, the vendor will either round the figure to the nearest whole number or give you a sweet with your change.

The rupee is not terribly stable against foreign currencies and has fluctuated between Rs66 and Rs101 to the pound since 2010. The exchange rates given below were correct at the time of going to print, but you are advised to check the latest rates online, in the newspapers or with the banks before changing money.

£1 = Rs99   €1 = Rs81   US$1 = Rs59

WHAT TO CARRY Currency controls prevent you being able to exchange Indian rupees abroad. Consequently, you will not be able to buy rupees from a bureau de change before you go.

There are several ways to get rupees once you have arrived in India: withdraw them from an ATM; get a cash advance on your Visa or MasterCard in a bank; or change foreign notes with a local bank or money agent. ATMs are widespread in the larger towns and usually well stocked. Many of them are inside small booths but accessible 24 hours if you swipe your bank card in the lock on the door. Before you leave home, check with your bank as to their charges for accessing funds from abroad as these can mount up quickly.

Hotels and travel agents are increasingly able to process card payments, which reduces the amount of cash you will need to carry. That said, the card machines are dependent on the electricity and phone lines working, and you will always need cash in hand for taxis, meals and buying small items in the shops.

Although travellers' cheques were popular in the past, they are increasingly difficult to change. It is normally only possible to process them in the larger banks and even then you will usually get a poor exchange rate.

CHANGING MONEY Money changers are as omnipresent as mosquitoes, and every town has a wealth of places where you can change foreign currency, from banks to travel agents to cyber cafés. US dollars, euros and sterling are all easily exchanged; other currencies are exchangeable but you may have to haggle harder for a fair rate.

Changing larger denomination notes (fifties and hundreds) tends to be easier than fives and tens as they are considered less likely to be forged. For the same reason money changers also have a preference for dollar bills printed after 2006. Try to keep your foreign currency notes flat and clean: those that are torn or marked (even with cashier's pen) may not be accepted.

BUDGETING

Whether you are scraping by on a backpacker's budget or have a king's ransom to spend, J&K has plenty of options for you.

Though the area is perhaps not quite as cheap as some other parts of India, backpackers can survive on Rs600–700 per day. For this you'll be able to get a dorm bed or share a basic twin room in a guesthouse, eat simple, vegetarian meals and travel by public buses. Now and then you'll be able to have a beer, and you'll have change to make donations when sightseeing in gompas and temples. Walking, either for pleasure or to get from A to B, is of course free.

With a daily budget of Rs1,500–2,000 you can travel comfortably, sharing a room in a mid-range hotel, eating varied meals in restaurants (where tipping is typically 10%) and travelling in a mixture of buses and shared taxis. If you keep your costs down in the towns, you'll then be able to afford to do some trekking, especially if you have your own equipment and are happy joining a group.

Costs start to rise if you want to get away from the main towns. Taxi rates are relatively high but are frequently your only means of getting somewhere. Tented camps in the Nubra Valley and southern lakes charge disproportionate sums for what you actually get and as there's an absence of food shops and restaurants you'll probably have to pay for a hotel meal plan. In such areas, budget an additional Rs2,000 per person per day.

At the upper end of the scale, Leh, Srinagar and Jammu all have hotels with rooms of upwards of Rs8,000 per night. Hiring a car and driver maximises your flexibility, and you may consider taking a domestic flight if time is of the essence. Genuine pashminas and silk Kashmiri carpets are more affordable here than elsewhere in the world but they still come with a hefty price tag, and of course you have to pay to ship the latter home.

To give you a sense of small spends, the following prices were accurate for basic items at the time of writing.

Bottle of water (1 litre)	Rs10
Bottle of beer (0.5 litres)	Rs80
Fresh juice (0.3 litres)	Rs30
Genuine pashmina	Rs4,000+
Mars bar	Rs40
Papier mâché box (small)	Rs100
Petrol (1 litre)	Rs78
Phone call (local)	Rs5
Phone call (international)	Rs10
Plate of *momos* (vegetarian)	Rs80
Postcard	Rs15
Stamp (international)	Rs20
Tailor-made shirt	Rs1,000
Tailor-made suit (three-piece)	Rs8,000
Wi-Fi (an hour)	Rs40

GETTING AROUND

J&K is a large state and transport infrastructure is relatively poor. Journeys by road are often long and uncomfortable, regardless of your means of transport, as even the national highways are badly maintained and narrow; accidents and road closures are frequent. Take local advice on the latest journey times, depart early in the morning if you have a long way to travel and make sure you've got a really good book (other than this one, obviously) to help pass the hours.

BY PLANE Jammu, Leh and Srinagar all have civilian airports and domestic flights link them together, as well as with other parts of India. Flights are most regular in the summer months when customer demand is highest (and prices also increase), so you may need to book well in advance to guarantee a seat. The flight from Srinagar to Leh takes 44 minutes and costs from Rs4,870 each way; flights between Jammu and Leh take 1 hour 20 minutes and tickets start from Rs5,000.

Tickets can be booked online via the Indian travel portal www.yatra.com (which includes tickets for India's budget airlines) and the individual airlines' websites (see page 36 for contact details), as well as from airport ticketing desks and through local travel agents.

Security is particularly strict on flights originating in J&K due to terrorism fears, so check airline baggage regulations before travelling. Note that you are usually required to have both a print-out of your ticket (even for e-tickets) and your passport in order to gain access to the departure terminal.

BY ROAD The best roads in J&K are the national highways: NH1A in the west between Jammu and Srinagar, and NH1 from Srinagar to Leh via Kargil. These roads carry a mixture of trucks, taxis and private vehicles, as well as frequent military convoys driving between the different military bases. Though mostly covered with tarmac, the surfaces are far from smooth, with pot-holes a common hazard. In the narrowest sections there is not space for a vehicle to overtake, and high passes are forced to close when it snows.

Away from these highways, the road conditions deteriorate further. Many roads are unmade, making for very slow progress, and some quite important routes, including the main road from Kargil to Zanskar, are closed completely throughout the winter months, reopening again only in late spring.

By bus The JKSRTC (*www.jksrtc.co.in*) operates a reasonable network of buses between J&K's main towns, and they typically stop in the larger villages *en route* too.

Public buses are the cheapest way to travel and depending on the type of bus (standard, deluxe, coach, etc) you might even get your own seat. Larger items of luggage (and occasionally additional passengers) travel on the roof, so buy a small padlock for your rucksack or case and keep valuables inside the bus with you.

Given the winding roads and tendencies of the bus drivers, you may consider taking anti travel sickness medication, even if you don't normally feel nauseous in the car. It may also come in handy for other passengers, as will wet wipes and tissues, and given your close proximity to them it's in your own best interest to share.

HOW FAR IS...?

Jammu to Kargil	497km
Jammu to Leh	727km
Jammu to Padum	737km
Jammu to Srinagar	293km
Leh to Kargil	234km
Leh to Padum	474km
Leh to Srinagar	434km
Srinagar to Kargil	204km
Srinagar to Padum	444km
Padum to Kargil	240km

Details on individual bus routes, journey times and ticket prices are given in the *Getting there* sections of each chapter in Part Two. However, as a guide for a standard coach or bus ticket (one way), prices start from:

Gulmarg to Srinagar	Rs24	Pahalgam to Srinagar	Rs190
Katra to Jammu	Rs38	Sonamarg to Srinagar	Rs190
Jammu to Katra	Rs38	Srinagar to Gulmarg	Rs24
Jammu to Patnitop	Rs150	Srinagar to Jammu	Rs230
Jammu to Srinagar	Rs230	Srinagar to Kargil	Rs373
Kargil to Padum	Rs350	Srinagar to Leh	Rs919
Kargil to Srinagar	Rs357	Srinagar to Pahalgam	Rs190
Leh to Srinagar	Rs919	Srinagar to Sonamarg	Rs190
Padum to Kargil	Rs350	Srinagar to Yusmarg	Rs180
Patnitop to Jammu	Rs150	Yusmarg to Srinagar	Rs180

By taxi   Leh, Kargil and Zanskar all have their own taxi unions, which set rates and other taxi-related regulations, including which taxis can go where. The regulations are designed to protect local drivers from outsiders stealing their business, but can be infuriating for visitors forced to change taxis to continue their journey or prevented from using their original car and driver for both outward and return journeys.

That said, you quickly get used to the system and the fixed rates remove the usual hassle of haggling over price. Taxis can be either cars or minivans and drivers have to be registered. The drivers frequently speak a few words of English and some are knowledgeable about local sites and culture, acting as informal guides for their passengers. They know where to stay and where to eat and, on the whole, we consider the standard of driving to be high by regional standards.

If you have a car and driver for several days, it is appropriate to tip the driver at the end of your trip, even if you've prepaid an agent for a package. We work on the basis of Rs200 tip per day and it's always gratefully received.

Full details on the routes, driving times and prices are given in the *Getting there* sections of each chapter in Part Two. For hiring a small car or van, minimum one-way prices on the inter-city routes are given below. Note that due to the fact fares are set by the individual taxi unions, prices sometimes change depending on the direction you are travelling.

Jammu to Srinagar	Rs4,500	Leh to Srinagar	Rs11,855
Kargil to Leh	Rs6,515	Padum to Kargil	Rs11,000
Kargil to Padum	Rs11,775	Srinagar to Jammu	Rs4,500
Kargil to Srinagar	Rs5,847	Srinagar to Kargil	Rs5,800
Leh to Kargil	Rs5,983	Srinagar to Leh	Rs11,500

Self-drive   Though it is possible to hire just a car in India, more often you get a car and driver together (see *By taxi*, above). It is likely then that if you are driving yourself you have bought or imported your own vehicle, or are driving the car of a friend.

EU driving licences (which include UK photo-card driving licences) are valid in India, though you may wish to get an International Driving Licence before leaving home. These are available from the RAC and some larger post offices and cost about £7.

If you are bringing your vehicle into India from another country, you will need to purchase a *carnet de passage en douanes*, or 'carnet' for short. This document,

'Nothing comes for free in India – you'll never hitchhike there!' These were the words of encouragement I received as I prepared to leave Lahore in Pakistan to make for the Indian border.

But in fact hitchhiking in India's mountainous north proved rather straightforward. This may in part have been down to the advantage of having a white face and thus becoming an object of interest to many who picked me up. But beyond that, in India there seems a general appreciation of the concept of hitchhiking.

Perhaps the practice doesn't exist in quite the same way as in Europe, but standing by the side of the road with thumb outstretched seems to do the trick, while Indians seem to translate the enterprise through the use of the word 'lift' – pronounced 'leafed'.

There were a few occasions when the driver seemed bemused by the concept of a 'lift' without payment, but it is always a good idea in Asia to clarify before the start of the journey whether you expect to pay.

If you do not, the phrase 'rupee nahi' (literally: money none) will clarify your intentions and cause the driver either to speed off in a bemused rage (seemingly indignant that someone could envisage being given a ride without wishing to pay for the service) or to invite you in with a welcoming shrug of the shoulders.

Beyond this, the same rules and advice apply to Kashmir as to anywhere else in the world. Top tips include standing in a visible position (not the middle of the road), making sure there is space for drivers to pull in on either side of where you are standing, and having a few words of the native language under your belt (20 words can get you a surprisingly long way) to ease with negotiations over direction and any monetary contribution you do or do not wish to make.

Patience, as ever, is a virtue when hitchhiking. Try to make sure your driver takes you to a helpful spot, although this may be hard to communicate. Where possible, aim for petrol stations or main roads leading out of town (in the direction you wish to travel), and make sure you have a map.

It is never possible to recommend hitchhiking without a word of caution, due to the inherent risks involved, but this writer believes that it is both possible and a lot of fun, wherever you are in the world.

also available from the RAC, is a waiver for import duty and guarantees you will remove the vehicle from India at the end of your trip. The cost of the carnet is determined by the value of your vehicle and full details are available on the RAC's website (*www.rac.co.uk*).

The rules of the road are theoretically very similar to those in the UK, and vehicles are supposed to drive on the left. The reality is that people drive wherever there are fewest pot-holes and rules are typically observed only when a policeman is watching. Driving anywhere in India, and especially in the mountainous parts of J&K, is not for the faint-hearted.

By bike You would have to be exceptionally fit and not just a little bit mad to consider cycling in Kashmir. The roads are badly maintained, the motorists homicidal and the altitude is an additional hurdle. In spite of all this, you will see cyclists on the road. All of them are foreigners, and most of them are undertaking epic bicycle journeys across India, across Asia or round the world.

It is possible to hire bicycles in Leh. These are mountain bikes rather than road bikes, and rentals are typically by the day, though you can request longer packages. Demand and wear a helmet, regardless of how silly you think you look, and make sure you have spare inner tubes and the tools required to fix a punctured tyre. Do not, under any circumstances, cycle at night or be tempted to undertake other vehicles, regardless of how slowly they are moving.

If you are considering bringing your own bike to Kashmir, take all the spare parts you could possibly need with you. The boneshaking roads take their toll on bikes as well as bodies, and so replacement parts will be available locally. If you forget something or something breaks, it would have to be couriered to you from Delhi or even from abroad.

MAPS J&K has been well mapped. The majority of the roads appear on national road atlases, free tourist maps show the major towns and tourist sites, and specialist trekking maps show the topography and trekking routes.

General maps of the area are available in bookshops in Leh, Jammu and Srinagar as well as in souvenir shops elsewhere. If you require a specific map (and in particular large-scale trekking maps) you would be advised to order them before leaving home to ensure you can get the one you want. If you plan to do extreme trekking beyond the established routes, military-grade maps produced by cartographers from the Soviet Union are held in some national libraries and can be scanned or photocopied, though they are not commercially available.

When looking at state-wide maps, be cognisant of the fact that many of those published in India do not show the Line of Control (LoC) with Pakistan. All parts of Greater Kashmir, including the states of Azad Kashmir and Gilgit-Baltistan, are

SELF-DRIVE CHECKS

- Drive a car that is common in the local area: you won't stand out and if you break down the parts and expertise to repair it are more likely to be available.
- Check you have a spare tyre, jack and wheel wrench. Spare oil and water, a tow rope, a jerrycan of fuel and a shovel are also highly advisable.
- If you have the option, get central locking, electric windows and air conditioning: they give you greater control over what (and, indeed, who) comes into the vehicle with you.
- Make sure you know the rules of the road and have a good idea about where you are going. Tell someone you trust your route and your expected time of arrival.
- Carry your driving licence and any vehicle documentation with you at all times. Photocopies are useful for handing to police and other interested parties.
- Ensure there is a first-aid kit, food and plenty of drinking water in the boot in case of emergencies.
- A mobile phone is essential in the event of an accident or a breakdown you can't fix by the side of the road. Unless you have a garage's number already, your best bet would be to call a large hotel in the nearest town or city and ask them for a recommendation.

You wake up in a tent, under a bridge or in a bush and think, 'Where shall I go today?' Mounting your steed, bags loaded behind you and only a map in front, all you have to do is choose. Overland travel by motorbike is quite possibly the most liberating form of travel: there's something about being able to reach out and touch what's around you.

Kashmir is wild country and driving here in or on anything is not to be underestimated. Forging these roads from mountains that are constantly trying to reclaim them is an ongoing task and as such many areas are not metalled. At the time of research, many roads, including key stretches such as the Zojila Pass between Kargil and Srinagar, were still unsurfaced. Trepidation is advisable, but if historic and frankly amazing-sounding names mean that you just can't help yourself, then here's some advice.

Take care with the seasons. Some parts of J&K are affected by the monsoon, and large parts of the state are under thick snow in winter. When the snow begins to melt, the roads all around Leh as well as many other areas churn into mud. Rain adds weight to the soil and this season often sees the most landslides, which can stop your journey for days. Last time I rode in Kashmir it froze, then snowed hard and I had trouble escaping Manali with my fingertips intact, so avoid the winter months too.

Few local bikes are safe in this region so it is best to source a suitable bike and fly it (or, even better, ride it) to Kashmir. If you have to buy or hire locally, look for something with long suspension, a front disc brake, a big front wheel and a rack or other way of carrying your kit, as keeping it on your back is not a good idea. Before you leave, make sure you check the lights and horn (the louder the better), the front and back brakes (it's a long way down those precipices), the suspension (you're going to need it), and that the chain is in good condition with plenty of oil. Make sure the wheels are round (seriously) and, if you're going on broken roads, that you have knobbly or new tyres with lots of tread. If the bike looks too old, is making particularly odd noises or rattles on tarmac, find something better. Traffic is rare and mechanics are only to be found in big towns. There are more fulfilling things than finishing an epic journey with your bike in the back of a truck.

Before you leave ask yourself lots of questions. What's my fuel range? Do I know how to repair a puncture? How will I navigate? What if it snows? Do people know where I'm going and what time I'll check in with them? Do I have more than enough clothes to be warm and dry? Will I need a sleeping bag?

Be aware of the distances and the time it takes to travel between them. Kargil to Padum is only 240km (150 miles) but can easily take a motorcyclist two, or even three, days to travel safely, especially as you should be off the road before it gets dark. *En route* you can be struck by anything from falling debris to a herd of goats. If that sort of thing excites you, get to it.

shown included within India's borders, causing confusion for visitors who would in reality not be able to cross the LoC but would have to travel south to Wagah, enter Pakistan with a Pakistani visa, and again travel north from there.

ACCOMMODATION

J&K offers all manner of accommodation, from mats on dirt floors to luxury hotels, monastic cells to floating palaces. In peak season the best options can get booked up well in advance, but you'll always be able to find a room somewhere, at a price you can more or less afford.

ESSENTIAL EQUIPMENT
Spare key
Puncture repair kit
Engine oil
Covers for baggage rack
Basic tools (spanners, pliers, screwdrivers)
Emergency food and water
Reliable map and compass (1:500,000 or less)

EXCEPTIONALLY USEFUL EQUIPMENT
Duct tape
WD40 and grease
Zipties
Spare throttle and clutch cables
Spark plugs
Spare bulbs

CLOTHING
Helmet with visor, goggles or sunglasses (for dust)
Thick bike gloves (& thin inner gloves for when cold)
Hardwearing jacket
Jeans (or similar) with over-trousers
Sturdy walking boots or biker boots
Thermal layers
Fleece jacket

The kit listed here is the absolute minimum for a short ride. Anyone wishing to go a long distance should read *The Adventure Motorcycling Handbook* by Chris Scott for practical information on bikes, preparation and maintenance, as well as known trips and overland adventure stories. The website www.horizonsunlimited.com is an unparalleled resource for up-to-date overland information, and www.advrider.com gives plenty of inspiration.

Don't drive after dark, and keep it rubber side down.

Bryn Kewley travelled with us on our first trip overland to Afghanistan, caught the overland bug, and spent the next two years motorcycling all of the way from the UK to Singapore, including through Kashmir.

If you're travelling on a shoestring, find a buddy so you can split the room rates. The cheaper guesthouses and many homestays offer rooms, often with breakfast included, for less than Rs500, and many of the monasteries have space where visitors can stay in exchange for a small donation. Look out too for the hotels aimed at domestic pilgrims: in Jammu in particular there are a number of hotels with dormitories as well as private rooms. Providing you have your own tent, camping is usually free.

In the budget and mid-range sections you have a great deal of choice. The majority of guesthouses and small hotels fall into these brackets, as do the smarter homestays. You will frequently get one or more meals included with the price of your room and can expect to have electricity and an attached bathroom with running water. The hot water may come from a geyser. Rooms in these price brackets can vary spectacularly, so do look around at your options before making a final decision.

In the upmarket category you'll find larger hotels, tented camps and also many of the houseboats. J&K offers visitors the opportunity to stay in places they would not normally be able to afford, and the houseboats in particular offer great value for money. The tented camps, however, are generally overpriced: you pay a premium for the novelty value and some don't even have the facilities of a budget hotel.

Luxury accommodation is typically only available in the largest towns and cities. The best of Srinagar's houseboats are certainly luxurious and the likes of the Taj Vivanta and Fortune Riviera hotels are replete with all mod cons. Here you are paying not only for the surroundings but also for professionally trained, English-speaking staff who anticipate your every need.

EATING AND DRINKING

Food and drink varies between districts. In Ladakh and Zanskar the local diet is largely vegetarian and Tibetan *thukpa* (soup with noodles) and *momos* (steamed dumplings filled with vegetables or cheese) feature heavily. Although in Leh your options are diverse, in smaller towns and villages you will be limited to what is produced locally.

Moving west to Kargil and Kashmir, the Muslim population eats a far richer diet with plenty of lamb and chicken. Indian take-away favourites such as *rogan josh* (braised lamb cooked in a gravy of shallots, yoghurt, garlic, ginger and flavoured with spices) is a Kashmiri signature dish, and Kashmiri naan (flatbread stuffed with raisins and nuts) will also be familiar to curry fans.

EATING OUT Leh and Srinagar, and to a lesser extent Jammu, have a wide range of restaurants serving all manner of international and Indian cuisines. Many of these restaurants are targeted at tourists and business travellers, although there is an increasing trend for middle-class locals to eat out on special occasions too.

The smartest restaurants tend to be in the top-end hotels and they are open to non-residents as well as hotel guests. You may need to book a table at weekends but can expect well-presented, tasty food and good service. You may also be able to drink alcohol with your meal (see below).

In other restaurants you'll find a huge range in quality, from the sublime to the horrific. The restaurants listed here were reasonable or good when we visited, but do still take up-to-date recommendations from other travellers and look out for places that are packed with diners, as that tends to be an accurate sign.

Even where the food is delicious, service may be slow. Be patient initially, but if things are getting ridiculous, do prompt the manager or kitchen staff as it's not uncommon for orders to be forgotten or for customers to be queue-jumped by later but more pushy arrivals. Service is rarely included, except in the more expensive establishments. If you have received good service and want to leave a tip, 10% or rounding up the bill to the nearest Rs100 is standard.

DRINKING Alcohol is not widely available in J&K. Drinking isn't forbidden by law, but neither the Buddhist populations of Ladakh and Zanskar nor the Muslim majority of Kashmir drink heavily. You are unlikely to see much alcohol for sale in the shops but some of the tourist-orientated restaurants do serve bottled beers and the larger hotels have bars with a range of wines and spirits. Being drunk in public is culturally unacceptable and in any case makes you vulnerable to accidents, mugging and other misfortunes. Driving under the influence of alcohol is illegal.

THE *WAAZWAAN*

A traditional feast with as many as 36 courses, the *waazwaan* is served to guests at Kashmiri weddings. The host can show great hospitality to his assembled guests, the chefs can demonstrate their mastery of Kashmiri cuisine, and visitors can not only taste regional delicacies but will go home considerably heavier.

Sharing in the *waazwaan* reinforces a sense of community. Family members bring around a jug of water for the ritual washing of hands before the meal. Guests sit in groups of four and eat from a shared plate.

Key dishes in the *waazwaan* include:

- *Rogan josh* (see above)
- *Yakhni* (lamb shanks cooked in yoghurt)
- *Rista* (lamb meatballs in spicy red gravy)
- *Tabakh maaz* (fried rack of lamb)
- *Syoon pulaav* (meat pulao)
- *Lyodur tschaman* (cottage cheese cooked in cream and turmeric)
- *Dum aloo* (whole potatoes cooked in gravy)
- *Nadir-waangan* (lotus stems with aubergines)
- *Sheekh kabab* (spicy minced lamb skewers)
- *Gushtaaba* (lamb meatballs cooked in oil, milk and yoghurt)

An almost reverential approach to tea more than compensates for the lack of beer, perhaps, and sits particularly well with British visitors. The two most popular local types of tea are *noon chai* or *sheer chai*, which is green tea with milk and salt, and *kahwah*, a delicious and light green tea made with saffron and almonds.

PUBLIC HOLIDAYS AND FESTIVALS

India has a vast number of public holidays, but many of them are only celebrated in particular states or by one religious community. The three main secular holidays are **Republic Day** (25 January), **Independence Day** (15 August) and **Mahatma Gandhi's Birthday** (2 October). These are celebrated nationwide. Banks and government offices will be closed, and the sale of alcohol on these days is forbidden.

In J&K various religious occasions are also celebrated as public holidays. Dates are typically set according to the lunar calendar and so change from one year to the next. Prominent Hindu festivals include **Holi** (spring festival where coloured dyes are thrown in the streets), **Dussehra** (Hindu festival dedicated to worshipping the goddess Durga, usually in September or October) and **Diwali** (the autumn festival of lights).

MONASTERY FESTIVAL DATES 2014–16

The monastery festivals offer what is by far and away the best opportunity to see Ladakhi traditions such as masked dances, sacred dances, processions and oracle predictions. If you do have flexibility in your travel dates, plan ahead to be able to incorporate a visit to one of the larger monastery festivals such as Hemis, Thiksey or Lamayuru.

The dates of festivals are based on the Tibetan lunar calendar and so change from one year to the next according to the Western calendar.

	2014	2015	2016
Chemre	20–1 November	9–10 November	28–9 November
Dakthog	5–6 August	26–7 July	12–13 August
Diskit	22–3 October	17–18 February	TBC
Hemis	6–7 July	26–7 June	14–15 June
Karsha	24–5 July	14–15 July	TBC
Korzok	29–30 July	18–19 July	5–6 August
Ladakhi Losar	22 December	11 December	29 December
Lamayuru	24–5 June	14–15 June	TBC
Leh	27–8 February	17–18 February	7–8 February
Likir	27–8 February	17–18 February	7–8 February
Markha	19–20 December	TBC	TBC
Matho	15–16 March	4–5 March	22–3 March
Nyoma	20–1 November	TBC	TBC
Padum	20–1 November	TBC	TBC
Phyang	25–6 July	14–15 July	TBC
Spituk	29–30 January	19–20 January	8–9 January
Stok	10–11 March	28 February–1 March	18–19 February
Temisgang	13 June	3 June	22 May
Thiksey	9–10 November	29–30 October	17–18 November
Tibetan Losar	1 March	19 February	9 February
Yargon	4–5 March	23–4 February	TBC

The dates of the Muslim festivals of **Ashura** (Shi'a Muslim day of mourning for the martyrdom of Husayn ibn Ali), **Eid al Fitr** (the end of the holy month of Ramadan) and **Eid al Adha** (the feast of sacrifice) are calculated according to the Islamic calendar.

PHOTOGRAPHY *John E Fry (www.fryfilm.com)*

Taking pictures in India and particularly Kashmir throws up quite a number of important considerations when it comes to choosing the right gear and looking after it while you record your subcontinental adventure. I hope my tips below help you capture your experience fully, the way you want to, and come home with some great photographs.

ETIQUETTE As in any country, it is always polite to ask before taking someone's photo, and Kashmir is no exception. If you are using a long lens this may not be necessary because they may not notice you taking the picture from a distance, but if you can it's still wise to ask permission first, then take a few shots quickly to be sure of capturing a good expression, and giving yourself options later. Do not worry excessively about photographing children in Kashmir, as they are usually happy to pose and there is absolutely no risk to them or you in you doing so.

Again, as in most countries of the world, pointing any sort of camera in the direction of anything military, border crossings or governmental buildings is generally to be avoided. It is not worth having your camera kit seized just for the sake of an otherwise useless picture of a typical colonial office, or an old tank.

ADVERSE CONDITIONS The most common problem in hot countries is **humidity**. Humidity and temperature changes can cause condensation on and inside your lenses and camera almost instantly when going into the heat from your air-conditioned hotel room or vehicle (should you be lucky enough to enjoy either).

If you can, try to slow down transitions between hot and cold areas, and wrap up your gear to insulate it against temperature and moisture. In most cases, if your lens or viewfinder has become misty with condensation all you need to do is leave it to acclimatise for a few minutes, then give them a wipe with a lens cloth. Should the worst happen and condensation get inside your lens, one thing to try is leaving it in front of a hairdryer for ten minutes or so, allowing the warm flow of air to push the moisture out.

Another particular problem for cameras, lenses and other equipment in India is **dust**, **sand** and other **dirt**. Keeping a close eye on your lens caps, changing lenses as little as possible and keeping all your gear in a bag or camera case when not in use will all help to minimise the ingress of potentially damaging grains. Sand and grit is of course pretty abrasive, and can easily scratch your lenses and LCD screens. Always carry a small air blower, lens pen & cotton buds to clean your kit whenever you can, for if particles are left they can work their way into lens gears, between elements and into connectors while moving around in the bag.

If you are heading up the mountains, taking pictures in the **snow** can confuse cameras occasionally. Due to the way automatic exposure systems measure the amount of light they are faced with, they see light colours such as snow (and wedding dresses incidentally) incorrectly, as if the scene itself has more light in it, and consequently underexposes the image. Low temperatures will also drain your batteries more quickly than usual, so make sure you have at least one if not several spare, and the same with memory cards. You never know when a memory card or battery may develop a fault, so generally you should always take as many spares as you can.

If you are shooting on a digital camera, as most are, you should take a test picture of the scene you wish to capture, and adjust your exposure accordingly, using either

2

Exposure Compensation (a feature present on the vast majority of cameras, big and small), or manually exposing the next frame. We can easily do this now with digital, so why not shoot a few and adjust until you get it right, and from then on even in unusual situations you know roughly where the ideal exposure setting lies with minimal adjustment.

If you are shooting on film then I would suggest overexposing in these environments 0.7–1.5 stops, or if you are shooting transparency, overexposing by 0.3–0.5 stops. Better to slightly overexpose a negative, but slightly underexpose a transparency.

RECOMMENDED EQUIPMENT

Cameras Because there is now such a wide range of types of camera from which to choose, depending upon your budget, ability and ambition, I am going to divide them into three categories. The general advice is the same whether you choose digital or film cameras.

Compact cameras The advantage of small compact cameras, such as Canon's popular Ixus range or Nikon's Coolpix, is that they are very small, easy to use, produce stunningly good results in most conditions, and are easy on the budget. The disadvantages are mainly when it comes to controlling the picture, as many functions are automatic only. This can lead to under- or overexposure and even out-of-focus pictures in difficult or unusual conditions, such as high-contrast situations in strong Indian sunlight or in low contrast such as in the snow at the Gulmarg ski resort. Read reviews in photography magazines or online to identify the sort of features you need, then go into a store and try a few models out. The best camera for you is the one you can happily use most easily.

Bridge cameras This relatively new concept of putting an interchangeable lens system on a compact body opens up many of the creative possibilities of larger SLR cameras, within a very small form factor only slightly larger than a compact. These typically have larger image sensors, which coupled with the interchangeable lenses give more options for composition due to the shallow depth of field and lens field of view options this combination offers.

To make full use of the system, though, you will need to buy and carry several lenses, which while much smaller than SLR lenses still take up a bit of space, and add to the danger of dust getting into the camera when you change the lenses. They do have a lot of the ease of use of compact cameras though, so if you aspire to shoot more creative pictures than a compact allows, but are a little daunted by a full-size SLR, a bridge camera might be the best choice for you. Again, try a few out and see what works best for you.

SLR cameras The big advantages of SLRs are an optical viewfinder and mirror, showing you exactly the view that will be captured through the lens, a larger and more sensitive image sensor, a very wide variety of lenses, and fully manual controls. Certain types now offer additional clever features, but to be honest a lot of these are fairly gimmicky and will end up being used very little or not at all.

To make best use of these cameras you will need at least a few good lenses, so your camera bag may end up feeling rather heavy. I have offered a few suggestions for lenses and keeping the weight down on the opposite page. You should change lenses as little as possible to avoid particles of dust and dirt getting into the body of the camera and ending up on the sensor, which is of particular concern in India due to the warmer, drier climate and lower standards of cleanliness compared with Europe or America.

Don't get too caught up in the camera itself, as many produce very similar pictures. Instead (as with any camera) concentrate on how it feels in your hands, how easily you find it to get to the controls you will actually use, and if it supports the sort of lenses you want to use. With SLRs particularly (but not exclusively), it is the lenses that make the pictures, not the camera. Speaking of which...

Lenses Should you be fortunate enough to own an SLR system, there are ways to minimise what you take with you and the amount of lens changing you need to do. For example, some of the new compact high-zoom lenses can replace an entire bag full of f2.8 ones. For smaller chip SLRs (DX) there are a few very good 18–200mm lenses. For full-frame (35mm sized) sensors, my favourite is the Nikon 28–300mm AFS VR, which replaces my 28–70mm f2.8 AFS, my 80–200mm f2.8 AFS, and a 300mm, so that's at least three large, expensive lens field of views covered by just one!

The trade-off is the maximum aperture and arguably build quality, but if you have a full-frame sensor the difference in depth of field is minimal, and as there is a lot of light around in the subcontinent it is unlikely you will miss the couple of stops of extra light an f2.8 or faster lens would give you.

If you are into wildlife or particularly enjoy 'sniping' candid shots from a distance, a longer zoom such as Nikon's 80–400mm VR is an excellent choice, although you can't add a teleconverter. There is a Canon 100–400mm but it's bigger and heavier than the Nikon.

I would probably still take a 50mm f1.8 as well because it's very small and inexpensive, and can offer you that tiny depth of field if desired, plus a few extra stops of light if you need them. It's always a good idea to have at least one spare lens anyway and you can get away with a 50mm for most things if you have to.

An ultrawide would also be a useful addition, but not essential. An 18mm on DX, or 28mm on full frame, are wide enough for most things, but if you like wide angles and if you have the space in your bag, an ultrawide would be your third lens; something like a 14mm prime for FX, or a nice compact and surprisingly excellent Tokina 11–16mm for DX, or maybe a 16–35mm or 18–35mm depending on your budget. The trick is not to overuse wide-angle lenses; you should always be trying to mix close-ups, mid-shots and wides to tell a full and interesting story of where you have been.

Remember not to get too caught up with shallow depth of field and maximum apertures. Firstly because in such a beautiful place as Kashmir you want to see most things in focus anyway, and secondly because all lenses produce their optimum results in the middle of their aperture range, at least a couple of stops from either end. On an f2.8–22 lens, for example, its sharpest images will be captured from about f4 to f11.

Flash Using flash creatively and artistically can be a real art. Luckily in Kashmir there is a lot of ambient sunlight around so you shouldn't need much flash (which will drain your batteries), but if you do, here are a few tips.

Generally, turn the automatic flash off unless it's really dark or you need to see a specific detail, such as a carving or painting, but be aware of the reflection of the flash back off the subject – you may need to take the picture from a different angle.

Try to avoid direct flash if you can; it is very unflattering to faces particularly, and results in harsh exposure drop-off leaving backgrounds very dark, sometimes to the point of invisible.

If your flash does not tilt itself, use your hand or a bit of card to push the flash up towards the ceiling, which will result in light reflecting down on to the subject creating a much more even spread and much more flattering illumination of the subject. We are used to light coming from above, be it from ceiling lights or indeed the sun, so bouncing the flash off the ceiling automatically looks more natural and pleasing to the eye than direct flash, which tends to look as if you are shining a torch directly at your subject.

Sometimes, and depending on your camera, the flash won't be powerful enough to bounce off the ceiling, so turn it off and try to put your subject in front of some other light source, such as a window or lamp. If there's no option or no time, of course use the flash directly, but be aware that it won't look as nice as natural light or bounced flash.

With such stunning vistas, interesting characters, incredible colours and vibrant life to photograph in Kashmir, take pictures in the daytime with the sun behind you, switch the flash off and relax in the evenings!

Video With many digital stills cameras now offering the ability to shoot video, you will probably be tempted to use this to capture some of the exciting sounds and movement in Kashmir, so here are a few general tips.

The trick is to approach each video shot principally as if it were a still photograph. Line up your shot, compose and expose the scene, then record just five or six seconds of that view on video. If there is something moving in the scene to keep your attention, or a sound you want to capture, or if you are filming something specific that is going to be doing something, then keep the camera rolling a bit longer, but don't keep shooting without a reason to. Many people come home with holiday videos that consist of lots of very long clips, which frankly are very boring to watch back and don't give an accurate representation of the environment or them.

Think like a photographer and film lots of views and subjects as short clips, and try to shoot them as sequences as if you were watching a short slideshow on each place, with a distinct beginning, middle and end. Again, get a variety of shots in your sequences, a big wide to set the scene, a medium shot of something interesting that's going on, and a couple of meaningful close-ups. Remember to get a few shots of yourself too, telling the camera how you are feeling at the time (good or bad), your personal highlights of the day, and what you are looking forward to doing next.

You don't have to film a lot to cover what you want to, but you do have to shoot enough in as many short shots as you can to give a full picture of where you went or what you did. And the same is true, of course, for your stills.

LITTLE THINGS One thing to keep in mind: take pictures of the little things. It's often the small details that get missed in the wide expansive views and colourful scenes in Kashmir, but the things that jog your memory most effectively are often the little things, such a bright piece of clothing, an unusual door handle or an especially beautiful carving. Don't forget to capture some of these details, as well as the big, more typical holiday pictures.

DON'T GET TOO CAUGHT UP IN THE PHOTOGRAPHY! Enjoy yourself taking pictures, but do remember to put the camera down and enjoy the experience too. You are going to an amazing place, full of beautiful sights to photograph, but also tastes, smells, sounds, people to meet, new experiences and unusual places to explore. It is easy to want to record everything so you don't forget it, but sometimes putting the camera away and concentrating more on where you are and all the things the camera cannot capture commits those things to memory even more effectively than taking a photograph.

Enjoy taking the pictures, be as creative as you can, but don't worry if your shots are not perfect. Unless you aim to sell them then all they will be are aids to memory and to show friends and family, so do try to create as full memories as you can by not hiding behind the lens all the time – I say this from experience!

MEDIA AND COMMUNICATIONS

The legacy of Kashmir's troubles is seen most clearly in its strict control of communications infrastructure, especially the red tape surrounding getting SIM cards for mobile phones, restrictions on mobile phone use, and the regularity with which internet services are switched off by the government.

NEWSPAPERS India's main English-language newspapers, including the *Times of India* and the *Hindustan Times*, are all widely available in Jammu and Srinagar, and you can usually also get copies in Leh. The *Kashmir Times*, the oldest newspaper in the state, is published daily in Jammu, and *Greater Kashmir* (a daily publication) and the *Kashmir Observer* are both published and distributed in Srinagar. Newspapers are not typically for sale in smaller towns and villages in J&K due to the challenges and costs of distribution.

TELEVISION Televisions are widespread in hotels, restaurants and middle-class homes across J&K, but they only work when there's electricity so you'll frequently be left stranded halfway through a film or favourite soap opera.

Most users have a satellite box for the television, giving access to a large number of Indian and international channels in English as well as regional languages. The most accessible local news channel for foreign viewers is CNN-IBN, a collaboration between CNN and the Indian Broadcasting Network.

PHONES Making phone calls in J&K can be a source of great frustration. SIM cards from outside J&K (including those of international operators) are blocked from working in the state; getting a mobile phone SIM card is complicated and time-consuming; and pay as you go customers cannot send or receive text messages on their phones.

The easiest way to make a local phone call in J&K is to use a standard trunk dialling (**STD**) landline. Booths are plentiful in villages and towns and usually clearly marked with a sign, most hand-painted on a yellow background, that says 'Get STD here' or words to that effect, leading to no end of giggles. Calls will cost you around Rs5 a minute. Note that STD lines do not have the capacity to make international calls.

There are two main ways to make an international call. You can either use an international subscriber dialling (**ISD**) landline or, if there is an internet connection, a voice-over IP (VoIP) system that uses software such as Skype. In both cases international calls will cost around Rs10 a minute.

It is possible to get a local **SIM card**, albeit with reduced functionality (see page 97). To apply for a pay as you go SIM you will need to provide a photocopy of your passport and visa, four passport photos, a photocopy of the ID of a local resident (your hotelier or head of your volunteering programme may be able to help), and also their contact telephone number. It is theoretically possible for your SIM card to be activated the next business day, but in practice three to five days is normal, and seven to ten days is not uncommon, especially in Leh. When you buy a SIM card it comes with some minutes included: for reference purposes, Aircell's Rs60 SIM card includes 80 minutes of talk time; the Rs80 card includes 120 minutes.

INTERNET   J&K's access to the internet is increasing: there are now cyber cafés in all of the major conurbations, and more and more hotels and restaurants are providing Wi-Fi. That said, this is only of any use when the broadband is actually working. The government frequently turns off the service, supposedly due to security concerns; the cables providing broadband to Kargil and Leh have been buried too close to the surface and so are frequently damaged by rockfalls and inclement weather; and the regular electricity blackouts knock out the local hubs in any case. During one 12-day stay in Leh in summer 2013, internet services were up and running for just two hours. This is apparently not uncommon.

A small number of cyber cafés and travel agents, particularly in Leh, have satellite internet systems which, though still subject to the vagaries of the electricity supply, does at least avoid the problems of government interference and broken cables. This service is more expensive to use and slow, but can be used as a stopgap when no other service is available. Cyber cafés with a satellite uplink are specified in the relevant town's chapters.

POST   India's postal service, India Post, is a remarkable if bureaucratic institution with post offices in all towns and in many larger villages: look out for the dark red signage. In the larger post offices, particularly those that serve a lot of tourists, you may find an English speaker.

The post offices' principal role is to sell stamps: an international stamp for a postcard costs Rs20. Delivery is slow (you may well arrive home before your postcards do) but cards and letters do seem to arrive eventually. Parcels can also be sent through India Post, but this is a time-consuming process, as items have to be wrapped in cloth, stitched up and sealed with a wax seal, in addition to completing the usual customs paperwork. You are not permitted to stitch up your own parcel in advance of coming to the post office, but this does at least keep tribes of (mostly) affable old men in work. Information on the postal service in J&K is available online at www.jkpost.gov.in.

BUSINESS

The same legislation that governs land ownership covers other forms of property too, and consequently foreigners and individuals from other parts of India must have a local partner in order to set up a business in J&K.

J&K is rich in **mineral resources** (see *Geology*, page 3) and there are commercially viable reserves of coal, gypsum, bauxite, lignite, graphic, magnetic and limestone.

Though the mining sector is as yet underdeveloped, several mineral extraction projects have been identified as suitable for private investment, and the state government is able to provide information on these (see website, below).

The three **core areas for business growth**, however, are agriculture, handicrafts and tourism. Jammu and Kashmir state has been declared an Agri Export Zone for apples and walnuts, the land and climate in Kashmir is suitable for the commercial growing of flowers for both the domestic and international markets, and products such as saffron, cherries and strawberries all attract a high mark-up. Agriculture in the state is largely unmechanised and plots are unconsolidated.

To support the handicrafts sector, an Export Promotion Industrial Park has been established at Kartholi, Jammu and a similar park is being set up at Ompora, Budgam. The purpose of these parks is to effectively market and export traditional products such as papier mâché items, carpets, embroidery and pashmina shawls. The industry requires better co-ordination and marketing, both within India and overseas, as despite high price tags for items in the shops, little of the profit is seen by the producers, leading to a decrease in the number of artisans and a de-skilling of those who are still making crafts.

Tourism is, and will remain for the foreseeable future, the main source of income for the state. Although highly competitive, particularly in the hotel and travel agent sectors, there are still niches where new companies can profit. These include working with the tourism directorate in Srinagar to introduce a greater variety of watersports on Dal Lake, and providing courses and equipment for winter sports and other activities.

Businesses in J&K typically follow western business hours, though you may find that some shops are closed on Friday afternoons when their proprietors and staff go to the mosque for Friday prayers. Great attention is given to **relationship building** in business, and you may be invited to join potential business partners or clients for lunch, a party at home, or even to go on holiday with them. This is about getting to know each other better, and it can be the deciding factor in whether or not you get a contract. Be warm, be open about your expectations and boundaries, and be patient. Everything happens on India time.

Information about investing in the state, including opportunities and incentives, is available from the **government website** http://business.gov.in/investment_incentives/jammu_kashmir.php.

BUYING PROPERTY

Unlike other parts of India, non-residents of J&K cannot buy land or property in the state. This applies to Indian nationals from other parts of the country as well as to foreigners. This historic legislation, which led to the boom in houseboats in Srinagar (see page 199), and subsequently an article of the constitution was designed to protect the local population from dispossession and an influx of outside labour.

Those outsiders who still wish to purchase land in J&K do so through local intermediaries who hold the title on their behalf. Though the law offers such individuals little protection, such private arrangements often work well and enable outsiders to own and operate guesthouses, holiday homes, etc.

Before contemplating buying property in J&K, you should consult a local lawyer who fully understands the state's complex bureaucracy. You may also need the help of a local real estate agent: try **Alhassan Associates** (✆ *0194 247 1403*) in Srinagar or **RV Realtors** (✆ *0191 245 0077; www.rvrealtors.in*) in Jammu.

SHOPPING

J&K is a paradise for shopping, with some of the most beautiful (and, frequently, affordable) handicrafts anywhere in India made and sold here. In J&K, even budget travellers can purchase papier mâché boxes and decorations, painstakingly painted by hand with intricate patterns. Scarcely more costly are the hand-carved wooden boxes and small statues, crafted in Srinagar's backstreet workshops, and, of course, the tiny packets of dark red saffron, grown, picked and dried at Pampore. Brightly coloured cotton or wool scarves, and Buddhist trinkets from the Tibetan markets, are similarly affordable and take up little room in your suitcase.

If you have a little more to spend, consider buying a unique piece of Ladakhi silver jewellery set with coral, turquoise or lapis lazuli. Antique pieces command a premium, but modern replicas are often just as attractive. Fake pashminas are everywhere (you'll learn to spot them from their coarser texture and garish colours), but reputable retailers do have authentic cashmere shawls with prices starting from around Rs4,000. They naturally come only in shades of cream, grey and beige (the colours of the goats), though it is possible to get other colours if they've been dyed. Many of the more expensive pashminas are decorated with very fine embroidery sewn by hand. If you are concerned that you don't know what you're looking at and might be cheated, the J&K government arts emporiums in Leh, Jammu and Srinagar have a small selection of real pashminas and the prices are fixed.

Kashmir is famed for its hand-knotted carpets made from wool and/or silk. Prices for quality pieces start from around US$500 and the sky really is the limit. If you are contemplating buying one, take time to learn to differentiate between the varying qualities and to get a fair idea of prices. Village Arts and Crafts in Leh (see page 94) and NCE Carpets and Pashminas in Srinagar (see page 201) both have highly knowledgeable staff and a wide range of quality carpets. They can also arrange to ship your carpet home.

ARTS AND ENTERTAINMENT

Unlike other parts of India where music and dance spectacles and other forms of entertainment are laid on for tourists, in J&K this is less common: you can see masked dances during festivals in Ladakh's monasteries, but these retain their spiritual meaning and are for the benefit of monks and pilgrims as much as for casual spectators.

In high season there may be concerts and other performances laid on for visitors in J&K's larger towns, so look out for advertising posters and ask around. These are typically one-off, ticketed events and are sometimes set in splendid surroundings such as the Shalimar Gardens. Although international performers rarely make it to J&K, you may well be able to see leading Indian musicians perform. If you are attending such events in Srinagar, expect security to be tight. In and around Leh, though, it's a little more relaxed.

The best entertainment, however, is usually to be found at weddings and other private parties: fortunately these are lively affairs with hundreds of guests, and you will frequently be invited to join in the revelry even if you've only just met the host (or indeed one of his distant relatives). Seize the opportunity with both hands, dress up for the occasion and enjoy the food, music and dancing. Kashmiris really know how to party.

Although cinema (and Bollywood) is an India-wide obsession, there are relatively few cinemas in J&K. If you want to watch the latest blockbuster, your best bet is Jammu, where there is a cinema (see page 233). Cultural films and documentaries are sometimes shown at LAMO in Leh (see page 100).

J&K is, on the whole, a conservative state and lewd behaviour, revealing clothing and intoxication with drugs or alcohol are unacceptable. Although you may not be publicly chastised for such actions, they reflect badly on other visitors and will embarrass and offend your hosts.

Specific religious observances are required at the different places of worship (see below) and these should be observed out of respect: although you are visiting sites as a tourist, they are usually still active places of pilgrimage and prayer for devotees and should be treated as such. In all cases you should remove your shoes, dress conservatively (shorts are not acceptable attire for men or women, however hot the weather) and refrain from using bad language, smoking and public displays of affection.

BUDDHIST MONASTERIES Circumambulate a Buddhist gompa or temple in a clockwise direction. Bow your head towards the Buddha as a mark of respect when entering a temple, and when sitting do not point your feet at a monk, nun or statue. Do not touch statues or paintings and do not walk between someone who is praying and the idol towards which they face. Rather than shaking hands with a monk or nun, instead greet them by putting your hands together with the palms flat and bowing slightly with your hands near to your forehead. It is acceptable for non-Buddhists to pray, meditate and light candles in Buddhist temples, and it is polite to make a small donation for the upkeep of the monastery and its inhabitants when you leave.

HINDU TEMPLES Hindu places of worship should also be explored in a clockwise direction. Devotees will typically ring a bell as they step across the threshold to alert the gods to their arrival, and visitors are invited to do likewise. If you are offered a *tilak* (a red mark on the forehead that denotes a blessing) or a piece of *prasad* (food that has been offered to the gods), it is polite to accept whether or not you are a believer.

MUSLIM MOSQUES AND SHRINES Foreign visitors are often cautious about visiting mosques and shrines, but there is no need to be: guardians and congregations are typically welcoming and if there is a restriction on the entry of non-Muslims (for example for logistical reasons during prayer time), you will be advised accordingly.

Women must cover their hair when entering a mosque. Any scarf will do, and you may be able to borrow one if you don't have something to hand. Do not disturb or photograph people who are praying or walk in front of them. Keep noise to a minimum.

PRIVATE HOMES In private homes you will usually be expected to remove your shoes at the door. It is polite to take a small gift for your hosts (chocolates or other sweets are perennially popular), to chatter excitedly even if you don't share a word in common, and to tuck in enthusiastically to whatever food or drink is served. Do not touch food with your left hand as it is considered dirty.

If you see something that you don't understand, ask. People are generally open to explaining their religious and cultural practices and, in a place like J&K, they are used to dealing with people from different cultures. Be polite in your approach and genuine curiosity will more often than not be met with genuine answers.

TRAVELLING POSITIVELY

The single most important thing you can do for J&K is to visit, to explore, to spend your money, and to share your positive experiences with others when you return home.

Nicole Hydrick

Like most less-cynical travellers, I had wanted to be in holy places, sense sacredness and feel solicitude in some small degree, but the immediate experience of manic India had often overwhelmed subtler impressions and inhibited connection within me and with others. It was only when I reached Leh that I was finally able to feel in an immediate way, in a way that now feels quite distant from 'real' life.

The first surreal day at Mahabodhi was the day I met the Venerable Sanghsena, the monk behind all the initiatives and the whole community at Devachan. He told me I would help get him a cable car for the Mahabodhi International Meditation Centre (MIMC). He prophesied that I would be the first to ride in this feat of modern engineering and would possibly listen to a *dhamma* talk on the way up to the restaurant and gift shop at the summit. Though I had written a couple of grants in my time, I had no experience with cable cars, and am, in truth, acrophobic. But all these things would materialise because Sanghasena wills things into existence. Knowing and wanting to please in this context requires openness and flexibility.

On the other hand, at Mahabodhi volunteers actually end up doing exactly what they want to do, and although conditions are very basic, volunteers with initiative can be quite ambitious in their projects. Not being hugely prepared myself, it helped when I arrived having multiple options to piggyback on the efforts of recent volunteers who had, among other things, begun designing gardens for the meditation centre, creating media for fundraising and promotion, teaching various subjects in the residential school as well as the nunnery and monastery, and helping with visual and dramatic arts events. If, at the end of any day, I felt confused at all or frustrated in how I spent my time, I could certainly talk to Lobzang, my co-ordinator, Sanghasena's younger brother and self-proclaimed black sheep of his family. I came to him with complaints, usually about the impossibility of working without internet or teaching lessons with no prep time, and ended up having long and earnest conversations with him about religion and climate change.

In the end, the experience is unpredictable and parts of the day that seem peripheral are most memorable. My husband, who volunteered teaching life skills at the school, doesn't remember his lessons as much as he remembers watching the kids in free moments and feeling amazed that they knew so well how to amuse themselves and maintain interest in everything. We remember trying to reason through what went on in their minds at the morning assembly through the *dhamma* prayers. We wondered who chose the topics for short presentations, why the obsessions with Mount Rushmore, or Elvis, or the atomic bomb? Still all a mystery.

We think of what we could have done better. We should have brought more materials on the plane, especially for the school. We should have prepared a month's worth of lesson plans. We should have stayed away from the *dal*. More often, we think of the people and miss those associations. Our regrets are subsumed completely and seemingly through the will of those others who were so patient with us and ready to receive anything we could contribute. They are the same with anyone willing, and anyone who can go should go, if only to know these people for a brief and mysterious time.

Kashmir has been conflict-free for several years and yet the perception both in the international press and among the general public is that it is still unsafe to travel there. This view will only change when people see the state for themselves and start spreading the word that it is a beautiful, fascinating place and very much open for tourists.

If you are keen to volunteer, there are plenty of opportunities to do so. One particularly effective NGO in Ladakh is the **17000ft Foundation** (*www.17000ft.org*), which provides improved infrastructure, teacher training and volunteer teachers to schools in the remotest parts of the district. It is also possible to arrange teaching placements at many of the monastery schools, including at Likir (see page 149).

Volunteering opportunities are also available on a variety of projects with the **Ladakh Women's Alliance** (*http://womenallianceladakh.org*), the **Students' Educational and Cultural Movement of Ladakh** (*www.secmol.org*) and at the **Mahabodhi International Meditation Centre** (see box, opposite).

J&K, and in particular the mountainous areas, has a fragile ecosystem and this needs to be recognised and protected by tourists as well as the local population.

There is little capacity for recycling waste and so heaps of plastic bottles, tin cans, etc already mar the landscape on the outskirts of towns and in some popular picnic spots. Do not add to the problem. Reduce the plastics that you use and carry your non-biodegradable waste away with you. Water and electricity are also in short supply, so be sparing in what you use.

STUFF YOUR RUCKSACK – AND MAKE A DIFFERENCE

www.stuffyourrucksack.com is a website set up by TV's Kate Humble which enables travellers to give direct help to small charities, schools or other organisations in the country they are visiting. Maybe a local school needs books, a map or pencils, or an orphanage needs children's clothes or toys – all things that can easily be 'stuffed in a rucksack' before departure. The charities get exactly what they need and travellers have the chance to meet local people and see how and where their gifts will be used.

The website describes organisations that need your help and lists the items they most need. Check what's needed in Kashmir, contact the organisation to say you're coming and bring not only the much-needed goods but an extra dimension to your travels and the knowledge that in a small way you have made a difference.

Part Two

THE GUIDE

3

Leh

Telephone code: 01982

Life in Ladakh centres on the mountain town of Leh, spilling out into the surrounding villages as Leh continues to expand. Most visitors to Ladakh start or finish their journey here, and the seasonal influx of both foreign and domestic tourists gives the area a cosmopolitan air.

Ladakh's capital is a bustling hub with the rare combination of reasonably developed tourism infrastructure and a number of well-preserved tourist sites. If you arrive by air you'll need a few days to acclimatise to the altitude, but it's an easy place to spend time, especially during the summer months, and there are plenty of options for accommodation, food and entertainment.

The best way to get a feel for the city is to start out in the bustling bazaar and then climb the spaghetti-like tangle of streets between the bazaar and Leh Palace. The streets are far too narrow for a car to get through, so you have a glimpse into times gone by: men struggling uphill with handcarts laden high with vegetables; women baking flatbreads in ovens open to the street; and crowds of schoolchildren racing and shrieking along, excitable but good-natured street dogs in pursuit.

HISTORY

Leh was historically a small trading post on the southern spur of the Silk Road that linked Tibet and Ladakh with central Asia, and more southerly parts of the Indian subcontinent with China. Part of Greater Ladakh, it was an independent territory but a regular battlefield for Chinese, Mongolian and Tibetan forces from the 8th century onwards.

Leh was a relatively small and politically insignificant settlement when compared with neighbouring Shey (see page 126), but the relocation of the Ladakhi royal residences here in the 16th century, first to the Tsemo Fort and then Leh Palace, put it on the map. The town's growing prestige was demonstrated in its new architecture, and particularly in the gompas and mosques. Large houses were built for officials and the aristocracy at the foot of the palace, and these structures, many of which date from the 17th century, are the heart of the Old Town today.

The first European to visit Leh was the Englishman William Moorcroft in the 1820s, who came here *en route* to Bukhara, now in Uzbekistan. Moorcroft signed commercial treaties with the local government, opening Ladakh up to British trade, and ultimately published an account of his travels under the wordy title *Travels in the Himalayan Provinces of Hindustan and the Punjab, in Ladakh and Kashmir, in Peshawur, Kabul, Kunduz and Bokhara, from 1819 to 1825*.

After independence, foreigners were banned from travelling to Ladakh and the restrictions were not lifted until 1974. Leh began to expand at great speed, with both the military and tourist sectors investing in infrastructure development. Growth accelerated in the 1990s as tourists unable to travel in Kashmir headed for

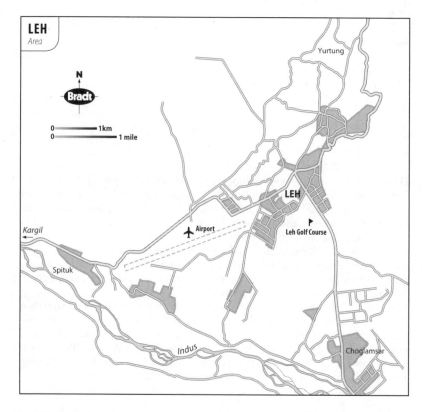

Ladakh instead, and many of Srinagar's hoteliers, souvenir sellers and restaurateurs relocated their businesses to Leh.

GETTING THERE AND AWAY

How you reach Leh will be dictated by your budget and the time of year. In the winter months all options are unreliable, as snow closes the road out in both directions and flights are frequently delayed, rescheduled or cancelled entirely. Even July and August are not immune to occasional bouts of inclement weather, so allow plenty of time for hold-ups.

BY AIR Leh's airport (*IXL*; ✎ 251 783) lies to the south of the city, situated between Leh town and Spituk. All flights into and out of Leh depart early in the morning, supposedly due to poor visibility later in the day. Even so, flights are frequently cancelled due to bad weather, putting pressure on availability as passengers are bumped on to the next flight, sometimes displacing others who have bought tickets.

Several airlines, including JetKonnect and Go Air, fly from Delhi daily. The flight takes 75 minutes and costs from Rs5,165 one-way. Prices increase substantially in high season and flights get booked up well in advance. Air India also operates an occasional service from Srinagar (55 minutes; from Rs4,870 one-way).

The airport terminal is a small and unprepossessing building, but the delivery of bags to the carousel is relatively efficient and a lady hands out foreigners' registration forms to fill in while you wait. Bring a pen, write in the usual details (passport number, visa number, etc) and hand it in at the desk on the left as you leave.

Outside the terminal you'll find a small crowd of taxi drivers jostling fairly good-naturedly for your attention, but also a pre-paid taxi booth. The 3km ride into central Leh costs Rs220, of which Rs20 is the booth's handling fee.

BY ROAD There are two roads linking Leh with the rest of the world. They are open in the summer and autumn months only. The Srinagar–Leh road winds its way 434km via Kargil and, until the opening of the Zoji La Tunnel at an as yet unspecified date, it is open only when there is no snow or rockfall. The tourist information centre in Srinagar (see page 195) can advise you as to the current status of the road and any planned closures, as can the police station in Drass (see page 187). In addition to Zoji La (3,540m), the road also crosses Fotu La (4,147m). You can also reach Leh driving the 473km from Manali in neighbouring Himachal Pradesh (see page 40). This is the main overland tourist route but it's a hard road with four high passes, two of which, Lachulung La and Tanglang La, are over 5,000m. If you are driving your own vehicle, note that the last fuel pump on the road is at Tandi, 107km north of Manali. Ensure that you have sufficient fuel to complete the drive to Leh.

Although categorised as national highways (NH1), both of these access routes are slow. The tarmac is often broken, overtaking is difficult, and bad weather, avalanches

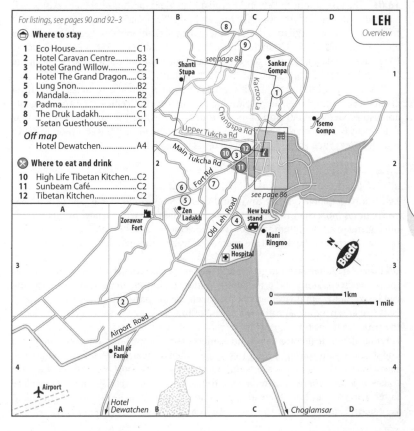

For listings, see pages 90 and 92–3

LEH
Overview

🛏 **Where to stay**

1 Eco House.................................C1
2 Hotel Caravan Centre............B3
3 Hotel Grand Willow................C2
4 Hotel The Grand Dragon.....C3
5 Lung Snon...............................B2
6 Mandala...................................B2
7 Padma.......................................C2
8 The Druk Ladakh....................C1
9 Tsetan Guesthouse...............C1

Off map
    Hotel Dewatchen..................A4

❌ **Where to eat and drink**

10 High Life Tibetan Kitchen....C2
11 Sunbeam Café.........................C2
12 Tibetan Kitchen.....................C2

and breakdowns frequently block the road. It is theoretically possible to drive between Srinagar and Leh in a day, leaving around 05.00 and arriving after 19.00, but it is better to break your journey in Kargil. Coming from Manali you should spend the night around Keylong (see page 40). It is another full day's drive from Manali to Delhi.

Buses Long-distance buses are the cheapest way to reach Leh, if not the fastest or most comfortable. The J&K State Road Transport Corporation (SRTC) (*www.jksrtc.co.in*) operates standard and de luxe coaches on the Srinagar–Leh road from early June until mid-November. The standard coach (Rs919) departs from Srinagar at 07.30 and reaches Leh at 13.00 the following day, stopping for the night in Kargil. If there are enough passengers, the de luxe 18-seater coach (Rs1,330) runs along the same route. Accommodation in Kargil is not included in the fare.

Buses from Manali to Leh take around 19 hours and typically break the journey at Keylong or Sarchu. The Himachal Pradesh Tourism Development Corporation (HPTDC; *www.hptdc.nic.in*) runs daily tourist coaches from 1 July to 15 September. One-way tickets cost Rs1,600/2,200 (without/with accommodation). HPTDC also operates an onward connection to Delhi (Rs1,220) in air-conditioned Volvo coaches.

HPTDC buses for Manali (with connections there for Delhi) depart from the HPTDC bus stand in Main Bazaar [86 B3]. Other long-distance bus and coach services, for example to Kargil and Srinagar, depart from the main bus stand by SNM Hospital.

Taxis The taxi unions in Leh and Kargil dictate rates for long-distance taxis as well as local routes, and if you are travelling along the Srinagar–Leh road you may have to change taxis at Kargil in order to comply with taxi union rules. Leh-based drivers charge from Rs16,355 to Manali, Rs5,983 to Kargil and Rs11,855/13,940 to Srinagar (one day/ two days). Return rates are available on some but not all routes: check the LTOCL list (see box opposite) for the latest options.

If want to pre-book your taxi, it's easiest to do so by contacting one of Leh's travel agents (see pages 85–7). If you are happy to share the vehicle, the travel agents are also proactive about finding other tourists travelling the same way on similar dates. This is particularly helpful if you have a limited budget but still want to get to remoter areas such as the Southern Lakes (see page 138).

GETTING AROUND

Leh is a reasonably compact town, and even if you decide to stay on its outskirts, you're never more than 15 minutes' drive from Main Bazaar. Journeys by bus and car often grind to a halt in traffic as badly parked vehicles cause bottlenecks in the already narrow streets, but the drivers are adept at squeezing through the tiniest of gaps.

ON FOOT It is often faster to get around the central parts of Leh on foot than by car as the traffic creeps along and is frequently stationary. Indeed, in the Old Town walking can be your only option as many of the streets are too narrow for a vehicle to pass.

If you are spending a protracted period of time in Leh, it is worth getting to know the pedestrian cut-throughs as these will significantly shorten your walk. The alley running alongside the stream behind Rainbow Guesthouse links Karzoo to Changspa and shortens your walk by a good 15 minutes when compared with following the road. Likewise, the footpath opposite the Moravian Mission School cuts off three sides of a square if you are continuing to Zangsti. You can walk from Main Bazaar to Leh Palace faster than you can drive there and, providing you are fit, it is also just a short (albeit very steep) climb up the hairpin footpath from the palace to the Tsemo Fort.

It is generally safe to walk around central Leh, even after dark, although you should of course take standard precautions. The traffic moves slowly but at night you should carry a torch to make sure you can be seen by motorists and also so that you can see the drains, broken paving and other trip hazards that could easily break an ankle.

BY BUS A small number of minibuses run from the main bus stand to Main Bazaar, and also link the suburbs with central Leh. There is, however, little difference between these minibuses and the shared taxis. You are not guaranteed a seat and your baggage may have to travel on the roof, but you will typically pay less than a quarter of the taxi fare (see below).

BY TAXI Leh's taxis are mostly minivans that seat around five passengers comfortably. Drivers typically speak a few words of English and their vehicles are generally clean. Taxis congregate around Leh Taxi Union (see page 84), the bus stand (see opposite) and the airport (see page 80), and there are usually a handful on Changspa or up by the palace too. If you prefer to call a cab in advance you can contact the taxi union or speak to one of the below-listed taxi drivers directly.

LEH TAXI FARES 2014

The following official taxi fares have been published by the Ladakh Taxi Operatives Co-operative Ltd (LTOCL). They are calculated from the main taxi stand on Ibex Rd [86 B3], differentiated by vehicle type, and updated on a yearly basis. A copy of the latest rates list is available either from the LTOCL office by the taxi stand, or from the J&K Tourist Office. Taxi drivers tend to keep a copy in the front of their vehicle too.

The rates below are given in Rs.

Destination	Innova, Xylo Drop/Return	Scorpio, Qualis Drop/Return	Eco, Van, Sumo Drop/Return
Ag Ling	203/262	194/251	186/240
Changspa	115/149	110/142	105/136
Choglamsar	299/387	286/371	274/355
Chubi Katpar	122/158	117/151	112/144
Gangless	263/343	252/328	241/314
Gompa village	229/296	220/284	210/271
Gyamtsa	347/451	332/432	318/413
Housing Colony	107/139	103/133	98/127
Khagshal	158/205	151/197	144/188
Leh Palace	176/229	169/220	162/210
Sabu Gompa	282/368	270/353	259/337
Sabu Oracle	NA/520	NA/499	NA/477
Sabu Zong	670/872	642/836	614/799
Shambala Hotel	152/198	146/190	140/181
Shanti Stupa	198/257	190/246	181/236
Skalzang Ling	160/208	153/199	147/191
Skara	152/198	146/190	140/181
Sankar	152/198	146/190	140/181
Tsemo	215/278	206/267	198/255
Yurtung	166/217	159/208	152/199

Leh GETTING AROUND

3

The Leh Taxi Union (*Ibex Rd;* ☏ *252 723*) is a co-operative that regulates the town's taxi drivers and fares. It publishes an annual fare list (see box, page 83) and can arrange you a driver directly. Rates are charged from point to point, or you can hire a taxi for a half-day (from Rs903) or full day (from Rs1,806) and take it wherever you please within the city.

For reliable and patient taxi drivers, we thoroughly recommend English-speaking Tsewang Rigzen (m *946 904 9347*) with his large, jeep-like vehicle, and also Thinles (m *962 296 2197*) and Hussein (m *990 698 3886*). The latter two both have minivans, comfortably seating five and four passengers respectively, and they charge in accordance with the LTOCL rate list. Thinles and Hussein do not, however, speak English, so you'll either need to get good at charades or ask someone else to explain where you want to go.

BY MOTORBIKE Exploring Leh and its environs by motorbike is incredibly popular and other road users are generally used to the vagaries of bikers. Leh's bike-hire companies do not require you to show a bike licence but simply to answer in the affirmative the question 'Can you drive?'

It goes without saying that there are significant risks associated with motorbikes. Hire rates include helmets and, in some cases, elbow and knee pads too. Wear them: your helmet is no use tied to the back of the bike. For general tips on biking in Kashmir, see box on pages 60–1.

Himalayan Odyssey [map, page 88] Mentokling Complex, Zangsti Rd; m 946 920 6777; e himalayanodyssey@yahoo.in. Comes highly recommended & offers motorbike touring packages that include homestay accommodation.
Karmic Journeys [86 A3] Zangsti Rd; m 962 298 0973; e rinchen.wangail@gmail.com. Just 1 of a number of bike-hire firms along Zangsti, Rinchen & stocks Bullets (Rs1,100/day), Pulsars (Rs800/day) & automatic scooters (Rs700/day).
Planet Himalaya [map, page 88] Changspa Rd; m 959 696 7182; e thabkas@gmail.com. Well established & professional, Project Himalaya can supply Royal Enfields (Rs1,100/day) & Pulsars (Rs600–800/day) among other options. Rates include elbow & knee pad hire & a discount of Rs100/day is available for longer hire periods.

BY MOUNTAIN BIKE Well-maintained mountain bikes are available to hire through Eco Travels [map, page 88] (*nr Wonderland Restaurant, Changspa Rd;* m *985 880 6864;* e *ladakhecotravels@gmail.com*). If you fancy the thrill of biking down Khardung La (see page 108) but quite understandably cannot face the slog of getting up there, they will rent you a bike and drop you at the top for Rs750. The adrenaline-fuelled ride back down to Leh takes around five hours and is certainly not for the faint-hearted or those suffering from vertigo, but has some of the most impressive views around and a definitely unrivalled brag factor.

A good selection of mountain bikes is available from Himalayan Bikers (*Changspa Rd;* m *946 904 9270; www.himalayan-bikers.com*). They charge Rs400–600 per day for bike hire (depending on the bike chosen), including hire of a helmet and bike lock. They offer a similar trip down Khardung La for Rs1,400, Rs400 of which is the cost of the Inner Line permit (not included in Eco Travels' price; see also box, page 107).

TOURIST INFORMATION

The state-run J&K Tourist Office [86 B3] (*Ibex Rd;* ☏ *252 297;* ⊕ summer only 10.00–16.00) is a nice idea but falls short of where it needs to be in terms of materials and even more so in regard to customer service. It's worthwhile popping in here for

mountaineering, mountain biking & trekking. The owners are knowledgeable & enthusiastic.

Ladakhi Women's Travel Company [map, page 88] Upper Tukcha Rd; ☏ 257 973; m 946 915 8137; e ladakhiwomenstc@gmail.com; www.ladakhiwomenstravel.com. Owned & run by women, the company has all-female trekking guides but is happy to arrange treks & tours for men & women. It uses local homestays wherever possible & is focused on responsible tourism.

Moonlight Travels [86 B2] Gompa Complex, Old Fort Rd; ☏ 202 332; m 941 921 9555; e info@ ladakhtravels.com; www.ladakhtravels.com. Director Nawang Lhundup is a bundle of energy, a charismatic individual who makes customer service a priority. In addition to trekking & expeditions he offers a number of more unusual options including

a springtime apricot flower tour popular with Japanese tourists, & treks in the bureaucratically challenging Karakoram Range.

The Ladakh Tours (See ad, page 106) [86 B2] NAC Complex, Main Bazaar; m 962 297 5440; e info@theladakhtours.com; www.theladakhtours. com. New, attentive outfit offering personalised tours & treks for small groups. Highlights of its programme include the Chadar winter trek & motorbike expeditions to Pangong Tso.

Zanskar Thema Tour (See ad, page 179) [86 B2] Hemis Complex, Zangsti Rd; m 946 972 7778; e vstobchazar@yahoo.co.in; www.zanskar-thema-tour.com. Specialist in Zanskar region offering ready-made & tailored packages. Options include trekking & mountaineering, horse trekking in both Ladakh & Zanskar, jeep safaris & cultural tours.

If you only require airline ticketing and nothing else, Jet Airways [86 C3] (☏ 250 999) and City Ticketing Office [86 C3] (m 962 245 3737) are both located on the eastern side of Main Bazaar. Jet Airways (☏ 253 754) and Indian Airlines (☏ 252 255) also have ticketing desks at the airport.

WHERE TO STAY

Leh has a wide variety of places to stay, from homestays and basic guesthouses to upmarket hotels. Accommodation options at the upper end of the scale tend to have electricity round the clock (provided by a backup generator when the main supply goes out), both hot and cold running water in the bathrooms, and a restaurant on site. They offer meal plans should you wish to eat all your meals at the hotel.

The majority of cheaper guesthouses and hotels are situated in Changspa, Karzoo and around Main Bazaar. They are conveniently located if you're reliant on getting around on foot, with both sites and restaurants nearby. The downside of these properties is that they can be noisy, both due to traffic and other guests, and some of the rooms are cramped. You may want to have a look at several places before checking in.

For a key to accommodation price codes, please see the inside front cover of this guide and page 62.

All listings are included on one of the three city maps: accommodation around Main Bazaar and Fort Road is mapped opposite, while Karzoo and Changspa options can be found on the map on page 88, unless otherwise stated. Page references for accommodation found in other areas are included below.

AROUND MAIN BAZAAR

See map opposite. Main Bazaar is a bustling part of town, rather crowded & noisy but in the thick of the action & well located for both sightseeing & onward transport.

🏠 **Hotel Khangri** (35 rooms) Old Fort Rd; m 941 917 8207; e info@hotelkhangri.com; www.hotelkhangri.com. Though unassuming

from the roadside, Khangri's internal courtyard is a pleasant enough spot for b/fast or a coffee. Rooms are unexciting but a decent size & with reasonable furnishings & clean linens. Wi-Fi included. **$$$$**

🏠 **Hotel Lingzi** (24 rooms) Old Fort Rd; ☏ 252 020; m 962 231 8987; e lingzihotel@ gmail.com. Very centrally located, this hotel has a wonderfully painted lobby, large rooms (all with satellite TV) & a terraced garden. Staff are helpful & there's a small restaurant on site. Wi-Fi included. **$$$-$$$$**

🏠 **Hotel Tsomori** (10 rooms) Fort Rd; 253 622; m 941 917 8029; e tsomori@yahoo.com; www.ladakhtsomori.com. A stone's throw from Main Bazaar, Tsomori is surprisingly quiet. Staff are helpful, there's free Wi-Fi & the owners also have a travel agent of the same name next door. **$$$**

🏠 **Kunga Guesthouse** (12 rooms) Zangsti Rd; 250 726; m 979 767 3621; e kungahotel@ rediffmail.com. Tucked back from Main Bazaar, Kunga is in a convenient position & rooms are reasonable. The building next door was being rebuilt at the time of going to press, causing some noise, but work should be finished by mid-2014 & it will add an extra 15 rooms to the hotel. B/fast included. **$$$-$$$$**

KARZOO

See map below. Some of Karzoo's hotels feel a little far from the town centre, but they're cheaper than those in the Main Bazaar & less overrun with gap-year students than Changspa.

🏠 **Hotel Naro** (18 rooms) Karzoo Rd; 252 481; m 941 921 8214; e paldan.naro@hotmail.com. At the far end of Karzoo & right next to The Ladakh (see opposite), Naro is in a quiet spot & is popular with motorcyclists due to the ample parking. Meals are available in the dining room; discounts are offered to independent travellers so be sure to ask. **$$$$**

🏠 **Royal Ladakh** (27 rooms) Upper Karzoo Rd; 251 646; e hotelroyalladakh@gmail.com; www.hotelroyalladakh.com. Definitely the smartest option in Karzoo, it's an attractive, well-kept hotel

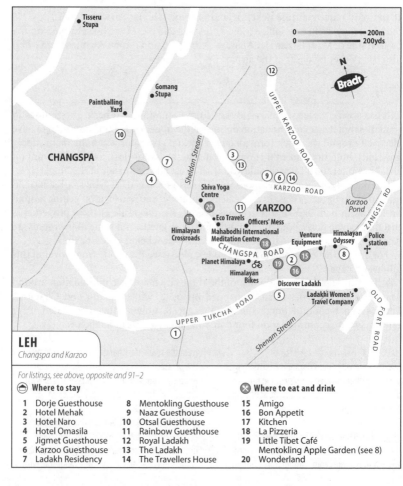

LEH
Changspa and Karzoo

For listings, see above, opposite and 91–2

🛏 **Where to stay**

1	Dorje Guesthouse	
2	Hotel Mehak	
3	Hotel Naro	
4	Hotel Omasila	
5	Jigmet Guesthouse	
6	Karzoo Guesthouse	
7	Ladakh Residency	
8	Mentokling Guesthouse	
9	Naaz Guesthouse	
10	Otsal Guesthouse	
11	Rainbow Guesthouse	
12	Royal Ladakh	
13	The Ladakh	
14	The Travellers House	

❌ **Where to eat and drink**

15	Amigo
16	Bon Appetit
17	Kitchen
18	La Pizzeria
19	Little Tibet Café
	Mentokling Apple Garden (see 8)
20	Wonderland

at the end of a quiet lane. Staff are attentive but not fussy; rooms are large, light & have fine views. Best option in this price bracket. **$$$$**

🏠 **The Ladakh** (14 rooms) Karzoo Rd; ✆ 252 627; e hoteltheladakh@gmail.com; www.mountaincalladventure.com. Slightly cheaper than its neighbour, Hotel Naro, the Ladakh is also rather more chaotic. All rooms overlook the courtyard garden but the place feels somewhat cramped. **$$$$**

🏠 **Naaz Guesthouse** (8 rooms) Karzoo Rd; m 946 970 2410. Right on the road, Naaz has the feel of a college hostel. There's no real outdoor space to sit, but rooms are light & all have en-suite bathrooms. A little overpriced. **$$$**

🏠 **Dorje Guesthouse** (12 rooms) Upper Tukcha; m 962 295 7511; e dorje_guesthouse@hotmail.com; www.dorjeguesthouse.com. Charming Dorje and Konchok welcome guests to their family home in a quiet location. Split over 3-storeys, many rooms have views of the Shanti Stupa, Tsemo Fort or Stok Kangri range. A Ladakhi breakfast is served in the garden, & Dorje can arrange trekking through Ladakhi Yeti Travels (see page 86). **$$–$$$**

🏠 **The Travellers House** (8 rooms) Karzoo Rd; ✆ 252 048; e leosami@hotmail.com. Probably the friendliest of the 3 guesthouses on this stretch of the road, Travellers comprises several buildings in a garden. The girl who runs it speaks English & is charming. B/fast available on request. **$$**

🏠 **Rainbow Guesthouse** (14 rooms) off Karzoo Rd; ✆ 252 332; m 941 917 8644; e rainbowgh@rainbowghleh.com; www.rainbowghleh.com. Far & away our favourite budget option in Leh is tucked along a quiet side street & built around a lush garden. Rooms & bathrooms are basic but clean & there's running water round the clock. The English-speaking staff are friendly & helpful. In the older of the 2 buildings there are a few cheaper rooms with a shared bathroom costing just Rs300. A footpath gives swift access to Changspa Road. **$–$$**

🏠 **Karzoo Guesthouse** (10 rooms) Karzoo Rd; m 979 750 7683. One of the cheapest options in Karzoo, this guesthouse is in a large, pleasant-looking house set in a garden. The owner can arrange basic travel agent services. The slightly more expensive rooms have attached bathrooms. **$**

CHANGSPA

See map opposite. This is Leh's tourist hub: you don't come to Changspa so much to experience the local atmosphere as to share in the backpacker vibe.

🏠 **Ladakh Residency** (22 rooms) Changspa Rd; ✆ 258 111; m 941 917 8039; e info@ladakhresidency.com; www.ladakhresidency.com. Changspa's smartest option is efficient if a little lacking in personality. There's no AC but rooms have fans. Plenty of secure parking. B/fast & Wi-Fi included. 10% service charge on all room rates applies. **$$$$$**

🏠 **Hotel Omasila** (40 rooms) Changspa Rd; ✆ 252 119; e hotelomasila@yahoo.com; www.hotelomasila.com. Cheaper & with oodles more character than the neighbouring Ladakh Residency, Omasila is a true haven in what can be a hectic part of town. Open year-round, rooms at the back of the property have striking mountain views. Mature fruit trees & patio plants give way to an organic vegetable garden that provides supplies for the kitchen. Central heating in winter. 24hr hot water. Wi-Fi included. **$$$$**

🏠 **Jigmet Guesthouse & Hotel** (25 rooms) Lden Malpak, Upper Tukcha Rd; ✆ 253 563; m 962 296 5846. Just 5mins' walk from Main Bazaar, Jigmet is a simple set-up in a quiet location. Guesthouse rooms are half the price of those in the hotel. Meal plans are available, though you're better eating somewhere else in town. **$$$–$$$$**

🏠 **Mentokling Guesthouse** (3 rooms) Nr Police Station, Zangsti Rd; m 985 839 9142. Attractive whitewashed building with carved wooden windows & quiet orchard garden in a convenient location. Rooms are large, modern in appearance & clean, & there are plans to extend the accommodation to 10 rooms shortly. The Indian Mountaineering Foundation (see page 99) has its office downstairs. Wi-Fi included. **$$$**

🏠 **Hotel Mehak** (20 rooms) Opposite Moravian Mission School, Changspa Rd; ✆ 256 110; m 941 917 8664. Conveniently located but somewhat dark hotel on the eastern side of Changspa. Staff are pleasant & speak English. Wi-Fi included. **$$**

🏠 **Otsal Guesthouse** (16 rooms) Past bridge, Changspa Rd; ✆ 252 816; e otsalguesthouse@hotmail.com. At the far end of Changspa is this large, popular guesthouse & its neighbouring restaurant. Rooms are large & reasonably clean; dbl & sgl rooms available. The secure courtyard is convenient if you need to lock up your bike overnight. **$**

FORT ROAD

See map, page 81. Accessible & tourist-orientated but slightly quieter than Main Bazaar, Fort Rd is a good option if you plan to get around on foot.

🏠 **Hotel Grand Willow** (36 rooms) Fort Rd; ☎ 251 835; m 941 917 8242; e grandwillow@ yahoo.co.in; www.grandwillowladakh.com. Large, traditionally styled hotel spread across 3 floors with quiet rooms facing away from the street & overlooking the garden. The central heating is a godsend if you are visiting Leh in the winter months. Wi-Fi included. **$$$$**

🏠 **Padma Hotel** (15 rooms) Goji Gherger, Fort Rd; ☎ 252 630; m 941 917 8171; e padmaladakh@ gmail.com; www.padmaladakh.net. Tucked back on a pedestrian alley running parallel with Fort Road, this eco-conscious guesthouse has pleasant staff & a laid-back feel. B/fast is served in the garden. Wi-Fi included. **$$$$**

🏠 **Lung Snon** (6 rooms) Opposite Mandala Hotel, Fort Rd; ☎ 252 749; m 941 921 9607; e lungsnon@gmail.com. Friendly, family-run guesthouse serving delicious organic meals. There's hot water around the clock &, as the owner works at the hospital, always a doctor on call. Views from the garden encompass Stok Kangri & Khardung La. The 2 sgl rooms are slightly cheaper. **$$**

OTHER AREAS

See map, page 81. Some of Leh's pleasantest hotels are in the slightly outlying area. If you have your own transport (or are happy to walk further or take a cab), they offer better value for money &, in many cases, attractive surroundings.

🏠 **Hotel Caravan Centre** (See ad, page 78) (30 rooms) Skara; ☎ 252 282; m 941 918 1260; e caravan@yahoo.co.in. One of Leh's oldest hotels, Caravan Centre has been updated to keep in step with modern expectations. In a quiet location amid pleasant gardens, it's a good spot to relax away from the bustle of the town. Rooms are comfortable, bathrooms immaculate & the staff attentive. Buffet meals served in the attractively painted dining room.

The owner is a mine of information. Friendliest option in this price bracket. B/fast & Wi-Fi included. **$$$$$**

🏠 **Hotel The Grand Dragon** (47 rooms) Old Leh Rd; ☎ 257 786; m 962 299 7222; e hotel@thegranddragonladakh.com; www. thegranddragonladakh.com. Leh's closest approximation of a 5* hotel has a liveried doorman & impressive entranceway. The management is accommodating but this does not translate to the general staff. Facilities include a shop, restaurant & 24hr café. The food is overpriced & uninspiring, but it provides pleasant surroundings for afternoon tea. B/ fast included. Wi-Fi costs Rs200/hr. **$$$$$**

🏠 **The Druk Ladakh** (26 rooms) Shanti Stupa Rd, Yurtung; ☎ 251 702; m 941 917 8448; e reservation@thedrukladakh.com; www. thedrukladakh.com. Conveniently located for Shanti Stupa but sadly not much else, the Druk is on the very edge of Leh in an attractive setting. There's a certain arrogance among the upper-level management, but regular staff are polite & attentive. Suites start from Rs8,000. B/fast included. 10% service charge on all room rates applies. **$$$$$**

🏠 **Eco House** (12 rooms) Nr Sanskar Gompa; m 990 697 7846; e stanzin@ecologicalfootprint. in. Leh's 1st eco hotel is a brand-new option for 2014. Owned & run by the Ecological Footprint team (see *Local tour operators*, page 85), the ecological credentials are 2nd to none, as is the customer service. Highly recommended. **$$$$**

🏠 **Hotel Dewatchen** (13 rooms) Ag Ling; e tanzin.norbu@gmail.com. South of the city, not far from the airport, is this quiet haven where you can while away days in the garden looking out across fields. Rooms are simple but comfortable & the home-cooked meals are delicious. Highly recommended for anyone seeking peace. Enquiries & bookings should be made through Mountain Tribal Vision (see page 30). **$$**

🏠 **Tsetan Guesthouse** (11 rooms) Upper Changspa; ☎ 224 9125; e tsetan_n@yahoo.com; www.tsetanguesthouse.com. A little away from the centre, Tsetan is quiet & set among beautiful gardens. It's clean, friendly & the slightly more expensive rooms have attached bathrooms. **$–$$**

✖ WHERE TO EAT AND DRINK

You won't find haute cuisine in Leh but, as the majority of visitors are either backpackers on a budget or carbohydrate-hungry trekkers, that should come as no surprise. Both of these groups are well catered for, with a high concentration of cheap and cheerful, if slightly scruffy, restaurants serving all manner of meals along Changspa and around Main Bazaar. If you're looking for somewhere a little more upmarket to impress a date, your choices are somewhat limited: try Bon Appetit for a romantic mountain panorama, or Tibetan Kitchen for a lively atmosphere. Both serve excellent food, and Bon Appetit even has wine and cocktails on the menu.

The restaurants listed below cater almost entirely to the tourist trade and so are open from May to October only unless otherwise stated. They open for breakfast (muesli, porridge and banana pancakes are the not terribly imaginative menu staples) around 07.00 and remain open throughout the day, closing as the last patrons leave sometime after 22.00. Once the daylight fades you'll frequently be dining in the dark if the power fails, although a few of the larger restaurants are able to run their lights off a generator if need be.

As Ladakh's local population is predominantly vegetarian, as are many of the Indian tourists, all of the restaurants listed here have both vegetarian and non-vegetarian (i.e. meat) dishes on their menus. In many cases the vegetarian options outnumber the non-vegetarian, and they're almost always delicious.

RESTAURANTS
Around Main Bazaar
See map, page 86. For a really cheap, fast snack, check out the kebab stands (⏰ evenings only; £) on the corner of Main Bazaar & Old Fort Rd.

✗ **Il Forno** Gompa Complex, Old Fort Rd. Rooftop restaurant with great views of Leh Palace & the Old Town, always packed with foreign clientele. Lavazza coffee available. Generally needs a good clean & spruce up to make the most of the location. Try to avoid the toilets. $$

✗ **Leh View Restaurant** Next to SBI, Main Bazaar. Leh View has 2 floors: an inside restaurant & the roof terrace above. Head for the latter for an uninterrupted view straight up at the palace. Tables on the Old Town side are the best. In daytime enjoy the set b/fasts from Rs110 & take your camera. After dark it's no less atmospheric as the muezzin calls the faithful to prayer from the neighbouring Jama Masjid. $$

✗ **Chaska Maska Restaurant** Old Fort Rd. The only restaurant we've found in Leh serving south Indian food. Pop in for crispy dosas stuffed with spiced potatoes, & pretty passable idli & uttapam. If you haven't had enough of them yet, you can also get a plate of steamed momos. $–$$

✗ **Momo La** Zangsti Rd. Tiny momo café with just 2 big tables, shared by whoever turns up. Watch the momos being made in the galley kitchen & pick either from the menu or have the momos of the day. You pay by the plate: veg momos are just Rs80. $–$$

Changspa and Karzoo
See map, page 88.

✗ **La Pizzeria** Changspa Rd; m 941 918 4409. Popular, if rather overpriced, pizza joint with an entirely foreign clientele. 11-inch pizzas cost Rs210–390 depending on the toppings, & salads, lasagne & cannelloni also make a welcome appearance on the menu. $$$–$$$$

✗ **Bon Appetit** Off Changspa Rd; ☎ 251 533; ⏰ lunch & dinner only. By far & away the best continental cuisine in Leh. Dishes vary from well-done classics to slightly more unusual variations: think pizza margarita with sundried tomatoes, or a caramelised onion & mutton burger. There's a strong line-up of mocktails (Rs150) & cocktails (from Rs160), & you can also try local specialities like the delicious, vitamin-rich sea buckthorn juice. Follow the red signpost down the footpath from Changspa Road. $$$

✗ **Amigo** Opp Moravian Mission School, Changspa Rd; m 946 970 9455. Authentic Korean restaurant with rooftop setting. Korean staples such as ramen noodles cost Rs170; dishes such as backsook (Rs450) & jimdak (Rs356) are for 2 people to share. Check out the daily specials board. $$–$$$

✗ **Kitchen Restaurant** Changspa Rd; ☎ 253 670. Relaxed roof terrace restaurant with a varied menu & young clientele. The decorative Marco Polo sheep's skull, lit up at night, is a little disturbing as far as décor goes, but the staff are friendly & the food, though a little bland, is pleasant enough. Wi-Fi, we're assured, is coming soon. $$

✕ **Mentokling Apple Garden Restaurant** Nr Police Station, Zangsti Rd; m 985 839 9142. Pleasant garden restaurant tucked behind the Mentokling Guesthouse. There's plenty of shade beneath the fruit trees, parasols & canopy, so it's a prime spot to sit with a Kingfisher beer & read or wait for friends. Service is glacial but the banana pancakes are worth the wait. Free Wi-Fi. $$

✕ **Wonderland** Changspa Rd; m 962 297 2826. Though rather unprepossessing at street level, the interior staircase ascends to a large roof terrace where gentle Himalayan flute music sets the laid-back scene. The extensive menu incorporates everything from excellent Italian bruschetta laden with garlic & olive oil to Tibetan thukpa (noodles in soup). Nothing happens in a hurry but the dishes are tasty & prices are fair. $$

Fort Road

All listings are on the map on page 86 unless otherwise indicated.

✕ **Dreamland** Above Dreamland Trek & Tour, Fort Rd; ☎ 255 089; www.dreamladakh. com. Upmarket inside restaurant & open-air roof terrace serving a range of international dishes but specialising in Kashmiri *waazwaan* (see box, page 63). Mocktails cost Rs110. Free Wi-Fi. $$–$$$

✕ **Summer Harvest** Behind Dreamland, Fort Rd; m 990 698 6556. Though it describes itself as a Tibetan restaurant, you should come to Summer Harvest for its Indian dishes, which are quite possibly the best in Leh. Our favourites are the shahi paneer & malai kofta, accompanied by plenty of garlic naan. The vegetarian dishes here are highly recommended. $$–$$$

✕ **Tibetan Kitchen** [map, page 81] Fort Rd; m 979 765 7181. Set back from the street behind a row of buildings, this is rightly Leh's most popular restaurant. The garden tables are invariably packed & if you don't arrive early you'll have to stand & wait. The building is influenced by traditional Tibetan architecture & the menu ranges from fresh trout to succulent Afghan kebabs. $$–$$$

✕ **Chopsticks Noodle Bar** Raku Complex, Fort Rd; m 941 917 8652. Recently relocated to larger premises by the river, Chopsticks has a reasonable menu of loosely Chinese dishes as well as excellent momos & other local favourites. It's spotlessly clean & service is efficient. The large tables outside may be shared by several groups of guests. $$

✕ **High Life Tibetan Kitchen** [map, page 81] Cnr Fort Rd & Main Tukcha Rd; m 941 956 5905; e stanzin-ningbo@yahoo.com; ☉ Apr–Oct. Atmospheric courtyard garden with a daily specials board & varied menu that includes Mexican dishes. We enjoyed the soppa de Azteca, a spicy tomato soup with tortilla chips & sour cream (Rs110). $$

CAFÉS

🖥 **Café Sutra** [map, page 86] NAC Complex, Main Bazaar. Homemade cakes & proper coffee served at tables on the 1st-floor verandah. For a bit of a treat, try one of the muffins for Rs40. The bookshelf of secondhand titles is worth a browse too.

🖥 **Lala's Art Café** [map, page 86] Old Town. From the outside you'd be forgiven for thinking you're in the wrong place, but climb the crumbling stone staircase & you'll reach a Leh institution. A standard menu of teas & coffees is supplemented by the opportunity to try Tibetan butter tea, served in a miniature wooden churn, accompanied by traditional Ladakhi breads.

🖥 **Little Tibet Café** [map, page 88] Changspa Rd. Tiny & very basic café serving locally bottled fruit juices (inc apricot & sea buckthorn juices) as well as tea & coffee.

🖥 **Lonpo House** [map, page 86] Below Leh Palace. Right at the top of the steep climb if you come to the palace on foot, Lonpo House is run by the Himalayan Cultural Heritage Foundation (m 941 921 8013; e office.hchf@gmail.com). Situated in an atmospheric old building, the roof of which is held aloft by 4 hefty wooden pillars; guests sit on carpets on the floor & are served tea, coffee & soft drinks at low tables.

🖥 **Open Hand** [map, page 86] Library Rd. If after weeks of rice & dal you cry at the sight of lettuce, this is the place for you. Proper coffee, juices & divine homemade cakes, salads & wraps, all served in a laid-back atmosphere with indoor & outdoor space & free Wi-Fi. While you're there, be sure to check out the Open Hand shop (see opposite).

🖥 **Pumpernickel Bakery** [map, page 86] Old Fort Rd. Leh has a profusion of so-called German bakeries, but Pumpernickel is head & shoulders ahead of them all. A wonderful Sikh gentleman with a radiant smile lovingly doles out apricot crumble, chocolate cake & his own delicious take on apple strudel, & if you want to eat in you can sit back & enjoy a reasonable coffee & light lunch.

Sunbeam Café [map, page 81] Opp Hotel Grand Willow, Fort Rd. Climbing the slightly rickety staircase to the roof brings you to this charming café with checked tablecloths & Chinese paper lanterns. Variants of noodles feature heavily on the menu, but it's also one of the few places in Leh where you can get a calzone.

ENTERTAINMENT AND NIGHTLIFE

Weekly **film showings** take place at LAMO (see page 100) each Friday at 16.00. The programme is composed predominantly of documentaries, usually with a social or environmental angle.

Other than this, there are no formal entertainment and nightlife options. What you will find during the high season, however, are locally advertised party nights and other such events, especially in the restaurants on Changspa. Look out for posters and chat to other travellers to find out what's happening where.

SHOPPING

With the exception of locally produced handicrafts, all of the goods for sale in Leh are imported either from other parts of India or from China: even basic foodstuffs and household items frequently come all the way from Jammu. For this reason prices are typically higher than elsewhere in India and you may see only a limited selection of items, though shops here are still better stocked than in other parts of Ladakh.

SOUVENIRS There is no shortage of souvenir sellers in Leh, though the range, quality and prices are distinctly variable. We've selected the retailers below because they have stock that is a little out of the ordinary, or their profits support local NGOs.

Handicraft Industrial Co-operative Society [86 B3] Old Fort Rd; ⏰ 11.00–19.30. Simple selection of locally made stock, including sea buckthorn textiles & low tables finely carved or brightly painted with Tibetan dragons. A large, hand-carved table that packs flat for ease of transport costs from Rs7,000.

J&K Government Arts Emporium [86 C2] Main Bazaar; ⏰ 10.30–18.30, closed 13.00–14.00. Next to the Jama Masjid, this small, state-run emporium has fixed prices, giving you a good idea of what you should be paying elsewhere. There's limited stock but they do have some attractive papier mâché pieces (Christmas decorations are Rs240 for 3) & genuine pashminas in natural colours from Rs4,000.

Jigmat Couture [86 B4] Old Fort Rd; m 969 700 0344; e jigmatcouture@gmail.com; ⏰ 10.00–20.00. Jigmat Couture really demands a category all of its own: encompassing both high-end fashion & family heirlooms, its artistic textiles are quite simply priceless. Their accessories have featured in photo shoots for French *Vogue* & every line can be customised to ensure it is not only unique but has the perfect fit. Even if you're not in the market to buy, go in & take a look.

Ladakh Rural Women's Enterprise [86 B2] NAC Complex, Main Bazaar; m 990 699 1375; ⏰ 10.00–20.00. Tiny shop stuffed with knitted hats & socks, felt toy yaks & Bactrian camels, colourful slippers & other woollen items. All items are made by local women & profits go back to them.

Open Hand [86 B4] Library Rd; m 962 205 5896; www.openhand.in; ⏰ 07.30–21.30. Large & friendly shop & accompanying café selling fair trade clothes, toys & other gift items. Products are made by marginalised & rescued women who receive training & a living wage for their work. We couldn't resist the gorgeous, brightly coloured toy elephants (Rs310) or the more unusual monk and nun dolls (Rs600) made by nuns at the Dolma Ling nunnery in Dharamsala.

Silk Route Arts & Crafts [86 C2] Next to SBI, Main Bazaar; m 962 293 6736; ⏰ 08.30–20.30. Small, well-organised shop selling a selection of high-quality carpets, embroideries & shawls from Kashmir & central

3

Asia. The pashminas are authentic & the owners not too pushy.

⬛ Tibetan Refugee Market [86 B2] Next to SBI, Main Bazaar; ⊕ 08.00–21.00. This open-air market has numerous stalls selling colourful beads, turquoise & silver jewellery, prayer wheels & other nicknacks. The vendors are usually open to negotiation over price. There are several similar sites within Leh, including on Fort Road close to the Tibetan Kitchen restaurant & in the southern part of Main Bazaar. In all cases the stock & prices are similar.

⬛ Utpala Arts & Natural Dyes Centre [86 B2] Hemis Complex, Zangsti Rd; ✆ 244 035; m 941 921 8589; ⊕ 10.00–20.00. Sells a range of natural fibres coloured with vegetable dyes

& handwoven to make attractive clothes & accessories.

⬛ Village Arts & Crafts (See ad, page 78) [86 B3] Fort Rd; m 990 656 6330; e wangnoomuzafar@gmail.com; ⊕ 10.00–21.30. The best selection of Kashmiri carpets in Leh. Both wool & silk carpets available. Designs can also be made to order. Owner Muzafar Wangnoo speaks excellent English & French & has an intimate knowledge of carpet making. Payment can be made by Visa & MasterCard. Highly recommended.

⬛ Wali Curious [86 B2] Opp NAC Complex, Main Bazaar; ✆ 257 015; e walicurious@yahoo. co.in; ⊕ 09.00–21.00. An Aladdin's cave of Ladakhi jewellery (antique & modern) including beautiful pieces of lapis lazuli, turquoise & coral.

TREKKING GEAR If you're in need of serious trekking equipment, from four-season sleeping bags and trekking poles to Gore-tex jackets and hiking boots, go to **Himalaya Adventure Store** [86 B2] (*Goji Complex, Main Bazaar;* ✆ *258 609;* m *990 699 7072;* e *himadvstore@yahoo.com;* ⊕ *11.00–22.00*). It keeps a wide range of stock in different sizes, and the branded items are genuine. Cold-weather clothing and Nepalese knock-off North Face rucksacks (more suitable for casual travellers than serious trekkers) are also available from **Mountain Wear** (*Changspa Rd;* m *969 722 9434;* ⊕ *07.00–22.00*).

If you would rather buy than rent your trekking gear, **Venture Equipment** [map, page 88] has a tiny shop at the eastern end of Changspa Road.

BOOKS Leh is the only place in Ladakh where you'll find a good selection of bookshops selling English-language titles, maps and postcards. The shops below are particularly well stocked.

⬛ Himalayan Book Shop [86 A3] Raku Complex, Fort Rd; ⊕ 08.00–20.30. Carefully chosen selection of books on Buddhism, trekking maps & Ladakhi language guides. Closes early if there's a power cut.

⬛ Ladakh Book Shop [86 C2] Next to SBI, Main Bazaar; ✆ 256 464; m 986 811 1112; ⊕ 08.30–21.30. Very large collection of coffee-table books, maps, guides & non-fiction titles, with

a small number of novels in English too. Agents for the Delhi-based publisher Hanish & Co. Shop is on the 1st floor of the building.

⬛ Lehling Book Shop [86 C3] Main Bazaar; ✆ 244 192; m 962 298 000; ⊕ 08.00–20.30. Friendly shop packed floor to ceiling with English-language books, postcards & stationery. Prices are theoretically fixed, but the owners are happy to negotiate a discount if you are buying several items.

PHOTOGRAPHY Several small shops around Main Bazaar offer photo printing and passport photography, and also stock a small selection of memory cards, batteries and generic chargers. The two below are the most helpful, and the staff speak a little English.

⬛ R K Studio [86 B2] Cnr Old Fort Rd & Main Bazaar; m 729 897 4715; ⊕ 08.00–21.00. Also does Forex.

⬛ World Digital Color Lab & Studio [86 C3] Opp post office, Main Bazaar; ✆ 253 160;

⊕ 09.30–21.00. Efficient service & fair prices: passport photos are Rs40 for 4 or Rs60 for 8; 4x6 photo printing is Rs10 per image. Look out for the Kodak shop sign.

FOOD Leh has no supermarkets as such, but there are a number of small dried and packaged goods stores where you can pick up snacks and other stores for trekking. They tend to be fixed price and have a limited range of items. Check the 'best before' dates before buying, as tins in particular may have been sat around for rather a long time.

🏬 **Chospa Supermarket** [86 C2] Main Bazaar; ⏲ 08.30–21.00 Mon–Sat, 08.30–18.00 Sun. Basic store selling packaged foods, spices by weight, cosmetics & hair products, & a freezer of ice cream that may or may not have defrosted in the most recent power cut.

🏬 **Modern Bazaar** [86 B3] Fort Rd; ⏲ 06.00–23.00. Tucked into a corner & more reminiscent of a garage than a food store, this shop nevertheless sells dried & tinned goods, snacks & soft drinks. You can buy bottled water in bulk.

ACTIVITIES

Whatever your interests, there are plenty of things to keep you occupied in Leh. The majority of options are, inevitably, only on offer during the summer months, though you're welcome to meditate year-round.

MEDITATION The best place in Ladakh to do a meditation course is at the **Mahabodhi International Meditation Centre** (☎ 264 372; e *infomimc@gmail. com; www.mahabodhi-ladakh.org*) in Choglamsar, just outside Leh to the south. The centre can accommodate as many as 50 people on retreat at any one time, and regular three-day meditation courses are scheduled throughout the summer, both for beginners and for more advanced students. More information about the centre is available on page 74.

The centre also has a smaller but very convenient **Leh branch** [map, page 88] (m *962 295 7460;* ⏲ *09.00–19.30 Mon–Sat*) on Changspa Road, which hosts daily meditation classes with yoga, and also public talks.

MOUNTAIN BIKING AND MOTORCYCLING Bike hire is big business in Leh and there are numerous companies offering everything from pushbikes to 500cc Royal Enfields. See *By motorbike,* page 84, for more details.

PAINTBALLING One of Leh's more unexpected options is nonetheless popular with gap-year students (and most other people after a few beers). Just past the bridge on Changspa Road, at 3,524m, **Paintballing Yard** [map, page 88] (m *990 634 3834/959 698 1936*) is apparently the highest paintballing site in the world. Prices start from Rs400 for safety gear, markers and 20 balls; Rs350 gets you an additional 30 balls. Call to arrange a game as there are no fixed opening times.

RAFTING White-water rafting on one of Ladakh's many rivers is a popular attraction and easily arranged from Leh. Although many of the regular travel agents (see pages 85–7) do offer rafting packages, you'll have a better experience if you arrange it through a specialist operator, and indeed many of the other operators only act as middlemen in any case. The companies below can arrange one-day river excursions or much longer trips.

Splash Ladakh (See ad, page 163) [86 B2] Gompa Complex, Old Fort Rd; m 962 296 5941/7123; e gangakayak@yahoo.com; www. facebook.com/reachsplashladakh. River-rafting specialist with highly trained staff & well-maintained equipment. Safety is improved by the presence of outriders in kayaks. Regular expeditions on the Indus & Zanskar rivers. Request the wonderful Raju as your guide. Kayaking also available.

TNE Adventure Rafting m 962 299 6536; e rregmirafter@yahoo.com. Firm of competent Nepali rafting guides with summertime river expeditions around Leh.

YOGA Though there are not as many opportunities to study yoga in Leh as in other parts of India, a few companies have spied a gap in the market and are offering classes for tourists. Daily yoga classes combined with meditation are also available from the Leh branch of the **Mahabodhi International Meditation Centre** on Changspa Road (see page 95).

Gravit Yoga [86 A2] Raku Complex, Fort Rd; m 999 931 6648; e elevateyogaclasses@gmail. com. Daily Ashtanga yoga classes at 08.00 & 09.30. Each session lasts 75mins & costs Rs200. Teachers are certified by Yoga Alliance International.

Shiva Yoga Centre [map, page 88] Nr Wonderland, Changspa Rd; m 849 281 4196. 5- & 7-day classes starting every Mon & daily drop-in sessions of Ashtanga (07.30) & Hatha yoga (09.00 & 16.00). Reiki treatments, meditation sessions & month-long yoga teaching courses also provided.

OTHER PRACTICALITIES

COMMUNICATIONS

Internet Leh's internet providers give an erratic service, with the central system often down for hours (and even days) at a time, especially if the cable from Srinagar has been damaged by flooding or rockfalls. A few of the hotels and restaurants have password-protected Wi-Fi for customers, but otherwise you'll need to visit one of the **cyber cafés** listed opposite.

For photocopying, scanning and more sophisticated printing, including decent-quality business cards (Rs400 per 100), your best bet is likely to be Tsewang Tolden at **Digital Impressions** (*Fort Rd*; m *962 298 9885*; e *tsewang22@ gmail.com*).

CT Cyber Café [86 B2] Khawaja Complex, Main Bazaar; ✆257 220; ⊕ 09.00–22.30. Small, rather dark internet cafe also offering STD phone calls for Rs5/min & ISD landline calls for Rs10/min.

Discover Ladakh Cyber Café [map, page 88] Changspa Rd; ✆252 471; ⊕ 07.30–23.00. Half a dozen computers & Wi-Fi costing Rs1.50/min as well as printing & CD & DVD burning. Also does Forex & cash advances for Visa & MasterCard holders.

Get Connected [86 C2] Next to SBI, Main Bazaar; m 990 697 1071; ⊕ 09.00–22.00. Internet café charging Rs10 for up to 10mins, Rs60 for 1hr. VoIP calls cost Rs10/min.

Peace Cyber Café [86 A3] Zangsti Rd; ⊕ 07.30–23.00. Terminals with a satellite uplink – the internet works (albeit slowly) even when the rest of Leh is without a connection. Wi-Fi costs Rs40/hr; use of the satellite connection is Rs90/hr. Tea & coffee are available from the adjoining café.

Potala Cyber Café [86 C2] Main Bazaar; ✆252 111; ⊕ 09.00–21.30. 12 computer terminals with internet access for Rs1.50/min. Also offers printing & scanning (Rs10/page), STD & international phone calls.

Wi-Fi Internet Café [86 C3] Opp post office, Main Bazaar; m 959 673 0570; ⊕ 08.00–23.00. Small, friendly internet café charging Rs50/hr.

Post Leh has two central post offices, the most useful (a relative concept) of which is the **Tourist Post Office** [86 C3] (*cnr Main Bazaar & Ibex Rd*; ⊕ *10.00–18.00 Mon–Sat*). Postcards cost Rs15 and an international stamp for a postcard is Rs20. Many of the other services listed on the wall (including STD phone calls) are not actually available here, and the post office staff working on the afternoon when we visited didn't speak any English.

Telephones Getting a **SIM card** anywhere in J&K is a bureaucratic nightmare (see page 70), and Leh is no different. If you are determined to go ahead, they are sold by **Aircell** [86 C4] (*Main Bazaar*; ✆251 132; ⊕ *10.00–18.00 Mon–Sat*). You will need to submit four passport photos, photocopies of your passport and that of your local sponsor, and getting a connection frequently takes up to four working days. **Top-up** is available from numerous stands around Main Bazaar and Changspa: look out for the logo of your service provider.

If you need to make a call but do not have your own handset or SIM, STD and VoIP lines are widely available in all parts of the town, including at all internet cafés (see above). Almost all international calls are routed via the web, so bear this in mind if the internet goes down. Expect to pay Rs10 per minute. Public telephones are all marked as STD (local calls) or ISD (international calls).

HAIR AND BEAUTY The dust and heat of India inevitably take their toll, even before you go trekking, so now and then a bit of pampering is in order, if only to keep you looking vaguely presentable. **Aaina Beauty Parlour** [86 A3] (*Library Rd*; m *969 773 2003*; ⊕ *10.00–21.30*) is run by English-speaking Rajni & her husband, and together they offer manicures and pedicures, haircutting, facials, threading, head massage and a variety of other treatments for both men and women. They also sell a small range of cosmetics including lip salves.

LAUNDRY Most hotels and guesthouses will wash your clothes, albeit for an inflated fee. If you need to arrange laundry yourself, however, go to **Wonder Wash** [86 A6] (*behind Namgyal Shunu Complex, opp FCI bldg, Airport Rd, Skalzang Ling*; m *979 773 8380*). It uses borehole water, so your clothes will end up cleaner than if the *dhobi* dunks them in the river. Alternatively, **Highland Dry Cleaning** [86 B2] (*Zangsti Rd*) is a little more expensive but situated in the centre of town. As well as washing it also, as one might expect, does dry cleaning, for which you'll pay Rs150 for a wool jacket, Rs200 for a down-filled jacket & Rs600 for a sleeping bag.

MEDICAL Leh is the only place in Ladakh with reasonably well-developed medical services. Staff typically speak English, standard medications are readily available, and you can get treatment for most illnesses and injuries.

✚ **Het Ram Vinay Kumar Chemists** [86 C2] Main Bazaar; ✆ 252 160; ⏰ 10.00–21.00 Mon–Sat, closed 14.00–16.00 for lunch. Near the Jama Masjid, this is Leh's best-stocked chemist. The pharmacist is helpful & speaks good English. Antibiotics & altitude sickness medication are sold over the counter without need for a prescription. Stocks cosmetics, baby products & food supplements.

✚ **Ladakh Physiotherapy & Rehabilitation Centre** [86 B2] Behind Splash, Gompa Complex, Old Fort Rd; m 962 227 0829; e rigzindolkar@gmail. com; ⏰ 16.00–20.00. Friendly clinic with 2 qualified physiotherapists. Treatments for neck, shoulder & back pain, & sports & trekking injuries. Rs250/hr.

✚ **Potala Medicos** [86 C3] 1st Flr, Batta Complex, Main Bazaar; m 990 699 8525; ⏰ 09.00–10.00 & 17.00–19.00 Mon–Sat, 17.00–19.00 Sun. Dr Tashi Thinlas runs this daily polyclinic, akin to a GP's surgery.

✚ **SNM Hospital** [81 C3] Nr main bus stand; ✆ 252 014. Large & well-run district hospital with competent staff in most specialisms. If you require treatment for altitude sickness, you'll likely be brought to the SNM. Doctors here, though sympathetic, are rightly weary of dealing with those who have ignored advice about acclimatisation & then got into trouble.

MONEY Foreign exchange is widely available in Leh, with everyone from travel agents to cyber café owners cashing in on the business. Below are listed four banks with 24-hour ATMs, though there are frequently queues to use them and they often run out of cash before everyone has been served, in which case you'll need to get a cash advance on a Visa or MasterCard.

$ **HDFC Bank** [86 C4] Main Bazaar; ⏰ 10.00–16.00 Mon–Fri, 10.00–13.00 Sat. 24hr ATM.

$ **J&K Bank** [86 B3] Cnr Ibex Rd & Old Fort Rd. 24hr ATM.

$ **Paul Merchants Ltd** [86 B2] Khawaja Complex, Main Bazaar; ✆ 255 309; m 729 854 0340; e pmlleh@paulmerchants.net; www. paulmerchants.net; ⏰ 10.00–20.00. Part of a

nationwide chain of Forex offices. Also processes Western Union transfers.

$ **PNB** [86 C2] Main Bazaar. 24hr ATM.

$ **SBI** [86 B2] Main Bazaar; ⏰ 10.00–16.00 Mon–Fri, 10.00–13.00 Sat. Forex during branch hours only; 24hr ATM. Note that in the winter months the branch opens & closes 30mins later.

REGISTRATION Visitors arriving in Leh by air are expected to fill in the foreigners' registration form, which contains virtually the same set of information you'll have provided on arrival in India. Fill in approximate dates if you don't yet know when you'll depart: like with so much of India's bureaucracy, you're obliged to submit the form at the airport desk but the chances are it'll then disappear into a storage room, never to be seen again.

PERMITS For those travelling from Leh to the Nubra Valley, Dha Hanu or the Southern Lakes, it is necessary to get an Inner Line permit (see box, page 107) before leaving Leh. If you decide to apply for the permit yourself, you will need to find at least two other people to apply with you.

Take your passport, photocopies of your passport, a print-out of your intended itinerary and a covering letter addressed to the **Deputy Commissioner's Office** (*LAHDC, Nr SNM Hospital*; ✆ *252 010*; ⏰ *09.00–17.00*). Applications need to be submitted before 15.00. The permit itself costs Rs20 with an additional Rs10 donation to the Red Cross. The permit will usually be issued on the same day. If you are short of time or need additional people to apply with, give your paperwork to a local travel agent (see pages 85–7) as they seem to be able to rustle up the requisite additional people and can get the permits at great speed, sometimes even at the weekend.

If you plan to climb one of Ladakh's many peaks, you'll need to buy a permit from the **Indian Mountaineering Foundation** [86 B1] (☏ *253 437; www.indmount. org*) whose office is hidden behind the Mentokling Guesthouse (see *Where to stay*, page 89). Peak fees are calculated according to height and start from US$50. You can apply through a local travel agent (see pages 85–7) but it's easy enough to do it yourself and, providing the peak is under 7,000m (above which requires special permission from Delhi and hence months of paperwork and hassle) then formalities can be completed in under an hour. Take with you half a dozen photocopies of your passport and visa, and also the name and contact details of your guide, as he/she will be responsible for you on the mountain.

WHAT TO SEE

OLD TOWN   Leh's Old Town appears on the World Monuments Fund's list of the 100 most endangered sites. Natural erosion of the mud-brick buildings in the wind and rain is the principal threat, though the pressures of modern urban life – unregulated building, motor vehicles, the need for proper sanitation, etc – are all taking their toll.

Leh Palace complex   [86 D1] Towering across Leh and viewable from almost any street corner in the town, **Leh Palace** (*Namgyal Hill;* ☏ *252 297;* ⊕ *dawn-dusk; entrance fee Rs5/100 local/ foreigner, video camera Rs25*) seems to feature on every postcard, and quite rightly so. Purportedly modelled on the Potala Palace in Lhasa (though at just nine storeys considerably shorter) the mud-brick and wood structure is undoubtedly impressive, albeit in places in a poor state of repair.

Leh Palace was built by Sengge Namgyal in 1600 and took three years to complete. It has more than 100 rooms (though many of them are no longer accessible) and when inhabited was divided into two distinct areas: animals were stabled and fodder, dried meat and vegetables were stored on the lower levels, while the upper floors housed the royal apartments, reception halls, throne room and private prayer hall.

Inside the palace there is sadly now little to see: none of the rooms are furnished with the exception of the colourful **prayer room**, one wall of which is lined with carefully wrapped sacred manuscripts. Enlargements of early 20th-century photographs of Ladakh and Tibet line some of the corridors, and temporary exhibitions are displayed in what was once the **audience hall**. From some of the lower terraces you can survey the carved **wooden balconies** and window frames that are a local speciality.

The highlight of visiting the palace is the view from the roof. The rooftops of storeys eight and nine (the latter of which is accessed via a ladder) have **panoramic views** across to Stok Kangri and the Shanti Stupa, and further up the cliff to the Tsemo Fort and Gompa. The skies seem to be clearest in the morning, and if you come at this time you'll not only avoid the midday heat but also have the palace virtually to yourself.

There are no signs to indicate the function of different areas, which makes a local guide an essential addition if you want to properly understand the palace's layout and history. Wear proper footwear, as many of the floors and staircases are uneven, and be sure to carry a torch as many of the interior corridors are unlit.

From the town centre you can reach the palace either by taxi (Rs162–170 one-way; Rs210–229 return), which will drop you right by the entrance, or by walking the clearly signposted route through the Old Town. Take the path from Main Bazaar that leads away from the Jama Masjid, and follow it to the left just past Lala's Art Café. A short way further on the palace is confusingly signposted both to the left and the right: the path to the left is a short cut but somewhat steeper. The short cut brings you past LAMO (see below), Lonpo House (see page 92) and up through the courtyard of the Chokhang Vihara Gompa (see opposite).

Ladakh Arts and Media Organisation   [86 D1] (*Below Leh Palace;* \ *251 554;* e *info@lamo.org.in; www.lamo.org.in;* ☉ *11.00–17.00 Mon–Sat; entrance fee Rs20/50 local/foreigner*) LAMO lies immediately below the palace complex, and you'll pass right by if you approach the palace via the short cut (see above).

Opened in 2010 in two sensitively restored buildings dating from the 17th century, the LAMO centre comprises multiple exhibition spaces, a study centre and library. A charitable trust, it exists to conduct outreach programmes, research, workshops and exhibitions into Ladakh's visual culture, performing arts and literature.

The main focus of the centre from a visitor's perspective is the **temporary exhibition**, which changes each summer. Previous exhibitions have examined the cultural heritage of Leh's Old Town, the production and craftsmanship of pashminas, and the early mapping of Leh by foreign travellers. Images and maps are drawn from the centre's extensive visual archives and supplemented by related artefacts. All the displays are accompanied by well-written captions and information boards (all of which are in English), and the knowledgeable staff are happy to chatter about the various projects they're undertaking with the local community.

Tsemo complex   [81 D2] Looking down even on Leh Palace, the Tsemo complex is the small collection of white and red buildings perched like a bird's nest at the high point of the mountain and encircled by streaks of primary-coloured prayer flags. It is possible to drive up (*15 mins; Rs198–215 from the taxi stand*) but rather more popular is the 15-minute steep climb along the zigzag footpath from Leh Palace. Do not attempt this climb if you are already suffering from the effects of the altitude.

The solid, dark red structure at the base of the complex is the **Tsemo Gompa** (☉ *07.30–19.00; entrance fee Rs20*), where a monk sits in the shade selling tickets and reminding visitors to circumnavigate the site in a clockwise direction. The gompa houses the two-storey **Maitreya Buddha**, whose serene expression is visible only when you are standing at its feet, and surrounding prayer rooms decorated with slightly nightmarish **murals** of demons.

Climbing past the gompa brings you to the **Tsemo Fort** (☉ *08.00–18.30; entrance fee Rs20*), a simple, whitewashed building bedecked in coloured prayer flags that flutter in the wind. Inside the dark, wooden prayer room is a miniature stupa flanked by two multi-faced female statues. Devotees prostrate themselves here in prayer, so be careful not to stand in their way.

Make sure you take a walk around the rickety-looking (but fortunately perfectly stable) covered walkway around the outside of the prayer hall. The views down across Leh are quite simply breathtaking, especially when the mountains are clearly visible too, and the prayer flags add an elegant and wholly appropriate frame to any photos you take.

Central Asia Museum   [86 D2] A remarkable modern structure on the edge of the Old Town, the museum's building has been inspired by traditional Ladakhi

architecture and made from stone and wood carved by local craftsmen. Although it was inaugurated in 2011, funding troubles have delayed its opening and it was still closed to the public at the time of going to print. It will ultimately showcase trade artefacts and house a library.

Guru Lhakang Shrine [86 C2] (*Free admission but donations welcome*) This Buddhist shrine dates from the early 17th century and is situated southwest of the palace in the lower part of the Old Town. Constructed on a rectangular plan and with walls up to 70cm thick, the original timber frame and paintings were damaged by water but then restored in 2004–05 with the help of the Tibet Heritage Fund, which has a detailed report on the conservation work on its website (*www.tibetheritagefund.org*). There are some modern murals and also a **statue of Guru Rinpoche**.

MAIN BAZAAR
Chokhang Vihara Gompa [86 B2] (*Opp SBI, Main Bazaar; free admission but donations welcome*) If you spend any time around Main Bazaar, or indeed have ventured up to the palace, the chances are that you'll have caught a glimpse of the golden, pagoda-like roof of the Chokhang Vihara Gompa poking out above the surrounding flat-roof buildings: it is by far the most attractive piece of architecture in the vicinity.

Entering through the gate brings you into the large, shady courtyard that surrounds the gompa itself. Take a look at the small **library** and, if it's of interest, go in, take tea and have a chat at the office of **Ladakh Buddhist Association**: it's straight across the square. From the open area to your left you'll have an unobstructed view up to Leh Palace and Tsemo Fort, and it's a peaceful place to sit and reflect. You can fill up your water bottle for a few rupees at the clearly marked **drinking-water tap**.

The gompa itself (confusingly also known as Tsug Lhakhang and the Choskhang, Jokhang or Soma Gompa) was built in 1956 to celebrate the Buddha's 2,500th birthday. The temple contains an important image of the **Sakyamuni Buddha** (the historic Buddha) made in Tibet in 1959, the same year that the Dalai Lama fled into exile.

Jama Masjid [86 C2] Leh's Jama Masjid, or Friday Mosque, stands in the corner of Main Bazaar. Non-Muslims are welcome to come inside providing they are appropriately attired and behave in a respectful manner (see *Cultural etiquette*, page 73), though it is best if you do not visit on a Friday afternoon when prayers are in progress.

The mosque was built in 1666–67 by the Mughal emperor Aurangzeb, a religious zealot in comparison with his predecessors, who was nonetheless responsible for some fine sacred architecture, including the wonderful Badshahi Mosque in Lahore. The construction of this mosque accompanied the signing of a treaty between the Ladakhi king Deldan Namgyal and Aurangzeb to jointly oust Mongol forces from Ladakhi soil.

Much of what you can see today is sadly not original. The mosque was largely rebuilt (and expanded) from 2002–05, so it is in essence a modern building, albeit with a few historical features.

The Jama Masjid serves Leh's Sunni community. A second mosque for Shiite Muslims, the **Inumbra Mosque**, is further south along Main Bazaar.

CHANGSPA AND KARZOO
Gomang Stupa [map, page 88] (*Changspa Rd; free admission*) Non-backpackers can be forgiven for avoiding Changspa, but in doing so they risk missing out on this

tiny and easily accessible gem. The whitewashed complex is thought to date back more than 1,000 years and there are some fine Mani stone carvings dotted around the place. Given its proximity to the town centre it is surprising how few people come here; those who do tend to be praying or meditating.

Shanti Stupa [81 B1] (*Shanti Stupa Rd;* ⊕ *05.00–21.00; free admission but donations welcome*) One of Leh's most iconic images is the view west across the town to Shanti Stupa. The snow-white dome shines out against its dusty, mountain backdrop, drawing your eye.

Shanti Stupa is a relatively recent addition to Leh's skyline and its shape and decoration are somewhat different from others in the area, no doubt due to the era of its construction and the fact that it was Japanese Buddhists rather than locals who paid for its construction. Relics of the Buddha are contained within the stupa's base, making it an important pilgrimage site as well as a tourist attraction, and there are some brightly painted relief carvings visible from the terraces that encircle the structure.

Shanti Stupa is one of Leh's most popular tourist sites, so if you want to appreciate it without hordes of other people, you need to get there early. We came around 06.30, just as it was getting light, and had the place almost to ourselves for the first hour.

OTHER AREAS
Tisseru Stupa [map, page 88] (*Gyamsa Rd; free admission but donations welcome*) In the northwest of Leh and easily combined with a visit to Shanti Stupa is the far older Tisseru Stupa, a crumbling brick-built structure reminiscent of a fairly squat ziggurat. It dates from approximately the 11th century (though some archaeologists have dated it as late as the 1400s) and was once part of a complex of more than 100 temple buildings.

The name Tisseru (also written as Tisuru) comes from Tibetan and means 'yellow rock'. Legend has it that an evil spirit used to occupy the site, causing death and disease among the local population and their livestock, but that the king wisely constructed the stupa on top of the sprit's lair and thus protected the community.

The stupa is built on a metre-high foundation block; the upper structure is tiered. It is thought that there were once nine terraced levels (making it similar in appearance to the tiered stupa in Paro, Bhutan), but only the lowest ones survive. It is possible to make out some of the floor plan, specifically the positions of shrine rooms and corridors, but the mud-brick construction has largely crumbled, leaving us to speculate at its former glory.

Zorawar Fort [81 B3] (*Fort Rd*) This is the fort that gives Fort Road its name and yet sadly few visitors ever come down into Skara to check it out. The fort was built by Thanedar Magna in 1836 on the orders of Wazir Zorawar Singh (1786–1841), whose statues and pair of cannons mark the entranceway. The fort itself is built of mud bricks and is still in use by the Indian armed forces: you may well be invited to join the officer on duty for lunch or tea.

Inside the fort is the small **Army Museum** (⊕ *Apr–Oct 10.00–19.00, closed 13.00–16.00; Nov–Mar 10.00–17.00, closed 13.00–15.00; entrance fee Rs10*) dedicated to the Dogra warriors. Cross the bridge over the dry moat, go through the arched gateway and then turn immediately right along the red path. The museum is on your left. If it is locked, continue along the path to the barracks and ask someone to open it for you.

The museum's **lobby** is decorated with regimental flags, shields and well-written information boards about three prominent military figures: Mehta Basti Ram, Raja Gulab Singh, and General Zorawar after whom the fort is named. There's an interesting black and white photograph of Zorawar's final resting place in To-Yo, Tibet.

The room on the right is the **information room**. Here you will find boards, again clearly written, detailing the 1st Ladakh Campaign (1834–36) and the region's subsequent consolidation, the Baltistan Campaign (1839–40), and the Tibet Campaign (1841). A small number of artefacts, including leather and metal shields and a steel and brass breastplate, the design of which seems hardly to have changed since the Classical period, add visual interest to the display.

The **artefacts room**, on the opposite side of the lobby, has rather more to see, though without so much background detail. Of particular interest here are the cabinet of metal wine and tea pots; the **collection of musical instruments** (including the oboe-like *shahnai* and several pairs of *bhugjal* or cymbals); and the set of rather intimidating gladiator-like masks. There are also a few dusty items of traditional costume, and a case of finely worked silver jewellery and other small items.

Mani Ringmo [81 C3] (*nr the new bus stand*) Mani stones are oversized pebbles inscribed with the Avalokiteshvara mantra: 'Om mani padme hum'. Often stacked into cairns or, in this case, a long wall, they're typically found by roads and rivers. Travellers passing by add their own stone to the pile as an act of devotion. You should circumnavigate the wall in a clockwise direction and think of the stones as a collection of prayers slowly added to over hundreds of years.

Nezer Latho [86 B6] (*nr the main bus stand; free admission but donations welcome*) The Nezer Latho shrine is south of Main Bazaar but still well within the limits of the town. The shrine itself, which is linked to the gompa at Spituk, is an unprepossessing whitewashed cube a steep climb atop a barren, rocky hill, but its raised position offers superb views across the town to Leh Palace and Tsemo Gompa or, in the other direction, towards Stok Kangri.

Nezer Latho is accessible only on foot: if you're coming by taxi or minibus you should ask the driver to drop you at Leh Main Gate and follow the footpath up the hill.

Hall of Fame [81 B4] Leh's Hall of Fame (*Airport Rd; ⊕ Apr–Oct 09.00–19.00; Nov–Mar 09.00–17.00; entrance fee Rs10/50 local/foreigner*) is an army-run venue on the opposite side of the road to the cantonment. The exhibits commemorate the events and heroes of the 1962 Sino-Indian War (see *History*, page 14) and also the 1999 Kargil War (see box, page 187). Unless you have a particular interest in these conflicts, it's probably not worth coming here specially.

AROUND LEH

Leh is a convenient starting point from which to explore neighbouring towns and villages, many of which are easily accessible by public transport.

SANKAR GOMPA [81 C1] Just 2km to the west of Leh in the hamlet of Sankar is the Sankar Gompa (*free admission but donations welcome*), which belongs to the Gelug-pa sect. Some 20 monks, attached to the main monastery at Spituk (see page 104) live and worship here.

Built in the 19th century during the lifetime of the previous Bakula Rinpoche, the three-storey gompa houses a richly painted *dukhang* dedicated to the White Tara and also to Kangyur Lhakhang. The **murals** depict scenes from monastic life and there are also fine images of Avalokitesvara, Tsongkhapa and Vajrabhairava.

A taxi to the gompa from Main Bazaar will cost you from Rs140 one-way or from Rs181 return.

SPITUK Almost overlooking Leh airport, **Spituk Gompa** (☉ *07.00—18.30; admission fee Rs30*) is perched in a superb position atop a hill, overlooking the Indus. Climb right to the top of the site where a monk sits outside a small temple, ringing his bell and directing visitors into the inner sanctum. The temple's interior is dark and slightly eerie, decorated with grotesque masks, flickering bulbs and shrouded statues. The military clock looks somewhat out of place here. The antechamber is filled with oil lamps, flames dancing above a floor sticky with oil.

Standing outside the temple you are rewarded with impressive views in every direction, and especially across the airport towards Leh.

CHOGLAMSAR To the south of Leh, just past Spituk, is the sprawling settlement of Choglamsar, a village inhabited almost entirely by Tibetan refugees that is an important regional centre for Buddhism. Here you can visit the **Tibetan Children's Village** (TCV), home to more than 100 orphans, and also the only **Bon Temple** in Ladakh (*Regional Tibetan Bon Cultural Centre, Tibetan Refugee Camp #1, Sonamling, nr Zampa*). Inaugurated in 1994, adherents to the ancient Bon religion follow aspects of both ancient Hindu and Buddhist rituals.

Those interested in learning more about Buddhist philosophy and in serving the local community should plan to spend some time at the **Mahabodhi International Meditation Centre** (*MIMC, Dewachan Choglamsar;* ✆ *264 372;* e *infomimc@gmail.com; www.mahabodhi-ladakh.org*). Founded by the Venerable Bhikkhu Sanghasena in 1986, the centre not only offers meditation teaching and inter-faith programmes but also plays a vital, practical role in the local community with schools and hostels for 500 underprivileged children, a monastery and nunnery, a care home that caters to the aged, disabled and destitute, a hostel for the blind, a public healthcare centre offering Western, Chinese and Tibetan treatments, an adult literacy programme, and environmental projects such as solar energy and organic food production. MIMC actively encourages foreign volunteers to come, stay and work on its projects, in particular to teach English in its schools. For information on volunteering opportunities, see page 74–5. The centre also has a small branch in the centre of Leh (see page 95), where meditation and yoga classes are taught.

Most importantly, however, when the **Dalai Lama** comes to Leh (which he does not infrequently), he lives in Choglamsar and delivers his *puja* or teaching

---

BON

Bon is not a distinct religion in its own right but an offshoot of Tibetan Vajrayana, or Tantric, Buddhism. Legend has it that Guru Shenrab, a Tibetan prince, began his journey looking for a horse that had been stolen by a demon, but ended up on the path to enlightenment.

Bon was originally a shamanistic and animistic faith. Shamans were thought to be possessed by either demons or spirits, sometimes those of ancestors, and to receive divine visions, especially when they retreated into the wilderness. It then developed into Yungdrung Bon, at which stage there are clear parallels with other forms of Tibetan Buddhism.

Today Bon has relatively few followers. It was estimated that there were 300 Bon monasteries in Tibet immediately prior to the Chinese invasion, but it is unclear how many of these survive. Elsewhere in the world there are Bon monasteries in Nepal and in India, the most significant of which is at Dolanji in Himachal Pradesh.

THE 14TH DALAI LAMA

Our first exposure to the Dalai Lama was as children watching *Seven Years in Tibet*. This 1956 documentary, which later was remade as a film starring Brad Pitt, depicts the boy Lhamo Döndrub, who was identified as the 14th Dalai Lama at the age of two.

The Dalai Lama is a high lama of the Gelug school of Tibetan Buddhism. The position is primarily as a spiritual leader, though the current Dalai Lama also served as the head of state for the Tibetan Government in Exile until his retirement from that post in 2011. When one Dalai Lama dies he is reincarnated, and it can take two to three years to identify the next reincarnation. Visions and omens guide the lamas to the child, who must then pass various tests to confirm he is indeed the Dalai Lama.

The current, 14th Dalai Lama was born in eastern Tibet in 1935, the son of a farming family. He was one of seven children to survive into adulthood, and his eldest brother had already been identified as a reincarnation of the Lama Taktser Rinpoche. His home was seen in a vision and then sought out, and when presented with an array of objects, the young boy was correctly able to identify those that had belonged to the 13th Dalai Lama. He was then formally recognised as the Dalai Lama and given the title Jetsun Jamphel Ngawang Lobsang Yeshe Tenzin Gyatso (Holy Lord, Gentle Glory, Compassionate, Defender of the Faith, Ocean of Wisdom).

The Dalai Lama's childhood was split between the Potala Palace and his summer residence at Norbulingka. He had both monastic and secular tutors, and was eventually awarded a Lharampa degree, the equivalent of a doctorate in Buddhist philosophy, at the age of 23. He was by this time already the temporal ruler of Tibet, having been enthroned in November 1950 at the age of 15. In this early period of his rule, the Dalai Lama worked alongside the Chinese government, ratifying the Seventeen Point Agreement for the Peaceful Liberation of Tibet, attending the National People's Congress and meeting with Chairman Mao. By 1959 the relationship had deteriorated significantly, however, and the Dalai Lama was forced to flee for his life at the outset of the Tibet Uprising. He sought asylum in India and formed the Government of Tibet in Exile in Dharamsala. Around 80,000 refugees followed him into exile, and he has spent much of the following decades appealing at the United Nations for the rights of Tibetans.

The Dalai Lama has not returned to Tibet in more than 50 years. He continues teaching Tibetan exiles and travelling extensively within India and abroad, engaging in inter-faith dialogue with the Pope, Archbishop of Canterbury and other senior religious figures. He was awarded the Nobel Peace Prize in 1989 and is vocal on peace, human rights and environmental issues. His Twitter handle is @DalaiLama; he announces some appearances through tweets.

sessions at the Ladakh Buddhist Association's Showground. The sight of thousands of people crossing the dusty fields on foot and then sitting entranced before the teacher is like something out of the Bible, and the comparison is further enhanced when monks and other volunteers start to feed the crowds with *prasad* and to hand round steaming cups of Tibetan butter tea.

Advertised well in advance and typically starting at 08.00, the Dalai Lama draws crowds of well over 100,000 people and his sermons are delivered in Ladakhi and

Tibetan but also translated into English. You'll need to stand close to the front to hear the English version, so arrive early.

It is highly advisable to bring a mat to sit on as the ground becomes swampy if it has rained, an umbrella or hat to protect you from the sun, and to wear plenty of sunscreen. A bottle of water and a few snacks wouldn't go amiss if you plan to stay for the whole session. Note that you will be gently frisked by security on the way into the ground. You are not allowed to carry cigarettes.

Getting there and away Getting to and from Choglamsar is relatively straightforward, except on *puja* days (see pages 104–5) when every man and his dog is on the move and you'll need to get as far as you can by taxi or bus and then complete the journey on foot. Minibuses leave Leh every 15 minutes from 07.00–20.00. Tickets cost Rs10. Alternatively, if you prefer to travel by taxi, then you will pay Rs290–316 one-way or Rs377–411 return.

4

Khardung La and the Nubra Valley

The Nubra Valley and Khardung La, the mountain pass you cross to reach it, lies to the north of Leh, in the north-eastern corner of Ladakh towards the border with China. The road from Leh (the imaginatively named Khardung La Road) winds its way initially along a vibrant green valley where each irrigated field is lined with shade-giving trees. Substantial houses and large white stupas dot the landscape. Small streams cascade over rocks. The road then begins to climb, gently at first but then becoming steeper, the hairpin bends contorting across the hillside. The loose scree slopes are barren and dry, only the red, iron-rich rocks breaking up the dusty, brownish grey.

AROUND KHARDUNG LA

SOUTH PULLU Some 14km before you reach the top of Khardung La is the smattering of prefab buildings known as South Pullu. There is a **military checkpoint** here and you are required to show both your passport and your Inner Line permit (see box below). There is also a basic **first aid** post.

After South Pullu the road surface deteriorates substantially: expect boneshaking pot-holes and regular hold-ups as road crews with bulldozers work to clear the latest rockfall and widen the road sufficiently that two cars can pass. There's nothing to do but sit back and admire the view.

INNER LINE PERMITS

The Inner Line permit is the government-issued travel document that enables non-Ladakhis (both Indian and foreign nationals) to travel to parts of Ladakh that are close to the Chinese border. It is compulsory to have the permit if you wish to travel to Khardung La, the Nubra Valley, the Southern Lakes or Dha Hanu, and the permit will be checked at numerous police posts and army checkpoints along the road. Make sure you have plenty of photocopies (four to six should be fine) that you can leave at the checkpoints if required.

The only place to get the permit is in Leh. You can apply yourself at the District Commissioner's office or, with far less hassle, ask a local travel agent to do it for you (see pages 85–7). The permit is valid for just seven days for foreigners (up to 21 days for Indian nationals) and cannot usually be extended. In order to make an application there must be more than two people in the group submitting paperwork. However, once you have the permit there are no restrictions on you travelling alone. Travel agents will usually be able to find additional people also in need of permits if you're travelling on your own.

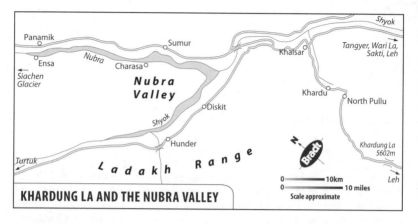

KHARDUNG LA AND THE NUBRA VALLEY

KHARDUNG LA Khardung La is the top of the world, at least if you believe the signposts. Supposedly the highest motorable road on earth (though with a few close contenders), it climbs to 5,602m, and so it's not only the views that will leave you breathless. It's a hugely popular destination for domestic tourists, the majority of whom come here on a day trip from Leh, but also the principal route via which people access the Nubra Valley.

Getting there and away By far and away the easiest way to reach Khardung La (and get back again) is by **taxi** from Leh, 40km to the south. The return journey will cost you Rs1,909–2,117 and there are always plenty of other tourists willing to make the trip if you want to share a ride. The journey is just shy of 40km and takes anywhere from one to three hours each way depending on the weather, road condition and whether or not you have to wait for rocks to be cleared.

Almost as popular is to get to Khardung La by bike. **Motorbike hire** in Leh costs from Rs600 per day, including helmet (see page 84), but given the combination of rough road surface and altitude the journey wouldn't be advisable for complete novices. Those with thighs of steel and strong nerves may also consider getting a lift to the top of the path and then **mountain biking** back down to Leh: rates start from Rs400 per person (see page 84).

If you do plan to travel by motorbike or mountain bike, leave early in the day so that you will be off the pass by nightfall. Travel slowly and be aware of the impact that the altitude will have on your physical and mental capacity: we had to evacuate one motorcyclist off the pass after he became very sick indeed. Don't forget to wear a helmet and take a scarf and sunglasses to keep the dust out of your eyes and mouth.

The road is open daily, albeit with delays, from 1 June to 31 October. In the winter months it is often closed without prior notice, both due to snowfall and for essential maintenance.

✕ Where to eat and drink The **Rinchen Cafeteria** claims to be the highest in the world and yet somehow still manages to boil water for tea. The plastic cups are tiny and the liquor sickly sweet, but it's Rs10 well spent, especially if you have an unexpected stop here while they blast the road below. There are a few basic snacks on sale, but a quick chat with the soldiers who make up the bulk of the clientele is definitely more rewarding than the catering.

What to see The principal attraction of Khardung La is the pass itself and the views from either side, either looking back towards Leh or down into the Nubra

Valley. **Glaciers** are currently visible in two places (though given the rate at which they are melting this may sadly be the only edition of the guide in which this is the case) and on a clear day you have a fine view of Stok Kangri too.

If there's still air in your lungs you can scramble up to the small prayer flag-strewn **shrine** overlooking the road, or browse the **souvenir stand**. Music and chanting blares out of the loudspeakers, giving a party atmosphere, and of course you need to stop and pose for a picture in front of one of the two road signs declaring the height of the pass.

NORTH PULLU Coming down off the pass in to the valley, the first settlement you reach is North Pullu, which is about 16km (10 miles) away from Khardung La. It is a small army encampment belonging to the Ladakh Scouts, who seem to spend much of the day sitting lazily by the stream and dangling their feet in the water. The tarmac, which is noticeably absent as you cross Khardung La, restarts just before you reach North Pullu.

The other sign of development here is the presence of three cafés catering to passing tourists. They are all in the second part of the village, past the whitewashed buildings with their camouflage-painted roofs. Two of the **cafés**, identifiable only by their collections of aged patio chairs, serve hot tea and soft drinks; the third proclaims itself a **Garden Restaurant** and also has rooms to rent (**$**).

KHARDUNG Khardung village is a fairly miserable ribbon development and the first civilian settlement after the pass. If you're on foot or cycling you might be tempted to stop at the **Maitreya Mid-way Café** (**$**) or the even more grimy **Skitchan Restaurant & Guesthouse** (**$**) next door, but otherwise drive straight through.

THE NUBRA VALLEY

Easily accessible from Leh and yet far enough to feel like you're getting out into the wilderness, the Nubra Valley is one of the most popular destinations for trekkers and quite rightly so: the views are splendid, routes are varied, and the infrastructure is reasonably well developed if you do want a hotel and a hot meal on the valley floor.

Although the valley takes its name from the River Nubra, there are actually two rivers in the Nubra Valley: the Shyok River originates in the Rimo Glacier and

4

winds its way from Pakistan, across the Line of Control (LoC) and through the villages of Turtuk, Hunder and Diskit. The Nubra River is its tributary, flowing out of the Siachen Glacier south through Panamik and Sumur. The confluence of the two rivers is just to the east of Diskit, and they continue on in a southeasterly direction, ultimately joining the Indus.

Historically the Nubra Valley was of great importance as a trading route: it was only after independence in 1947 that the trade routes were severed. Camel caravans travelled the length of the Karakoram range to China and into central Asia: the descendants of these pack animals are the Bactrian camels now used to give rides to tourists on the sand dunes outside Hunder.

DISKIT *Telephone code: 01980* The largest settlement in the valley, Diskit has grown up around the gompa of the same name. Tucked between the cliffs and the river, it's an attractive place to base yourself if you want to explore Nubra's cultural sites, though you'll also find it a convenient break in your journey when trekking or continuing by road to Turtuk. The tree-lined lanes are pleasantly dappled with shade and it's an easy stroll to the river and back. The vast Maitreya Buddha (see page 112) surveys his domain munificently: everywhere you go you'll be under his watchful gaze.

History Diskit's written history begins in the 1400s, though it was undoubtedly inhabited long before this and travellers and traders would also have passed through. The local ruler, Nyigma Gragspa, supported Sharap Zangpo in the building of the gompa (see page 112) and in the century that followed the combined palace and monastery was heavily fortified in order to withstand invaders, including the Mongol general Mirza Muhammad Haidar Dughlat Beg. Although Mirza Haidar was defeated, it was as a result of intervention by the King of Leh, and so Diskit came under his influence too. Local chieftains grew rich on the trade with Yarkand and made territorial gains in Baltistan, as well as fighting against the Mughals.

Getting there and around Unless you have entered the valley **on foot from Phyang** (see page 113), you will reach Diskit by road having come across Khardung La. Shortly after the village of Khalsar the main road splits in two: the right fork crosses the river to Sumur and Panamik; the left fork continues on to Diskit and Hunder.

It's a 118km **drive from Leh** to Diskit. It takes around seven hours but inevitably longer if snow or rocks have blocked the road. In the summer months minibuses leave three times a week (Tuesday, Thursday and Saturday) from Leh's main bus stand at 06.00, reaching Diskit in the early afternoon. The fare is Rs151 per person.

Due to the greater flexibility and comfort, most visitors choose to travel to Diskit by car, either hiring a taxi themselves or riding in a shared jeep. At the time of going to press, the Ladakhi Taxi Operatives Co-operative Ltd (LTOCL) offered a number of options for getting to the valley: a basic day return from Leh to Diskit and Hunder started from Rs6,721; travelling from Leh you could combine Diskit and Hunder with Sumur and Panamik over two days from Rs8,005; and if you wished to travel from Leh to Diskit, on to Turktuk and back again (also over two days), rates started from Rs9,939.

Travelling on within the valley, there are **minibuses** twice a day (08.00 and 15.00; not Sunday) from Diskit to Sumur (2 hours; Rs30) and the 08.00 bus continues on to Panamik (2½ hours; Rs45). More frequent are the minibuses shuttling the short distance between Diskit and Hunder (Rs10). From the bus stand at Diskit jeeps can be hired to Hunder (Rs250), Sumur (Rs1,050) and Panamik (Rs1,800).

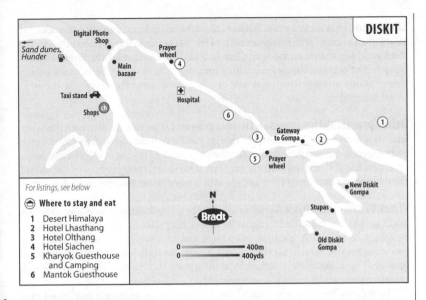

Sand dunes, Hunder
Digital Photo Shop
Prayer wheel (4)
Main bazaar
Taxi stand
Shops (ch)
Hospital (+)
(6)
Gateway to Gompa (3) (2)
(5) Prayer wheel
(1)
New Diskit Gompa
Stupas
Old Diskit Gompa

For listings, see below

⌂ **Where to stay and eat**

1 Desert Himalaya
2 Hotel Lhasthang
3 Hotel Olthang
4 Hotel Siachen
5 Kharyok Guesthouse
   and Camping
6 Mantok Guesthouse

N
Bradt
0 ————— 400m
0 ————— 400yds

⌂ **Where to stay and eat** Diskit has the greatest variety of accommodation options in Nubra, rivalled only by Hunder. Hotels and camps here predominantly target Indian domestic tourists and so offer combined packages of rooms and meals. The following establishments are all marked on the map above.

⌂ **Desert Himalaya** (25 tents) Beneath Diskit Gompa; (01982) 253 588; e deserthimalayaresort@gmail.com; www. deserthimalayaresort.com. Luxury tents erected on hard standing with views up towards the Maitreya Buddha & mountains. Every tent has its own immaculate bathroom with shower. It is a shady site, you can fish for rainbow trout in the pond, & come nightfall there is a bonfire & option to BBQ. The on-site restaurant seats 80. Note that all bookings incur a 10% service charge. **$$$$$**

⌂ **Hotel Lhasthang** (10 rooms) Beneath Diskit Gompa; 200 043; m 946 917 6104; e norboolasthang@yahoo.com. The sister property to Hotel Olthang (see below), this slightly more expensive hotel opened only in 2013. The large, light rooms are complete; the landscaping of the grounds is in progress. The dining hall has impressive views across the valley & a generator ensures constant power. All rooms have en-suite bathrooms. **$$$**

⌂ **Hotel Olthang** (21 rooms) 220 025; m 946 917 6104; e hotelolthang@yahoo.com. Probably the longest-established hotel in Diskit,

Olthang has a central location & small courtyard garden. All rooms have attached showers but there's hot water only in the morning. A backup generator guarantees the electricity. Meals are available on request. **$$$**

⌂ **Hotel Siachen** (4 rooms) Behind prayer wheel; 220 004; m 941 937 2016. Basic hotel in the centre of the village, hidden behind a tall wall. The welcome is less warm than at Mantok Guesthouse (see below), but it is perfectly serviceable if all you want to do is sleep. **$$**

⌂ **Mantok Guesthouse** (4 rooms) Nr Sub District Hospital; 200 039; m 946 978 6980. Tsewang Dorjay & his family live in the same peaceful compound as their guesthouse & it really feels like home: the sunflowers are lovingly cultivated & fodder for the animals is piled on the roof. Guest rooms are large & clean, & meals are freshly prepared to order, often with vegetables from the garden. **$$**

⌂ **Karyok Guesthouse & Camping** (15 rooms) Opp Hotel Olthang; 220 050; m 946 917 6131. Quiet compound close to the gompa with 2 guesthouse buildings (old & new) & ample space for tents. Camping costs Rs200; rooms start from Rs300. **$**

4

Shopping Diskit has a small **bazaar** selling basic consumer goods and packaged foods, the centre of which is just south of the main road. You are unlikely to truly need anything that is on sale here, but in a desperate situation the **Digital Photo Shop** might come in handy for burning memory cards to CD. There is also a short run of **shops** selling sweets and soft drinks as you leave the village on the road towards Hunder.

Other practicalities The **Sub District Hospital** is located in Diskit, on the lower road. It is somewhere between a GP's surgery and a polyclinic, but does have its own ambulance, X-ray machine and the capacity to handle (at least at a very basic level) emergencies. If you need medical care but it is not an emergency, you can attend the daily outpatient clinic ($\oplus$ *10.00–16.00*). Several of the doctors speak English.

What to see The **Diskit Gompa** clings to the rugged cliffside, and somehow has done so for centuries. Built originally as a royal palace in the 15th century, the buildings were heavily guarded with huge watchtowers and two heavy wooden gateways, one of which survives. Close to the location of the lower gate (now removed) is a chessboard etched into the stone: this is how the guards would entertain themselves in their downtime.

The palace's defences were clearly effective: only once were they penetrated by a Mongol chieftain, and even then his victory was short-lived. The unlucky chap was caught in the palace temple and decapitated. His head and one hand were then offered up to the temple guardian: this grisly gift was clearly accepted, as the fortifications have not subsequently been breached. The body parts remain in the temple to this day.

The monastery was founded by Lama Sharap Zangpo, a disciple of Tsongkhapa, and its 120 or so monks follow the Gelugpa school of Tibetan buddhism. Like Thiksey Monastery (see page 128), Diskit is also under the direction of successive reincarnations of Skyabsje Khanpo Rinpoche.

Diskit's **New Gompa** is slightly below the main monastery, away from the cliff face and closer to the river. The gompa itself is of little architectural or historical interest but there are two things you cannot avoid (in one case literally) seeing here. The **photang of the 14th Dalai Lama** houses an exhibition of antique *thangka* paintings, and a vast **Maitreya Buddha** (also known as the Gyalwa Chamba) tops the site. Some 30m tall and painted in gold and garish colours, the statue dominates the surrounding landscape and is clearly visible from both directions along the valley. It is a relatively recent addition to the landscape having been inaugurated by the Dalai Lama only in 2010. Standing at the Buddha's feet you feel both dwarfed and humbled, but at the same time thrilled by the panoramic views.

If you have the time and inclination, you can also step inside the first-floor **temple** built into the Buddha's plinth. Though far less ornate than many of Ladakh's other temples, it nonetheless houses three interesting statues: of the Buddha himself; of the Tantric Buddhist master Guru Padmasambhava (AD 717–762); and of Tsongapa (1357–1419), founder of the Gelupa, or Yellow Hat, sect of Tibetan Buddhism (see page 135). There are also a number of smaller, gilded statues and sacred manuscripts wrapped in colourful fabric and protected behind glass cabinets.

You can visit both gompas on a single ticket (costing Rs30) that has to be purchased from the elderly monk in the shed at the fork where the road to the two sites divides. Don't worry about missing him: he'll have watched you all the way up the hill and be ready to spring out as soon as you draw near. The money is used for the restoration and maintenance of the monastery buildings and so falls somewhere between an entry fee and a donation.

Around Diskit Leaving Diskit on the road towards Hunder brings you to Nubra's **sand dunes**. It's possible to go **camel riding** here on Bactrian camels, the legacy of Ladakh's historic Silk Road ties. Renting your own camel (moderately trained) costs Rs350 for half an hour and, although you're half a world away, you can still fulfil every Lawrence of Arabia fantasy you might ever have indulged in.

HUNDER *Telephone code: 01980* Hunder is a strange place: you get the sense that it wouldn't exist if it weren't for the military and the tourists. The army camp and the tented camps lie side by side (though thankfully each unaware of the other) and there's nothing to see in the village itself, though the nearby sand dunes and Chamba Buddha are intriguing.

History Though today's settlement at Hunder is relatively new, there has been continual habitation in the local area since at least the 7th century AD. It is likely that rock carvings such as the Chamba Buddha (see page 114) were created beside the river as markers to guide traders and pilgrims as they travelled through the valley: think of it as a kind of early signpost.

Getting there and away
By road Hunder is set back to the right of the main road as you travel northwest from Diskit but it is clearly signposted so you won't miss it. When you reach the army base, turn left and this brings you into the centre of the village.

If you are hiring a taxi to reach Hunder, the LTOCL's rate card applies: the cheapest option is to arrange a return trip from Leh to Diskit and Hunder; prices start at Rs6,721 per vehicle. You'll have no trouble finding people to car-share with in Leh.

Far cheaper is the thrice-weekly minibus from Leh to Diskit (see page 110), which takes seven hours and costs Rs151. Some of these buses do continue on to Hunder but if not you can take the more regular local bus (Rs10) between the two villages, or hire a jeep from Diskit bus stand (Rs250).

On foot It is also possible to walk the fairly flat 7km route from Diskit to Hunder in a little over an hour but, providing you have the time, stamina and inclination, it is possible to reach Hunder on foot by trekking from Phyang: this completely removes the need to come across Khardung La. This wonderful four- to six-day (depending on route) trek is of moderate difficulty. Starting at Phyang village, you climb first to Phyang Phu and then on to Lasermo La, which at 5,205m is the physical high point of the hike and offers superb views down along the Shyok Valley. The trek continues through fragrant meadows where nomads graze their flocks to the Hunder Dok villages before descending through the Hunder Gorge to Hunder itself.

Tashi and Cristina of Hidden North (*www.hiddennorth.com*) live in Phyang itself and so are well placed to arrange the trek for you and to guide you through these passes. Their immaculate guesthouse (see page 146) also makes the perfect start or end point for your trek.

Where to stay and eat Hunder features on the tourist trail solely because of its accommodation options: there really is little else here. The upside of this is that you have numerous options to choose from, some of which are quite luxurious, and when things are quiet you can haggle for a substantial discount.

Organic Retreat Nubra (20 tents) ✆200 118; **m** 946 917 6076; **e** organicretreat@hotmail. com; www.nubraorganicretreat.com. Hunder's luxury accommodation option is this deluxe tented camp set among apple & apricot orchards. There's an organic vegetable garden to supply the kitchen, hammocks by the stream, bonfires each evening &, if you're feeling more energetic, a badminton court. STD phone calls can be made here. **$$$$$**

🏠 **Chunka's Camp & Resort** (13 tents, 5 rooms) m 990 699 9996. Solar-powered tented camp & guesthouse. All tents have attached toilets & hot & cold running water. Meals are homemade & organic. Bonfire & evening entertainment available on request. **$$$$**

🏠 **Karma Inn** (21 rooms) ☎ 221 042; m 941 961 2342; e karmaleh@yahoo.co.in; www. hotelkarmainn.com. Manicured lawns surround this large, well-run hotel. Rooms are large & those on the top floor have superb views. Most have balconies. There's 24hr hot water. Extra beds in the family rooms cost Rs1,165; rates can be discounted by up to 20% so make sure you ask. **$$$$**

🏠 **Nubra Ethnic Camp** (23 tents) ☎ 200 096; m 941 951 8128; e nubraethniccamp@gmail. com; www.campsofladakh.com. Comfortable tents

with en-suite bathrooms, electricity & easy chairs on the deck. The camp's in a shady garden setting & staff are attentive. Meals available. **$$$$**

🏠 **Himalayan Guesthouse** (7 rooms) ☎ 221 131; m 946 917 7470. Whitewashed bungalow set in a delightful garden where only the crowing cockerel might disturb you. Meals are made with homegrown vegetables & herbs. Rooms are clean & there is hot water in the bathrooms. **$–$$**

🏠 **Mehreen Guesthouse** (2 rooms) m 946 917 2690. Tucked behind a small stupa & prayer wheel in the centre of the village, Kheykhey Malo & her family welcome paying guests & campers to their home, an old house built over 3 floors. The garden is lovingly tended with heavily laden apricot trees, & pot plants on the stairs. Meals available on request. **$**

✗ **Café 125** By the main gate of the army base. Serves tea, soft drinks & biscuits. If you're caught short, there's a public toilet next door, though only the brave should enter. **$**

Around Hunder
Returning to the main road and continuing 4km towards Turtuk brings you to the **Chamba Gompa**, which is on the right-hand side of the road just before the bridge. The gompa is, at least by Ladakhi standards, unremarkable from the outside but it is thought to date from the 15th century and there is a large, if rather severe-looking, golden Buddha inside, as well as some attractive frescoes. As rather fewer tourists venture here than, say, at Alchi (see page 151), you'll have plenty of time to look at the wall paintings without being chivvied on by the crowds.

On the opposite side of the road, a short scramble down from the track leading away up into the hills, is the Chamba Buddha. Look for the small shrine on the patch of grass: the Buddha is immediately to its left. Only the head and torso of the statue remain, and even they are rather weathered, but you can still make out its erstwhile size and glory, and the skilled craftsmanship that went into its creation. Dating of the Buddha is sketchy, but it is thought to have been made sometime between the 7th and 10th centuries and to have originally stood in excess of 2m tall.

TURTUK
Telephone code: 01980 At the north western end of the valley, Turtuk is the furthest point in Nubra that foreigners are allowed to visit, even with an Inner Line permit. The severing of historic overland trading routes by the LoC has turned it into a quiet backwater, a place to sit back and relax beneath hundreds of apricot trees in terraced gardens. The apricots are ripe in August, adding colour to the scene and also giving you the opportunity to gorge yourself with handfuls of fruit. Turtuk is only a small place but it is divided into three distinct areas: Turtuk Farul is inhabited by Nurbakshi Muslims; it is segregated from Turtuk Yul, home of the Sunni Muslims, by a small tributary to the Shyok; and there is a third area, Turtuk Chuthang, on the banks of the Shyok River.

History
It is likely that Turtuk was once a trading post for merchants travelling across the Karakoram range, though little of that period of its history is visible today.

It is its more modern history that shapes what you see: until 1971 Turkuk was part of Pakistan. Unlike other parts of Nubra that are predominantly Buddhist, almost all of Turtuk's population is Muslim, with 70% of them following the Nurbakhshi school of Sufi Islam. Due to its proximity to the LoC, foreigners were prevented from travelling to Turtuk until as late as 2010.

Getting there and around Turkuk is at the end of the line: it is close to the LoC and so foreigners can get there only by travelling along the road running parallel to the river from Hunder. As yet, it is not possible to cross the LoC from Pakistan to Turtuk.

A weekly bus (Saturday) comes the 212km from Leh and costs Rs242 but it may be more convenient to take the minibus from Leh to Diskit (see page 110) and then change for the local minibus from Diskit to Turkuk, which departs at 14.30 every day except Sunday and returns the following morning at 06.00. The journey takes 3 hours 30 minutes and costs Rs100 each way.

The majority of people come by car, however: the LTOCL's fares start from Rs9,939 for a trip from Leh to Diskit and Turtuk and back. It is also possible to get a taxi from Diskit, for which you should expect to pay around Rs3,500 one-way, and a third more to go and come back.

Local travel agents There is no formal travel agency in Turtuk but Ataullah at Turtuk Holiday Camp (see below) is able to make transport and accommodation bookings and also to arrange cultural tours and trekking guides.

Where to stay

Turtuk Holiday Camp (8 tents) Turtuk Chuthang; m 990 699 3123; e turtukholiday@gmail.com; ⊕ Jul–Sep. Situated in a quiet spot with basic but clean facilities. The hospitable staff will set up your dinner in a gazebo by the river & can also arrange for you to enjoy a traditional Balti meal with a family in the village. **$$$**

Maha Guesthouse (11 rooms) Turtuk Farul; ☎ 248 040; m 962 298 2145; e sales@turtuk-ecoresort.com; www.turtuk-ecoresort.com.

Clean & comfortable guesthouse set in an organic garden. Shared bathrooms have hot & cold running water. Multi-cuisine restaurant uses ingredients from the garden. Also pitches tents (**$$$**) in the summer months. **$$–$$$**

Rangyul Guesthouse (6 rooms) Turtuk Farul; ☎ 280 016. Family-friendly guesthouse with delightful hosts. Meals are served in the dining room or out in the garden. More rooms under construction. **$**

Where to eat

Turtuk is a Balti village, so grasp the opportunity to eat traditional Balti food with both hands. The walnut and buckwheat breads served with herby yoghurt, mulberries and sun-dried tomato chutney are especially delicious. The guesthouses and tented camp serve both Balti and Indian dishes; check whether or not meals are included in your rate. The only café in town is the Selmo Restaurant (**$**), which sounds rather grander than it is. It serves instant noodles and a few other basic snacks.

If you come during Ramadan, note that the local people will be fasting from dawn until dusk, so meals may not be served during daylight hours.

Shopping Small stalls in the market sell attractive stone figurines while the local blacksmiths produce finely worked brass bangles inlaid with red and green enamel. This kind of jewellery is unique to Baltistan and therefore makes a memorable souvenir or gift.

4

What to see Turtuk has a number of sites that, though not marketed at tourists, are nonetheless of interest. There are no formal opening times or entry tickets: just turn up and ask politely to see inside. If you're fortunate, someone will give you a guided tour, in which case it is appropriate to give them a tip and, in the case of the mosques or gompa, leave a small donation.

Turtuk Yul Mosque has been reconstructed on the site of a 16th-century mosque. It is shared by both of Turtuk's Muslim communities and therefore is particularly busy during Friday prayers. Unusually, the mosque's interior is particularly decorative. Turtuk's second mosque, the **Tsangzer Mosque**, was built only in 2011 and is in a prominent position on the hillside: climb up here for superb views of the valley.

The 300-year-old **Khan's Palace** is an attractive wooden structure that is to this day the home of Mohammad Khan Kacho, the latest member of the Yagbo dynasty of Chhorbat Khapulu. The family can trace its lineage back more than 1,000 years and the khan is a gracious and well-informed host.

Turtuk does have a small **gompa** but it is not an old one: there are no longer any Buddhists in the village and so this one was built in 1972 to serve the needs of Buddhist soldiers in the Indian army who had been posted on the LoC. Inside is a simple fresco showing the Buddha flanked by two Padmasambhava figures.

If you happen to be in Turtuk on Navruz (Persian New Year, 21 March), check out the annual **polo match** and related celebrations that last for a period of ten days. The feats of horsemanship on show will make you want to cover your eyes while still peaking through the cracks in your fingers so that you don't miss a move.

SUMUR *Telephone code: 01980* Sumur is a pleasant, green place that takes its name from the three rivers (*sum* = three; *yur* = rivers) that converge near here. It's the home of the impressive Samtanling Gompa (see opposite) and also a few sand dunes, which though less dramatic than those between Diskit and Hunder still offer the chance for camel riding. The town itself is unremarkable, but it is a convenient and pleasant spot to break your onward journey.

Getting there and around There is a minibus from Leh to Sumur two days a week (Thursday and Saturday) that departs from Leh's main bus stand at 06.00. The journey takes six to seven hours and tickets cost Rs101. It is also possible to take the minibus from Leh to Diskit (see page 110) and then take the local minibus (daily 08.00 and 15.00) from Diskit back along the road you've just come in on to the crossroads and then turn north to Sumur. It takes just under two hours and costs Rs30.

Taking a car and driver from Leh you can combine Diskit and Hunder with Sumur and Panamik over two days from Rs8,005.

Where to stay

Mystique Meadows (23 tents, 4 rooms) m 941 917 8254; e mystiquemeadows.ladakh@ gmail.com; www.mystiquemeadowscamp. com. Choose between conventional tents & Mongolian yurts in this well-run camp located close to the monastery. All of the tents have attached toilets & are pretty spacious. A backup generator ensures electricity supply after dark. Multi-cuisine meals & cultural show available on request. $$$$

Valley Flower Camp (17 rooms) m 941 917 8844; e valleyflowercamp@gmail. com; www.lehladakh.valleyflowercamp.com. Deluxe tent camp in a quiet setting. Well-maintained tents with king-size beds, clean linens & backup generator for power. Dining tent seats 50 people. $$$$

AO Guesthouse (6 rooms) Next to J&K Bank; m 946 973 1976. In a shady garden in the centre of the village lie several buildings given over to paying-guest accommodation. It's a quiet spot, back from the main road, and you're welcome to camp if you have your own tent. Ground-floor rooms are cheaper than those upstairs. **$–$$**

⌂ **Sand Dune Leisure Park** (up to 20 tents) Off main road; m 941 985 0985. On the outskirts of the village & clearly signposted, this simple tented camp has an enviable riverside location that goes some way to making up for the lack of facilities: portaloos are as fancy as it gets & the tents are reminiscent of those used by 1950s Boy Scouts. There's a basic on-site restaurant serving Indian & Chinese cuisine, a herd of Bactrian camels to ride, a bonfire in the evenings, & you can pitch your own tent for just Rs100. The friendly Goan manager speaks reasonable English. **$**

✗ **Where to eat** There are two simple restaurants in the centre of Sumur: **Gyal Restaurant** and **Larjey Restaurant**. They're both cheap and not terribly cheery and could do with a good clean. You'll find them by the junction with the bank.

Other practicalities There is a branch of **J&K Bank** (🕐 10.00–14.00 & 14.30–16.00 Mon–Fri, 10.00–13.30 Sat) in the centre of Sumur. It's on the junction by the colourful prayer wheel.

What to see Clinging to the cliff face between Sumur and the neighbouring village of Tigga is the **Samtanling Gompa** (🕐 08.00–12.00 & 13.00–18.00) and immediately around it a smattering of even more gravity-defying shrines.

Founded in 1846 by Lama Tsultim Nyima, his incarnations continue to direct this Gelugpa monastery today. Some 60 monks, plus neophytes, live a life of strict asceticism: unlike monks in other monasteries they do not dance, make offerings or have any personal possessions, including books or clothes.

The gompa is set into the hillside and best approached on foot alongside the Mani wall. There are three principal dukhangs or temples: in the **Men Dukhang** you'll find elaborate murals showing the 35 Buddhas; in the **Mandala Dukhang**, which, ironically, does not contain a single mandala, are two vast statues of the Buddha, wall paintings and numerous smaller statues; and in the **Old Dukhang** are yet more murals, again showing the 35 Buddhas as well as scenes from the life of the Buddha, his disciples and the various protective guardians. If you continue up the hill behind the gompa you come to a large **bas-relief** depicting two boddhisatvas and stupas.

PANAMIK *Telephone code: 01980* Famed for the curative properties of its hot springs, Panamik has the potential to become a miniature resort, though as yet it is someway from realising that dream. In the meantime it is the access point for the holy lake of Yarab Tso and also the Ensa Gompa.

Getting there and around Most visitors to Panamik hire a car and driver from Leh and thus pay for a package from LTOCL (see pages 83–4). If you are reliant on public transport, it is easiest to take the minibus from Leh to Diskit (see page 110) or Sumur (see opposite). The same local minibuses that go from Diskit to Sumur continue north to Panamik and the journey takes three hours. On the return journey to Diskit, the minibus leaves Panaik at 15.00.

Alternatively, take the Saturday bus to Charasa or the Tuesday bus to Khimee, both of which depart from Leh at 06.00 and stop in Panamik *en route*. Tickets cost Rs166 and Rs169 respectively.

Panamik itself is a small enough village to explore on foot. If you plan to go to Yarab Tso you have to trek as there is no road access, and the same applies to the last part of the journey to Ensa Gompa, as there is only a footpath from the road up to the gompa itself.

🏠 Where to stay and eat

Accommodation options in Panamik are inexpensive but very basic. If you have time, you may want to look at several options, as cleanliness and service seem variable.

🏠 **Nobula Guesthouse** (4 rooms) 📞 247 013. Between the hot spring & the centre of the village, this family-run guesthouse is set in a colourful garden with patio tables & mountain views. Meals are available on request. Rooms with a shared bathroom are cheapest at just Rs500. **$$**

🏠 **Hot Spring Guesthouse** (4 rooms) 📞 247 043. Attractive bungalow in a pretty garden. Rooms with a shared toilet are Rs300. **$**

Panamik has a third accommodation option, the **Banka Guesthouse & Campsite** (📞 247 044) in a secluded spot at the bottom of the valley. It was, however, locked up when we visited, and we have been unable to establish when it's likely to reopen.

Other practicailities

There is a **primary healthcare centre** on the right-hand side of the road as you enter Panamik from Sumur. Staff do not speak English and facilities are basic, but in an emergency and when you have no independent transport, it would be the best place to wait while doctors are called out from the hospital in Diskit (see page 112).

What to see

Panamik is famed for its **hot spring** (🕐 *dawn–dusk; entrance fee Rs20*), a naturally occurring sulphur bath that is said to have medicinal properties, particularly for the treatment of rheumatism, but is sadly rather underwhelming to look at. Panamik's Women's Alliance has taken over management of the site and has overseen the construction of a modern, segregated bathhouse. Other buildings, including a small café, should be completed during the lifespan of this edition.

In the centre of the village are an exquisitely painted **wooden gateway** and **prayer wheel**, both in vivid colours. Continuing past them along the main road brings you to the **Memorial of BSF Mountaineers** on the edge of the village. It's a well cared for site inscribed with the names of those who have died while climbing locally.

Around Panamik

There are two significant sites around Panamik, neither of which can be reached by road: even if you start your journey by 4x4, you'll have to finish it on foot.

Yarab Tso is a sacred lake 90 minutes' walk from Panamik village. No river flows into the lake, so the source of the water is unclear. Perhaps early people thought it to be a miracle. Yarab Tso's holiness also comes from the belief that a person born in auspicious circumstances will be able to look into its waters and see clearly the gompa at Lhasa. We did have a look, but sadly our stars are not properly aligned.

On the opposite side of the river from Panamik is the **Ensa Gompa** where an elderly monk lives out his days, most of them in silent solitude. If you have a vehicle, pass through Panamik and continue along the main road for 3km until you reach the police checkpoint. Turn left on to the Kobed Bridge Approach Road and then cross over the river. Once on the far bank, turn left. Beware that the road condition here deteriorates significantly.

From here you must continue on foot. Follow the track between the cliff and the riverbank until you reach a large field surrounded by a wall. Cut across the field and then take the steep trail up the track on the left. The narrow valley takes you straight up to the gompa. In total the walk should take not more than three hours from Panamik and substantially less, of course, if you drive the first part of the way.

Only five monks still live at Ensa, though the monastic community was once far

Panchen Lhachun was a Buddhist monk born in the Nubra Valley. Returning home from his studies in Lhasa, he began to teach but this brought him into conflict with a Muslim cleric. The cleric attacked Panchen Lhachun, cut him in two with a sword and threw the pieces in the river. Half of the body floated ashore here and was encased in the stupa; the rest was found and placed in the gompa at Tinger.

In the 1960s, the state of the stupa at Charasa had deteriorated considerably and it was decided to reinter the body in a new structure. Much to the surprise of the monks and other spectators, the body (specifically the torso and one arm) was perfectly preserved. A photo of the mutilated corpse was taken by a local man and is kept for posterity in the monastery.

larger. The buildings are partially renovated and include a **lhakhang** with two statues of the Buddha, one wearing a crown; a slightly depressing **dukhang** with murals and statuary; and a **second dukhang** that is on the verge of collapse and has some badly decayed murals featuring the White Tara, Red Amithaba, the Buddha and his disciples.

CHARASA   *Telephone code: 01980*   Once the capital of the ancient kings of Nubra, Charasa is scarcely visited by tourists as it has no bridge and thus takes a long time to reach, but with its palace ruins and two monasteries, this is an unfortunate oversight.

Getting there and away   The daily minibus that leaves Diskit at 15.00 for Sumur and Panamik ends its journey in Charasa around 20.00. Walking from Panamik to Charasa is possible with an optional detour to Ensa, but as it takes around eight hours, you'll need to allow a full day. In winter it is possible (and far faster) to cross on foot directly from Sumur to Charasa across the frozen river in just half an hour. The minibus has to go past Panamik to the bridge and then double back on the other side of the river, necessitating a drive of around five hours.

Where to stay and eat   There is not currently an official place to stay. You may be able to arrange bed and board with a local family, but you'll have to turn up and ask.

What to see   The first of Charasa's gompas is the **Serdun Gompa**: its monks belong to the Gelugpa school and it's related to the monastery at Diskit. The main temple is dedicated to Panchen Lhachun, a Buddhist scholar from the 15th century, and the remains of his body are said to be encased in the golden stupa alongside his statue.

Charasa's second gompa, **Singkhar Gompa**, houses just one monk and some small statues. It is attached to the gompa at Hemis. Alongside it are the ruins of the Winter Palace, which belonged to the ancient kings of Nubra. The remains you see here date from the 17th century but were built upon the foundations of much older buildings, supposedly by the Ladakhi King Nyima Namgyal who stayed occasionally here to pay his respects at Panchen Lhachun's stupa.

4

FOLLOW BRADT

For the latest news, special offers and competitions, subscribe to the Bradt newsletter via the website www.bradtguides.com and follow Bradt on:

- www.facebook.com/BradtTravelGuides
- @BradtGuides
- @bradtguides
- www.pinterest.com/bradtguides

top left Slaty-headed parakeet (*Psittacula himalayana*) (DH/FLPA) page 7

top right Black-necked crane (*Grus nigricollis*) (KW/FLPA) page 7

above left Long-tailed minivet (*Pericrocotus ethologus*) (JH/FLPA) page 7

above right Eurasian golden oriole (*Oriolus oriolus*) (DH/FLPA) page 7

left Jungle cat (*Felis chaus*) (TA/FLPA) page 7

below The Bactrian camels seen in the Nubra Valley are the descendants of the pack animals that once travelled the length of the Silk Road (f9/SH) page 110

above left The 12-terraced Nishat Bagh in Srinagar is one of the famous Mughal Gardens, built in accordance with traditional Persian landscape design inspired by the Islamic view of heaven (J&KT) pages 204–5

above right Originally a trading post on the Silk Road, today Leh is the capital of Ladakh, home to a bustling bazaar and remarkable historical sites such as Tsemo Fort and Leh Palace (I/FLPA) pages 79–103

left Jammu's Mubarak Mandi complex was once the royal seat of the region's rulers, and its architecture is a riot of European Baroque, Mughal and Mewari styles (J&KT) page 236–7

below Shey Palace sits atop a rocky outcrop surrounded by artificially irrigated fields and holy fish ponds (J&KT) pages 126–8

top   Padum is the main base for treks in the remote
           Zanskar Valley (ND/SH) pages 169–74

above right Kashmir is famous for its hand-knotted wool or silk
               carpets, here sold in a Srinigar back-street (AJ/SH)
               page 72

below right The latest member of Ladakh's royal family still
               spends the summer at Stok Palace, while one wing
               has been converted into a museum showcasing
               royal artefacts and paintings (J&KT) pages 123–6

above left The 7m Chamba Buddha in Kartse Khar is thought to have been carved by visiting Buddhist missionaries in the 7th or 8th century (J&KT) page 164

above right Sacred Buddhist texts are protected in the temple at Karsha Gompa (MEP) page 175

left The Sun Temple near Mattan was built in the 8th century AD and contains a number of well-preserved carvings (MEP) page 218

below Inaugurated by the Dalai Lama in 2010, the enormous Maitreya Buddha surveys the landscape around Diskit (MEP) page 112

above   Precariously positioned at the mouth of a cave deep within a river gorge, the remote Phuktal Gompa is accessible only on foot (I/OK/FLPA) pages 178–9

above right   Jammu's Shri Raghunathji Temple is the largest complex of its kind in northern India (AJ/SH) pages 237

below right   The Jamia Masjid in Srinagar has 370 pillars built from wood from around the city, while the pagoda-like design reflects the regional influence of Tibetan Buddhism (PL/SH) page 206

below   Monastery festivals provide the best chance to witness Ladakhi cultural traditions: here Buddhist monks carry ceremonial instruments at Lamayuru Gompa (Z/SH) page 64

above   J&K's most popular sport is undoubtedly polo, and games draw vast crowds of spectators (J&KT) page 25

below   Artistic traditions from carpet making to woodcarving are still practised in the backstreet workshops of Srinagar, while the city's floating vegetable market is a photographer's dream (MEP and PL/SH) pages 200–1 and 203

top Choglamsar is populated by Tibetan refugees, and the Dalai Lama visits the village on occasion, drawing in thousands of faithful from all over the region (MEP) pages 104–6

above Traditional Ladakhi dress features jewellery and headdresses inlaid with turquoise, coral and lapis lazuli (JK&T) page 24

below The Ladakh Festival is a major celebration of regional culture and a good opportunity to see traditional costumes, archery competitions and masked dances (AJP/SH and JK&T) page 26

above Views don't come much more dramatic than at Basgo, where the ruins of the palace cling perilously to the cliffs at a point where the Indus Valley narrows (MEP) pages 148–9

5

Southern Ladakh

Some of J&K's wildest, most remote and most beautiful scenery is to be found in the south of Ladakh. Here the human population is scant, especially as you move away from the monasteries, but the mountains and lakes roar across the landscape, ripping up the land into jagged peaks through which mighty rivers flow.

It is here that you will find some of Ladakh's most famous monasteries: the striking Thiksey Gompa with its vast Maitreya Buddha; perennially popular (if overly commercialised) Hemis; and dark Thagthog, the only Nyingmapa monastery in Ladakh. They lie almost side by side with holy fish ponds, carved stone Buddhas and two royal palaces, offering a rich cultural experience for visitors.

It is the natural sights that draw us back, however: the southern lakes of Pangong Tso, Tso Moriri and Tso Kar may be far from habitation and along pretty awful roads, but their turquoise waters and unspoiled surroundings more than justify the bumpy journeys out to reach them. Likewise, some of the most popular treks are to be found in the Markha Valley, which is more easily accessible from Leh.

Destinations in this chapter are explored in the following order: sites south of Leh on or close to the Leh–Keylong Rd (NH1); Chemre and Thagthog; the Markha Valley; and lastly the three southern lakes of Pangong Tso, Tso Kar and Tso Moriri. Most journeys within southern Ladakh will start in Leh, and you will have to pass through the towns along NH1 to reach either Markha or the lakes.

STOK   *Telephone code: 01982*

Just 15km to the south of Leh is the beautiful village of Stok, a settlement on the banks of the River Indus that is watched over not only by Stok Kangri but also the imposing Stok Palace. It's easy to see the sites in a day, and to get here and back from Leh, but the village also serves as the starting point for ascents on the peak.

HISTORY   In the early part of its history, Stok was simply the site of a monastery: there has been a gompa here since at least the 14th century, and houses and smallholdings grew up around it to provide goods and services for the monks. Stok came to prominence in 1834, however, when General Zorawar Singh annexed Ladakh. King Tsepal Tondup Namgyal was forced to abandon his palace in Leh and having done so he relocated the royal family to Stok: his descendants still live in a wing of Stok Palace today.

GETTING THERE AND AWAY   The road from Leh to Stok is in good condition and covered with tarmac along the route. It narrows to the width of a single vehicle once you reach the outskirts of the village, but there are plenty of places to pass.

Minibuses shuttle back and forth from Leh to Stok twice a day, departing from Leh's main bus stand at 09.00 and 17.00 and returning at 10.00 and 18.00. The journey takes around 30 minutes and costs Rs20.

121

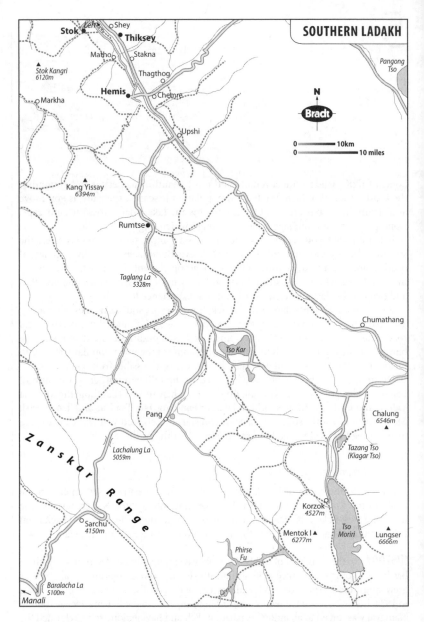

Stok
Leh
Shey
Thiksey
Matho
Stakna
Stok Kangri
6120m
Thagthog
Hemis
Chemre
Markha
Upshi

N
Bradt

0 ———— 10km
0 ———————— 10 miles

Kang Yissay
6394m

Rumtse

Taglang La
5328m

Chumathang

Tso Kar

Chalung
6546m

Pang

Tazang Tso
(Kiagar Tso)

Lachalung La
5059m

Z a n s k a r   R a n g e

Sarchu
4150m

Korzok
4527m

Tso
Moriri

Lungser
6666m

Mentok I
6277m

Phirse
Fu

Baralacha La
5100m
Manali

If you prefer to take a **taxi**, a drop-off at Stok Palace from Leh starts from Rs485 and a return journey from Rs625. If you choose to combine Stok with other destinations, you can visit Stok and Stakna from Rs1,387; Stok, Stakna and Matho from Rs1,589; and Stok, Hemis, Thiksey, Shey, Matho and Stakna in a very long day (but better split over two) from Rs2,540.

🏠 **WHERE TO STAY** Given the proximity of Stok to Leh, most people choose to come here on a day trip rather than stay the night. There are, however, some quite pleasant accommodation options should you choose to buck the trend or be planning an early morning departure on the Stok Kangri trek. It is also theoretically possible to stay at the small **Thagspa Guesthouse** but unfortunately there was no-one there when we visited: you'd have to turn up and see.

🏠 **Hotel Skittsal** (24 rooms) \ 242 049; e hotel@skittsal.com; www.skittsal.com. Built in a traditional architectural style, Hotel Skittsal is the smartest place to stay in Stok. Rooms are large, though not terribly light, & the staff are friendly. They're happy to keep your luggage for you while you're trekking, which comes in handy. **$$$$**

🏠 **Hotel Highland** (15 rooms) \ 242 005; e tangdul@yahoo.co.in. A stone's throw from the palace, Hotel Highland is run by Tsering Angdu & his family. Rooms are clean & well maintained with attached bathrooms. Most of the clients are trekkers & the owners are involved in sending doctors & dentists on treks to provide healthcare in remote villages. **$$$**

✖ **WHERE TO EAT** There is a simple **cafeteria** by the main entrance to Stok Palace, which served tea, soft drinks and snacks. It seems clean enough and the views from the tables on the terrace are impressive but we had horrific food poisoning after eating the fried egg and instant noodles, so our advice would be to give the food a miss.

Beneath the palace in the central part of the village is the **Ladakhi Kitchen** (m *990 698 8325*). It's clearly marked on a signboard on the main road: follow the alleyway by the sign. Opening times are inconsistent but during summer should roughly match those of the palace (see below). The name is a reference to its former use: today the stocky, fortress-like building houses an exhibition of *thangka* paintings.

WHAT TO SEE The principal attraction in Stok itself is **Stok Palace**. This 77-room residence was built in the 1830s to house Ladakh's royal family, the Namgyals, and the latest member of the family, Queen Deskit Angmo, still lives here in the summer months. She has converted one wing of the palace into the **Palace Museum**

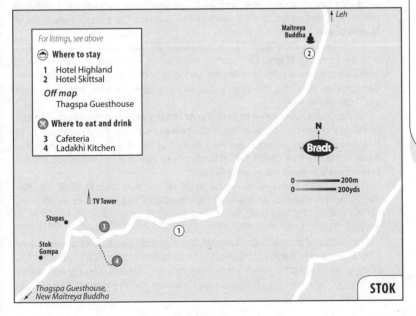

For listings, see above

🛏 **Where to stay**
1 Hotel Highland
2 Hotel Skittsal
Off map
   Thagspa Guesthouse

✖ **Where to eat and drink**
3 Cafeteria
4 Ladakhi Kitchen

Maitreya Buddha

↑ Leh

N

Bradt

0 ———— 200m
0 ———— 200yds

TV Tower

Stupas

Stok Gompa

Thagspa Guesthouse, New Maitreya Buddha

STOK

(⏰ *May–Oct 08.00–13.00 & 14.00– 19.00; entrance fee Rs50*) that is open to the public and showcases royal artefacts and items of anthropological interest.

The museum is arranged around an **internal courtyard** decorated with pots of geraniums and the rather musty heads of an ibex and a sheep. Climbing the staircase to the first floor brings you to the temple and exhibition galleries.

The **temple** is a light room where daylight streams through the windows and from a skylight in the roof. The roof is supported on wooden pillars and the woodwork is finely painted, though it needs some restoration work to remove the decades of dust and reveal the colours in their former glory. Exhibited here are gilded statues and a large number of silken banners.

Next door to this is a room of **armour and weaponry**, both of which look quite Mongol in style. In addition to the chain mail you can closely examine the quivers,

CLIMBING STOK KANGRI

Stok Kangri (6,120m) has India's highest trekkable summit, so it should come as no surprise that it's a firm favourite with tourists during the summer months and base camp can get quite crowded.

It is possible to climb Stok Kangri any time from July to November, though due to the deteriorating weather conditions, July to September is the optimum period. Even then, temperatures at base camp fall to below freezing at night, so you'll need to have suitable clothing and equipment.

The trek takes six or seven days and starts from the village of **Shang** (3,657m) where enterprising locals sell biscuits and other small snacks to the trekkers. The first day's climb leads you first along a jeep track and then along trails to the flat plateau at **Shang Phu** (4,343m). It's only a little over 11km but trekking guides typically allow six hours.

On day two you cross **Shang Phu La**, the first high-altitude pass on the trek, which is at 5,115m. The 8km of trekking take you at first through a narrow valley lined with juniper bushes, then into open grasslands with snow-capped peaks on the horizon and superb views down to Matho Gompa. You camp for the night at **Matho Doksa**.

Day three is a short day of no more than four hours walking, and it begins with an ascent of **Matho La** (4,850m) from where you have an uninterrupted view of both Stok Kangri and Matho Kangri (6,100m). You also look down on **Gangpoche** (4,435m), the grassy plateau criss-crossed with streams where you'll spend the night.

On day four you'll ascend to **Stok Kangri Base Camp** (4,968m). Visually this is probably the most spectacular day of the trek as on a clear day you can see right across to Khardung La (see page 108), as well as into the Mankarmo Gorge. For much of the day Stok Kangri itself is hidden from view, but as soon as you see the prayer flags you know you're getting close.

Depending on how well you've acclimatised, you may want to insert a **buffer day** here. This will also give you greater flexibility if there is bad weather as, having got this far, you don't want thick cloud cover spoiling your view from the top.

Not everyone attempts the **summit**, but if you do you'll need to get to bed early as the ascent begins at midnight. The air is thin and there are two stretches of snow to traverse, for which you'll need to use crampons. Though not strictly necessary, some trekkers choose to use ropes too. On the summit day you can slingshots and shield. Two garishly coloured dreamcoats that Joseph would have been proud of are displayed here too, though they would surely have drawn too much attention on the battlefield.

The **royal kitchen** is stuffed full of copper and brass cooking and serving vessels. The kettles are particularly finely worked. Take a look at item 32: it's a copper steamer for cooking *momos*. On the shelves are also small quantities of silver and porcelain.

The other rooms in the museum display a high-quality collection of *thangka* paintings, some of which are 300 years old; printing blocks for producing holy books; gruesome ceremonial items including part of a skull and a trumpet made from a human thigh bone; a collection of hats; and some beautiful murals painted on plaster and wood.

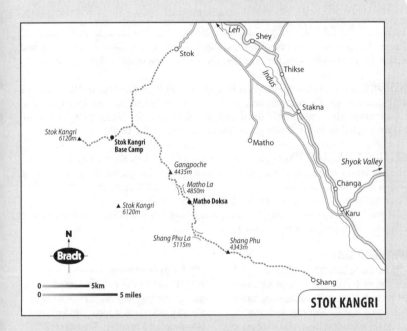

expect to spend at least 14 hours walking, and 16 hours is not uncommon, especially if you're having trouble with the altitude.

On the final day of the trek you'll descend from base camp to **Stok** (3,615m). The descent is fairly rapid, usually taking around five hours, and it's best started early in the day as it includes crossing back and forth across the river on a number of occasions. The volume of water increases as the day progresses. Highlights include passing through the gorge at Mankarmo, which you'll have seen in the distance earlier on in the trek, and returning from the barren mountainsides into the lush green fields that are irrigated on the valley floor.

Note that the timings given here are those suggested by local trekking guides who are used to guiding domestic tourists with little mountain experience. If you are moderately fit and have trekked in similar conditions before, you can expect to complete the trek in five days or less.

Although you can take photos of the outside of the building, photography inside is prohibited.

Situated above the palace is **Stok Gompa**, a 14th century Gelugpa monastery founded by Lama Lhawang Lotus. In addition to several temples (one of which is claimed to be the oldest in Ladakh) and stupas is the **library**, which contains 108 volumes of the Buddha's teachings, as well as other sacred manuscripts. The monastery has some ancient wall paintings that include depictions of the Sakyamuni Buddha, White Tara and a 1,000-handed and 11-headed Avalokitesvara to whom the monastery is dedicated. The monastery becomes particularly busy during the **Stok Guru Tsechu Festival** (see page 64 for dates).

Last but not least, a large new **Maitreya Buddha** was under construction not far past the gompa. You can get there on foot or by road, and it should be completed sometime in 2014.

SHEY   *Telephone code: 01982*

Famed for its palace and holy fish pond, Shey is only a short distance from Leh and makes for an interesting excursion either on its own or *en route* to Thiksey and Hemis.

HISTORY   Shey was the first capital of Ladakh and its earliest ruins date from the 10th century AD. The fort was built by Ladakh's first king, Lhachen Spalgigon, and its successor, Shey Palace, remained a royal residence of the Namgyal dynasty until they relocated to Stok following the Dogra invasion in the 1830s.

GETTING THERE AND AWAY   Regular **minibuses** leave Leh throughout the day for Shey, at least every hour during daytime in summer, though less frequently in the winter months. It's a drive of just 15km (9 miles) and takes no more than half an hour, as the road surface is very good. Tickets cost Rs20.

If you prefer to hire a **taxi** from Leh, a one-way ride starts from Rs355 and you can go to Shey and back from Rs461.

WHERE TO STAY

Besthang Guesthouse (3 rooms) 267 556. This wonderful, homestay-style guesthouse is set in a traditional Ladakhi house among gardens facing the gompa. The bedrooms are large & groups can make use of the comfortable dormitory. One room has an attached bathroom & kitchen. **$**

Dokpa Guesthouse (7 rooms) m 979 748 5435. Yangdol, Phuntsog, their family & pet dog welcome long- and short-stay visitors to their friendly guesthouse set in a potage garden shaded beneath apricot & apple trees. B/fast, dinner & occasionally lunch included for guests only. **$**

WHERE TO EAT   On the opposite side of the road to the palace is **Shilkar**, a very basic café serving tea, soft drinks and snacks. It seems to have very irregular opening times, so don't count on being able to get anything to eat here.

WHAT TO SEE

Shey Palace   Once the royal residence of the Namgyal dynasty, Shey Palace inhabits an imposing position almost overhanging NH1. There is no designated parking so taxis stop by the roadside, from where it's a steep climb past a line of small prayer wheels to the palace's main entrance. While catching your breath at the top, be sure to turn around and look back at the idyllic surroundings provided by the artificially irrigated fields and the **holy fish ponds**. At certain times of day the palace is reflected in the water.

The façade of the palace rises dramatically above the visitor and is punctuated by numerous wooden balconies, prominent features in traditional Ladakhi architecture. Built during the reign of Deldan Namgyal (1620–40), the palace is atop the ruins of a far older fortified structure, parts of which are still visible. Climbing to the top of the site not only enables you to see these ruins close up but also to survey the **108 stupas** below. Among the stupas you'll also find the **Sakyamuni Temple** with its historic statuary.

The highlight for many visitors to Shey is the **Sakyamuni Buddha** inside the **Dresthang Gompa** at the top of the hill. Made from a mixture of copper and brass covered with gold plate, this 7.5m-tall statue is studded with precious and semi-precious stones. It is the largest metal statue in Ladakh and includes more than 5kg of gold. It was made in 1633 by a Nepalese sculptor and legend has it that the artist who painted the eyes did so with his back turned to the idol so that he did not show disrespect by staring into the eyes (and therefore the soul) of the Buddha.

Right on the road, almost beneath the palace, is a vast rock with an **early Buddha carving**. The images have been weathered by time and the elements, but if you look at them in the late afternoon, the shadows make the carving appear more prominent. Due to the angle of the rock face, you'll see the carvings best if you are passing through Shey to Leh: coming the other direction it's easy to drive straight past.

On the far side of Shey as you leave towards Thiksey you can't fail to spot the **Naropa Photang** on the left-hand side of the road. This vast field of white stupas surrounds the **nunnery** of the same name. The nuns welcome visitors and it makes a fascinating contrast to the monasteries you'll visit elsewhere in Ladakh.

THE SAKYAMUNI BUDDHA

The Sakyamuni, or Shakyamuni, Buddha is the historical Buddha, an Indian prince named Siddhartha Gautama who was born sometime in the early 5th century BC. The oldest surviving biographical manuscripts are not from until at least 400 hundreds years after his birth, but tradition has it that he was born into the Ksatriya family. His father was an elected chieftain from the Shakya clan, and his mother was a princess. The night he was conceived, Siddhartha's mother dreamed of a white elephant with six tusks, a sign that the child within her would be something very special indeed.

Siddhartha's mother died during or immediately after childbirth and so he was raised by his aunt. During his childhood and young adulthood he was sheltered from all suffering and given everything he could possibly want, including a wife and son, but at the age of 29 he left his palace to find out what went on in the world beyond its walls. For the first time he encountered the elderly, the sick and the dead. The experience shocked him and he gave up everything to become a mendicant.

Siddhartha took up yoga, fasted and tried to find enlightenment. These traditional paths gave him nothing: he had to find a new way. He developed instead the Middle Way, the so-called Noble Eightfold Path, which espouses the importance of having the right view, intention, speech, livelihood, action, effort, mindfulness and concentration. Siddhartha sat beneath a pipal tree and meditated for 49 days until, at the age of 35, he finally attained enlightenment.

For the remaining 45 years of his life, Siddhartha travelled and taught. His followers called him Buddha, the enlightened or awakened one.

The entrance to the *photang* is next door to the **Druk White Lotus School** (*www. dwls.org*), which shot to fame in the 2010 Bollywood film *3 Idiots* and counts both Richard Gere and Joanna Lumley as honorary patrons.

THIKSEY *Telephone code: 01982*

It's easy to overdose on gompas in Ladakh, but if you only visit one, make sure that it is Thiksey. Not only does it have a striking position and staggering views, but you get the sense that you are visiting a living, working monastery: it is much less commercialised than Hemis (see page 132) and although there are other tourists here, you'll feel part of the monastic community. Unusually, you're also permitted to take photos inside.

GETTING THERE AND AWAY Just 18km from Leh and a stone's throw past Shey, it is easy and advisable to combine Thiksey and Shey in a single day trip. **Minibuses** from Leh leave every half-hour or so during the summer months and the journey takes under an hour. Expect to pay Rs25.

Taking a **taxi** from Leh, LTOCL rates start from Rs355 one-way and Rs461 return. Hiring the car for a combined sightseeing tour of Shey and Thiksey starts from Rs824, and if you want to visit Hemis and Stakna too then prices begin at Rs1,935.

WHERE TO STAY

Chamba Hotel (30 rooms) Thiksey; 267 385; e kthiksey@gmail.com; www. thikseymonastery.org. Run for the benefit of the monastery, the black, white & red colour scheme of the building mirrors that of the gompa up the hill. The majority of rooms are considered deluxe & demand a high price tag, but there are also 8 standard rooms costing just Rs600. FB & room-only available. Wi-Fi included. **$$$$**

Chattnyanling Nunnery (6 rooms) Nyerma; m 990 698 5911; e tarahomestaybooking@gmail.com; www. ladakhnuns.com. Only 5mins' drive from Thiksey Gompa, the nuns of Nyerma run this small, quiet guesthouse in attractive surroundings. Rooms have attached toilets. B/fast & veg dinner included. Men & women welcome. Proceeds go towards education & upkeep of the nunnery. **$$**

WHERE TO EAT There is a medium-sized and apparently well-run **restaurant** ($) at the foot of the gompa serving breakfast, light lunches and dinners, as well as various snacks and soft drinks. Profits go to the monastery.

SHOPPING There is a well-stocked **souvenir shop** at the gompa (see below). In addition to postcards, books and calendars you can also buy T-shirts, garish clothing and various trinkets. Profits from the shop go towards the upkeep of the monastery.

OTHER PRACTICALITIES There is a small branch of **J&K Bank** on the road south from Thiksey. It is also possible to buy **Aircell** and **Airtel** talk-time from the roadside kiosks.

If you fall sick or need to buy medication, **Chamba Health Services** (*267 011*) has its premises at the main entrance to the gompa. The doctors here practise both Western and Tibetan medicine and they have a small pharmacy.

WHAT TO SEE If you are approaching by road, **Thiksey Gompa** (*267 005; www. thikseymonastery.org*) is best seen from the south: somehow it seems far more impressive than when driving the other way. Having left the main road to drive through Thiksey village, the road doubles back on itself and climbs to the foot of the gompa where there is a large and well-ordered parking area. From here you must proceed on foot.

You enter the gompa site through a **red gateway** painted with colourful *mandalas* (see box, page 130). Looking left you have unobstructed views across to **Stakna Gompa** (see page 131), then a line of buildings that include public toilets, and the gompa's restaurant and souvenir shop.

Here too is Thiksey's **museum** (⊕ *06.00–18.00, closed 13.00–13.30 & 16.00–16.15; entrance fee Rs30*). The museum ticket also gives you entry to the gompa itself. The museum is below ground level and the steps down to it are somewhat precarious, so proceed with caution and keep hold of small children.

The museum initially appears to be a single room but is in fact divided into three areas, the main room, a room of scrolls and books, and a third space containing assorted ceremonial tea vessels. In all areas the choice of exhibits is eclectic, with many of the items relating in some way to worship or spirit invocation. Look out for the trumpet made from a human thigh bone, the sound of which is supposed to drive away evil forces; portable altars; bows, swords and shields seized from Muslim invaders; and some fearsome ritual dance costumes.

From the museum you should continue up the steps to the gompa's **main courtyard** around which the most important temples are located. The courtyard is cloistered and the walls are painted with some attractive **modern murals**. Two small **Foo dogs** guard the space and a long, thin prayer flag flutters in the wind.

Go first into the **Temple of the Maitreya Buddha**, the Buddha of the future, the icon of Thiksey that adorns an infinite number of postcards. One of the finest Maitrya Buddha statues in Ladakh, the Buddha wears an expression of absolute serenity and the workmanship on the statue's crown in particular is quite exceptional. The smell of freshly cut wood mingles with the slow-burning incense, and the space is well lit with daylight streaming through large windows on three sides of the building. You are welcome to take photos of the Buddha (no flash) but should refrain from posing alongside it, as doing so is considered disrespectful.

Up the stairs to the left-hand side of the courtyard is a second **temple**. Murals here depict the guardians of the four cardinal directions: the white Yulkhor Sung (east); blue Phah Skespo (south); red Chanme Zang (west); and the yellow Natos Ses (north), whose accompanying mongoose spits out gemstones. You can take photographs here as long as you turn off the flash.

Far more so than the other areas of the gompa, this temple feels particularly old, and this feeling is only emphasised by the darkness. Many of the wall paintings here are in their original, unrestored condition, as is attested to by the occasional cracks and unfortunate water damage. On display here are two jade-green **ceremonial drums**, the monks' **yellow hats** (worn only on special occasions) and, on the back wall, a tantric *chakrasamvara* statue depicting a man and woman in a particularly intimate embrace.

Given the proximity to Leh, many visitors choose to come to Thiksey early in the morning to join the monks in this temple for prayers. You'll need to arrive before 07.00 and sit still and in silence for the duration of the meeting.

Behind the main temple room is a small **antechamber** with a collection of larger statues and a finely worked painting of a *begtse* or protector.

There are two further small temples here, less dramatic than those mentioned above but still worth visiting. The **gonkhang**, or Temple of the Protectors, is crowded and the air is thick with incense. The giant statues of the guardians are shrouded so you cannot see their faces. Also step inside the tiny **Tara Temple**, which is arranged like a Chinese curiosity cabinet with every little statue placed in its own cupboard space.

Before leaving the gompa make sure you see the picturesque row of **nine stupas** garlanded with prayer flags: on a clear day with a bright blue sky there are few sights that better epitomise Ladakh.

MATHO *Telephone code: 01982*

Matho takes its name from the Tibetan for 'much happiness'. As it is further back from the highway than some of the other monasteries it receives far fewer visitors, except for at festival time when Buddhist pilgrims and tourists alike flock here in their hundreds to see the oracles and hear their predictions for the coming year.

GETTING THERE AND AWAY Situated 26km from Leh, the approach road to Matho is long and straight towards the mountains; the gompa comes into view on the right-hand side above your usual line of sight. It's an arid, featureless landscape save for the old irrigation ditch that now lies dry.

Unlike Thiksey and Hemis, Matho is not on the main highway and there are only two buses a day directly from Leh to Matho. They turn around immediately on arrival, so aren't terribly helpful if you actually want to look around. If you are dependent on public transport, take the far more regular **bus** to Thiksey instead (see page 128) and then **walk** via Stakna (see page 131) to Matho. It's a pleasant stroll and will take you no more than 90 minutes.

Taking a **taxi** from Leh will cost you from Rs842 one-way and Rs1,095 return, or you can combine it with a trip to Stakna and Stok from Rs1,589.

WHAT TO SEE
Matho Gompa (m *962 295 5999; www.mathomonastery.com;* ⊕ *08.30–18.00, closed 13.00–14.00; entrance fee Rs20*) This is the only Sakya monastery in Ladakh. Sixty monks and 30 novices live in this gompa, which was founded in the early 15th century by the great Sakya Pandita Drungpa Dorje during his visit to Ladakh.

MANDALA PAINTINGS

The *mandala*, or wheel of life, depicts the Buddhist universe. It comprises three concentric circles.

In the innermost circle are depicted man's three greatest vices: there is the snake, which is symbolic of anger; desire is shown in the form of a cockerel; and then there is a pig, representing ignorance.

Moving outward, the middle circle depicts six realms. These are the worlds of the gods, demi-gods, ghosts, men, animals and, lastly, of hell.

The outermost circle is made up of 12 symbols that collectively represent the chain of cause and effect. Look in particular for the blind man who symbolises lack of knowledge; the house with six windows, one for each of our senses; the pain of an arrow to the eye; and the fate that awaits us all: a corpse being carried.

Mahayana Buddhists believe that the *mandala*, or *bhavacakra*, was developed by the Buddha himself as a teaching aid. You will find them either painted directly onto the walls of Tibetan Buddhist temples, or painted on canvas or paper and then hung up where everyone can see.

Tanzin Norbu (www.mountaintribalvision.com)

Matho Monastery has two oracles who predict the future. They are collectively known as Lha Rong-btsan, and on the 25th and 26th of the second Tibetan month (based on the lunar calendar) Matho celebrates their festival. People visit from all over Ladakh to witness the oracles in a trance.

The second day of the festival begins with a masked dance performed by the monks of Matho, which lasts for more than an hour before the oracles emerge.

Each year, the monastery chooses two monks to perform the oracle: these monks have to go through a month-long retreat in a dark room filled with barley grain offered by local villagers. On the day of the festival, the monks paint their bodies black from head to toe and wear thick, black wigs on their heads. Then, their eyes are covered with nine black blindfolds.

Before they go into their trance, monastery artists paint a fearful face of a deity on their stomachs, making sure to paint the deity's eyes at the very end. It is said that as soon as the eyeballs are painted in, the oracles begin to shake their bodies vigorously and jump up to run around the roof edge of the five-storey building of the monastery, their eyes still blindfolded. In their left hands, they hold *drilu* (the Tibetan bell) and in their right, the *daru* (a ritual drum), all the while performing acrobatic feats. Then they stand on the roof edge facing the main courtyard of the monastery where all the people wait for their blessing and prophesies for the whole valley, and listen for the method to remove any potential obstacles. After hearing these, all the people shout 'Ki-Ki-So-So-Lhar-Gyalo' (Victory to the Gods) three times. Then both oracles go around the monastery building and come down to the main court, standing on a platform, again giving their blessings and prophesies for the village. Once again all the people shout 'Ki-Ki-So-So-Lhar-Gyalo'.

Historians say that originally the two oracles were brothers who came from the Kham province of Tibet. When the Sakya Lama, Drungpa Dorje, came to Ladakh from Tibet, the two oracles accompanied him and the lama appointed them as protector deities of the Matho gompa.

For forthcoming festival dates at Matho Gompa, see page 64.

The buildings at Matho are generally in a poor state of repair, save for the modern **dukhang** built in 2005.

STAKNA

Perched like a crow's nest atop a hill by a bend in the Indus River, you could hardly wish for a more photogenic location than Stakna. The shape of the hill is said to resemble a tiger's nose, from where the gompa takes its name.

GETTING THERE AND AWAY Stakna's gompa is clearly visible from Thiksey, and the village lies just off the main highway between Thiksey and Hemis, half an hour's drive from the latter. The climb to the gompa itself is along a succession of switchback bends.

A single **bus** leaves Leh for Stakna, 25km (15 miles) away, each day at 07.00 and returns to Leh at 16.00. It is better, however, to take the bus to Thiksey (see page 128), as it has to turn around by the bridge crossing the Indus on the road to Stakna, from where you can **walk** to the gompa in 15 minutes.

By **taxi** from Leh you'll pay Rs653 one-way or Rs849 return but given that there is a limited amount to see here, you'll probably want to combine your visit with Matho and/or Thiksey.

✖ **WHERE TO EAT AND DRINK** There's nowhere to stay in Stakna but there is a small **tea stall** by the roadside. It's exceptionally basic but the cup of tea is welcome while you're waiting for the bus or to refresh yourself before the walk.

WHAT TO SEE The plain exterior of Stakna Gompa (📞 *267 577;* ⊕ *06.30–19.00, closed around 13.00–14.00; entrance fee Rs30*) belies what you'll find inside: bright and exquisitely painted **murals**.

The monastery was founded in the 1500s by a Bhutanese monk and scholar, Chosje Jamyang Palkar, and so the 35 or so monks who live here follow the Drugpa, or Red Hat, school of Buddhism, which originated in Bhutan. The monks who live here are welcoming of visitors and, though there is an entrance fee, it feels far less commercialised than neighbouring Hemis (see below).

The centrepiece of the gompa is the **16th-century prayer hall.** The paintings here have been sensitively restored and the colours are vibrant, making for some excellent photos, although you won't be allowed to use the flash.

HEMIS *Telephone code: 01982*

Probably the most famous, and certainly the richest, of all Ladakh's monasteries is Hemis. It has one of the most elaborate Buddhist festivals, the Tse Chu Festival, and it is claimed that a lost Gospel relating to the life of Christ is also secretly preserved inside.

GETTING THERE AND AWAY Hemis is on the main highway 43km south of Leh. The bus ride takes under two hours and the road surface is, at least by Ladakh's standards, good all the way. There are two direct **buses** that depart from Leh at 09.45 and 16.00 and return at 07.00 and 12.30.

Coming by **taxi** is slightly faster: allow 90 minutes. If you just want the car to drop you from Leh to Hemis then prices start from Rs1,078, and Rs1,565 to go there and back.

🏠 **WHERE TO STAY AND EAT** If you wish to stay at Hemis, the most atmospheric option is the **Hemis Monastery Guesthouse** (*12 rooms;* **$$**). Facilities are basic and there are mattresses on the floor rather than proper beds, but at least you feel you are getting the authentic monastery experience. The rooms are reasonably clean and prices are charged per person rather than per room, making it cost-effective if you're on your own. The downside is that you can't book in advance. It is also possible to **camp** at the gompa, for which there s a charge of Rs150 per person.

To the left of the gompa, a little down the hill, is the **Hemis Gompa Restaurant** (📱 *962 237 2915;* ⊕ *07.30–20.00;* **$$**). It is a little rudimentary but the setting among the trees is pleasant and you can hear the sound of the river. A parachute used as a tent protects you from the sun. Dishes are either Tibetan or Indian, and you can fill up on noodles for Rs110. A cup of black tea, much needed once you've been around the gompa, is Rs10.

SHOPPING There is a **gift shop** at Hemis Gompa where you can buy all manner of (probably) Chinese-made souvenirs you don't really want or need. Having monks selling T-shirts makes it feel rather crass and over-commercialised.

WHAT TO SEE When you arrive at Hemis Gompa (☏ *249 011*; ⊕ *08.00–18.00, closed 13.00–14.00; entrance fee Rs100*) your transport will most probably drop you in the gompa car park, from where there's the inevitable climb up steep steps to the ticket desk and an advertising board proclaiming that Hemis is the largest monastic institution in Ladakh. These two items sadly sum up the gompa perfectly: it's good at self-publicity, and the first thought of the management is on taking your money.

Passing the gift shop and lockers brings you into the **central courtyard** where the famous masked dances take place on festival days: you'll most likely recognise it from the postcards. A long, vertical prayer flag flutters on its pole, and to the right a line of **prayer wheels** are spun by absent-minded tourists and an occasional devotee or monk.

The **main prayer hall** was under renovation at the time of our visit and it was not possible to go inside: it should reopen in 2014. The outside of the hall has some attractive paintings and if you look up to the roof you'll see a line of skulls.

JESUS IN KASHMIR

During the late 19th century, a Russian aristocrat, writer, military officer and Great Game spy by the name of Nicolas Notovitch travelled to Ladakh and spent a prolonged period at Hemis Gompa in 1887. While there he claimed to have been shown a manuscript, written in Pali and brought to Hemis from Tibet, entitled Life of Saint Issa, Best of the Sons of Men. Notovitch translated the text into French and published it in 1894 with the title *La vie inconnue de Jesus Christ*, Issa or Isa being the Arabic form of Jesus.

The book caused outrage. It claimed that Issa came to India from Israel at the age of 14 and that he then studied Pali and the Buddhist texts. He returned to Israel aged 29 to preach, his study of Buddhism heavily influencing his teachings.

Though Notovitch was declared both a heretic and a fraud, and the noted German historian Max Mueller went as far as writing to the head lama at Hemis to question what Notovitch had written, two others followed in his footsteps and went to see the manuscripts for themselves. Swami Abhendananda, a disciple of the Indian mystic Ramakrishna, confirmed Notovitch's assertions and published his own book, *Kashmir O Tibeti*, in Bengali in 1922; and the Russian Nicolas Roerich visited Hemis in 1925, mentioning in his work the manuscript's existence.

If the manuscript is still here, the monks of Hemis are tight-lipped about it. Local people claim that there is a sealed room inside the monastery where only the most senior lama may enter. As he resides in Lhasa, the room and its contents cannot be reached.

On the other side of J&K, in the Kashmir Valley, a complementary tradition exists: that of Yus Asaf, the healer or shepherd. Here some Muslims believe that Yus Asaf was a preacher and prophet, the same Issa (or Jesus) mentioned in the Koran. An inscription once carved in what is locally known as the Temple of Solomon supports this view.

Yus Asaf lived in Kashmir in the 1st century and was buried in Srinagar in AD88. The first structure covering his tomb was built in 112 and the grave is aligned to point to the east and west as per the Jewish tradition: Muslim bodies are buried on the north–south axis. Alongside the tomb, carved into the stone are two footprints, each with marks above the toes that are said to be the scars of crucifixion. No other such footprints have been identified in Kashmir.

Perhaps the most intriguing items at Hemis are within the **museum**, which is downstairs from the courtyard. The items on display are an eclectic combination but include some fine statuary, turquoise masks, beautiful scroll cases decorated with gold filigree work, a cylinder for making butter tea, and a magnificent 14th-century conch shell with a silver and copper mouthpiece, the surface of which is embossed with a dragon and inlaid with pieces of turquoise, coral and lapis lazuli.

Note that you are not permitted to take photographs inside the gompa: cameras must be left in the lockers by the gift shop. The monks are very insistent about this.

CHEMRE *Telephone code: 01982*

Like all languages, Ladakhi has changed faster in its spoken than written form. Thus Chede Demchog Gompa (or Chemde for short) is in the village known as Chemre. Spread across the hillside and surrounded with a sprinkling of stupas, it's by no means the most striking of Ladakh's monasteries but a charming diversion nonetheless.

GETTING THERE AND AWAY Chemre is 40km from Leh in the Sakti Valley. There are several daily **buses** from Leh that stop in Chemre before continuing to Thagthog, and the journey takes around two hours. Expect to pay around Rs50 per person. By **taxi**, prices start from Rs1,535 for the return trip from Leh, though it'd be advisable to combine Chemre, Thagthog and Hemis, the price for which starts at Rs2,268.

WHERE TO STAY There is no formal accommodation at Chemre but there is space at the monastery where you can pitch a tent. As a matter of politeness you should ask the monks for permission and leave a donation: Rs150 per person is appropriate.

WHAT TO SEE Chemde Gompa was founded in the latter part of the 17th century by Lama Tagsang Raschen and is dedicated to Sengge Namgyal, king of Ladakh from 1616 until his death in 1642. It is home to 120 monks from the Drugpa school, and the chief lama here is also in charge at Hemis.

The principal part of the monastery is on three floors. On the ground floor is the **dukhang**, where the walls are brightly painted with seven rows of Buddha figures. A library of ancient manuscripts partially covers one section, and three large, antique *mandalas* are on display.

Above this is the **lhakhang** (in fact there are two lhakhangs here). The statues they contain have noticeably Mongolian features. On the top floor is a light room, recently painted with murals, in which you'll find an impressive **Padmasambhava statue** on its throne.

THAGTHOG *Telephone code: 01982*

Thagthog, or Tak Thok, takes its name from the cave where the Padmasambhava meditated and around which the gompa is built. The only Nyingmapa monastery in Ladakh, it has a very different atmosphere from the other gompas and some visitors have reported feeling a sensation of exceptional unease with physical symptoms, though the monks are friendly enough.

GETTING THERE AND AWAY It's 45km from Leh to Thagthog and the public **bus** runs to Sakti (passing through Thagthog) every day except Sunday. Allow two hours and Rs55 for the journey. By **taxi**, fares start from Rs1,760 return, though you may wish to combine your visit with a trip to Chemre (see above) and Hemis (see page 132).

WHERE TO STAY AND EAT There is a single **guesthouse ($)** at the foot of the gompa. It's run by the monks and theoretically always staffed, but in reality you'll have to ask around to find someone to open the gate for you. Rooms are simple but clean and have attached bathrooms. Breakfast and dinner are available on request.

WHAT TO SEE The reason for coming to Thagthog is to visit **Thagthog Gompa**. It has grown literally out of the rock: Padmasambhava is believed to have meditated in the cave, the cave became a shrine, and, eight centuries after his visit, in the mid-1700s, much of the monastery you see today was built. The new temple, just below the main complex, was consecrated by the Dalai Lama only in 1980, however, and so is not an original structure.

The **cave** is the physical and spiritual heart of the monastery. It's a small but not claustrophobic space and the walls are black and sticky with the oily soot of butter lamps. If you look closely you can make out eight painted circles, each one depicting a different manifestation of the Padmasambhava, but you'll almost need to press your nose to the wall.

The day we visited, a funeral service was taking place in the cave for a monk who had recently died. The monks and female participants in the ritual were chanting, incense was burning, and a younger monk created a web of string between his body and the ceiling of the cave, where coins, banknotes and playing cards were pressed into the roof as an offering to the spirit world. They were working to engage with a spirit, the nature of which did not feel entirely benevolent.

THE ORDERS OF BUDDHISM

In Ladakh there are four principal orders, schools or sects, of Buddhism represented. They are all variations of the Vajrayana path, a form of esoteric Buddhism that incorporates aspects of tantric Hinduism.

NYINGMAPA The oldest of Ladakh's four orders is the Nyingmapa, founded in the 8th century by Guru Padmasambhava, who is credited with bringing Buddhism from India to Tibet. Legend has it that he meditated in a cave at Thagthog (see opposite) and a monastery consequently grew up around the holy site. Thagthog is the only Nyingmapa monastery in Ladakh.

KARGYUD The Kargyud, or Order of Oral Transmission, dates from the 11th century but a hundred years later split further into the Drigungpa and Drugpa sects. The order is based on the teachings of a lineage of four scholars: Tilopa, Naropa, Marpa and Milarepa. Lamayuru and Phyang are both Drigungpa monasteries.

SAKYAPA The White Earth, or Sakyapa, order was founded at Sakya (in what is now Tibet) in 1073, and is based on the teachings of Indian yogis,

GELUGPA The Gelugpa, or Yellow Hat, is the most visible of Ladakh's Buddhist orders. It evolved out of the 11th-century Kadampa sect when the scholar Tsongkhapa (1357–1419) demanded reforms to restore what he saw as the purity of older ideas. His disciple Lama Lhawang Lhotos founded the Gelugpa sect at Likir.

Elsewhere in the gompa are some **historic frescoes**, a four-armed **statue of Avalokiteshvara** and an important collection of **ancient manuscripts** brought here by refugees from Tibet.

MARKHA VALLEY

The Markha River, a tributary to the Zanskar, has created one of the most scenic valleys in Ladakh, and it is quite rightly one of the region's most popular trekking destinations. Accessible via either Ganda La near Spituk, or from Gongmaru La near Hemis, much of the valley falls within the borders of the Hemis National Park. Most of the trekking routes are best attempted between July and September, though some are accessible until mid-October.

GETTING THERE AND AWAY Given that most people come to Markha to trek, it makes sense to travel to Spituk (see page 104) or Hemis (see page 132) and then cross the passes **on foot**. If you are short of time, however, or simply wish to visit

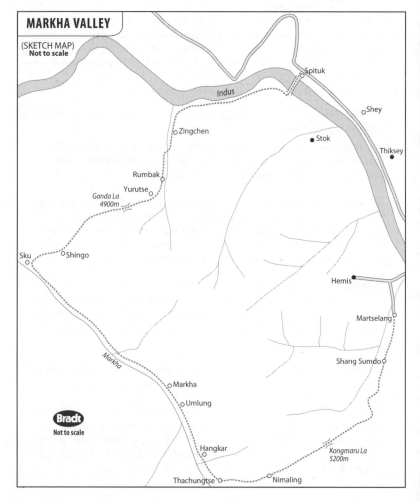

The trek starts at **Spituk** (3,307m), just outside Leh, on the bridge across the River Indus. It's a dusty three-hour tromp along the old jeep road up into the Zingchen Valley, then a further two hours along the Rumbak River (by which time the landscape is fresh and green) to the hamlet of **Zingchen** (4,560m; 14,960ft) where there is a campsite and, helpfully, a tea shop.

Zingchen is on the edge of the Hemis National Park and so, as you penetrate the reserve on day two, you can hope to catch a glimpse of mountain hares, marmots, wild dogs and foxes, as well as, if you're lucky, the Great Tibetan sheep and the Ladakhi urial. Climbing through the gorge brings you to a series of golden barley fields around **Rumbak** (4,050m), where blue sheep are occasionally visible on the slopes. A short distance on is tiny Yurutse, where there is a homestay, or you can continue on to the **campsite** (4,545m) at the base of Ganda La, which has majestic views of Stok Kangri.

On day three there's around six hours' walking, starting with a two-hour, zigzagging ascent of **Ganda La** (4,900m). Marmots and hares lark on the slopes, and stupas and prayer flags mark the top of the pass. Look to the west for the most impressive views, be sure to take some pictures, and then begin making your way down the trail to **Shingo** (4,200m), where there's a homestay if you need it, and thence through the gorge and back and forth across the stream to **Sku** (3,300m). There are some fortified ruins here, supposedly part of what was once a royal residence, that are worth having a look at too. There's one homestay here, and three more in the neighbouring hamlet of Kaya.

You need to allow for seven hours of walking on day four. The trail follows the Markha River for much of the way and passes several seasonal settlements used by the nomads. In each of these places there are small Buddhist shrines and many Mani stones. The valley is hot and exposed, which makes for a tiring day, but it ends in **Markha** (3,810m), the largest village in the valley, where you'll hopefully get a good night's sleep. If you've still got energy for sightseeing, there is a ruined fort and a small gompa.

Day five is culturally rich as you pass by both a ruined castle and the Techa Gompa, poised high on the cliff above Markha itself. The trekking trail weaves its way back and forth across the river to **Umlung**, from where you'll first see towering **Kang Yatse** (6,400m), then on through the meadows to **Hangkar** and finally the campsite at **Thachungtse** (4,250m). Allow six hours to reach the camp.

On the sixth day, from Thachungtse to the Nimaling Plateau, where nomads graze their sheep and goats, it's only a four-hour walk but the path is steep, as at 4,700m **Nimaling** is the highest campsite on the trek. Sweeping views take not only the Markha Valley but large parts of the Zanskar Range too, so if you're at all artistically inclined, this is the time to get out your camera or sketchpad.

The penultimate day of the trek starts with a crossing of **Kongmaru La** (5,200m), the physical high point of the journey. You descend from here into the **Shang Gorge** and proceed to **Chuskurmo**, a natural spring that is thought to have medicinal properties. The night is spent in the village of **Shang Sumdo** (3,660m).

Day eight brings you from the village along the jeep road to **Martselang** (3,450m), which connects to the main road. It's a pleasant stroll of just two hours, leaving plenty of time to reach your next destination.

Southern Ladakh **MARKHA VALLEY**

5

the valley on a day trip, you can take a **taxi** from Leh. Driving to Rumbak-Zingchen via the bridge at Spituk will cost from Rs1,217 return; to get there via the bridge at Choglamsar will cost from Rs2,307 return.

LOCAL TRAVEL AGENTS Though almost any of the travel agents in Leh (see pages 85–7) will be able to arrange a trekking package or trekking guide for you in the Markha Valley, we can particularly recommend **Dreamland Trek and Tour** (*www.dreamladakh. com*) and **Ladakh Yeti Travels** (*www.ladakhyetitravels.com*). Both companies are well organised, professional and their guides know Markha like the backs of their hands.

WHERE TO STAY AND EAT An offshoot of the Snow Leopard Conservancy India Trust (see box, page 10), **Himalayan Homestays** (*www.himalayan-homestays.com*) has organised a series of excellent homestays throughout the Hemis National Park, many of which are in the Markha Valley. Visitors are rotated around different homes in each village to ensure the money benefits as many local families as possible. You'll pay Rs800 per person for a warm bed and delicious, home-cooked meals, and it's the best way to get to know local people and their way of life. There are currently homestays in Rumbak, Yurutse, Shingo, Kaya, Sku and Chilling.

If you have lightweight equipment and/or porters to carry it, **camping** is also a viable option. There are a number of designated camping spots (local guides know where they are), and you can also often arrange to camp in someone's field or on the outskirts of their village. Always ask permission if you do this, and be prepared to make a small payment (Rs100 or thereabouts).

WHAT TO SEE You come to the Markha Valley to see the scenery and the wildlife, and to trek. The trekking options are numerous and varied: local tour operators in Leh will be able to make recommendations based on your level of fitness, interests and the amount of time you have available. The trek outlined in the box on page 137 is our particular favourite.

SOUTHERN LAKES

The southeastern part of Ladakh, running up towards the Chinese border, is sprayed with picture-postcard lakes and, if you've had your fill of monasteries, retreating to the shores to watch the waters lapping around your toes, or staring up into a seemingly endless star-filled sky, is just what the doctor ordered.

Unless you have a lot of time available, you'll probably need to choose either to visit Pangong or to go to Tso Moriri and Tso Kar lakes. Both require a long and uncomfortable car journey, and as getting there and back from Leh is expensive your decision may well be shaped by whom you can share a car with.

The road south from Leh to the lakes is the main Leh–Manali road, National Highway 1 (NH1). It splits at Karu, an army base that also hosts a small line of **shops** and **cafés**. From here it is 110km to Pangong, 115km to Tso Kar and 175km to Tso Moriri.

Due to the proximity of the lakes to the Indo-Chinese border, you are required to have an Inner Line permit (see box, page 107) to travel there. If you do not have a permit (and the requisite number of photocopies), you will not be allowed to travel past the police checkpoints.

PANGONG TSO People frequently come to Pangong and say that it leaves them spellbound. The backdrop to many a Bollywood movie, including parts of *3 Idiots* with Aamir Khan and *Dil Se* starring Shah Rukh Khan, the colours of the water change constantly, mesmerising the viewer. A visit during the full moon is unforgettable due to the silver-white reflection on the surface of the lake.

Getting there and away From May to September there is a bi-weekly JKSRTC **bus** from Leh to Spangmik, a village on the shore of Pangong Tso, which departs from Leh on Saturday and Sunday at 06.30, returning to Leh the following morning at 07.00. It costs around Rs200 each way and the journey takes at least eight hours, and more if you have a flat tyre or other delay.

If you need more flexibility in your timing, a seat in a **shared taxi** will cost Rs1,000–1,500 each way, and hiring a **taxi** for yourself will cost from Rs6,556 if you go there and back in a day, or Rs7,804 if you go one day and return the next.

Where to stay and eat
Pangong's two principal **tent camps** are both operated by Camps of Ladakh (see page 85) and fit into the upmarket (**$$$$**) category. **Camp Whispering Waves** (15 tents) is on the southern shore of the lake at Spangmik, the furthest point where foreigners are permitted to go. All tents are carpeted and have en-suite bathrooms, and multi-cuisine meals are served in the communal dining tent.

The second camp, **Camp Water Mark** (15 tents), is also at Spangmik. The cleanliness and comfort require particular mention, as does the standard of the food. Hot water is available in the mornings on request.

If you are looking for something cheaper, there is a functional but uninspiring **PWD Government Resthouse** (**$$–$$$**) and also the rather more friendly **Gomgma Homestay** (m *946 953 4270;* **$**), both of which are in Spangmik. In Tangste you can stay affordably at the **Dothguling Guesthouse** (*opposite the health centre;* **$**), and in Lukung **Eco Huts** has both private and dormitory tents with prices starting from Rs400 per person (Rs600 including meals). You will need to turn up in person to see if there is space, as due to the lack of mobile reception it is not possible to book in advance.

You should eat your meals where you stay, or bring food with you from Leh, as there is little to buy locally, except for the traditional *chang*, homemade barley beer, which will set you back about Rs15.

What to see Pangong Tso (*Tso* meaning lake) is an endorheic lake: a closed basin with no river flowing out from it. A natural dam has closed off the river leading into the Shyok; the only water leaving the lake does so through seepage and evaporation. At its longest point it measures 134km and it straddles the border of India and China, leading to an occasional skirmish along its shores.

The lake water changes colour markedly depending on the time of day and the season: in bright sunlight at midday you might see it in vibrant turquoise; looking back from a distance in the afternoon it might be royal blue; and up close, staring into the water when it's overcast, of course it's a brackish brown. In spite of its salinity, the lake freezes completely in winter.

There are few, if any, fish in the lake but this doesn't stop large numbers of migratory birds resting here in the summer months: they feed on crustaceans and the herbs and scrub growing in the marshy patches at the water's edge. Bar-headed geese and Brahmi ducks are both common sights, and it is hoped that the lake will soon be recognised as a wetland of international importance.

TSO KAR The smallest of the three main lakes is Tso Kar, an attractive salt lake whose tourist potential is yet to be fully realised: the development of hotel and restaurant infrastructure is far behind that at Tso Moriri, for example, but the resulting lack of other tourists undoubtedly has its own charm.

Getting there and away The drive from Leh to Tso Kar is almost entirely along NH1 and driving the 155km takes around seven hours. When the road forks at **Upshi**, continue along the road heading right towards Manali. You will also pass through **Gya**, where there is a small gompa across the river (use the rickety footbridge) from the village, and **Rumtse**, from where it is a demanding seven-day trek to Tso Moriri if you feel so inclined.

South of Rumtse you must cross the **Taglang La Pass** (5,359m). The views are probably best when driving north along the road, but whichever way you are driving you should stop to take in the views, as the mountainside and twisted shoelace of a road simply seem to fall away beneath you. Don't try to do anything here too quickly as the altitude takes its toll, even if you've already acclimatised in Leh.

The last settlement before you reach the turn-off for Tso Kar is **Dipling**. It's far from impressive, composed as it is of just a row of temporary-looking buildings and tents serving basic meals. Some 2km further on is the grandly named **Dipling Restaurant**, a solitary tent serving tea and *momos*, and it is here that you leave NH1 and turn left onto the track for Tso Kar.

If you are driving between Tso Moriri (see opposite) and Tso Kar, there is a largely unmade road between the two lakes. Providing it is dry it's not an uncomfortable ride and the views are superb. The distance is only around 50km but it takes a full three hours. You may well be asked to pick up hitchhikers in one of the villages *en route* and to take them as far as NH1 as there is no public transport locally and few other vehicles pass this way.

Where to stay and eat Tso Kar village is less developed than the settlements at Pangong Lake and Tso Moriri, and probably wouldn't exist at all if it weren't for the passing tourist trade. There are a small number of mud-brick buildings but your options for eating and sleeping are all under canvas. Camps of Ladakh operate the upmarket **Pastureland Camp** (*30 tents;* **$$$$**) from a superb location and it is particularly popular with birdwatchers. The **Tso Kar Resort Camp and Restaurant** was still being constructed when we visited but looks as though it will ultimately be a reasonable place to stay.

Rice and dal lunches, instant noodles, tea and inflated-price snacks are available from **Tso Kar Restaurant** (**$**), a round, white tent with a few tables inside. There's the slightly gruesome (but still impressive) skull and horns of a long-dead sheep immediately outside the entrance.

What to see A short scramble above the village, away from the lake, brings you to **Tso Kar Gompa**. The building itself is neither particularly old nor particularly interesting but it offers a fine vantage point from which to survey the lake and its mountainous backdrop, and this is what justifies the climb.

The smallest of the three principal southern lakes, **Tso Kar** itself is a saline lake conjoined with its smaller sister, Startsapuk Tso. Though the lakes' inlets contain fresh water, the lakeshore is covered with a thick, white crust of salt which gives the lake its name (*kar* meaning white). Changpa nomads used to collect this salt, process it and export it to Tibet.

Tso Kar is far less visited than Tso Moriri and Pangong, but it is a fine place for birdwatching. Black necked cranes, which have a wingspan of 2.5m or more, come here to lay their eggs, as do Brahmi ducks and great crested grebes.

TSO MORIRI In our opinion, Tso Moriri is the most beautiful of the three lakes, though there'll inevitably be plenty of people to argue otherwise. It's best seen early in the morning or late in the day when the shadows are long, and you'll need to walk a short way from Korzok around the shore to be able to appreciate the pristine environment and peace. Some 34 species of bird, including 14 waterbirds, are found in the Tso Moriri Wetland Conservation Reserve (see page 143), as are snow leopards, Tibetan wolves, great Tibetan sheep and marmots.

Getting there and away The **drive** south from Leh is 215km and takes as much as eight hours, as long and painful sections of it are on unmade roads. Leaving by 10.00 at the latest will ensure you reach Tso Moriri when the lake and surrounding mountains are at their most photogenic, swathed in a warm afternoon light.

Significant (though by no means substantial) settlements *en route* include **Upshi** where the road forks: you can stop here for steamed momos or an omelette at **Padma Restaurant** ($) and pick up snacks for the road in the small **shops** before heading out of the village to the left (the right fork takes you to Tso Kar and then on to Manali and, eventually, Chandigarh).

At riverside **Chumathang** there is a decidedly dusty-looking **hot spring**, a **bar** serving Kingfisher beers and various noxious local spirits, and two cafés, **Skit Tsau Restaurant** ($) and the marginally more presentable **Paradise Restaurant** ($–$$). Both are fine for a quick snack, and there is a very basic **public toilet** up the hill behind the row of shops if you've been knocking back the beers. Look right as you leave Chumathang and you'll see one of the flimsier-looking **footbridges** in the area: it's probably only held together by the prayer flags.

Past Chumathang is the **Mahe Bridge**. Here you must cross the river even though the main road continues along the left bank. The road to Tso Moriri crosses the bridge and sweeps around to the right, with dry, gorse-like bushes on the valley floor and purple and yellow flowers scattered across the slopes.

Travelling to Tso Moriri by road, you will need three copies of your Inner Line permit (see box, page 107). You will be required to present these at the police checkpoints at Upshi and Mahe Bridge, and to the Indo–Tibetan Border Police at Korzok. The latter will also require you to sign a form stating the number of cameras and GPS units in your vehicle, and confirming that you are not carrying a satellite phone.

If you do not have your own vehicle, there are three **buses** a month from Leh, departing on the 10th, 20th and 30th at 06.30. You would, however, need to wait a full ten days for the return bus, or arrange for a car to bring you back. It would better suit those planning to drive in and trek out. The bus fare is Rs219.

Where to stay and eat All of Tso Moriri's accommodation options and places to eat are in the small village of Korzok, the only permanent settlement on the lakeside. Business here is seasonal and the variety of places to stay limited, but you'll have no difficulty finding a warm(ish) bed and hot meal, even if you turn up unannounced.

Tso Moriri Camp (*15 tents, 5 huts; Korzok Village;* \ *(011) 4058 0334;* e *info@ campsofladakh.com; www.campsofladakh.com;* **$$$$**), run by Camps of Ladakh (see page 85), is the first of the tented camps you see on the right as you enter Korzok. It's the only one we'd consider staying in: the others are more akin to refugee camps than holiday homes. Here you'll find simple but comfortable tents with plenty of blankets for the cold nights. Every tent has an attached bathroom with proper toilet and running water. Meals are served buffet-style in a large maharaja's tent. If you haven't packed for inclement weather, they also sell colourful, hand knitted socks for Rs200/pair.

5

The best **budget accommodation** is at one of nearly a dozen **homestays ($)** in the village, each of which has two to three rooms and will provide all your meals. Homestays are marked with white signs: simply knock and see if they have space. **Rosefinch Homestay** is on the main street; **Reshank Homestay** is below the road and has clear views of the lake. You can also pitch your own tent at the **campsite ($)** on the far side of the village. There is a temporary toilet block and water seems to come from the stream. Two of Korzok's scruffier tent camps unfortunately block your view.

If you are not staying in Korzok but need to stop here for a meal, your best option

RUMTSE–TSO MORIRI TREK

The trek from Rumtse to Tso Moriri traverses spectacular, wild scenery where a smattering of nomadic settlements will be your sole human encounter. Best completed between June and mid-October, it's a challenging trek that climbs to a maximum elevation of 5,000m and takes seven days.

Starting at **Rumtse** (4,095m) on the Leh–Manali Highway, two hours' drive south of Leh, the first day of the trek follows the road as far as the Government Bungalow, then cuts up the trail on the right-hand side of the valley, past some old army buildings, and then to the river. It's necessary to cross both the river and the stream to its left before continuing along the valley to the campsite at **Kyamar** (4,383m). In total it'll take you not more than four hours.

Day two starts with a slow ascent of **Kyamar La** (4,870m). Take time to look out for the mighty Indus River snaking by below. When you finally catch your breath at the top, the track splits in two: you need to follow the path to the right that crosses a small stream and then climbs **Mandalchan La** (4,996m). It's a steep descent from the top of the pass to the campsite at **Tisaling** (4,800m). Allow five hours for this section of the trek.

The third day starts gently enough but the climb is steady and ultimately brings you out on top of **Shingbuk La** (5,016m), one of the physical high points of the trek, from where it is possible to see across to Tso Kar. By evening you will be at **Pangunagu** (4,398m) in the sparsely populated Tso Kar basin. Again you should allow five hours for the day's walking.

Tearing yourself away from the campsite may be tough, but you can console yourself with the fact that the first two hours of day four are around the rim of the lake on the dusty but little-used jeep track. A sandy trail then takes you away from Tso Kar, winding through irrigated fields to the campsite at **Nuruchan** (4,500m). You should have plenty of time to picnic, birdwatch and generally idle along the way, as it will take you no more than four hours.

Day five is the shortest day with just three hours of walking. There's a straightforward river crossing first thing, followed by a gentle climb up **Horlam Kongka La** (4,712m). Coming down the other side you have to cross several small streams to reach the campsite at **Rjungkaru** (4,668m) where it is likely you'll meet Tibetan nomads grazing their flocks.

The penultimate day is the longest: allow six hours. The day begins with a strenuous ascent of **Kamayur La** (5,125m), and once you've covered that pass the trail continues to another slightly smaller one, **Gyama La** (5,100m). The rest of the day is spent making your way downhill, across a few small streams, to **Gyama Lhoma** (4,895m), which is the base camp for the Korzok Pass.

Start out early and follow the stream through the wild flower meadows to the top of **Yalung Nyaulung La** (5,450m). By mid-morning you'll be standing at the is **Lhasa Restaurant** ($) in the centre of the village. The fare is unimaginative but portions are hot and filling and prices are reasonable.

What to see The **Tso Moriri Wetland Conservation Reserve** is the official name given to Tso Moriri lake. Some 19km long and 3km wide, it is the largest high-altitude lake in the Himalayas and is fed with water from the Pare Chu. At its deepest the floor of the lake is 105m beneath the surface of the water. The shore is at 4,595m above sea level.

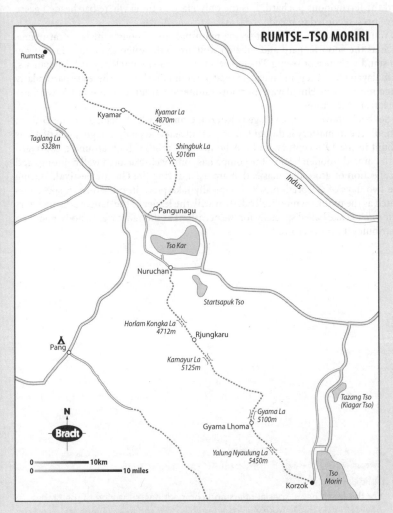

RUMTSE–TSO MORIRI

Rumtse

Kyamar
Kyamar La
4870m

Taglang La
5328m

Shingbuk La
5016m

Indus

Pangunagu

Tso Kar

Nuruchan

Startsapuk Tso

Horlam Kongka La
4712m
Rjungkaru

Pang

Kamayur La
5125m

Tazang Tso
(Kiagar Tso)

Gyama La
5100m
Gyama Lhoma

N

Bradt

Yalung Nyaulung La
5450m

0 ──── 10km
0 ──── 10 miles

Korzok

Tso
Moriri

top surveying the panoramic views not only of Tso Moriri but of the surrounding mountains too. This is the reward for your effort. The trek ends with a steep descent along the Korzok Phu River into **Korzok Village**, where the creature comforts of Tso Moriri Camp (**$$$$**; see page 141) await.

Nobody comes here for the statistics, however. You come here for the scenery and for the wildlife. The turquoise waters of the lake reflect the snow-capped peaks that surround it, the many colours of the rocks and water a veritable artist's palette. Though at first glance you'd think the land supports little vegetation, on closer inspection you will see marshes with multiple species of sedges and reeds, as well as pastures that support grazing livestock.

Birdlife thrives here, and the lake supports a number of rare species including black-necked cranes, brown-headed gulls, great crested and black-necked grebes, and the ferruginous pochard. It is the only place in India where bar-headed geese have been recorded to breed.

You have a strong chance of seeing **mammals** too. Though the large carnivores such as the snow leopard and Tibetan wolf are, more often than not, elusive, you do stand a chance of seeing Tibetan gazelles and Goan antelopes, the Tibetan ass, Himalayan blue sheep and nayan (a type of mountain sheep). There are particularly large numbers of Himalayan marmots sauntering around on the hillsides a little back from the shore.

Set back above Korzok village is **Korzok Gompa**, which belongs to the Drugpa school. The monastery is thought to be around 300 years old, though much of it was rebuilt in the 19th century, and it is home to 35 monks. Built around a courtyard with painted wooden beams, the gompa has some well-executed wall paintings and a collection of grotesque masks that are used during the **Gustor Festival.** During the two days of celebration, which typically take place in midsummer, spectators watch as the monks symbolically destroy evil: the leader of the dancing dismembers a *storma* (a cake baked specially for the occasion) as though it were a body, and then distributes it for the crowd to eat.

6

Leh to Mulbekh

Northwest of Leh, National Highway 1 (NH1) runs parallel to the River Indus, sharing the valley that the mighty river has carved out for itself. In this chapter we'll explore the sites along the road, and those that are (fairly) accessible either side.

This northern part of Ladakh is a natural adventure playground. Visiting adrenaline junkies can pit their strength and skills against the rivers while white-water rafting and kayaking, or explore yet more of the trekking routes linking the Ladakh and Zanskar ranges. Driving on the main roads is straightforward enough, but get away from NH1 and you'll be testing your off-road skills, fording rivers and traversing rocky ground.

Some of Ladakh's richest cultural sites are found here too: Likir is a lively monastery where novice monks giggle and play beneath the watchful eye of a vast, golden Buddha; the beautifully carved and painted shrines at Alchi date back to at least the 12th century and are remarkable for both their age and state of preservation; and the settings of Basgo and Lamayuru, each among rugged, rock landscapes, are truly sights to behold, not to mention masterpieces of architecture and engineering. Continuing north into Kargil district you'll find some of the largest and most impressive standing Buddhas in the world, reminiscent of those destroyed by the Taliban at Bamiyan in Afghanistan. There's also the opportunity to visit the fascinating Brokpa villages of Dha and Hanu where the people have a distinctive culture and claim descent from the troops of Alexander the Great.

PHYANG   *Telephone code: 01982*

Set in a picturesque side valley a short distance back from what is now NH1, Phyang's gompa rises dramatically out of the earth, dominating its surroundings. Look past the gompa, however, and you'll find a higgledy-piggledy patchwork of yellow and green, the irregular layout of fields interspersed with thin, willowy trees, single-storey houses topped with drying fodder, and contentedly grazing *dzo*.

GETTING THERE AND AROUND There are three **buses** a day between Leh and Phyang: they depart around midday, and in the evening, but leave when they are ready rather than at a specific time. The journey takes approximately 45 minutes (depending on the number of request stops), and the fare is Rs25 to the gompa or Rs30 to the top of the village. If the altitude is getting to you, the same buses can be used to get from the gompa to the guesthouse; otherwise it is half an hour's walk.

If you prefer to take a **taxi** from Leh, prices start from Rs649 for a drop-off and Rs843 to go there and back.

There is also a rewarding **trek** from Hunder in the Nubra Valley to Phyang (see page 113).

WHERE TO STAY AND EAT As far as we're concerned, there is only one place to stay in Phyang: the **Hidden North Guesthouse** (*8 rooms*; \ *226 007*; m *941 921 8055*; e *office@hiddennorth.com; www.hiddennorth.com;* **$$**). Perched at the top of the village with what have to be among the best views in Ladakh, the guesthouse is run by a charming Ladakhi-Italian family who have been in the tourism business since the 1990s but opened this guesthouse (which is also their home) and campsite only in 2010.

Open year-round, the guesthouse has broadband internet and immaculate bathrooms. If you're taking your meals here (which are delicious), expect lively conversation in your choice of English, French, German, Italian or Ladakhi. Husband Tashi is an experienced trekking guide and can arrange a variety of treks and tours, including a five-day trek from Phyang to the Nubra Valley, through his travel agency **Hidden North Adventures** (*contact details as for guesthouse*).

If you prefer to be closer to the monastery, the **Chirpon Camping Site** (\ *226 009*; m *941 921 9412*; **$**) has plenty of space to pitch your tent and also offers one room with an attached toilet (**$**).

WHAT TO SEE No-one knows exactly how old Phyang Gompa (\ *226 005*; ⊕ *c08.00–20.00; entrance fee Rs50*) is. The monastery was founded in 1515 during the reign of King Jamyang Namgyal, but there may well have been a settlement here prior to this. The bulk of the buildings were constructed two decades later. Some 70 monks reside here today.

Parking is at the rear of the gompa, and from here you climb a steep slope that passes beneath a yellow **gateway** topped with two golden (but anatomically questionable) deer. On your left is the gompa's **carpentry workshop** where everyday items such as new window frames and doors are being made, and set against the wall are several slabs of stone etched with stupas and Tibetan script.

At the top of the slope, where you may well have to stop to catch your breath (blame the altitude), the new parts of the monastery are to your right and the older, more interesting parts are to your left. It is traditional to circulate a Buddhist temple or gompa in a clockwise direction (see *Cultural etiquette*, page 73), so visit the old part first.

The old part of the gompa is a bit of a warren: expect to get lost. Wherever you walk, watch your head and your feet, as doors are low and the floors and stairs are very uneven.

Your first port of call should be the **main prayer hall**, which is accessed up a decidedly rickety wooden staircase from the internal courtyard. A single monk stands guard in the antechamber, collecting entrance fees (see opposite) and ensuring no photos are taken inside.

The prayer hall is a particularly dark space, the only light entering through the doorway and a single window beneath the roof. The ceiling is supported on a dozen red pillars, evenly spaced, and as your eyes adjust to the gloom, the fabulous **murals** start coming into focus. Predominantly depicted in shades of red and green, the facial characteristics of these 200-year-old figures are in some cases decidedly Mongol. A trio of brocade silk banners further break up the room, and along the back wall devotees leave Rs10 offerings at the feet of ten statues of varying sizes, each one representing a significant figure in the development of Tibetan Buddhism.

Making your way carefully back down the staircase and out of the courtyard, turn left. Immediately on your right is a pair of short, red doors with brass knockers. These doors are kept locked, so if there's no monk present to let you in, you'll need to return to the prayer hall and ask.

This lower room contains the much-advertised highlight of the gompa: finely preserved **16th-century wall paintings**. For us, however, the accompanying objects were also of great curiosity: look out for the grotesque, tiger-legged statue of four-armed Mahakala who converted four demons to Buddhism; a ceremonial drum and severed goat horns; and Mongolian spears and shields left as offerings by warriors who visited here.

Working your way around now to the modern part of the gompa, you'll see more of the monks, as this is where they live and work. The western end of the building has some impressive **modern decoration**, with hundreds of garish colours and patterns competing for your attention, and also three newly painted **stupas** set alongside a fourth, red reliquary reminiscent of a Royal Mail post box.

Around Phyang   Leaving Phyang west on NH1, you pass a number of intriguing sites, starting with the dramatic **confluence of the Indus and Zanskar rivers**, where a number of popular rafting trips begin (see *Rafting*, page 96). The small **Gurudwara Sri Pathar Sahib** attracts a small number of Sikh devotees and an occasional tourist, but most visitors to the area drive straight on to the clearly marked **Magnetic Hill**. This optical illusion makes it appear that cars are rolling up hill, defying gravity, and it's a popular diversion for domestic tourists in particular.

NIMMU   *Telephone code: 01982*

Though you would never plan your itinerary to incorporate Nimmu, there are a few helpful things here if you're passing through. It's a ribbon development that's grown up to service the local army base at the western edge of the village, and also those travelling along NH1.

The only proper hotel in Nimmu is **Hotel Takshos** (❨ *225 064;* **$$**), which has a fair-sized garden restaurant where tour buses occasionally stop. **Wimbledon Continental**

(225 656) and **Nilza Guesthouse** also both offer basic rooms with shared bathrooms (**$**) but you have to call in to see if they have space, as they don't have phones.

The central part of the village is composed of a run of largely un-signed shops on both sides of the road. Here you'll find **Norling Restaurant** (**$**), which does cheap Tibetan dishes and also STD calling. Several shops along from here (facing away from Leh) is a pharmacy, the **Rafta Medical Hall** (⊕ 09.30–18.30). On the opposite side of the street is the slightly larger and cleaner **Namgyal Restaurant** (**$–$$**), which also sells bottled water and fresh juices, a **public toilet** (far from the worst we've seen), an un-named store selling mobile phone credit, and an **SBI ATM** (⊕ 24hrs).

As you're leaving the town westwards, take a quick look at the unusual **sky blue stupa** and also the larger, crumbling **white stupa** that is gradually being engulfed by the army base. Refrain from taking photos of the latter.

BASGO   *Telephone code: 01982*

Few places in the world can boast a landscape as dramatic as that at Basgo. The village takes its name from a rock the shape of a bull's head (*ba-mgo*) and it is situated at a point where the Indus Valley narrows, the fort and monastery temples clinging precariously to the cliffs above.

HISTORY   The history of Basgo can be traced back to the 15th century with the construction of the Rab-brtan Lhartse Khar (Divine Peak of Great Stability), the rock-top citadel whose ruins are still visible today. It is possible that sections of an older, 11th-century, structure are underneath, but it is is not known for sure. The citadel was the residence of Gragspa Bum, ruler of Lower Ladakh, who alternated his capital between Basgo and Tingmosgang.

The gompa's Chamba Lhakhang dates from this early period of construction, and later buildings were added to the complex during the reigns of Tsewang and Sengge Namgyal in the 16th and early 17th centuries. The first European visitor, a Portuguese named Diego d'Almeida, visited Basgo in 1603, appreciating it in all its glory.

Basgo was besieged by Mongol forces for three years in the late 1600s and thanks to its natural water supplies and carefully stored food reserves survived the ordeal. When Basgo was attacked by the Dogras in 1834 it was not so lucky, however: the buildings were ransacked and many of the treasures they contained carted off by the soldiers.

GETTING THERE AND AWAY   Basgo is situated 42km from Leh and it's a good road to travel along, unless of course you get stuck behind a military convoy. If you do not have your own transport, you'll be dropped on the main road about 20 minutes' walk from the monastery.

This side road winds past small houses to the river, which you'll have to wade across or, if you're in a car or minibus, ford. Fear not, it's only mid-shin deep. A new, steel bridge has been partially constructed but until the road up to it on either side has been completed, it is essentially useless. There was no sign of construction work taking place when we visited, so getting wet feet may be your only option for quite a time to come.

Taxis can be hired from Leh from Rs1,041 one-way or Rs1,351 return.

WHERE TO STAY AND EAT   There are several unassuming but convenient places to stay in Basgo. The small but reasonably well-kept **Chamba Guesthouse & Restaurant** (**$**) is on the main road, quite a trek from the gompa. Other options include the **Lagang Guesthouse** (225 102; **$**) and **Tsering Khangsar Guesthouse**

φ *225 108;* $), both of which are in the village itself. For a greater variety of options, including mid-range hotels, you'll need to continue on to Likir or go back to Leh.

If you want a quick snack, try the basic but easily accessible **National Highway Restaurant** (φ *225 648;* $$), which is on the main road.

WHAT TO SEE Basgo Gompa was founded in 1515 but much of what you see dates from a century later. Perched on top of a rocky crag above a jade green oasis, this crow's nest of a gompa seems to be pushing organically up out of the ground. In fact, sadly, the movement is the other way round: as our guide told us emphatically, 'it is melting'. With every passing year the elements take their toll, the rains dissolving the baked mud bricks, until one day in the not so distant future the gompa and surrounding buildings will return to the earth whence they came.

There are four main parts to the complex, the most impressive of which is the **Chamba Lhakhang** (*entrance fee Rs20*). The oldest of the three temples, it is built mostly from mud brick and mud mortar, with some additional sections of compressed earth, which is why it is so fragile. The incredible **wall paintings** inside were commissioned by King Tsewang Namgyal in the 16th century and so are a little newer than the building. It is thought that this is the only temple from the period to survive with its murals intact. Look out for the Buddhas of the past, present and future; a depiction of the Drugpa scholar Padma Karpo; and panels showing the king and his courtiers.

The temple's central hall has an exquisitely **painted ceiling**, supported on colourful **wooden columns**, beneath which is a three-storey **Maitreya Buddha**. It is made from clay but covered with gilt.

The **Serzang Khakhang** (*entrance fee Rs20*) takes its name from the copper-gilded **Maitreya Buddha** it houses. Though the idol was actually built earlier, it was gilded on the orders of Sengge Namgyal in 1622 and Queen Khatun, his mother, donated the precious stones used in its ornamental crown and bracelet. Beautiful brocade silk covers the lower part of the statue.

The third of the temples is the rather squat-looking **Chamchung Lhakhang**, a small structure dedicated to protector deities. Given its similarity in design to a Balti mosque, some academics have suggested that this may have been its original purpose, though it certainly was used as a Buddhist temple soon after. The temple has recently been restored.

Surrounding the temples are the ruins of the **palace**. Unlike the gompa buildings, no maintenance work was ever done here, and indeed the wooden beams that supported the roofs were likely repurposed for other buildings. It is still possible to appreciate, however, the scale of the site and what an impression it must have made on early visitors.

In India you inevitably spend rather more time than you'd like in the toilet, and many of those experiences are unrepeatably horrid. What a pleasant surprise, then, to find Basgo's **loo with a view**! Step into the cubicles next to the gompa's parking and the windows open out on to one of the finest scenes around. Just don't step into the hole while you're staring enthralled into the distance.

LIKIR *Telephone code: 01982*

Likir is utterly charming and our stay at the monastery school (see page 150) was one of the most pleasurable experiences we had while researching this book. Staying the night also gives you the chance to explore the gompa later on in the day (or, indeed, early in the morning) without the presence of other tourists.

GETTING THERE AND AROUND There is a daily **bus** direct from Leh to Likir, which departs around 04.00. Far more frequent are the buses to Saspol and other locations further along the highway: you can take one of these and get off at the crossroads to Likir. It's a total distance of 52km along a well-maintained road (excluding the last bumpy 6km side road if you continue from the crossroads to Likir itself) and the journey takes 2 hours 30 minutes. Tickets cost Rs100.

Heading in the opposite direction, if you stand on the main road you can hail one of the buses going to/from Lamayuru. This journey also takes 2 hours 30 minutes and costs Rs100 per person.

Likir village and gompa are a ten-minute drive from the main road along a largely unmade track. You can walk this route but it's hot, dusty and takes well over an hour. Consequently, hitchhiking here is common. If you're in a car, it's likely you will be asked for a lift.

WHERE TO STAY

Hotel Lhukhil (24 rooms) 227 137; www.nomindhomestay.com. Modelled apparently on a Chinese temple (though you'll have to use your imagination), Likir's best hotel lies a short distance below the gompa. Rooms are attractively decorated & all have en-suite bathrooms. You can take your evening meal sat out in the garden looking across at the mountains or, a few hours later, at an impressively clear array of stars. B/fast included. (In the same building is also the No Mind Homestay (m 941 989 2237; www. nomindhomestay.com) where you can participate in yoga & meditation retreats.) Both the hotel & the homestay are open from May to Oct only. **$$$**

Dolker Tongol (3 rooms) Above gompa; 227 141. A short walk past Chhume (see next listing) is this similar guesthouse with top-floor views down towards the gompa. Prices are charged pp rather than per room. B/fast & dinner included. **$$**

Chhume Guesthouse (2 rooms) Above gompa; m 990 697 3732. Just a stone's throw from the Maitreya Buddha (see opposite), this family-run guesthouse has basic rooms with a shared toilet. Additional 1st-floor rooms were under construction at the time of going to print. Camping in the garden also possible. B/fast & dinner inc. **$-$$**

Gompa School (4 rooms) Above the teachers' quarters are several clean guest rooms offered 1st to volunteers at the school and then to other visitors. Water is from a tap in the yard & the toilets (one Western, one squat) are round the back, but this is more than compensated for by the fun & games of the 26 boy monks. You can also join them for dinner. No charge is made for accommodation or meals but a donation is appreciated: Rs500 for a room & evening meal is appropriate.

WHERE TO EAT AND DRINK There is a small, outdoor café, the **Namglal Restaurant** (**$-$$**), next to the gompa's parking. The menu has an unremarkable selection of Indian and Chinese dishes, and more often than not only noodles are available, but the redeeming feature is undoubtedly the filter coffee.

Free black tea is served to all visitors at the **Gompa School**. Free drinking water is also available from the clearly marked tap in the gompa's parking area.

SHOPPING There is one small shop in Likir, located by the gompa's parking area. It sells sweets, crisps, biscuits and bottled soft drinks in lurid colours, but that's about it.

WHAT TO SEE One of the oldest monasteries in Ladakh is **Likir Gompa** (⊕ *May–Oct 08.00–13.00 & 14.00–18.00; Nov–Apr 10.00–13.00 & 14.00–16.00*). It was founded in 1065 during the reign of King Lhachen Gyalpo, and then rebuilt 700 years later. There are around 70 adult monks living here as well as 26 boy monks who are studying. They come here from the age of six. Today the monks follow the Gelugpa school of Buddhism, but prior to the 15th century the monastery was connected to the Tibetan Kadampa order. The head lama is the brother of the Dalai Lama, though he's permanently absent from Likir.

The most striking thing at the gompa is the 23m **Maitreya Buddha**. This golden statue stands out above the monastery buildings, surveying the land around, and was completed in 1999. The best place to photograph it from is the roof of the monastery school: there's a ladder from the first floor.

The entrance to the **Main Dukhang** is beneath a covered veranda painted with the guardians of the four directions. Inside you'll fine a throne for the head lama, stupas containing statues of Avalokitesvara and Aitabha, and three very large statues: two of the Sakyamuni Buddha and a third of the Maitreya Buddha. The ancient *thangkas* attached to the walls are unrolled only during the winter festival. One shows the Sakyamuni Buddha and the other Likir's guardian deity.

The **New Dukhang**, diagonally across the courtyard, is around 200 years old. It too has a painted veranda but, unusually, the figures here are not the four guardians but instructional scenes showing lamas how to behave and how to wear their robes. Inside too the walls are richly painted with more modern murals including the 1,000-armed Avalokitesvara, the 35 Buddhas and the 16 Arhats (those who have achieved nirvana).

Outside the New Dukhang is a ladder leading to the **zinchen** above. This is the head lama's room and it is where the Dalai Lama stays when he visits. It's an Aladdin's cave of *thangkas*, statues and other curios. Particularly fine are the 21 variations of the White Tara.

ALCHI *Telephone code: 01982*

Alchi is one of Ladakh's foremost cultural attractions on account of its superbly preserved frescoes, many of which date from the early medieval period. As the monks are no longer in residence, and it's a key stop on package tours in the summer months, it can feel overly touristy: try to get here early or late in the day when it is not crowded, and appreciate it as you would a museum rather than as a living monastic community.

HISTORY Alchi's position, tucked back from the historic caravan route that winds through Ladakh, has been its saving grace. After the monastery was founded in the 11th century it was a relatively wealthy place (as attested to by the superb murals) but attracted little attention from outside. When the Dogra invasion came in the 1830s, many of Ladakh's monasteries were sacked but Alchi passed beneath their radar, and consequently the frescoes survived.

GETTING THERE AND AWAY There are three **buses** a day from Leh to Alchi, and it would also be possible to take any bus heading between Leh and Kargil on the highway (for example the bus from Leh to Lamayuru; see page 159) and to get off at the turn-off to Alchi, walking the last 4km. From Leh it is a 70km, three-hour journey for which you should expect to pay Rs120.

Taxis from Leh to Alchi cost from Rs1,690 one-way and from Rs2,197 return. You can combine Likir, Alchi and Lamayuru in a long return day trip from Rs4,768, or add Phyang, Basgo, Rezdong and Dah to that itinerary (split over two days) from Rs9,182.

WHERE TO STAY Accommodation in Alchi is considerably more expensive than in the surrounding villages on account of the popularity of the gompa as a tourist attraction. You might, therefore, consider staying elsewhere (eg: 19km away in Likir; see page 149) and visiting Alchi for the day, especially if your budget is tight. At the time of going to print, **Hotel Lower Ladakh** (m *941 996 1025;* **$$**) seemed to be undergoing some building work, but it should reopen in time for the summer 2014 season.

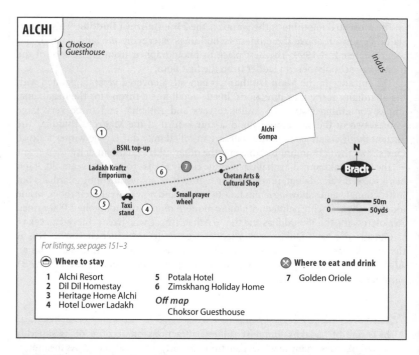

ALCHI

Choksor
Guesthouse

Indus

Alchi
Gompa

BSNL top-up

Ladakh Kraftz
Emporium

Chetan Arts &
Cultural Shop

Small prayer
wheel

Taxi
stand

N

Bradt

0 — 50m
0 — 50yds

For listings, see pages 151–3

Where to stay

1 Alchi Resort
2 Dil Dil Homestay
3 Heritage Home Alchi
4 Hotel Lower Ladakh
5 Potala Hotel
6 Zimskhang Holiday Home

Off map
Choksor Guesthouse

Where to eat and drink

7 Golden Oriole

Alchi Resort (22 rooms) 227 177;
m 941 921 8636; e alchiresort@gmail.com; www.
alchiresort.tripod.com. Close to the taxi stand,
Alchi Resort comprises a large house behind which
are a number of bungalows set a little too close
together. It seems rather chaotic & in need of
updating but is nonetheless popular with domestic
tourists who have bought their room & all meals as
a package. **$$$$**

Zimskhang Holiday Home (16 rooms)
227 086; m 941 917 9715; e zimskhang@
yahoo.com; www.zimskhang.com. Norboo Gaitsan
& his team run this pleasant guesthouse midway
between the taxi stand & the gompa: it's on the
pedestrian street so you'll need to carry your bags.
Rooms are clean & in season you can relax with
a freshly squeezed apricot juice in the garden.
$$$$

Heritage Home Alchi (13 rooms) 227
125; m 941 981 1535; e heritagehomealchi@
rediff.com. Heritage Home is situated right on
the doorstep of the gompa but hence accessible

only on foot. It's an attractively carved building
with substantially more character than the other
accommodation options. Wi-Fi included. **$$$**

Potala Hotel (11 rooms) m 941 988
0182. The Potala may have seen better days, but
carpets & linens are clean despite being worn.
The bathrooms are reasonable & have running hot
water; the bedrooms are large & light. You can take
meals sat among the fruit trees in the garden if so
inclined. **$$$–$$**

Choksor Guesthouse (12 rooms) 227
084; http://hotelalchichoskorleh.com. Situated
1km from the gompa back towards the main road
& therefore less convenient than other choices,
Choskor is nevertheless a pleasant place to stay with
mature gardens & a roof terrace. Meals are available
on request. The guesthouse is set back from the road:
stop at the prayer wheel & look for the turquoise
building with stained wood window frames. **$$**

Dil Dil Homestay (2 rooms) 227 100.
Alchi's most basic option is central & cheap but the
shared bathroom requires a stiff stomach. **$**

WHERE TO EAT AND DRINK The best meals in Alchi are to be had at **Zimskhang
Holiday Home** (see above). The large garden restaurant is popular with tour groups;
there are plenty of tables, most of them in the shade, and the menu is wide, if
unimaginative. Take a good book to read and enjoy a Kingfisher beer (Rs100) while

you wait for your food as it's invariably understaffed and service is consequently at a snail's pace, albeit willing.

Meals are also served in the garden of **Heritage Home Alchi** (see opposite). It's a shady spot and the red and white gingham tablecloths give it a cutesy feel. Both this and the restaurant at Zimskhang fit into the cheap and cheerful (**$$**) price bracket.

If all you want is a coffee or a quick snack, **Golden Oriole** (aka the German Bakery) is a reasonable alternative. Situated slightly further along the pedestrian street, they serve a variety of fresh juices, milkshakes and *lassis* as well as homemade cookies (Rs20) and croissants (Rs40). Everything looks as though it could do with a good scrub, but the free Wi-Fi might tempt you in regardless.

SHOPPING The pedestrian street between Alchi's taxi stand and the monastery is lined with shops and stalls selling all manner of naff, rather pricey souvenirs, including the usual selection of turquoise beads, bundles of prayer flags, bangles, incense, grotesque masks and occasional wooden puppets. You won't find anything unique for sale here and will have to haggle hard for anything approaching a fair price. The appropriately named **Ladakh Kraftz Emporium** and, situated closer to the monastery, **Chetan Arts and Cultural Shop**, are probably the pick of the bunch.

OTHER PRACTICALITIES On the rare occasions when the Indian phone company BSNL is actually providing an internet service, you can get free **Wi-Fi** at Golden Oriole (see above) and Heritage Home Alchi (see opposite). Mobile **phone top-up** is available from an unnamed shop by the taxi stand: look for the BSNL advertising in the window.

WHAT TO SEE The monastery complex of **Alchi Chhoskhor** (🕐 *08.00–18.00, closed 13.00–14.00; entrance fee Rs20/50 local/foreigner*) is composed of six temples, stupas, Mani stones and monks' cells. Tradition has it that Alchi was founded by Rinchen Zangpo (see box, page 155) during his visit to Ladakh in the early 11th century, though the earliest surviving buildings date from around 200 years later. Although it remains a holy place first and a tourist attraction second, the monks no longer live here: it is cared for by Gelugpa monks from Likir.

The oldest of the temples at Alchi, and indeed one of the oldest in Ladakh, is the **Sumtsek Lhakhang**, which dates from 1217. This three-storey structure is built in a traditional Tibetan style but decorated with delicate woodcarvings and fine, tapered columns more typically associated with the artisans of Kashmir. Inside, the wall by the door is covered with 1,028 blue Buddhas, and some of the statues set into niches are as much as 5m tall. The quality of the frescoes is unrivalled, though in places modern restoration work has been poorly executed.

Roughly contemporary to this is the **dukhang** at the centre of the complex. The wooden door is believed to be original, and hence is more than 800 years old. Here 1,000 small Buddhas are painted on to the walls alongside numerous *mandalas*, divinities (both male and female) and protectors of the temple.

The newest of these three temples (though only by a decade or so!) is the **Jampe Lhakhang**, which experts have inferred dates from around 1225. The interior here is less well preserved (probably due to the proximity to the river), but there are still some striking items: the four images of the boddhisatva Manjushri (from which the lhakhang takes its alternative name, the Manjushri Temple) sat back to back atop a vast platform; further images of Manjushri seated on a lion throne, flanked by lions, wearing a crown of flowers, and bedecked in jewels; and a painted wooden ceiling.

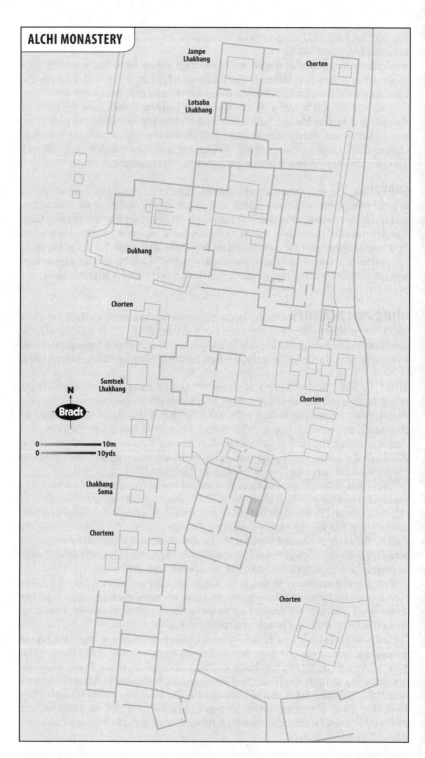

ALCHI MONASTERY

Jampe Lhakhang

Chorten

Lotsaba Lhakhang

Dukhang

Chorten

Sumtsek Lhakhang

Chortens

N

Bradt

0 ——— 10m
0 ——— 10yds

Lhakhang Soma

Chortens

Chorten

Visiting Alchi, Mangyu or Lamayuru, you cannot help but come across the name of Rinchen Zangpo, the Lotsawa, or 'Great Translator'.

Born in Guge in 958, Rinchen Zangpo was ordained at the age of 13 and travelled across India numerous times in search of ancient Buddhist scriptures. He studied at the leading centres of Buddhist learning, returning later to Kashmir and Tibet with the texts that he would then translate.

During his lifetime, Rinchen Zangpo is credited with building 108 monasteries and temples, and in doing so reviving Buddhism in Tibet and Ladakh. He engaged the services of 32 Kashmiri artists to decorate the monasteries he founded, and so we have him to thank for the oldest artworks at Alchi, Basgo, Lamayuru, Nyarma and Sumda, among others.

En route to Tibet once again in 1042, Rinchen Zangpo met Saint Atisa and the two entered into a lengthy debate as to the nuances of the sacred texts. Rinchen Zangpo realised that his earlier translations had missed certain subtleties of meaning, and so at the ripe old age of 84 he became a student once again. He died aged 98 in 1055.

Note that it is not permitted to take photographs inside the temples, and you should also refrain from smoking or drinking alcohol while in the complex.

Southwest of Alchi, away from the Chhoskhor, is the **Shangrong Lhakhang**, part of a complex of stupas and other small structures that date from the 1400s. On the verge of collapse in 2007, it has been temporarily repaired by the Achi Association (*www.achiassociation.org*) pending further work when funding allows. The interior frescoes, which include an illustration of the 84 Mahasiddhas and several important inscriptions, are among the few surviving examples linked to the Drigung school of art.

Around Alchi Two hours' walk west of Alchi is tiny **Mangyu**. To reach it you must cross the small bridge across the Indus and follow the track past the village of Gera into a gorge. The track ascends from the right bank of the stream. The way, though not marked with signposts, is fairly clear due to the number of feet that have walked this path before. You chance upon the gompa quite suddenly as it is low-lying and pretty well camouflaged behind the rocks.

It is likely that **Mangyu Gompa** was founded by Rinchen Zangpo at roughy the same time as Alchi, though it is a much smaller complex. There are four principal temples, each housing interesting statues, and also a number of murals, though less well executed than those in Alchi.

If you prefer not to walk, there is a weekly **bus** from Leh to Mangyu (*summer 13.30 Sat; winter 13.00; Rs113*). A **taxi** can be hired from Rs2,043 one-way or Rs2,655 return, though it is probably best to combine it with a trip to Alchi and Likir from Rs3,164.

ULETOKPO *Telephone code: 01982*

Uletokpo is a resort town, an attractive spot by the river with three excellent places to stay for those travelling between Leh and Kargil. It is also the closest settlement to the 19th-century Rizong Gompa and its sister nunnery, Chulichan.

GETTING THERE AND AWAY The road from Alchi to Uletokpo is in good condition and predominantly surfaced with recently laid tarmac. Unlike Alchi, Uletokpo is on the National Highway, so any of the **buses** running between Leh and Kargil (or villages along the route) have to pass by: you can ask any of them to stop here and, if they have space, have them pick you up.

By **taxi**, LTOCL offers a two-day trip to Basgo, Likir, Alchi, Rezong, Uletokpo and Lamayuru from Rs6,415. Alternatively, you can go there and back from Leh from Rs1,898 one-way or Rs2,467 return.

WHERE TO STAY AND EAT Visitors are advised to book a meal plan at their camp if staying in Uletokpo. The food in all three places listed below is superb.

Uley Eco Resort (70 rooms) m 941 917 8088; e uleyadv@gmail.com; www.uleyecoresorts. com. Similarly luxurious to sister property Uley Ethnic Resort & home to some very funky huts. There's nothing to choose between them in terms of levels of service or eco-friendly credentials. The Eco Resort rents out bikes & you can white-water raft virtually from the doorstep. **$$$$–$$$$$**

Uley Ethnic Resort (31 tents, 15 cottages) 253 640; e ulecamp@gmail.com; www. uleresort.com. Laid out across a large area of apple & apricot groves overlooking the river, this has to be one of the most photogenic holiday camps in Ladakh. The wooden cottages, which resemble alpine chalets, have hot water thanks to solar panels on the roof. Meals are homemade, organic & delicious. Highly recommended. **$$$$–$$$$$**

West Ladakh Camp & Resort (17 tents) Run by Camps of Ladakh (see page 85), West Ladakh is set amid a 20-acre ranch on the bank of the Indus. All tents are en suite & bathrooms have hot water. Multi-cuisine meals are served in a communal tent or out in the garden. **$$$$**

WHAT TO SEE Uletokpo offers easy access to the river and is a popular starting point for **white-water rafting** trips. Although you can arrange these through the local resorts/camps, you will probably be charged a premium for doing so: it is better to contact Splash Ladakh in Leh (see page 96).

Around Uletokpo

Other than to have a relaxing break amid stunning scenery, the reason for staying in Uletokpo is that it is just 5km from the **Rizong Gompa**, also known as the Yuma Changchubling. This is a relatively new monastery, established by the Lama Tsultim Nima in 1831, although there was a hermitage here before. Some 40 monks from the Gelugpa order reside here and they follow the strict Vinaya rules: they are not allowed to leave the monastery unless seriously ill; in the hours of darkness they are forbidden to leave their cell, which has neither bedding nor a fire; they may not touch anything handled by women (including family members); and they may have no personal possessions. The gompa comprises a number of attractive whitewashed buildings. Among the items preserved here are a **statue of the Mahakala** (a protector deity prominent in both the Buddhist and Hindu pantheons); **relics** of the gompa's founder; and, in the Thin-Chen shrine, **frescoes**.

A further 2km on from the gompa is the **Chulichan Nunnery** where younger nuns follow a curriculum of Tibetan language classes and meditation, and older nuns work in the fields, spin yarn and press apricot kernels to make apricot oil. About 20 nuns live here, and the nunnery is subordinate to the monastery.

KHALTSI *Telephone code: 01982*

Khaltsi is a lively place, a market town where the majority of people you see are locals. It is the point, historically and now, where there has been a bridge across the Indus

River, and it is the point where the road from Kashmir first enters the Indus Valley. It's not necessarily a place you'd want to visit in its own right (though there is a gompa and the ruins of a fortress here; see page 158) but if you have your own transport and want somewhere to stretch your legs and have a cup of tea, it's a conveniently located option.

HISTORY The area around Khaltsi has been occupied for at least 2,000 years, and a fragmentary rock inscription discovered locally has been attributed to the Kushan king Vima Kadphises (r AD90–100). Roughly contemporary to this, other carvings thought to have been made by the Dards (see page 18) depict a man hunting antelope, and a woman carrying a basket upon her back.

The first major bridge on the site was constructed by the Dardic king Lha Chen Naglug in the mid 12th century. It must have revolutionised local transport and certainly would have been responsible for Khaltsi becoming a prominent local settlement. It was a shrewd move by the ruler, not only for the local economy, as he could charge customs duties on every shipment crossing the river to Khaltsi.

GETTING THERE AND AWAY Khaltsi lies 99km from Leh along NH1. There is a direct daily **bus** (departs 15.30 in summer & 13.00 in winter; Rs88), or you can take one of the buses heading to Lamayuru or Kargil. By **taxi** the fare from Leh starts from Rs2,601 one-way or Rs3,381 return. If you are approaching Khaltsi from the other direction, taxis from Kargil are currently priced at Rs3,810 one way, or Rs5.070 return.

The road through Khaltsi itself is currently unmade: it winds downhill to the river and then back up again as it enters the town. A new, steel bridge is currently under construction and, once completed, this will remove the need for the diversion. It is likely they will tarmac the approach road at the same time, making for an altogether more comfortable ride.

If you are approaching Khaltsi from the Kargil side (or indeed carrying on through the village towards Mulbekh), you will need to stop at the **police checkpoint** and show your passport. Formalities take a matter of minutes, though you may be asked to stay for tea and a chat.

Note that Khaltsi is also written as Khalsi or Khalatse on some maps.

WHERE TO STAY AND EAT Khaltsi is the kind of place you drive through rather than stop and spend an extended period of time. However, if you've missed breakfast and are ravenous, you might try the large, fairly clean **Punjabi Dhaba** (**$$**). Immediately across the street is the enchantingly named, though less enchanting-looking **NH1 Garden Café** (**$–$$**), but the Dhaba is probably a better bet.

If you need to stay overnight, the **Hidden Valley Guesthouse** (6 *rooms;* \ 224 047; m 946 973 6293; **$$**) is comfortable and clean. Owner Stanzin Dorjay and his family will also provide meals on request. You might also consider the larger **Hotel Namra** (*16 rooms; Temisgam;* \ 229 033; **$$**) close to Khaltsi.

OTHER PRACTICALITIES It is possible to buy mobile phone top-ups in Khaltsi and also to make STD phone calls: look out for the signboards along the main street.

WHAT TO SEE As you enter Khaltsi from the direction of Leh, **Khaltsi Gompa** is up a side road to the right. It's signposted so you won't miss it. It's a higgledy-piggledy structure that looks both to have grown out of the surrounding rock and to be collapsing once again into it.

There was once a **fortress** at Khaltsi, guarding the strategically important river crossing, though today scarcely anything is visible of the original structure. Some significant **petroglyphs** have been identified in the grounds, however, including an image of a yak charging at a snow leopard.

Around Khaltsi Immediately after Khaltsi's police checkpoint (see page 157) the road forks: the left fork (the main road) continues to Kargil and ultimately Srinagar, and the right fork is signposted for Batalik and Dha-Hanu. Taking the right fork brings you shortly to the **Domkhar Rock Art Sanctuary**. This outdoor museum encompasses some superb petroglyphs of human figures, stupas, animals and religious symbols and shows the artistic mastery of Ladakh's early people. They are akin in style to rock carvings further north on the Silk Road in Tajikistan and Kyrgyzstan.

DHA-HANU

Dha and Hanu are two settlements in the northern part of the Indus Valley, just before the LoC. They are the only two villages where it is possible for foreigners to meet the ancient Dards or Brokpa people (see page 18), who claim descent from the forces of Alexander the Great and who are ethnically, linguistically and culturally distinct from other groups in Ladakh. They are, in fact, more closely linked to the Kailash of Afghanistan. Though the area is undoubtedly beautiful and the culture unique, it can feel like a bit of a tourist trap.

GETTING THERE AND AROUND It's around 160km from Leh to Dha-Hanu, and as far as Khaltsi you are **driving** on the reasonably well-maintained NH1. After this point, however, the road condition deteriorates and progress is consequently slower.

The **bus** leaves Leh at 09.00 and arrives in Dha around 17.00. It drops you on the main road rather than in the centre of the village, so you have to continue the last section on foot (about 15 minutes). Tickets cost Rs216. It returns to Leh the following morning, departing from Dha at 08.30. It runs every day except Sunday.

There is a bus from Leh to Hanu on Fri only. It departs at 09.00 and costs Rs151 There is also a daily bus between Khaltsi and Dha. They journey takes 2 hours 30 minutes and tickets cost Rs80. There is currently no bus between Kargil and Dha.

By **taxi**, a one-way/return journey from Leh to Dha starts from Rs4,525/5,884, and to Hanu from Rs4,081/5,306. If you are planning to come here on a day trip, however, it is much faster and cheaper to come from Kargil: you'll pay around Rs2,000 one-way and Rs2,700 return.

If you wish to visit both Dha and Hanu, note that there is no public transport available between them: you would have to find a private vehicle to take you or, alternatively, walk the 8km.

 WHERE TO STAY AND EAT Simple rooms in a comfortable Tibetan house are available at **Skyabapa Guesthouse** (*4 rooms; Dha;* **$**). Meals are taken on the terrace.

OTHER PRACTICALITIES Due to the proximity of the villages to the LoC, it is necessary for visitors to have an Inner Line permit (see box, page 107).

Note that there is no mains electricity in Dha or Hanu: what power there is has to come from a generator, so be particularly sparing with what you use.

WHAT TO SEE Dha and Hanu are simple places and you come here to appreciate the landscape and to meet the people. There is a small **monastery** in Dha, built in 2009 on the site of an older building, which is notable not for its architectural features but because the Brokpa maintain many of their early beliefs, including respect for the Bon pantheon of gods (see box, page 104), alongside Buddhism.

Behind the monastery is a wild apricot orchard beneath which appear to be simply piles of rubble and stones: this is, in fact, what remains of the **fort** or palace at the centre of the first Brokpa settlement, founded in the first century AD.

The Brokpa have two important festivals, and if you are able to watch (or even participate in) them, they will be a high point of your trip. The dates are fixed to neither the solar nor lunar calendar, but do happen at roughly the same time of year. The Brokpa's **New Year** festival takes place at the start of January, and every third year at the start of October they celebrate **Bono Nah** with costumed dances and songs that describe the history of their people. The next Bono Nah celebration will be in 2016.

LAMAYURU *Telephone code: 01982*

Set in a lunar landscape befitting a science fiction movie, Lamayuru has one of the most striking locations in Ladakh. The gompa is one of the oldest and largest in the region, and it is a convenient place to spend the night *en route* from Kargil to Leh.

HISTORY Legend has it that Lamayuru was formed following the visit of the 10th-century Buddhist scholar and sage, Naropa. He drained the lake that filled the valley, and then founded the gompa, which he built with Rinchen Zangpo (see page 155).

GETTING THERE AND AWAY Lamayuru is situated 111km from Leh and 153km from Kargil. It's on NH1, just to the east of Fotu La, which is, at 4,108m, the highest point on the highway. The road surface in both directions is reasonable and so the going is good: Kargil to Lamayuru takes under five hours (though resurfacing was under way between Lamayuru and Mulbekh at the time of going to print, causing delays), and you should be able to get from Lamayuru to Leh in no more than six hours.

Whether you are starting from Kargil or Leh, the cost of reaching Lamayuru by **taxi** is roughly the same. Travelling from Kargil, taxis cost Rs3,390 one-way and Rs4,500 return. From Leh, prices start from Rs3,277 one-way and Rs4,238 to go there and back.

If you are coming from Leh by **bus**, you need to take the bus towards Kargil (which departs daily at 04.30) or Chiktan (departing at 08.00 on Tuesday, Friday and Sunday, returning the following morning). The ticket costs Rs120. The bus to Kargil has to come back again (obviously!), so you can pick it up as it heads to Leh, jumping off at Lamayuru. In this direction the bus leaves Kargil around 05.30 but it is worth checking at the bus stand the night before for confirmation as times can shift about an hour in either direction.

If you plan to come to Lamayuru from Zanskar, it is in fact as quick to **trek** as to drive: east of Rangdum there is a track across Kanjil La (5,255m) which links up with NH1 close to Lamayuru. A person of moderate fitness can complete this trek in two days.

WHERE TO STAY AND EAT
 Hotel Moonland (26 rooms) m 941 988 8598; e hotelmoonland@gmail.com. Large, comfortable hotel with a range of rooms & prices. Upstairs rooms have views of the mountains & monastery; those downstairs overlook the garden. There is a restaurant on site that serves reasonable meals, & Wi-Fi is available for Rs100/hr. Some staff

speak English. Ask for discounts in low season. There are 4 cheaper rooms with shared b/rooms. **$$$**
 Niranjana Guesthouse (20 rooms) Next to the gompa; 224 555; m 941 987 0872; e hotelniranjanalamayuru@yahoo.com. The super location at the foot of the gompa is Niranjana's saving grace. Staff are grumpy & you get far better

6

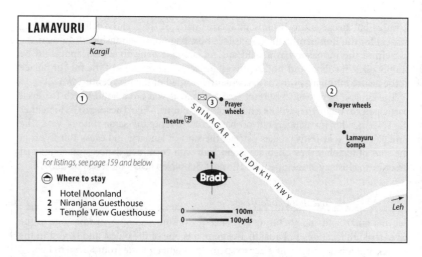

For listings, see page 159 and below

LAMAYURU

Kargil

Prayer wheels

Prayer wheels

Theatre

Lamayuru Gompa

SRINAGAR - LADAKH HWY

Leh

N

Bradt

For listings, see page 159 and below

◆ **Where to stay**

1 Hotel Moonland
2 Niranjana Guesthouse
3 Temple View Guesthouse

0 ————— 100m
0 ————— 100yds

value for money at Moonland. The restaurant is open to non-residents. Buffet-style meals are served in a large dining hall with an attractively painted ceiling. It's convenient, but don't expect much service. **$$$**

🏠 **Temple View Guesthouse** (15 rooms) 📞 224 529. Very basic rooms with shared bathrooms. Great views from the terrace up to the gompa. **$**

SHOPPING Woollen **handicrafts** made by the Women's Self-Help Group at Mundki (📞 252 944) are on sale at Niranjana Guesthouse (see page 159).

OTHER PRACTICALITIES Non-residents can use the Wi-Fi at Hotel Moonland. It costs Rs100 per hour and you can sit either in the dining room or out in the garden.

WHAT TO SEE The earliest parts of **Lamayuru Gompa** date to the 10th century, making it one of the oldest monasteries in Ladakh. It is also one of the largest, and at its peak it housed some 400 monks, though there are only around 150 still in residence.

You can drive right up to the gompa and, once inside, there are far fewer steps than normal, making Lamayuru relatively accessible for those with trouble walking (though it is still not really wheelchair-friendly). Inside the main building is a small, **cloistered courtyard** with bright modern murals, off which is a tiny room lit solely with butter lamps, and also a fair-sized **temple** with a lingering smell of incense. Large windows in the roof let in natural light, enabling you to properly appreciate the large Buddha statues with crowns made of silk, and the cabinets containing the 108-volume Tri-Pitaka scriptures, each one wrapped in orange cloth. Between the cabinets look out for the entrance to the **cave of Naropa**, where he is said to have sat and meditated. The dark **antechamber** contains more fine statues, two large silver horns and, unusually, a set of plastic toy animals.

A staircase off the courtyard leads you to smaller **prayer room** with much older wall paintings, two ceremonial drums (one with dragon finials), seven painted clay statues, three small stupas, and a collection of carved wax offerings.

Outside the main gompa building you will find a large number of **prayer wheels** and also larger **stupas** decorated with lions and phoenix.

Note that women are not permitted to remain on the monastery premises after dark and are also asked to take any used sanitary products with them when they leave.

Beneath the gompa on the main road is the **open-air theatre**, a showground where festival performances take place. Look out for the ornate gateway and colourful, pagoda-like building.

Around Lamayuru Just to the east of Lamayuru is the **moon landscape**, a naturally occurring geological formation that resembles the peaks of whipped meringue or, indeed, how one might imagine the surface of the moon to be.

MULBEKH *Telephone code: 01985*

Mulbekh is a small town, a stop along NH1 that would be unremarkable if it weren't for the presence of the enormous Maitreya Buddha carved into the rock face probably during the 8th century AD. Even if you are just driving through, you should stop for five minutes to appreciate this mighty work of art.

GETTING THERE AND AWAY Mulbekh lies 190km from Leh and 40km from Kargil on NH1. To reach there by bus you should take the daily **bus** between Leh and Kargil. Coming from Leh, the bus leaves at 04.30 and takes 10½ hours. Coming in from the Kargil direction, allow two hours for the journey.

If you prefer to travel by taxi, you have two options from Kargil. **Shared taxis** depart from the bus stand at 07.00 and should ideally be booked the night before. You'll pay Rs800–900 for a seat. If you prefer to have a **taxi** to yourself, a ride from Kargil to Mulbekh costs Rs1,140 one-way or Rs1,515 return.

Coming from Leh by taxi you will pay from Rs4,806 one-way or Rs5,624 return. If you are driving all of the way between Leh and Kargil, drivers will happily stop for a cup of tea or a bite to eat while you look at the Buddha.

If you are driving yourself, there is a rare **fuel station** 1.5km outside of Mulbekh on the road towards Leh. It belongs to Indian Oil.

WHERE TO STAY AND EAT No one was present at Mulbekh's guesthouses when we visited: it must have been a quiet day. The **Maitreya Guesthouse ($$$)** at the western end seems to be the best option, with solar-heated water, but the **Othsnang Guesthouse** (`270 028`) and **Othsal Guesthouse** (both **$–$$**) are certainly more central.

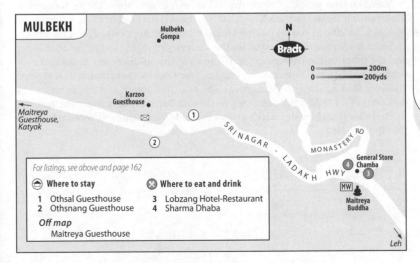

MULBEKH

Mulbekh Gompa

N

Brdt

0 ———— 200m
0 ———— 200yds

Karzoo Guesthouse

Maitreya Guesthouse, Katyok

①

②

SRINAGAR – LADAKH HWY

MONASTERY RD

General Store Chamba

④ ●③

MW

Maitreya Buddha

For listings, see above and page 162

🛏 **Where to stay**
1 Othsal Guesthouse
2 Othsnang Guesthouse
Off map
  Maitreya Guesthouse

✶ **Where to eat and drink**
3 Lobzang Hotel-Restaurant
4 Sharma Dhaba

Leh

Note that the **Karzoo Guesthouse**, though still marked with a sign, and a prominent local landmark, no longer rents out rooms.

The best of the local accommodation options is not in Mulbekh at all but 7km further on in Katyok. Even so, **Nun Kun Camp** (20 tents) (*Katyok;* ✆ *01982 251 676;* $$$$) is quite run-down and the staff aren't terribly friendly. You're better off carrying on to Kargil or Lamayuru.

For a very quick bite to eat if you are ravenous (but probably best avoided otherwise), you can get hot snacks and cold drinks at the **Lobzang Hotel Restaurant** (m *946 973 7773;* $) and the **Sharma Dabha** (m *946 924 0125;* $), both of which have excellent views of the Maitreya Buddha but leave something to be desired on the hygiene front. We stuck to Coca-Cola to be on the safe side.

SHOPPING There is a **general store** opposite the Maitreya Buddha where you can buy bottled water (Rs20) and chocolate (Rs10).

OTHER PRACTICALITIES There is a small **post office** where you can buy stamps and post letters (and that's about it) immediately next door to the Karzoo Guesthouse.

If you are caught short on your journey and can't stand the thought of going behind a bush, there is a **public toilet** right next to the Maitreya Buddha.

WHAT TO SEE The **Maitreya Buddha**, also known as the Chamba Buddha, is a 9m tall, deep relief carving cut into a large rock at the eastern end of Mulbekh, right on the main road. The combination of Shaivite symbolism and Kashmiri artistic influences (in particular the pronounced kneecaps) suggest that it was produced by Kashmiri Buddhist missionaries, possibly in the eighth century AD.

Though the statue is referred to as the Buddha, some art historians have argued that this is in fact a depiction of Avalokiteshvara, as the figure has four arms and also the symbols associated with him: a lotus flower, a vase of water, a string of rosary beads and a jewel held in one hand.

The modern **Chamba Lhakhang** (*entrance fee Rs20*) was built in 1975 immediately in front of the Buddha, with the frustrating consequence that you now either have to look at the statue cut off below the waist, or stand at its feet and get a distorted view of the body. It is guarded by a monk from Hemis.

Mulbekh Gompa is high up on the cliff, towering 200m above the western end of Mulbekh, but the access track to reach it is at the opposite end of town, just after the Maitreya Buddha as you're entering Mulbekh but on the opposite side of the road.

There are, in fact, two gompas on the site, one belonging to the Gelugpa order and the other to the Drukpa order. Historically this location was important as it enabled local rulers to guard the caravan route below: potential attackers were visible well in advance of their arrival. The principal gompa is a stocky structure, and certainly would have been easy to defend, but it is far less ornate than the monasteries elsewhere in Ladakh and so in reality you're unlikely to want to make the climb up here.

7

The Suru Valley and Zanskar

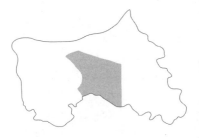

The region of Zanskar is a little slice of heaven, a place where the mountains reach up to kiss the sky. We were once told that only the pure of heart can reach here, and certainly the human population is thin on the ground. It's largely cut off from the outside world (and even now without road access in winter), and few tourists ever venture as far as Zanskar, but those who do are won over by the sheer scale of the scenery, the charm of the local people, and the absolute sense of peace.

From Kargil you reach Zanskar by travelling a long day's journey south by road through the Suru Valley, a softer environment where the road winds through well-tended fields. The impressive Buddha at Kartse Khar can be visited on a day trip from Kargil or *en route* to Zanskar, and the twin peaks of Nun and Kun make both a stunning backdrop to photographs and a formidable challenge for determined mountaineers.

This chapter sits here in the chronology of our guide for two reasons: culturally Zanskar has far more in common with Ladakh than with the Kashmir Valley; and though the principle access route is south from Kargil, it is also possible to get here on foot having trekked from near to Lamayuru on the Leh–Kargil road.

THE SURU VALLEY *Telephone code: 01985*

The photogenic Suru Valley stretches south from Kargil as far as Penzi La, the source of the Suru River. The road mostly follows the river's path along the valley bottom, and along it are strung simple villages where the people make their livings from the land. The valley is particularly colourful in late spring, when the slopes are filled with flowers, and at harvest time when the fields are full of men and women cutting and threshing their grain, and carrying it home to store for the winter.

Unlike Buddhist Zanskar, the population here is a mixture of Tibetans and Dards, the majority of whom are Muslim. Evidence of the area's historic Buddhist population does, however, survive.

KARTSE KHAR Kartse Khar (White Castle) was once a fortified town, though today it is no more than a village. The sole surviving feature that tells us of Kartse's former glory is the 7th- to 8th-century **Chamba Buddha**, a 7m-tall rock-cut Buddha similar in style and quality to the one in Mulbekh but far less well known. It is thought to have been carved by visiting Buddhist missionaries, and academics believe it was inspired by similar standing Buddha carvings in the Swat Valley (now in Pakistan) and Afghanistan, including the Bamiyan Buddha destroyed by the Taliban.

Getting there and away Kartse Khar is a little off the main road: you travel along the main Suru Valley road to Sankoo, a lively village 42km south of Kargil, then cross the river and continue east along a smaller side valley to Kartse, which is around 8km further on. There is a road all the way, but the surface quality deteriorates significantly after Sankoo. The **taxi** from Kargil costs Rs1,260 one-way and Rs1,680 return.

PANIKHAR Panikhar is a tiny place but there is a **J&K Tourist Bungalow ($)** here if you are cycling (or otherwise travelling slowly) and need to spend the night. The **bus** from Kargil to Padum (see page 170) passes through three times a week, otherwise you'll need to take a **taxi** (Rs1,865 one-way or Rs 2,480 return).

At **Damsna**, a pretty place with stone-built houses shortly before Panikhar, you'll get your first sighting of Mount Nun (see box, page 166). You will also need to show your passport at at least one police checkpoint along this stretch of the road to be allowed to continue.

PARKACHIK Most people will only ever pass through the village of Parkachik *en route* to Zanskar. If, however, you plan to climb Nun or Kun, the closest base camp is just 6km away.

Getting there and away Parkachik is itself an unremarkable village set to one side of a particularly rough stretch of road: it is rocky and often too narrow for two vehicles to pass. The main village is up the hill: follow the left-hand fork in the road as you are approaching from Kargil.

The thrice weekly **bus** from Kargil to Padum (see page 170) passes through, or you can hire a **taxi** (Rs2,960 single or Rs3,935 return).

Where to stay and eat There is one budget accommodation option in the village, the **Parkachik Alpine Hut ($)**, though there is also a flat area of grass by the river where you could ask to pitch a tent. The Alpine Hut is a J&K Tourism-run property with a local caretaker. Meals are available on request.

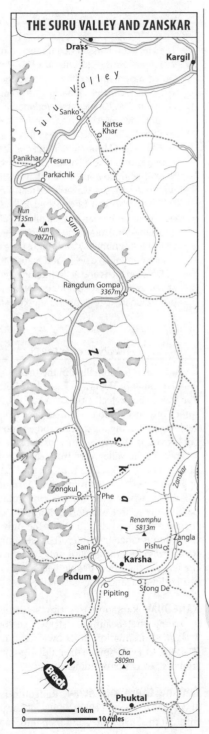

THE SURU VALLEY AND ZANSKAR

7

The Nun-Kun Massif encompasses a number of peaks, the three highest of which are **Nun** (7,135m), **Kun** (7,077m) and **Pinnacle** (6,930m). British and Dutch mountaineers first explored the area at the turn of the 20th century. The first ascent of Pinnacle was accomplished by husband and wife team Fanny and William Hunter Workman in 1906; Kun was climbed by the Italian mountaineer Mario Piacenza in 1913; and Nun was finally summited in 1953 by Bernard Pierre and Pierre Vittoz.

The Indian Mountaineering Foundation (see page 99) allots climbers with ascent routes, and all mountaineers must obtain a permit from them. At the time of going to print, the IMF fee for Nun or Kun was US$3,500 for six people. A reduced price is available for teams of three.

Base camp can be reached in a day's trekking from Tangole (midway between Panikhar and Parkachik) or Gulmatongo (midway between Parkachik and Rangdum), or via the Parkachik Glacier. Climbing is possible from June to October, though July and August are most popular. You will need to allow a minimum of 14 days to acclimatise at each level and complete an ascent.

Detailed plans and an indication of what you can expect are available online at www.nunkunexpedition.com. Nun Kun Expeditions are also able to arrange professional expeditions and supply all necessary paperwork and equipment.

ZANSKAR *Telephone code: 01958*

If you want to trek or climb in the Indian Himalayas, but are frustrated by the overly popular routes in Nepal and Ladakh, replete with queues of tourists and their rubbish, Zanskar is the perfect antidote. A subdistrict of Kargil, right in the heart of J&K, it is sufficiently inaccessible that first-time visitors to the region rarely make the effort to get here, preferring the quicker routes into and out of the Markha and Nubra valleys, but providing you are not in a rush, it is well worth the effort to get here.

Treks in the valley vary from easy day treks, such as the route across the valley floor from Zanskar's administrative centre, Padum, to Karsha, to numerous opportunities to create routes that have never previously been recorded. There are still places where even the trekking guides haven't been, and a single monk may be the only source of information that can supplement your map. In winter when the road is closed due to snow, the only way in and out of Zanskar is by doing the arduous Chadar Winter Trek (see box, pages 176–7) along the frozen Zanskar River, providing insight not only into the challenges of living in this landscape but the lengths that local people will go to in order to ensure that Zanskar's children receive an education.

RANGDUM Randgum is a tiny settlement in a stunning location, surrounded by strange but beautifully striped geological formations. Though probably not a planned destination in its own right, it is the key transit point into and out of Zanskar, and you can see the reddish gompa from miles away as it stands out starkly from its sandy surroundings.

Getting there and away Rangdum is approximately midway between Kargil and Padum, about 110km south of Kargil. Getting there takes a full day, mostly through the Suru Valley and then into Zanskar itself. Though paved in parts, much of the road is little more than a sand and gravel track and, depending on the time of year, you may well find that there are small streams to ford.

The **bus** from Kargil to Padum (see page 170) passes through Rangdum and you are welcome to get off there, though you may be asked to pay the full fare. Remember that the next bus will not come for two days and even then may not have space to pick you up, so factor this in to your onward journey.

It is more comfortable and flexible to take a car and driver from Kargil, splitting the cost between several people if you need to reduce the bill. A one-way **taxi** costs Rs5,720 and it is Rs7,600 return.

If you are travelling to Rangdum or into Zanskar proper from anywhere along the Kargil–Leh Highway, you might be surprised to learn that it is as fast to get there **on foot** as it is to drive, and the trek is perfectly feasible for someone of moderate fitness and agility. East of Rangdum there is a track across Kanjil La (5,255m) which links up with NH1 close to Lamayuru. The walk is easily completed in two days (or one and a half if you are really fast). Along the way you will pass through several valleys famed for their medicinal herbs: the Dalai Lama's personal *amchi* (see box below) is said to come here to collect plants.

There is a **police checkpoint** in Rangdum village where you have to present your passport, and another at the base of Rangdum Gompa.

Where to stay and eat

Nun Kun Deluxe Camp (*by Rangdum Gompa;* m *941 917 8401;* e *info@zanskartrek. com; www.zanskartrek.com;* **$$$$**) is the sister camp to the one outside Mulbekh (see page 162). Two things make Nun Kun a worthwhile place to stay: the spectacular views across the valley to the mountains with their colourful strata; and the excellent, home-cooked food. The tents themselves are comfortable enough but the shared toilet blocks need upgrading. Electricity is available courtesy of a generator after 19.30 only.

There are two simple **cafés** in Rangdum village where you can buy tea and small snacks. They also offer very basic accommodation (**$**), but there is no electricity and water is in buckets. Typically only the truck drivers stop here.

What to see   Rangdum Gompa (⊕ *08.00–19.00; donation Rs50*) is a 5km drive past Rangdum village: there is a road that skirts the edge of the valley, but most drivers prefer

THE MEDICINE MEN   *Tanzin Norbu (www.mountaintribalvision.com)*

Amchi means the medicine man. He is greatly respected in Tibetan, Ladakhi and Zanskari communities. The remote valleys of Zanskar and Ladakh were beyond the reach of Western medicine for centuries, and thus relied heavily upon the *amchi* of their villages to cure a wide range of diseases.

Amchi practise Tibetan herbal medicine. They are not only expert in diagnosing and curing disease, but also skilled in identifying Himalayan medicinal plants and medicinal preparation. *Amchi* use various methods to diagnose diseases, such as pulse, iridology, analysis of the tongue, and urine sampling. *Amchi* go though intensive training, only becoming qualified after five years of training.

During the summer, an *amchi* will go high into the mountains to collect various medicinal plants, flowers, roots and shoots, from which they prepare medicines after drying them in the sunlight.

to continue along the rough track straight across the (mostly dry) riverbed. The gompa is perched atop a rocky outcrop and clearly visible for quite some distance.

The monastery dates from the 18th century so it is relatively recent by Zanskari standards. A small number of monks belonging to the Gelugpa order live here, and though some people might tell you the donkeys sleep inside with them at night, this sadly seems to be a fallacy.

If you go into the **temple**, a small and very dark space, look out for the ceremonial cup made from a human skull.

Providing you ask, the monks are happy for you to climb up on the roof, which gives an interesting perspective not only on the gompa but also of the surrounding scenery.

ZONGKUL Up a side valley, some distance from the main road, is the quiet cave monastery of Zongkul, founded on the site where Naropa once meditated. It is rarely visited by tourists, but worth a half-day's excursion from Padum.

Getting there and away Zongkul is best reached by **taxi** from Padum (Rs2,700 return). By road you travel past Sani, staying on the west bank of the river as far as Tangkar, from where there is a signposted track, rough underfoot, into the side valley leading up to the gompa. Due to the twists, turns and poor surface, it's a 15-minute drive from this crossroads.

If you are coming **on foot**, you'll need to allow two hours for the walk from Phey, four hours from Sani, and six hours from Padum. Carry plenty of water as it is dry and dusty and for much of the way there isn't any shade.

What to see Tiny **Zongkul Gompa** (*donation Rs50*) is situated up a narrow track of crushed rock, not far from the village of Tangkar. Belonging to the Drukpa lineage, the monastery has grown up around a cave where Naropa is thought to have meditated.

The **cave** itself is at the centre of the monastery: it is a dark, claustrophobic place. The cave's roof is plastered with small coins, stuck with the oil from the butter lamps, and the footprints of Naropa are cut into the rock. There are six finely worked statues, five depicting the Buddha and one of Naropa.

Elsewhere in the monastery, there is an attractive **prayer room** with brightly painted wooden beams and columns, ceremonial instruments (specifically drums and trumpets), a collection of large paintings on cloth, and a line of statues. The statue of Lama Kunga Churlak (third from the left) is particularly unusual as he is shown with a beard and moustache. Monks are normally clean-shaven.

In the **smaller prayer room**, a square room in which the rock forms part of the roof, there is more natural light, showing off the painted statuary. The decorative cabinets in which the statues are displayed caught our eye: they are works of art in their own right.

The **library** contains hundreds of printing blocks that would once have been used for making religious manuscripts. Today all the Buddhist texts are printed on modern machines in Dharamsala, but the blocks are preserved nonetheless. The room also contains painted display cases decorated with silken banners in numerous colours and patterns, silver plates and a few other decorative items.

Check out the **glass swastika** embedded in the floor of the entrance hall when you leave. As in Hinduism, the swastika has been a sacred symbol in Buddhism for thousands of years.

Zongkul is a quite a dark monastery and the floors and doorways are very uneven. It is highly recommended that you bring your own torch and that you are careful of both your head and shins when making your way along the corridors, up stairs and through doorways.

Around Zongkul The closest accommodation to Zongkul is at Phey on the main road, two hours' walk from the Zongkul Gompa. Here it is possible to stay at either the **Darang Durung Guesthouse** (on the river side of the road) or the **ZDA Tourist Guesthouse** (behind the prayer wheel). Both have very basic facilities and fall into the shoestring (**$**) price bracket. They would also be convenient if you are hiking or coming by bike and won't make Padum before nightfall.

PADUM *Telephone code: 01983* The largest settlement in Zanskar, Padum is still only home to around 1,000 people. It is a pleasant place laid out either side of one main street, Mani Ringmo, and in the summer months it is fairly lively and a good place to meet other travellers: almost everyone trekking in Zanskar starts or finishes their trip here.

The local population is a mixture of both Tibetan Buddhists and Muslims, and this is reflected in the local culture. There is both a gompa and a mosque in town,

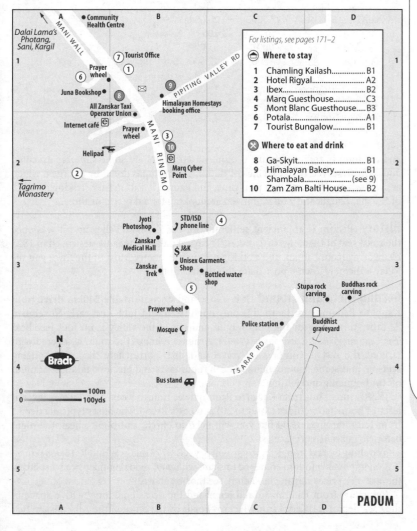

For listings, see pages 171–2

Where to stay

1	Chamling Kailash	B1
2	Hotel Rigyal	A2
3	Ibex	B2
4	Marq Guesthouse	C3
5	Mont Blanc Guesthouse	B3
6	Potala	A1
7	Tourist Bungalow	B1

Where to eat and drink

8	Ga-Skyit	B1
9	Himalayan Bakery	B1
	Shambala	(see 9)
10	Zam Zam Balti House	B2

PADUM

As in Leh and Kargil, the taxi union (All Zanskar Taxi Union), which is based in Padum, sets the official taxi fares. A copy of the latest rate list is posted inside its office on the corner of Mani Ringmo & Pibiting Road. The prices below for 2014 were correct at the time of going to print but will be revised at least on an annual basis.

All journeys listed here originate in Padum, and prices are given in rupees (Rs). You can book a taxi by going into the office, or by calling the office manager, Norboo, on his mobile (m 946 969 1683).

Destination	One-way	Return
Kargil	11,000	17,000
Karsha	800	1,200
Karsha Gompa	900	1,300
Leh	17,000	20,000
Pibiting	150	200
Rangdum	7,000	9,000
Srinagar	17,500	22,500
Stong De	800	1,200
Stong De Gompa	1,000	1,500
Zangla	2,000	2,700
Zongkul Gompa	2,200	2,700

and the food in the restaurants is quite varied. There are some superbly executed and well-preserved rock carvings of Buddhas and stupas down by the river, which are well worth a few hours of your time, and Padum is within easy striking distance of Karsha, Zangla and Zongkul if you are looking for a day trip or three.

History Padum is an ancient settlement in the Zanskar Valley and it was once the royal seat of the kings of Zanskar. The royal palace was sadly destroyed in 1823 by an army from Lahaul, and nothing of it now remains. Most of the town you see today – the new town – post-dates this destruction.

Getting there and around It is a long and uncomfortable 240km **drive** from Kargil to Padum, and the road is only open from mid-July until early November. At other times of year the only way in and out of the valley is on foot (see box, *The Chadar Winter Trek*, pages 176–7). Around 90km of the route is covered with tarmac; the rest is compressed gravel and dirt. Fortunately the ever-changing scenery, and some superb views of both mountains and glaciers, takes your mind off the bouncing and jolting.

JKSRC runs a **bus** from Kargil to Padum three times a week. The journey takes at least 14 hours (sometimes closer to 20) and costs Rs350. The buses typically depart from Kargil around 03.00 but you will need to check, and book a seat, the night before to guarantee a place.

Travelling by **taxi** from Kargil, you will pay Rs11,775 one-way and Rs15,660 return. It is often possible to find someone to share with you, reducing the price by splitting the cost. For prices starting in Padum, see the box above.

Returning from Padum, **shared jeeps** and the occasional lorry with a space in the back depart for Kargil from the crossroads by the office of the All Zanskar Taxi

Union (see box opposite). Drivers are frequently hanging around in the vicinity of their vehicle on the day before departure, but if not often leave a note affixed to the windscreen with their mobile number and planned departure time. If the vehicle is already full they may depart early, so do keep checking.

Helpful, patient and with a good command of English is Padum-based taxi driver **Tsering Mutup** (m *946 945 8059*) who has a comfortable 4x4 and can be hired both for the drive from Padum to Kargil and for more local trips.

Tourist information Tourist information is theoretically available from the **tourist office** [169 B1] on Mani Ringmo. It is, however, rarely open, has no obvious resources, and the single member of staff does not speak English. Staff at the guesthouses and at the Ibex Hotel (see *Where to stay*, page 172) are much better able to advise you about what to see and how to get there.

At the time of going to print, a new **tourist reception centre** was under construction slightly out of Padum on the road to the Dalai Lama's Photang, the building where he stays when he visits Zanskar. It should become fully operational during the lifespan of this edition and will likely replace the existing tourist office and Tourist Bungalow (see page 172).

Local travel agencies/guides There are a small number of competent local travel agencies in Padum, all of which focus on trekking. If you want to do a combination of trekking and sightseeing with a knowledgeable English-speaking guide, it is advisable to contact Tanzin Norbu at **Mountain Tribal Vision** (see page 30) before you go.

Zanskar Mountain Adventures Mani Ringmo. Trekking &, in the winter months, ski school. Call in for information & bookings.
Zanskar Trek [169 B3] Mani Ringmo; ☏ (01982) 252 153; m 941 917 8401; e info@zanskartrek. com; www.zanskartrek.com. Leh-based trekking agency with local office in Padum. Has own 4x4 vehicle for transfers.

Trekking guides The following trekking guides all come highly recommended and can be hired independently as well as through travel agents in Leh (see pages 85–7).

Himal Singh Magar m 979 764 1131; e himalallungeli@yahoo.co.in. Nepali trekking guide who spends the summer months in Zanskar. Good English.
Phunchok Mutup Kalyan m 962 295 8019; e kalyanmutup@gmail.com. Reliable trekking guide with good knowledge of Zanskar's cultural sites too.
Raju Khan e rajukhan.in34@yahoo.com. Warm, knowledgeable & with a fair command of English, Raju can usually be found at Hotel Ibex or the neighbouring Zam Zam Balti House when not in the mountains with clients.

⤵ Where to stay The accommodation options in Padum are the best in Zanskar, and very competitively priced. If you plan to be here in August, do try to book ahead as it can get very busy indeed. Homestays around Zanskar can be booked through the **Himalayan Homestays Booking Office** [169 B1] (*Pibiting Rd*; m *946 936 9406*; *www.himalayan-homestays.com*). They invariably fit into the shoestring (**$**) bracket and typically include dinner. All places to stay are shown on the map on page 169.

🏠 Marq Guesthouse (10 rooms) Off Mani Ringmo; ☏ 245 223; m 941 800 2171; e info@ marqinnzanskar.com; www.marqinnzanskar.com. Padum's best accommodation is run by a delightful English-speaking couple. Rooms are very clean & all have immaculate attached bathrooms. 24hr power is provided by a backup generator & water is solar heated. Wi-Fi included. **$$$$**
🏠 Chamling Kailash (18 rooms) Opp Prayer Wheel, Mani Ringmo; m 946 951 8874;

e kailashhotel2012@yahoo.com. Managed by Karsha Gompa, rooms are reasonable & set around a courtyard but in need of cleaning. Tea (Rs20) & sandwiches (Rs80) served. Camping ($) possible behind the hotel. Open 1 Jun–late Sep. **$$$**

🏠 **Hotel Rigyal** (10 rooms) Nr Helipad; m 946 922 4500; e hotel-rigyal@yahoo.com. Run by monks, this small hotel is kept exceptionally clean & camping is possible in the garden. No English is spoken but you should still be able to make yourself understood. **$$$**

🏠 **Ibex Hotel** (15 rooms) Mani Ringmo; ☏ 245 013; m 941 980 3731; e ibexpadumzanskar@gmail.com. Padum's most popular spot for foreign tourists benefits from its central location. Rooms are built around a pleasant courtyard. The manager is friendly & speaks good English. Meals are available on request but tend to take a while, as the hotel is short-staffed. **$$$**

🏠 **Potala Hotel** (4 rooms) Opp Tourist Office, Mani Ringmo; m 941 988 8056. Open from mid-May until mid-Oct, rooms at the Potala are clean & all have attached bathrooms. It plans to add another 4 rooms in the foreseeable future. The restaurant is open for non-guests too. **$$$**

🏠 **Mont Blanc Guesthouse** (4 rooms) Mani Ringmo; ☏ 245 183; m 946 923 9376. Simple guesthouse in the centre of town, set back from the main drag in a pleasant garden. Rooms are carpeted, with several sgl beds in each. **$**

🏠 **Tourist Bungalow** (12 rooms) Mani Ringmo; ☏ 245 017. If you can find anyone to let you in, the Tourist Bungalow is well situated, cheap & reasonably clean. If the tourist office (see page 171) by the main gate is locked, go into the accommodation block at the back left of the site & see if you can rouse someone from there. **$**

🍴 **Where to eat** All the restaurants in Padum are open for lunch and dinner unless otherwise stated: for breakfast it is easiest to eat in your guesthouse or hotel. All of these places are marked on the map on page 169.

🍴 **Ga-Skyit Restaurant** Mani Ringmo; m 946 936 9828. 1st-floor restaurant close to the crossroads. Dishes are mostly Tibetan, with a few Chinese & Indian options. **$$**

🍴 **Zam Zam Balti House** Mani Ringmo. Lively diner next door to the Ibex Hotel. There are good meat dishes on the menu as well as simple, often deep-fried snacks. **$$**

🍴 **Shambala Restaurant** Pibiting Rd; m 946 909 6716. 1st-floor restaurant serving Tibetan &

Chinese staples such as thukpa & chow mein. If you're looking for something simple, they also do reasonable omelettes. **$–$$**

🍴 **Himalaya Bakery** Pibiting Rd. Downstairs from Shambala Restaurant, this is the best of several bakeries in Padum. Though nothing exciting, the loaves of bread, savoury pastries & biscuits are helpful additions to your trekking provisions. Take-out only. **$**

Shopping Several general stores along Mani Ringmo sell basic dried and packeted food items. Only one of them sells bottled water; it's just past the Zanskar Trek office.

🏬 **Juma Book Shop** [169 A1] Behind Prayer Wheel, Mani Ringmo; ⊕ 10.30–19.00. Friendly store selling stationery & a small selection of games, books & trekking maps.

🏬 **Unisex Garments Shop** [169 B3] Next to J&K Bank; ⊕ 09.30–19.30. General clothing store selling waterproof jackets, gilets, fleeces, duffel bags, torches, multi-tools, padlocks & sunglasses.

Other practicalities

Communications Padum's **post office** [169 B1] (⊕ *Mon–Sat 10.00–16.00 daily*) is on Mani Ringmo, opposite the Ga-Skyit Restaurant. The red metal shutters are always down, even when the post office is open, so go in through the door on the right. Postmaster Angchuk franks mail with a metal stamp that he has to assemble one character at a time.

Padum's internet connection is erratic at best. There are two internet cafés on Mani Ringmo (both of them close to the crossroads) but they are rarely open. It is better to go to the **Marq Guesthouse** (see *Where to sta*y, page 171) where you can use the Wi-Fi.

STD and ISD phone calls can be made from the shop on Mani Ringmo, just before the driveway leading to Marq Guesthouse [169 B3].

Emergencies In the event of a medical emergency or other requirement for immediate evacuation, Padum has its own **helipad**, set just back from Mani Ringmo in the centre of the town.

Should you need police assistance, the **police station** [169 C4] (✆ *245 003*) is in the Old Town, close to the Buddhist graveyard and petroglyphs (see below). The regular police force is generally friendly and some of them speak English.

Medical Zanskar's largest hospital is the **Community Health Centre** [169 A1] (✆ *245 015*) beside the Tourist Office in Padum. The hospital is composed of two buildings: an outpatients clinic and a new building (opened in 2012) containing male and female wards, the casualty department and operating theatres. The hospital is well equipped for the region, with facilities including an X-ray machine and laboratory. In addition to several English-speaking surgeons and general medical staff, there is also a pharmacist and a dentist.

Almost opposite J&K Bank is the **Zanskar Medical Hall** [169 B3] (m *946 909 2711;* ⊕ *09.00–19.30*), a small pharmacy with an English-speaking pharmacist. It stocks most generic drugs as well as disposable syringes and scalpels contained in sealed packets.

Money There is no ATM in Padum and no official Forex facilities: individual merchants may agree to change dollars for you, but the rate is poor, so you are advised to bring with you all the rupees you are likely to need. The branch of **J&K Bank** on Mani Ringmo only has a local banking licence and therefore cannot change foreign currency or arrange cash advances. It is therefore useful as a local landmark only.

What to see If you've had your fill of gompas, Padum has a wonderful surprise: hidden in the north of the town by the river are two sets of **ancient petroglyphs** [169 D3]. Turning left off Tsarap Road, continue past the police station until the road bends round to the left. Continue straight along the footpath running parallel with the stone wall, and follow it round to the right: in front of you is an orange-coloured rock carved with **images of stupas**.

Behind the rock is a red-tiled pathway: follow it to the left and then downhill towards the river. This brings you to the **Five Buddhas Rock** [169 D3], so named because of the line of five Buddha carvings, each one sat meditating in the lotus position. At some stage in the relatively recent past the faces have been partly repaired with concrete, as have some of the limbs, but they are magnificent nonetheless.

Immediately to their right is a **standing Buddha** [169 D3] of around 3m tall, and at the base of the rock are various smaller human figures. The top section of the rock features several tiered stupas. Unlike the Chamba Buddha at Mulbekh (see page 162), you have an unobstructed view of the carvings and can even climb on top of the rock for impressive views in both directions along the valley.

Continuing down the steps, the rock face pointing towards the river has yet more petroglyphs, including a **meditating Buddha**, but these are substantially more weathered than the other carvings, and a large bush partially obscures several of the images. Stop for a while to sit on the rocks by the river and soak up the peaceful atmosphere: you're unlikely to be disturbed by anything other than a cow, and maybe the rushing of the water.

Padum does have a gompa too: the **Tagrimo Monastery** [169 A2]. Dating from the 17th century, it belongs to the Drukpa school. Its frescoes are in a good condition thanks to sensitive renovation works in 2005, and there is also a small library. The gompa is about 30 minutes walk from Mani Ringmo and overlooks the town.

Last but not least, Padum is home to the only **mosque** [169 B4] in Zanskar: it's the attractive green roofed building in the centre of town. Unlike the Shiite Muslims of the Suru Valley further north, Zanskar's small Muslim population are Sunni.

Around Padum
Pipiting Visible from much of Padum is Pipiting, the hill in the middle of the plain atop which sits a large **stupa** and small gompa, cared for by two monks from Karsha. The oldest part of this monastery dates back around 600 years. There are some fine wall paintings, and also three impressive statues of the Chamba Buddha, Padmasambhava and the 11-headed Chenrezi.

Sani It takes around two hours to walk the 8km (5 miles) back along the main road north from Padum to Sani, which is a small but attractive settlement with three sites that are well worth visiting.

On the opposite side of the road from the town is the **Sani Lake**. The lake itself would not be remarkable if it weren't for the large, modern Buddha statue rising from its centre. You can reach the island on which the Buddha stands by hopping from one stepping stone to the next. When we were visiting it was covered in scaffolding for cleaning, but this gave us the opportunity to get right up close and see the miracle: on the right-hand side of the Buddha's crown are three turquoise stones. The one at the bottom left (you'll need a telephoto lens or binoculars to see if from the ground) appears to have the face of the Dalai Lama naturally occurring in the pattern of the stone.

Sani Gompa is the only gompa in Zanskar to be built on the plain: all others are set into the mountain slopes. Though the current gompa dates only from the 17th century, there has been a religious community on this site far longer, as attested to by the Kanishka Stupa, which is thought to date from the 2nd century AD. Also of note here is a beautiful bronze statue of Naropa, housed in a small building behind the main gompa.

Sani is also home to **Kachod Ling**, a Buddhist nunnery belonging to the Drukpa order. It's a relatively small nunnery with only 14 or 15 nuns, the majority of whom are working in the village during the day. Their historic lhakhang has been sensitively restored and has some attractive wall paintings; and there is also a new dukhang.

VOLUNTEERING IN ZANSKAR

The majority of volunteering opportunities in Zanskar are linked to the schools. Sun School in Kargyak is supported by the Czech NGO **Surya** (*www. surya.cz*); the French NGO **Aaz** (*www.aazanskar.org*) sponsors 300 children at Pipiting School; and another Czech NGO, **MOST Civic Association** (*www. protibet.org*), has a presence in the valley too.

KARSHA Visible right across the plain from Padum, Karsha has an impressive location, set into the soaring cliff face as though its buildings were a succession of whitewashed crows' nests. The gompa is one of the friendliest we visited anywhere in Ladakh or Zanskar, and the views back down from it are second to none.

Getting there and away There is just one **bus** a day between Padum and Karsha: it leaves Karsha at 08.00 and returns the same day around 16.00. The journey takes 30 minutes and costs Rs20. A **shared taxi** also runs the same route with approximately the same departure times and price, but a shorter journey time (about 15 minutes).

If you want a private **taxi**, you need to take the car from Padum and get it to wait for you in Karsha, as there is no taxi stand there to pick up a different vehicle for the return journey. The return trip costs Rs1,200 (Rs1,300 to the gompa above the main village) and includes 90 minutes of waiting time while you explore.

You can also **walk** from Padum to Karsha via Pipiting in a little over two hours. Though it is flat, and hence easy walking, the plain is very exposed so make sure you wear a hat and carry plenty of water.

What to see The **Chamspaling Phagspa Shesrab Gompa** around which Karsha village has grown up is the largest monastery in Zanskar. It is a steep site, with the numerous storeys built higgledy-piggledy into the cliff, so if you do come by car, ask the driver to take you the long way round and drop you at the top.

There are three important figures in the history of Karsha's monastery: Phagspa Shesrab, the founder after whom it is named; Dorje Shesrab, who constructed the buildings you see today; and Shesrab Zangpo, who converted the monastery to follow the Gelugpa school.

There are around 150 monks at Karsha, as well as a number of novices who race around the monastery's courtyards, causing good-natured mayhem. It seems that relatively few foreign visitors come here, but we were made exceptionally welcome: the monks invited us to attend their afternoon prayers in their beautifully decorated temple and were happy for us to take photographs of them providing we sat still and were quiet. They also shared their lunch with us afterwards in the courtyard, which was a highlight of our trip.

Due to its raised position, the views from the gompa are superb: not only does the plain and river stretch out before you, but you can easily see Padum, Stong De and Pipiting, and in the background stretch out peak after snow-capped peak.

STONG DE Stong De, or Tongde, is midway between Padum and Zangla, on the opposite side of the river to Karsha. The principal reason for coming here is to visit the Marpaling Gompa, one of the holiest sites in the Zanskar valley.

Getting there and away It's a pleasant 12km **walk** from Padum to Stong De, and it'll take you around three hours. The daily **bus** from Padum to Zangla passes this way (Padum to Stong De takes an hour), or you can hire a **taxi** from Padum. The ride from Padum to Stong De costs Rs800 one-way, or Rs1,000 if you're going up to the gompa rather than just to the village.

Where to stay There are no formal accommodation options in Stong De. However, it is sometimes possible for individuals and small groups to stay at the gompa or with a local family. If you have a local guide, they will arrange this for you, otherwise you'll need to ask around when you arrive.

What to see The **Marpaling Gompa** is a 20-minute walk from Stong De village. One of the oldest monasteries in the region, it is said to have been founded by

Marpa himself (see box, pages 20–1) in 1052, hence its name. The current buildings date from the 13th century, and the three dozen monks who live here follow the Gelugpa school. There are also around 20 novices.

The oldest part of the gompa is the **dukhang**, where the murals are in poor condition due to their age, but still visible. More visually impressive are the paintings in the **main temple**, which show a large Sakyamuni Buddha surrounded by smaller

THE CHADAR WINTER TREK

If you think you're tough and want a challenge to pit yourself against, look no further than the Chadar Winter Trek, a six-day hike in sub-zero temperatures along the frozen Zanskar River from the appropriately named Chilling to Zangla. Night-time temperatures frequently fall to -35°C and rarely climb above -15°C even in the daytime, which is probably a reassuring thing given that you'll be walking on the ice. The trek is possible only in January and February.

The Chadar trek started out as a practical means for schoolteachers to get back to Zanskar after their Christmas break, the road from Kargil being closed in winter. *Chadar* means blanket of ice.

Chilling lies 64km from Leh and is really no more than a small collection of army huts near the end of the road. From the very start of the trek you are out on the ice, waddling like a penguin at first and then slowly gaining confidence and learning how to get your boots to grip. Day one requires just an hour of walking to reach the campsite at **Tilat Sumdo** (3,100m), which lies at, and takes its name from, the confluence of the Zanskar and one of its smaller tributaries.

On day two you'll cover less than 10km, but it takes a full six hours. In places where the ice is thin (your guide will know how to spot this, and you will swiftly become adept at recognising it too), you will have to keep to the edges of the river where the ice is thickest, sometimes clambering beneath the overhanging rocks, scrabbling on your hands and knees. Your day's destination is the campsite at **Shingra Koma** (3,170m), which lies directly beneath a steep and imposing rock wall.

The trek from Shingra Koma to **Tibb** (3,225m) is 15km and will take you around seven hours. It is probably the most tiring day of the Chadar trek but also the most beautiful, with the landscape a winter wonderland of frozen waterfalls and solid walls of ice. In the afternoon you pass through narrow gorges that at this time of year scarcely see any direct sunlight: it's bitterly cold and gloomy, but when you reach this point you know that you are only two hours from camp. Rather than pitching on the flat, you'll spend the night sleeping in a natural cave, snug with as many as eight other people.

Day four starts early and begins with a walk amid cliffs and gorges. The highlight of the day is undoubtedly the **Nerak Waterfall**: prayer flags and juniper bushes signal that you are close, and there's a small wooden bridge nearby. The **Nerak campsite** (3,390m) is up a small trail from the river. In total today's trek is 12km and takes seven hours.

From Nerak you trek to **Lingshed** (3,700m), a village that is only accessible when the ice is frozen. Here is there a Gelugpa monastery housing 60 monks; it's an important spiritual centre in the region. Today's trek will again take around seven hours. Camp here overnight.

On day six your destination is **Tsarak Do** (3,400m). It's a two-hour trek on solid ground from Lingshed back to the river, then a further five to six hours along the ice. There is a homestay in the village, or you can camp.

Buddhas, and an **antechamber** in which the Buddhas are painted unusually as white silhouettes on a black background.

ZANGLA Historically there were two kings in Zanskar: one had his capital at Padum, and the other ruled from Zangla. The latter's palace, now partially restored, is an obvious attraction, as is the Chanchub Choling Nunnery. In the summer

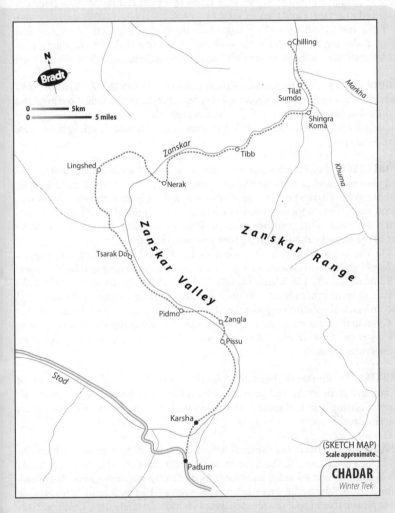

It is possible to walk from Tsarak Do to **Zangla** (3,491m) via **Pidmo** (3,429m) in ten hours providing you have the energy and leave very early in the morning, otherwise you will need to split this last part of the trek across two days. Highlights include passing through the gorge at Hanamur, and advancing on Zangla itself, the fort poised high and visible long in advance of your arrival.

If you wish to continue on foot all the way to **Padum** (3,657m), you will require one more day. The route goes via the village of **Pissu** (3,550m).

months you may also see nomadic families camping here with their flocks: they stop on the opposite side of the river when moving from pasture to pasture.

Getting there and away It's about 90 minutes' **drive** from Padum to Zangla along a reasonable (though unsurfaced) road. There is one **bus** in each direction (departing from Padum at 16.00 and from Zangla at 08.00) every day except Sunday, though it is more convenient to take a **taxi** from Padum (Rs2,700 return) if you need to get there and back in a day.

If you want to **walk** one or both ways, there are two possible routes, each of around 35km. Following the right bank, the walk takes seven or eight hours via Stong De; on the left bank via Karsha you can reach Zangla in seven hours.

🏠 **Where to stay** The **Dragon Guesthouse** (*3 rooms;* m *946 945 1481;* **$**) is more of a homestay than a guesthouse. Rooms are very basic but the rate includes both breakfast and dinner. Several families will host visitors in their homes: ask in particular for Tundup Tsering or Kalzang Chodak Namgyal. A bed and meals will cost no more than Rs500 pp.

What to see Zangla's principal attraction is the **Royal Palace**, a fortified structure that although now in ruins is the only indication we have of how Zanskari royals would have lived, their other palace in Padum having been completely destroyed. Some restoration work has been undertaken by a Hungarian organisation, but you'll still need to use your imagination. Twelve remarkable statues do survive in one of the ruined structures: make sure you hunt them down.

On the opposite side of the village is the **Chanchub Choling Nunnery**, a welcoming place with around two dozen nuns and a dozen trainee nuns. Here you will find an attractive **lhakhang** filled to the brim with religious books, and here as well as in some other rooms, colourful murals depicting a range of divinities and also an unusual painting of grotesque Mahakalas set against a black background.

Close to the nunnery is another curious site, the **Philaphug Hermitage**. It looks like a pile of ruins but is in fact a succession of small rooms, some of which are painted with frescoes.

PHUKTAL Breathtakingly beautiful Phuktal Gompa lies two days' trek south of Padum in a golden yellow gorge set back from the Tsarap River. It is well worth the effort of getting here, and indeed the journey itself is probably one of the best short treks in Zanskar.

Getting there and away There is a road going south from Padum, but only as far as the village of Raru. From here you must continue on foot, via either Anmu or Chatang to Purne, and thence to Phuktal. It is theoretically possible to walk from Raru to Phuktal in one day (it takes around 12 hours), but it is certainly more pleasurable to split the journey over two more leisurely days. Overnight, try **Stanzin Samphel's Homestay** (**$**) in Anmu, or camp.

What to see Clinging to the cliff around the mouth of a cave, **Phuktal Gompa** was founded by the famed translator Phagspa Sherab in the 12th century and, a century or so later, Sharap Zangpo (a disciple of Tsongkhapa, founder of the Gelugpa school) travelled to Zanskar to convert the gompa to the Gelugpa lineage. While in Phuktal Sharap Zangpo died, and his relics were interred in the **Sharap Zangpo Stupa**.

The gompa continued to play an important part in history, as it was here that the Hungarian linguist Alexander Csoma de Koros stayed for a protracted period when he visited Zanskar in the 1820s. Koros was the co-author of the first ever English–Tibetan dictionary, and a **plaque** at the gompa commemorates his contribution. It is due to Koros's link with the valley that a Hungarian NGO has supported the restoration of the palace at Zangla (see opposite) and other important cultural sites.

There are about 70 monks living at the gompa today, many of whom still wear the distinctive yellow hats of their order.

The Suru Valley and Zanskar   ZANSKAR

7

8

From Kargil
towards Srinagar

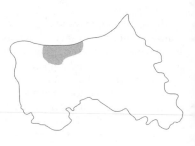

Far too often tourists race along the highway from Srinagar to Ladakh without pausing to see what's *en route*. Though the sites here may be lacking in publicity, scarcely mentioned in general tourist literature, this is an unfortunate oversight, as the area is home to a rich blend of Muslim and Buddhist cultures, fascinating historical sites and some stunning natural landscapes. The area is easily accessible, especially from Srinagar, and well worth taking time to explore.

This chapter covers the northern and central parts of J&K, the places close to the LoC in the Kargil District of Ladakh, and further west towards Srinagar in Kashmir. The three main conurbations in this region are Kargil, Drass and Sonamarg, ideal starting points for exploring the smaller, often overlooked sites that surround them.

KARGIL   *Telephone code: 01985*

Kargil's name will forever be associated with the Kargil War, a deeply sad state of affairs as the area has so much to offer. Kargil town lies in an attractive setting at the confluence of the Suru and Nallah Wakha rivers, and it has been at the crossroads of overland trading routes for centuries. The Munshi Aziz Bhat Caravanserai attests to Kargil's important position on the Silk Road, and the Munshi Aziz Bhat Museum has quite probably the most interesting collection of artefacts of any museum in the state.

Plan your visit to Kargil carefully and factor in the weather: the town experiences an extreme shift in temperatures between summer and winter. In July and August temperatures are very pleasant, usually in the mid-20°s C, but in the winter months it is not uncommon for it to be as cold as -20°C. Not all hotels provide heating.

HISTORY   Located almost equidistant between Srinagar, Padum, Skardu (now in Pakistan) and Leh, Kargil has been a trading post for centuries: goods passed through here from as far away as Turkey, Afghanistan and China, and Kargil's merchants profited from the sale of luxury goods such as silk, ivory and precious stones, as well as more mundane items. The surrounding territories were amalgamated into a single kingdom for the first time by Gasho Tatha Khan in the 9th century.

Kargil district came under Balti influence in the 16th century, during the reign of Ali Sher Khan Anchan, the Maqpon king whose capital was at Skardu. Kargil itself was developed as a garrison town by General Zorawar Singh during the Dogra invasion in the 1830s, and it was during this period that the foundations of the modern conurbation were laid down. Dogra control lasted until 1947.

After independence, the First Kashmir War (see page 14) and the resulting creation of the LoC dissected Baltistan, cutting Kargil district off from many of its

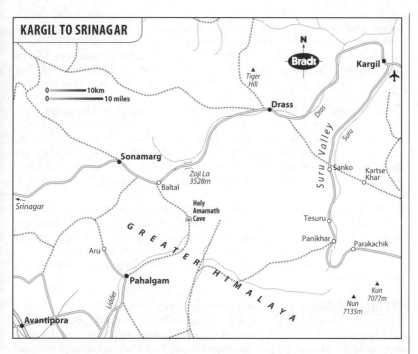

trading partners. The area was first opened up for tourists in 1974 and has grown steadily since this time, though the 1999 Kargil War (see box, page 187) inevitably had a detrimental impact on the local economy, and tourism in particular.

GETTING THERE AND AWAY Kargil lies roughly equidistant from Leh, Padum and Srinagar on NH1. It is currently accessible only by road, though it is hoped commercial flights might begin during the lifespan of this edition.

By road Kargil lies 204km (8–12 hours) from Srinagar, 234km (8 hours) from Leh and 240km (12–14 hours) from Padum. Though NH1, on which Kargil lies, is fairly well maintained and there are plentiful buses and taxis in all directions, the road towards Leh is snowbound in winter, and the Zoji La Pass between Drass and Srinagar is frequently closed due to bad weather. Bear this in mind when planning your trip.

By bus The J&K State Transport Corporation (JKSRTC) (*www.jksrtc.co.in*) operates standard and de luxe coaches on the Srinagar–Leh road from early June until mid-November, passing through Kargil. The standard coach (Rs357) departs from Srinagar at 07.30. If there are enough passengers, the de luxe 14-seater coach (Rs650) runs along the same route. Coming from Leh, buses depart from the main bus stand at 06.00.

JKSRC also runs a bus from Kargil to Padum three times a week. The journey takes at least 14 hours (sometimes closer to 20) and costs Rs350. The buses typically depart from Kargil around 03.00 but you will need to check, and book a seat, the night before to guarantee a place. The bus station is situated between Khumaini Chowk and the river, next to the bridge.

By taxi Kargil has three taxi stands, which can make things a little confusing. The **Main Taxi Stand** [183 C5] is on Khumaini Chowk, just south of the Islamia

School, and it's from here that you'll pick up a taxi or shared taxi for Zanskar, the Suru Valley or Ladakh. The **Old Taxi Stand** [183 C3] is further north on Khumaini Chowk, in the centre of Main Bazaar, and these taxis will ferry you around Kargil town and into the villages just outside. Finally, the **Drass Taxi Stand** [183 B1] handles taxis heading west to Drass and Srinagar. It's situated on the northern side of the town, on the road towards Srinagar.

The **Kargil Taxi Operators and Owners Co-operative Union** sets taxi rates for vehicles from Kargil. At the time of going to print, the cost of a one-way/return journey to major destinations is as follows: Drass Rs1,670/2,200; Lamayuru Rs3,390/4,500; Leh Rs6,515/8,670; Mulbekh Rs1,140/1,515; Padum Rs11,775/15,660; Pahalgam Rs8,910/11,850; Parkachik Rs2,960/3,935; Rangdum Rs5,720/7,600; Sonamarg Rs3,120/4,250; and Srinagar Rs5,847/7,780.

By air Kargil does have its own airport but at the time of going to print it was only used by military and private flights. It is hoped that during the lifespan of this edition it will reopen for commercial flights too, making not only Kargil town but the entirety of Kargil district, including Zanskar, very much more accessible.

The cost of getting from the airport to the centre of Kargil by taxi is Rs333/440 one-way/return.

GETTING AROUND The town's **minivans** ply its two main streets, running up and down to the bazaar. A single seat in a minivan will cost you Rs10; taking the whole vehicle costs Rs100. Note that later in the evening, especially if you are travelling away from the bazaar, you may be obliged to pay for the whole vehicle if there are no other passengers going in your direction.

Most of Kargil is accessible **on foot**. Walking from Bimathang to Main Bazaar will take no more than 20 minutes, and another ten minutes will get you to the museum.

TOURIST INFORMATION A tourist facilitation centre [183 C6] (✆ 232 721; www. jktourism.org) is operated by **J&K Tourism** in Bimathang, signposted from the bridge and not far from Hotel D'Zojila. Here we were able to get a free map of Ladakh but no other information was forthcoming: this will hopefully change during the lifespan of this edition. The centre also contains a restaurant (see page 184) and has rooms and a conference centre.

In the meantime, a better source of information, assistance and bookings is the **All Kargil Travel Traders Association** (*Hotel PC Palace, nr Old Taxi Stand;* ✆ *233 736;* m *946 922 1111;* e *allkargiltraveltrade2013@gmail.com*). Spearheaded by local travel agent Mohammad Hamza, it publishes tourist brochures and provides contact details for hotels, guesthouses and travel agencies in and around Kargil.

LOCAL TRAVEL AGENTS

Kazim Communications [183 C3] Old Taxi Stand, Khumaini Chowk. Air ticketing & railway reservations.
Sewak Travel Company [183 B3] Nr the Co-operative Bank, Khumaini Chowk; ✆ 233 736; e yasoobs9@gmail.com. Sightseeing, trekking & rafting packages as well as flight, train & hotel bookings. Manager Mohammad Ali speaks excellent English & has a detailed knowledge of local tourism options.

WHERE TO STAY Kargil doesn't yet have the wide range of accommodation options that you'll find in Srinagar or Leh, but standards are improving and there are already a number of options that are comfortable and well run, whether you're staying for one night or much longer. All places to stay are marked on the map opposite.

Main Bazaar

🏠 **Hotel Jan Palace** (18 rooms) Nr SBI, Public Pk Rd; 📞 234 135; 📱 941 917 6277; 📧 hoteljanpalace@gmail.com; www. janpalacekargil.com. Brand-new hotel in the town centre. Rooms & bathrooms are immaculate & hotel is well organised. Rooftop restaurant serves Kashmiri & international cuisine. Refreshing addition to Kargil's hotel scene. 10% service tax applicable. **$$$$**

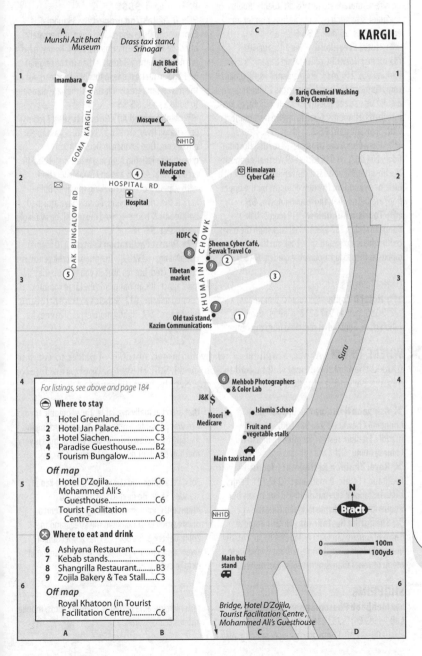

KARGIL

Munshi Azit Bhat Museum

Drass taxi stand, Srinagar

Azit Bhat Sarai

Imambara

Tariq Chemical Washing & Dry Cleaning

GOMA KARGIL ROAD

Mosque

NH1D

Velayatee Medicate

Himalayan Cyber Café

HOSPITAL RD

Hospital

DAK BUNGALOW RD

HDFC

Sheena Cyber Café, Sewak Travel Co

Tibetan market

KHUMAINI CHOWK

Old taxi stand, Kazim Communications

Mehbob Photographers & Color Lab

J&K

Noori Medicare

Islamia School

Fruit and vegetable stalls

Main taxi stand

NH1D

Suru

N

Bradt

0 — 100m
0 — 100yds

Main bus stand

Bridge, Hotel D'Zojila, Tourist Facilitation Centre, Mohammed Ali's Guesthouse

For listings, see above and page 184

🛏 **Where to stay**
1   Hotel Greenland.................C3
2   Hotel Jan Palace.................C3
3   Hotel Siachen.....................C3
4   Paradise Guesthouse..........B2
5   Tourism Bungalow..............A3

Off map
    Hotel D'Zojila......................C6
    Mohammed Ali's
      Guesthouse.....................C6
    Tourist Facilitation
      Centre.............................C6

❌ **Where to eat and drink**
6   Ashiyana Restaurant...........C4
7   Kebab stands......................C3
8   Shangrilla Restaurant..........B3
9   Zojila Bakery & Tea Stall......C3

Off map
    Royal Khatoon (in Tourist
      Facilitation Centre)...........C6

Hotel Siachen (See ad, page 191) (27 rooms) 232 221; m 941 917 6032; e hotel_siachen_kargil@rediffmail.com; www. hotelsiachen.com. Centrally located & very comfortable. Staff are polite & helpful; meals in the on-site restaurant are tasty & affordable. Rooms are quiet & heating is available in winter for an additional Rs750/day. $$$$

Hotel Greenland (See ad, page 191) (33 rooms) Nr LAHDC office, Main Bazaar; 232 324; m 962 219 2431; e greenlandkargil@gmail. com. Comfortable hotel split across 2 buildings on a quiet side street. Rooms are large & light, as are attached bathrooms. Good in-house restaurant with pleasant staff. $$$

Paradise Guesthouse (8 rooms) Hospital Rd; 204 067; m 946 923 9519. Virtually opposite the hospital, Paradise is a conveniently located (if a little noisy) option. The newer rooms on the upper floor are better than those lower down. $$

Tourism Bungalow (10 rooms) Dak Bungalow Rd; 232 328. Tucked back from the town centre, this is a pleasant spot. Look out for the 2 pet rabbits as they lollop around the garden. $–$$

Other areas

Hotel D'Zojila (53 rooms) Bimathang; 232 360; m 941 917 6212; e hotel_dzojila@ yahoo.co.in. Somewhat removed from the centre of town, D'Zojila is used predominantly by tour groups passing through. All rooms have attached bathrooms, 24hr hot water & fans but could do with a thorough scrub. There's a restaurant on site & the local muezzin gives a tuneful wake-up call. Wi-Fi included. $$$$

D'Zojila's 2nd property (35 rooms) Contact details as above. Will open immediately opposite the above in summer 2014. Rooms here are notably lighter & fresher than in the original building so request one in this block instead. All the new rooms are river facing & they are planning to build a pool. $$$$

Mohammed Ali's Guesthouse (2 rooms) Leh–Kargil Hwy; m 946 973 6736; e yasoobs9@ gmail.com. Due to open in Oct 2014, this guesthouse is being built in a traditional Ladakhi architectural style & has an enviable location with superb views overlooking the river, Bulbul Park & the cricket ground. Rooms have attached bathrooms & home-cooked meals will be available on request. $$

Tourist Facilitation Centre (10 rooms) Bimathang; 232 721. The phone at the centre is disconnected, but it's likely if you turn up they'll have space. It's an optimistically large complex, opened only in 2012, & there's a choice between 8 basic rooms & 2 slightly more expensive ones for VIPs. $$

✗ **WHERE TO EAT** As yet, Kargil has a relatively limited number of places to eat, and indeed the best food may well be had in your hotel. Still, the below options are fine for a quick eat and if you fancy a change of scene. See the map on page 183.

✗**Ashiyana Restaurant** Opp J&K Bank, Khumaini Chowk; m 946 973 8002. Clean & friendly 1st-floor restaurant offering Indian & Chinese menu. $$

✗**Royal Khatoon Restaurant** Tourist Facilitation Centre, Bimathang; 232 721. Large, clean restaurant serving multi-cuisine meals but frequently closed due to lack of business. $$

✗**Shangrilla Restaurant** Nr Co-operative Bank, Khumaini Chowk; m 946 944 8836. Visually underwhelming 1st-floor restaurant with a wide menu of vegetarian & non-vegetarian dishes that aren't actually available. The vegetable fried rice was passable & other diners were tucking in happily to chicken legs. Service with a smile is very much dependent on who is serving. $$

For a very quick and cheap eat, there are kebab stands ($) set up next to the taxi stand on Khumaini Chowk each evening, which send a divine smell wafting down the street; and the Zojila Bakery & Tea Stall ($) has a selection of sweet and savoury pastries which you can eat in or take out.

SHOPPING

Mehboob Photographers & Color Lab [183 C4] 232 535; m 941 917 6167; ⏱ 10.00–21.00. Photo processing & printing. Also sells rechargeable batteries, memory cards, mobile phones & accessories.

OTHER PRACTICALITIES
Communications

📧 **Himalayan Cyber Café** [183 C2] Hospital Rd; ✆ 234 017; ⏰ 10.00–20.00. Photocopying, printing, scanning & passport photos as well as internet access.

📧 **Sheena Cyber Café** [183 C3] Nr Co-operative Bank, Khumaini Chowk; 📱 946 973 6736; ⏰ 09.00–00.00. Well-run internet café with a dozen or so terminals & a reasonable broadband connection speed. Rs40/hr.

Post office Kargil has a large India Post office [183 A2], which lies at the junction of Hospital Road and Dak Bungalow Road.

Laundry If you've run out of clean clothes or have something that is dry-clean only, **Tariq Chemical Washing and Dry Cleaning** [183 C1] is next to the bridge in the northern end of the town.

Medical

✚ **Noori Medicare** [183 C4] Khumaini Chowk; 📱 941 927 1694. Well-stocked pharmacy with a daily doctor's clinic (⏰ 09.00–10.00 & 16.00–18.00).

✚ **Velayatee Medicate** [183 B2] Hospital Rd; 📱 941 934 2982; ⏰ 09.00–10.30 & 16.30–18.00. Small clinic equivalent to a GP's surgery.

Kargil has a large **hospital** [183 B2] (*Hospital Rd;* ✆ *232 382*) that is, by local standards, well equipped and has around 100 beds. Doctors generally speak English and most specialities are covered. The hospital is capable of handling A&E cases.

Money

💲**HDFC Bank** [183 B3] Khumaini Chowk. 24hr ATM. Branch will unofficially change sums up to US$500 for foreigners.

💲**J&K Bank** [183 C4] Khumaini Chowk. Small branch & 24hr ATM.

Some of the merchants in the **Tibetan Market** [183 B3] next to HDFC Bank will also exchange foreign notes for rupees. Ask around to get the best rate.

WHAT TO SEE Prior to the solidification of India's borders following independence in 1947, Ladakh's merchants traded goods the length and breadth of the Silk Road, from Turkey in the west to Mongolia in the east. The **Munshi Aziz Bhat Museum** [183 A1] (*Munshi Grong, Lankore;* 📱 *941 917 6061; www.kargilmuseum.org;* ⏰ *summer 09.00–18.00, winter closed; entrance fee Rs20/30 local/foreigner*) houses a gem of a collection. Also known as the Central Asian Museum, it is the undisputed highlight of Kargil town, and passionately curated by Aziz Hussain Munshi and Muzammil Hussain, descendants of the late 19th-century merchant Munshi Aziz Bhat (see page 186).

The first room of the museum displays **carpets and kilims**, many of which were made to be placed beneath a horse's saddle. The finest examples belonged to aristocrats and wealthy merchants and have come from as far afield as Kokand and Tajikistan. Of particular historical importance is the central Asian woven carpet decorated with eight tigers that belonged to Mohan Lal, assistant to Alexander 'Bukhara' Burnes. The room also contains **stone carvings** found at Kharcher Khar near Rangdum and dating from the 6th to 8th centuries.

The balance of the collection is in the main hall: items are grouped by type and clearly labelled in English with their approximate date and place of origin. Items of **costume** include British breeches, the name of their original owner still visible in ink on the waistband, and gowns and coats from Kashmir and Gilgit, Russia and central Asia. There are numerous **hats**, the earliest made in Mongolia in the 16th century, and also well-preserved examples of **shoes and boots**, including locally made *kratpa*, winter shoes sufficiently large that you could pack your feet around with straw to keep them warm.

Some of the most intriguing displays show local products and their foreign counterparts: **locks and keys**, European and Tibetan **medicines** (the latter with their original prescriptions) and **weaponry**. Central Asian **embroidered textiles** are exhibited alongside the British-made **embroidery threads** used to produce them.

The museum's **manuscript collection** is shown in an antechamber to the main hall. Highlights include Tibetan and Ladakhi texts on handmade paper and cloth that date back to the 14th century; what is quite possibly the earliest surviving Koran made in Ladakh; and various newspaper and magazine cuttings from the 1950s that offer insight into a bygone age.

Very little of Kargil's architectural heritage survives, but the **Aziz Bhat Sarai** [183 B1] (*between Khumaini Chowk and the river*) is a notable exception. Munshi Aziz Bhat (1866–1948), a prominent local businessman, built his three-storey caravanserai here in 1920. Horses and fodder were kept on the ground floor; goods were traded on the first floor; and visiting merchants were lodged on the upper floor.

This is the only known caravanserai remaining in Ladakh. Having been locked up for half a century, the artefacts and documents discovered here have formed the basis of the collection at the Munshi Aziz Bhat Museum (see page 185). The building itself is in a perilous condition, threatened not only by its own physical decay but also by financial pressure to demolish it and redevelop the site. Muzammil Hussain (e *muzammil@kargilmuseum.org*) is campaigning to save the caravanserai, hoping it might one day house the museum's exhibits and be preserved for future generations.

The majority of Kargil's population is Muslim and two places of worship are particularly attractive. The **main mosque** is towards the northern end of Khumaini Chowk, after the crossroads on the left, and it is also possible to visit the **Imambara** (*nr the Munshi Aziz Bhat Museum*), which is used for special celebrations at Eid.

Around Kargil
Some 15km outside of Kargil on the road towards Leh is the village of Pashkum where there are two ruined fortresses. The **Chuli Khar Fort**, set above the hamlet of Khardung, was built by the King of Pashkum, Habib Khan, in the late 17th century. Rather older is the neighbouring **Broq Khar**, the fortress of the Dard chieftain Kheva Khi Lde.

Rather than continuing straight back to Kargil, turn off the road towards Akchamal and continue to the village of Garpung where you will find the **Apati Buddha**. As impressive as the Buddha at Mulbekh (see page 162), it is at least 1,300 years old and also carved in relief from the rock.

The villages around **Bartalik** have only recently been opened to tourists, though to visit them you will still need to get an Inner Line permit (see box, page 107) before leaving Kargil. A motorable road connects Kargil and Khalsi, crossing the Haumutingla Pass (3,800m), and brings you to the villages of **Darchik** and **Garkon**, both of which are inhabited by Brokpa, an isolated tribal people of Dardic origin. Interestingly, unlike other tribal groups in the area, the Brokpa have not domesticated the cow, considering both her milk and dung to be taboo.

Further along the circuit, the people of **Shakar** and **Chiktan** are of Tibeto-Balti and Tibeto-Dardic origin, and are principally Muslim. Many local people still wear traditional dress and ornate accessories, especially at festival time, and at Chiktan you can also see the ruins of **Chiktan Khar**, the castle.

The Kargil War was an armed conflict that took place along the LoC between Indian and Pakistani forces between May and July 1999. The previous winter, Pakistani forces had been sent covertly to the Indian side of the line: it was initially claimed that these were rogue elements, or mujahideen, though senior Pakistani officers later confirmed they were regular troops.

The war itself, though short, had three distinct phases: the crossing of the LoC by Pakistani forces; the discovery of the incursion by Indian patrols, and India's subsequent mobilisation of troops; and finally direct conflict between the two sides. It was this final phase that was most serious and resulted in international pressure being brought to bear, as it is to date the only international conflict in which both sides were nuclear powers.

The exact number of casualties resulting from the war will probably never be known due to the covert nature of its early phase. Pakistan confirmed it lost 453 troops and India gave its official casualty figures as 527 dead, though non-military estimates from both sides can be twice as high.

DRASS   *Telephone code: 01985*

The town of Drass is a glorified army camp, where sunlight glints off the corrugated iron roofs. It is a fair-sized settlement and still expanding, but though there are interesting things to do in the environs, it's not a place where you'd want to stay any great length of time.

GETTING THERE AND AWAY Drass is situated on the NH1, just under a third of the way from Kargil to Srinagar. At the time of going to print, sections of the road close to the town were being widened and resurfaced, which though temporarily causing chaos, will ultimately result in a much better driving experience.

There is a police checkpoint at Mina Marg, to the west of Drass, where you have to show your passport and complete a Foreigners' Registration Form.

If you are travelling through Drass *en route* to Sonamarg and Srinagar, be sure to stop outside the police station (✆ *274 003*) to check the Zojila Pass noticeboard: this is updated daily and tells you the current status of the pass (whether it is open or closed); and if it is closed, why it is closed and when it is expected to open again. The same information can be gained by calling the police station.

To get to Drass from Kargil by **taxi** costs Rs1,670/2,200 one-way/return. It's 56km (35 miles) and usually takes just under two hours. If you are coming from Srinagar, it's still only157km but you'll need to allow at least six hours, and it can take as long as ten hours if there are delays at Zoji La (see page 189). One-way taxi fares from Srinagar start from Rs3,300, though it makes much more sense to take the taxi all the way from Srinagar to Kargil, just stopping briefly in Kargil.

Travelling by **bus**, you should take the daily JKSRTC from Srinagar to Kargil, jumping off at Drass. The bus departs from Srinagar at 07.30 and costs Rs357.

TOURIST INFORMATION A tourist information office is theoretically operated in Drass by **J&K Tourism** and is situated almost next door to the police station. When we visited, however, the dust was thick on the padlock.

⌂ **WHERE TO STAY AND EAT** Drass's accommodation options are really rather disappointing: unless you absolutely have to stay the night here, you'd be better off continuing on to Kargil or Sonamarg. Centrally located but really rather grim is the **Hotel Hill View and Restaurant** (*17 rooms*; m *941 937 7077*; **$$–$$$**), and only marginally better is **Dreamland Hotel and Restaurant** (**$$**), which is opposite the police station. For a quick snack, try **Mehfooz Bakery & Sweets** ($) on the main road.

OTHER PRACTICALITIES
Communications There are a number of small shops along the main road selling mobile phone credit and offering STD phone lines.

Medical There is a small **hospital** (☏ *274 016*) on the main road in Drass where you would be able to get basic medical attention in an emergency. For more minor incidents, and to buy medication, try **Zahoor Medicate** on the main road.

Money There is a branch of **SBI** (⊕ *10.00–16.00 Mon–Fri, 10.00–13.00 Sat*) opposite the police station on the main road. It's not possible to change money here, but there is an ATM. There is a second ATM, belonging to **J&K Bank**, next to the mosque.

WHAT TO SEE Drass is famed for its polo matches, and there is a large **polo ground** in the centre of the town. The polo season is in summer and games are reasonably regular, so ask around for forthcoming fixtures. In winter, sports fans can also watch **ice hockey**, usually played by teams from the Indian army.

On the outskirts of Drass (Kargil-side), situated at the bend in the road where the old NH1 road runs parallel to the new one, is a shrine with Buddhist prayer flags, an unusual sight in this predominantly Muslim area. Here you'll find an attractive **stone Buddha** around 1.5m tall, and also four other statues too badly weathered to identify. You'll need to pull back some of the prayer flags to see the statue properly, so be sure to put them back afterwards. We were told that the damage to the Buddha's face was caused some 12 years ago by a local man who objected to the presence of the idol and had it removed. When he and members of his family fell sick, they were concerned they were being punished for the act, and so returned the statue to its original location.

AROUND DRASS On the eastern side of Drass, 7km from the town, is the **Bhimbut Stone**. Legend has it that this is the petrified body of Bhim, the Pandava warrior whose exploits are central stories in the *Mahabharata* epic. Bhim, the second of the Pandava brothers, is credited with slaying all 100 of the Kaurava brothers in the probably mythical Kurukshetra War. The stone is becoming an increasingly popular place of pilgrimage for Hindus.

'War Tourism' is a growing attraction in the area for the domestic tourists who take tours to **Tiger Hill**, **Mushkoo** and **Tololing**. Those with a more general interest in the Kargil War, however, should stop only at the **Kargil War Memorial**, 5km east of Drass. It's an attractive monument constructed from red sandstone, and is inscribed with the names of Indian soldiers who lost their lives during the conflict. The giant Indian flag fluttering above is said to weigh 15kg, and there is also a small **museum** on site.

SONAMARG *Telephone code: 01942*

The town of Sonamarg sprawls out along a stunningly beautiful, lush green valley that is faintly reminiscent of Austria. The town thrives on domestic tourism, in particular

ZOJI LA

The Zoji La mountain pass lies between Drass and Sonamarg and, at 3,528m above sea level, it is the second-highest point along the Srinagar–Leh Highway. A thrilling ride around hairpin bends and with numerous dramatic drops to certain death, it's no mean engineering feat and understandably shuts frequently in winter months when ice and snow make it even more dangerous than usual. Several short cuts are possible on the way down only as their incline is too steep for vehicles to climb; the yellow bulldozers standing to attention, waiting for action, probably have to clear as many crumpled vehicles as piles of rock and snow.

A 14km tunnel beneath the pass is planned, and will enable the road to remain open year-round, but it is unlikely to be operational within the lifespan of this edition.

business from pilgrims heading for the Amarnath Cave. There are several well-established hiking routes, opportunities for white water rafting, scenic picnic spots and places for trout fishing. You can choose from a selection of well-run resort hotels and campsites, and getting here is hassle-free as it is easily accessible from Srinagar.

GETTING THERE AND AWAY Sonamarg lies 87km northeast of Srinagar along NH1 or, if you're approaching the town from the Kargil direction, 9km west of Zoji La.

In the summer months there is a daily tourist **bus** from Srinagar, which departs at 08.30 from the bus stand next to the tourist reception centre. The journey takes three hours and costs Rs380 return. Slightly cheaper, but much less comfortable, is the regular JKSRTC bus between Srinagar and Kargil, which passes through Sonamarg. In winter when the tourist bus is not running, this would be the only option.

By **taxi**, rates from Srinagar start from Rs2,025 and are set by the local taxi union. Given the number of people travelling to Sonamarg each day in summer, it is likely that you'll be able to find other people willing to share a car. Travelling by taxi is slightly faster than by bus: allow a little over two hours.

WHERE TO STAY Sonamarg has a large number of accommodation options, some of them very good. Prices can be high, however, and in the height of summer you'll need to book ahead to be sure of getting a room. July and August are particularly busy.

Hotel Sonamarg Glacier
(34 rooms) 241 7217; m 941 947 8432;
e hotelsonamargglacier@yahoo.com. Inspired by a Swiss chalet, the Sonamarg Glacier's rooms are wood panelled, warm & very comfortable. When the cloud lifts, there are chocolate-box views from the balconies. Bathrooms are immaculate & food in the restaurant is excellent. **$$$$$**

Namrose Resorts (30 rooms) m 979 792 1087; e namrose.resorts@gmail.com; www. namroseresorts.net. Large, comfortable rooms in an attractive modern hotel on the main road. Trpl-occupancy rooms available. Wi-Fi, satellite TV & AC included. **$$$$$**

Paradise Camping Resort m 941 907 4182; e paradisecamps@gmail.com; www. paradisecampingresorts.com. On the eastern outskirts of the town & has luxury tents with attached bathrooms. There's a multi-cuisine restaurant, electric blankets on the beds & evening camp fires. **$$$$**

Sonamarg Youth Hostel m 941 970 7307; e youthhostelsonamarg@gmail.com. Sonamarg's fairly new youth hostel is a part-timbered building on the eastern side of town. Dorms are large, light & clean, & beds cost Rs550. There is a restaurant serving vegetarian meals & the games room is popular in the evenings. **$$**

Kargil to Srinagar SONAMARG

8

189

WHERE TO EAT Three kilometres past Sonamarg on the road towards Srinagar is the **Island Retreat Restaurant** (**$$**), a clean, family-friendly place set back from the road by the river. The atmosphere is more pleasant than more crowded options in the town itself, the best of which is **J&K Tourist Cafeteria** (**$$**) on the main street.

OTHER PRACTICALITIES

Money There is a branch of **J&K Bank**, and also an **ATM**, on the main road in the centre of Sonamarg.

AMARNATH YATRA

The Amarnath *yatra*, or pilgrimage, is the principal draw for domestic tourists coming to this part of J&K: Baltal, not far from Sonamarg, is a popular starting point for the 102km trek through the mountains to the holy Amarnath Cave. The other possible departure point is Pahalgam (see page 218).

According to the Hindu texts, the Himalayas are the home of Lord Shiva, and it was inside the Amarnath Cave that he recounted the story of creation to his wife, the goddess Parvati. Inside the cave is a large ice *lingam*, a phallic structure that is associated with Shiva, as well as two smaller *lingams*, said to represent Parvati and Ganesh, the elephant-headed son of Shiva and Parvati. This is one of the holiest shrines of Hinduism, and it is possible that it has been a place of worship since 300BC.

Pilgrimage to Amarnath is only possible from late June until mid-August due to the inclement weather in the mountains. Even so, the route is frequently closed for several days during this period for safety reasons, and people do die each year on the way.

All would-be *yatris* (pilgrims) must register with the Shri Amarnathji Shrine Board (*www.shriamarnathjishrine.com*) prior to starting their pilgrimage. Non-Hindus are welcome to complete the pilgrimage route too, but still have to register and provide a medical certificate confirming they are in good health. Huts and tents are erected along the route to provide shelter, and ponies and porters can be hired to carry your baggage. You must trek with a group, not alone, and due to the physical challenges, children under 13, adults over 75 and women who are more than six weeks pregnant are not permitted to participate.

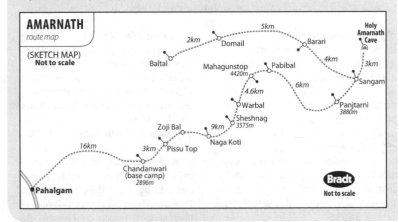

AROUND SONAMARG The area around Sonamarg is picture-postcard perfect: even in summer the surrounding peaks are sprinkled with snow, and their lower slopes are covered with meadows and pine forest. Local companies offer **white-water rafting** on the River Sindh, and it's also a popular spot for anglers as there are plenty of **trout** to catch.

The 4km climb to the **Thajiwas Glacier** takes around half an hour on foot and is by far and away the most popular short trek from Sonamarg. Though in all honesty most of the glacier has melted by summer, it is still a glorious place to walk or have a picnic. It is also possible to hire a pony and **horse trek** up here from the stand alongside the Hotel Sonamarg Glacier.

9

Srinagar and Gulmarg

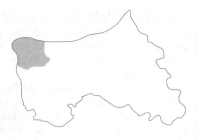

North of the Kashmir Valley, in the area around the sublimely beautiful lakeside city of Srinagar, and Gulmarg, the Himalayas' foremost ski resort, is an easily accessible part of J&K that should be an integral part of any itinerary. Whether you are drawn here by the houseboats and *shikaras*, the Mughal Gardens and other historical sites, the winter sports and trekking, or the golf, you'll quickly see why this was once India's premier tourist destination, and why there's now no reason it should not become so again.

SRINAGAR   *Telephone code: 0194*

If J&K is the crown of India, then Srinagar is the jewel in that crown. Breathtakingly beautiful as it rises from the mist that hovers in the early morning across the surface of the water in the lakes, the summer capital of J&K is a city rich in history and where history is worn lightly on the sleeve. Artistic traditions, from carpet making to woodcarving, are still practised in backstreet workshops; architectural masterpieces displaying an array of influences dot the skyline; and the houseboats, where British *memsahibs* played games of bridge, hippies smoked and the Beatles strummed away the hours under the watchful eye of Ravi Shankar, still float timelessly upon the water.

Srinagar is not trapped in the past, however: it is moving forward apace. Swiftly putting the militancy period behind it, tourism is not only reviving but also pushing into areas it has never been before. December 2013 saw the opening of the city's first cable car, transporting visitors to the Makhdoom Sahib Shrine, the new JKTDC Boat House is enabling people to try their hand at a variety of watersports, including sailing and kayaking, and the hill atop which the Hari Parbat fort is perched has been turned into an eco-reserve, a haven for local wildlife in an otherwise busy city.

HISTORY Though the Kashmir Valley has been inhabited since prehistoric times, and some claim that Srinagar itself is more than 2,000 years old, the earliest major archaeological finds were unearthed at Harwan, 21km from the centre of modern Srinagar. Dating from the early centuries AD when Kashmir was Buddhist is the base of a stupa and a chapel. Tiles excavated from the site show the central Asian influence on local costume, and the fragmented terracotta statues of the Buddha are from the Gandharan school of art.

The arrival of the Huns in the 6th century ended this era of civilisation, but the city did eventually recover, and by the late 900s it was capital of the Kashmir Valley. A succession of Hindu rulers would control the area until the mid 14th century, and many important religious sites, including the Shankacharya Temple, date from this period

Shah Mir (r1339–42), a Muslim warrior probably from the Swat Valley (now in Pakistan), defeated the last Hindu ruler and formed a dynasty that would rule for the next 200 years. The Jamia Masjid was constructed, as were many of Srinagar's

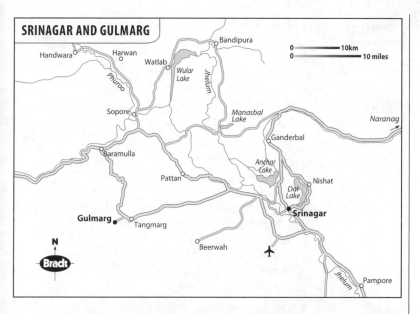

SRINAGAR AND GULMARG

most important shrines and, with the arrival of the Mughal emperors from the late 1400s onwards, the stunning Mughal Gardens were laid out.

The Mughal Empire disintegrated after 1707 and Srinagar was ruled first by the Durranis and then by the Sikhs. The 1846 Treaty of Lahore passed de facto control of the valley to the British, and their appointee, Gulab Singh, ruled the new princely state of Jammu and Kashmir from both Jammu and Srinagar.

As the summer capital of the state, Srinagar thrived economically and attracted huge numbers of tourists throughout the 20th century, including those travelling on the Hippie Trail. This period of wealth ended abruptly, however, when Srinagar became the focus of separatist violence in 1989, and clashes between the Indian security forces and militants continued throughout the 1990s.

Thankfully, Srinagar is once again a safe place to visit and FCO travel warnings have been lifted. Though the city and its people still bear the physical scars of the conflict, there is a growing sense of optimism: Srinagar is on the road to recovery, and the tourists are coming back.

GETTING THERE AND AWAY Srinagar is a regional transport hub and, although the railway does not yet reach the city, it is well served with flights, long-distance buses and taxis.

By road Although there are a number of bus stands in Srinagar, the principal one you will need is the **Tourist Bus Stand** [198 B4] (✆ 245 5107) next to the J&K Tourist Reception Centre. You should arrive at the bus stand at least half an hour before the scheduled departure to buy your ticket and get a seat.

At the Tourist Bus Stand arrive and depart long-distance de luxe coach services from/to **Delhi** (24 hours; Rs1,200/1,500 seat/bunk), **Jammu** (10 hours; Rs500), **Kargil** (7 hours; Rs555) and **Leh** (2 days with an overnight stop in Kargil; Rs1,050). From the same stand you can also take day trips to **Gulmarg** (2½ hours; Rs360 return), **Pahalgam** (3½ hours; Rs380 return), **Sonamarg** (3 hours; Rs380 return) and **Yusmarg** (2 hours; Rs360 return).

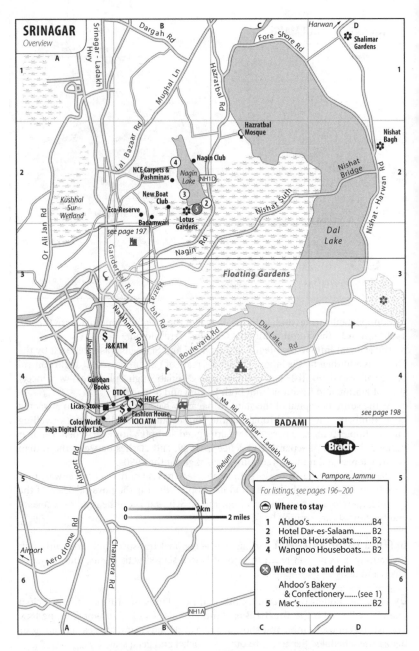

SRINAGAR
Overview

Shalimar
Gardens

Dargah Rd

Fore Shore Rd

Harwan

Mughal Ln

Hazratbal Rd

Hazratbal
Mosque

Nishat
Bagh

Nishat-Harwan Rd

Nagin Club

Nishat
Bridge

④ NCE Carpets &
Pashminas

Nagin
Lake

NH1D

New Boat
Club

③

② ⑤

Nishat Suth

Kushhal
Sur
Wetland

Eco-Reserve

Badamwari

Lotus
Gardens

see page 197

Dal
Lake

Nagin Rd

Hazratbal Rd

Ganderbal Rd

Floating Gardens

Or Ali Jan Rd

Nehru Rd

Jhelum

$ J&K ATM

Boulevard Rd

Dal Lake Rd

Gulshan
Books

DTDC

Licas Store

$ HDFC

① Fashion House,
ICICI ATM

$
J&K

Color World

Raja Digital Color Lab

Ma Rd (Srinagar - Ladakh Hwy)

BADAMI

see page 198

N

Bradt

Pampore, Jammu

Airport Rd

Jhelum

Chanpora Rd

Airport

Aerodrome Rd

NH1A

0 ————— 2km
0 ————— 2 miles

For listings, see pages 196–200

🏠 **Where to stay**
1 Ahdoo's..................................B4
2 Hotel Dar-es-Salaam..........B2
3 Khilona Houseboats..........B2
4 Wangnoo Houseboats.....B2

❌ **Where to eat and drink**
   Ahdoo's Bakery
   & Confectionery.......(see 1)
5 Mac's.....................................B2

Numerous **taxi firms** operate out of Srinagar, so you'll have both a choice of cars and, in low season, the ability to haggle somewhat on price.

By air Srinagar airport [194 A6] (*SXR*; ☎ *230 3000; www.srinagarairport.com*) is at the southern end of Aerodrome Road, on the southwestern outskirts of the city. **Air India**, **Go**, **Jet Connect** and **Spice Jet** all operate multiple daily flights to Srinagar from Delhi (70 minutes; prices from Rs4,600) and also daily flights from Jammu (40 minutes; prices from Rs3,657).

Note that even if you have an e-ticket, you will still have to show a print-out of your flight confirmation in order to be allowed inside the terminal building. You may also be subject to additional restrictions on hand baggage at times of increased security concern: check on your flight operator's website for details prior to departure.

Taxis from the airport into the centre of Srinagar cost Rs500 and are available from the Taxi Union Stand.

GETTING AROUND Depending on where you're going, the quickest way from A to B in Srinagar may be across the water. *Shikaras*, the gondola-like water taxis, cost Rs400 per hour, but for a short hop from Boulevard Road to your houseboat you'll pay around Rs60.

If you're staying on dry land, local **buses** criss-cross all areas of the city and tickets cost Rs5–6 depending on the route. You can hail a **taxi** or **auto-rickshaw** on the street with ease, and there are also a number of designated Tourist Taxi stands, including one opposite the tourist reception centre. A full day's sightseeing tour, including the Mughal Gardens, Shankacharya Temple and the Old City, will cost in the region of Rs1,750/1,950 for a non air-conditioned/air-conditioned car.

For a **radio taxi** at any hour of the day or night, call **Snowcabs** (📞 243 2432; *www. snowcabs.com*).

TOURIST INFORMATION The main source of tourist information in Srinagar is the **J&K Tourist Reception Centre** [198 B4] (*TRC Rd*; 📞 245 2691). A major new tourist complex is under construction immediately next door to the present buildings and, during the lifespan of this edition, it will open and provide all requisite tourist services under one roof.

In the meantime, the TRC offers a 24-hour information counter, a booking counter for JKTDC hotels and huts (🕐 *10.00–16.00*), a wildlife information counter (🕐 *10.00–16.00*), and staff can provide assistance with houseboat and hotel bookings as well as transport arrangements. In winter (🕐 *Nov–Mar 08.00–18.00*), it also sells tickets for the gondola at Gulmarg.

Tourist permits If you need a **wildlife permit** to visit **Dachigam National Park** (see page 207), you will ultimately be able to get it from the Wildlife counter in the new tourist centre (see above). For now, though, you have to go to see the chief wildlife warden (*Wildlife Dept, nr Lalit Grant Hotel*; 📞 246 2327; 🕐 *10.00–16.00 Mon–Fri; Rs25*). Similarly, **angling permits** are currently only available directly from the Fisheries Department (*Gogribagh*; 📱 959 609 8882). If you do not have the time to arrange these permits yourself, or would like them ready when you arrive in Srinagar, local travel agents will be able to get them for you.

LOCAL TRAVEL AGENTS

Alhabib Travels (See India Tourism ad, page 212) 12, 4th Flr, MS Shopping Mall, Kaka Sarai, Karan Nagar; 📞 250 3034; e sales@alhabibtravels. com; www.alhabibtravels.com. Run by 2 wonderfully hospitable & knowledgeable brothers, Imtiyaz Bhatt & Hyder Ali, Alhabib is an exceptional outfit. In addition to local travel arrangements in J&K, they offer transfers from Delhi & other hubs, & tours of the Golden Triangle.

Destination Paradise Tours & Travels (See ad, page 212) Dal Gate; 📱 985 879 4882; e latif@destinationparadisetravels.com; www. destinationparadisetravels.com. Proprietor Latif spent a number of years studying & working in the US before returning home to Srinagar. He's an attentive guide, thoughtful in his suggestions, & well informed about local history & politics. Winter sports & trekking packages are a particular speciality.

Fly Paradise (See ad, page 223) Hotel Paradise, Boulevard Rd; ☎ 250 0175; e flyparadisetravels@ gmail.com; www.flyparadisetravels.com. Young & enthusiastic, Sheikh Danish speaks excellent English & has imaginative ideas for excursions.

Johansen Travel Agency 7A, 1st Flr, Hotel Gulmarg Complex, Boulevard Rd; ☎ 213

3433; e rashid@johansentravels.com; www. johansentravels.com. Established in 1943, Johansen is the oldest travel agency in J&K. 60 years on it caters ably to both domestic & international tourists, has its own fleet of cars & can also provide expedition support.

RM Holidays Yatri Bawan Durganag Complex, Dal Gate; m 979 645 7999; e rmholidays@gmail. com; www.rmholidays.com. Small, Srinagar-based operator providing packages to various parts of J&K, & also car hire.

If you fancy exploring Srinagar and its highlights on foot and want a **local guide**, Renuka and Abeer of **Heritage Walks** (m *990 657 3224*; e *srinagar.walks@gmail. com*), both of whom are industrial designers, offer fascinating walking tours of the Old City that enable you to get under the skin of Srinagar. Focusing on either architecture or traditional arts and crafts, both guides are knowledgeable and passionate about preserving and promoting Srinagar's cultural heritage. Walks last several hours, are ideal for couples and small groups, and cost Rs2,000.

WHERE TO STAY

Srinagar has a wealth of accommodation options, some of which are world class. The city does become very busy in summer and around major holidays, however, so try to book as early as possible to ensure you get your first choice of houseboat or hotel. All listings are included on the maps; a cross-reference refers you to the correct map in each case.

Hotel Dar-es-Salam [map, page 194] (14 rooms) Nagin Lake; ☎ 242 7803; e info@ hoteldaressalam.com; www.hoteldaressalam.com. The only boutique hotel in Srinagar, Dar-es-Salam has superb views across Nagin Lake. Rooms are large, light & well maintained, & the attractive gardens run down to the lake. Central heating is available in winter. Travel desk can arrange water skiing & motorboat hire. $$$$$

Lalit Grand Hotel [map, page 198] (113 rooms) Gupkar Rd; ☎ 250 1001; e srinagar@ thelalit.com; www.thelalit.com. The only heritage hotel in Srinagar, the Lalit Grand is the former palace of Maharaja Pratap Singh, who built the main buildings in 1910. Notable guests include Gandhi & the Mountbattens, & you can follow in their footsteps with a stroll through the gardens. Facilities include indoor & outdoor swimming pools, a spa & several restaurants. Service is top-notch. $$$$$

Vivanta by Taj – Dal View [map, page 198] (84 rooms) Dal View, Kralsangi, Brein; ☎ 246 1111; www.vivantabytaj.com. The Taj rates as Srinagar's best hotel because of its position: the views down across the lakes & the city are

quite simply breathtaking. The décor is elegant & understated, the service world class. If you're going to blow your budget on a hotel, do it here. $$$$$

Ahdoo's Hotel [map, page 194] (24 rooms) Residency Rd; ☎ 247 2593; e ahdooshotel@yahoo. com; www.ahdooshotel.com. Ahdoo's lies between Residency Road & the river. Rooms are clean & cheerfully decorated. There is a small amount of parking on site. Wi-Fi included. $$$$

Hotel Akbar [map, page 198] (37 rooms) Dal Gate; ☎ 250 0507; e sales@hotelakbar.com; www.hotelakbar.com. We received a very warm welcome at Hotel Akbar, a large, clean property set around an attractive garden. Rooms are spacious & well equipped, beds are comfortable & the staff are helpful. Great location & an understandably popular choice. (Also consider Hotel Akbar's new sister property, Akbar Inn (behind Children's Hospital, Indra Nagar; m 941 901 6514; $$$$), a short drive from the lake.) $$$$

Hotel Paradise [map, page 198] (approx. 100 rooms) Boulevard Rd; ☎ 250 0663; e info@ hotelparadisesgr.org; www.hotelparadisesgr. org. Smack on Boulevard & with many rooms

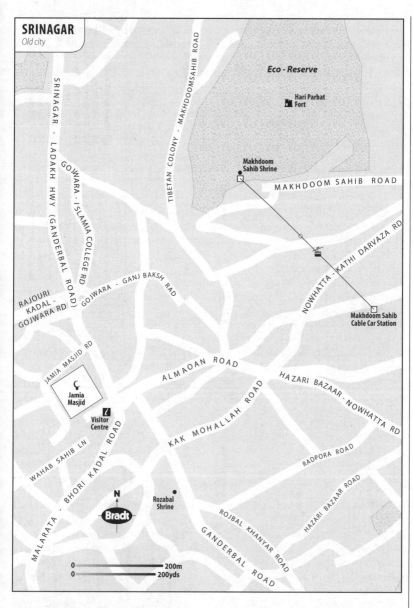

SRINAGAR
Old city

Eco - Reserve

Hari Parbat
Fort

Makhdoom
Sahib Shrine

MAKHDOOM SAHIB ROAD

SRINAGAR - LADAKH HWY (GANDERBAL ROAD)

GOJWARA - ISLAMIA COLLEGE RD

TIBETAN COLONY - MAKHDOOMSAHIB ROAD

NOWHATTA - KATHI DARVAZA RD

RAJOURI KADAL - GOJWARA RD)

GOJWARA - GANJ BAKSH RAD

Makhdoom Sahib
Cable Car Station

ALMAOAN ROAD

JAMIA MASJID RD

HAZARI BAZAAR - NOWHATTA RD

Jamia
Masjid

KAK MOHALLAH ROAD

Visitor
Centre

RADPORA ROAD

WAHAB SAHIB LN

MALARATA - BHORI KADAL ROAD

HAZARI BAZAAR ROAD

N

Bradt

Rozabal
Shrine

ROJBAL KHANYAR ROAD

GANDERBAL ROAD

0 ———————— 200m
0 ———————— 200yds

overlooking the lake, this huge hotel is a good mid-range option. Rooms are large & clean & you can negotiate good discounts from the rack rate out of season. We ate several tasty meals in the in-house restaurant, & there is a rooftop pool. Wi-Fi is available in public areas & the hotel offers free airport pickup. **$$$$–$$$**

Hotel Arjumand [map, page 198] (11 rooms) Dal Gate; 248 5578; m 959 635 9956.

Clean & conveniently located hotel with friendly staff. Substantial discounts available Nov–Mar. Wi-Fi included. **$$$–$$**

New Zeenath Guesthouse [map, page 198] (15 rooms) Dal Gate; 247 4070. Probably the cheapest accommodation option on Dal Gate, New Zeenath has large, light rooms & is clean. Some rooms overlook the lake, but they can be a little noisy. **$**

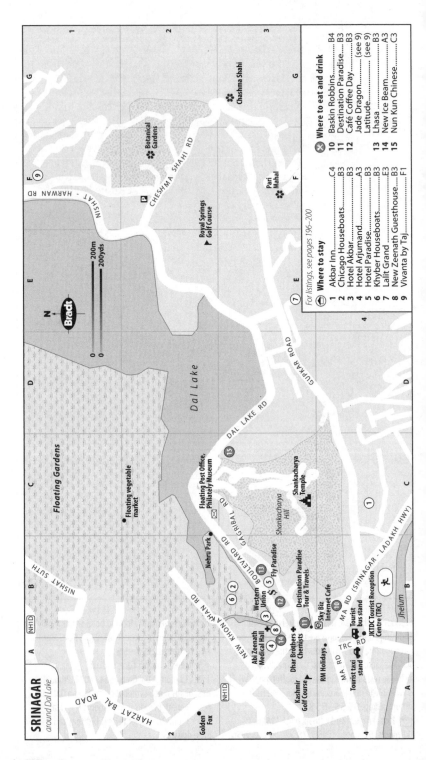

SRINAGAR
around Dal Lake

Bradt

N

0   200m
0   200yds

Floating Gardens

● Floating vegetable market

Dal Lake

Botanical Gardens

Chashma Shahi

Pari Mahal

P CHESHMA SHAHI RD

NISHAT – HARWAN RD ⑨

NISHAT SUTH

HARZAT BAL ROAD

NEW KHON A KHAN RD

Golden Fox ●

Kashmir Golf Course ▶

RM Holidays ●

Dhar Brothers Chemists

Abi Zeenath Medical Hall

⑭ ④

③ ⑧

Western Union

⑫

Destination Paradise Tour & Travels

⑪ Sky Biz Internet Cafe

Tourist taxi stand

Tourist bus stand

MA RD

TRC RD

JKTDC Tourist Reception Centre (TRC)

MA RD (SRINAGAR – LADAKH HWY)

Jhelum

⑥ ②

⑤ Fly Paradise

⑬

Nehru Park ●

Floating Post Office, Philately Museum ⊠

GAGRIBAL RD

BOULEVARD RD

Shankacharya Hill

Shankacharya Temple ✚

DAL LAKE RD

⑮

①

GUPKAR ROAD

Royal Springs Golf Course ▶

No trip to J&K could possibly be complete without a night (or, ideally, longer) aboard one of Srinagar's legendary houseboats, the beautifully carved cedar-wood structures that float romantically on lively Dal and quieter Nagin lakes. Originally built by the British to enable them to get around local restrictions on land ownership, the houseboats and the hospitality of the houseboat owners have become a Kashmiri institution, with many visitors returning year on year to spend their summers on the water.

There are quite literally thousands of houseboats in Srinagar, and they are regulated by the **Houseboat Owners Association** (↘ 245 0326; e khboa@ yahoo.com; www.houseboatowners.org), which also sets the prices for rooms and can make bookings on your behalf.

Having visited rather a lot of boats, those listed below are our absolute favourites and stand head and shoulders above the rest. That said, we couldn't visit all of them, so there will certainly be gems we've overlooked. Unless you're going on a reliable personal recommendation (and that hopefully includes ours), don't pre-book your houseboat, and especially not in Delhi. Packages are much more affordable if you arrange them directly in Srinagar, and you'll have the opportunity to look at several options before making your final choice.

🏠 **Chicago Houseboats** (See ad, page 212) [map, opposite] (6 rooms) Dal Lake; ↘ 247 7489; e chicagodallake@hotmail.com; www.chicagohouseboats.com. Houseboat owner Ajaz Khar lives with his family behind his 2 boats: he's the 4th generation of houseboatmen to welcome guests to Chicago. Hospitality is in his blood & you won't find a warmer welcome anywhere in the world. We felt like king & queen sleeping in his super de luxe-class houseboat & would readily have stayed for weeks. The best houseboats on Dal Lake. Wi-Fi included. $$$$

🏠 **Khilona Houseboats** (See ad, page 212) [map, page 194] (12 rooms) Nagin Lake; ↘ 242 2398; m 990 656 6331; www. cashmerehouseboats.com. Owned by another branch of the Wangnoo family (see Wangnoo Houseboats, below), Khilona's boats are large, lavish & immaculately kept. Brightly coloured cushions complement the rich cedar-wood walls. Highly recommended. $$$$

🏠 **Wangnoo Houseboats** (See ad, page 212) [map, page 194] Nagin Lake; m 979 610 6666; info@kashmirboats.com; www.wangnoohouseboats.com. Far quieter than Dal Lake, Wangnoo Houseboats is a sublime place to relax, read a book & watch the sun set across the water. Boat boy Din pre-empts your every need, the Wangnoo family are delightful hosts, & the meals served on board are delicious. Though each of the boats is lovely in its own way, if it's available, request the one-bedroom boat: it's a little slice of heaven. Wi-Fi included. $$$$

🏠 **Khyber Houseboats** [map, opposite] (6 rooms) Dal Lake; ↘ 213 3433; e info@khyberhouseboats.com; www.khyberhouseboats.com. Also highly recommended is Khyber Houseboats, whose comfortable boats have tastefully decorated interiors including chandeliers & wood panelling. Wi-Fi included. $$$–$$$$

All of these houseboats are able to provide a variety of meal options, and as meals are inevitably home-cooked and delicious, it's advisable to have your breakfast and evening meal aboard, even if you plan to be out and about during the day.

9

CAFES

If you just want a quick snack at the end of the day, **New Ice Beam** [map, page 198] (*Dal Gate;* ⏱ *09.00–late*) has a good selection of ice cream and snacks, and owner Ishfaq is keen to chat. **Baskin Robbins** (*MA Rd*) serves predictably fattening (and delicious) ice cream. Coffee and various iced drinks are available at **Café Coffee Day** (*Boulevard Rd*). For tasty sweets and pastries, try out **Ahdoo's Bakery** and **Confectionery** (*Residency Rd*).

✕ WHERE TO EAT Funnily enough, though Srinagar's hotel options are superb, the restaurants have some catching up to do. If you are staying on a houseboat, eat the wonderful, home-cooked meals on board; alternatively, opt for one of the tried and tested options below. Unless otherwise specified, restaurants are open all day. All listings are included on the maps; a cross-reference refers you to the correct map in each case.

✕ Latitude [map, page 198] Dal View, Kralsangi, Brein; ☎ 246 1111. Even if you can't afford to stay at the Vivanta (see page 196), go here for dinner, soak up the atmosphere & enjoy the incredible views. Latitude has floor to ceiling windows overlooking the lake & hills, service is slick, the multi-cuisine meals delicious. Alternatively, the hotel's other restaurant, Jade Dragon (⏱ 12.30–14.30 & 19.30–22.30), serves authentic Sichuan dishes in decadent surroundings in the same price bracket. $$$$$
✕ Nun Kun Chinese Restaurant [map, page 198] Dal Lake Rd. Set back from the road but still overlooking the lake, Nun Kun's food may not be authentically Chinese but is tasty nonetheless. $$$
✕ Lhasa Restaurant [map, page 198] Lane 3, Boulevard Rd; ☎ 250 0517. Popular, Tibetan-themed restaurant with indoor & outdoor tables. Both the Indian & Chinese menus are excellent & are written in English, & the AC keeps it cool in the summer heat. $$
✕ Mac's Restaurant [map, page 194] Nagin Lake Accessible only by shikara, Mac's Restaurant is tucked into edge of the floating gardens, just to the south of Nagin Lake. Though the food is nothing special, the location is fabulous, & it's for this reason if nothing else that you should come. $$

SHOPPING Of all the destinations in J&K, Srinagar undoubtedly has the best options for shopping. Famed for **handicraft production**, many of its artisans still have their workshops in the winding streets of the Old Town, and Heritage Walks (see page 196) can help you find them, to learn about the crafts and, of course, to recommend what to buy. Expect to go home with far more than you intended: thankfully both papier mâché and pashminas are light to carry. Carpets, however, will need to be shipped. For **camera accessories and photo printing**, there is a cluster of choices at Regal Chowk on Residency Road. The two best options are Raja Digital Color Lab [194 A4] (☎ 245 1748) and its neighbour Color World [194 A4] (☎ 248 0369), but if they don't have what you need then try Licas (☎ 247 2180), which is virtually opposite.

Note that most shops in Srinagar are closed on Friday afternoon when the proprietors go to the mosque for Friday prayers.

Golden Fox [198 A2] Nowpora; 📱 990 657 0993; ✉ goldenfoxfurriers@yahoo.co.in. Elderly Ghulam Nabi paddles across Nagin Lake to display his collection of handmade leather goods to houseboat guests. Soft suede purses start from Rs110, & leather handbags decorated with colourful embroidery are similarly a snip at Rs1,100. You can visit his factory or, more pleasurably, call him to visit you on your boat.
Gulshan Books [194 B4] Residency Rd; ☎ 247 7287; www.gulshanbooks.net. Quiet, AC store with good selection of English-language books & helpful staff.

Fashion House [194 B4] The Bund; 247 4808; ⏰ 09.30–20.00 Mon–Sat. Over the years we've had a lot of tailoring done in India, but nowhere has done a better job than Fashion House. The master has an eye for detail & his cutting of a blazer or gentleman's suit is perfect. Expect to pay Rs1,000 for a made to measure shirt, & around Rs8,000 for a three-piece suit. Highly recommended.

Mr Marvellous Nagin Lake. Cruising around Nagin Lake each morning in his bright red shikara you'll find Mr Marvellous, the aptly named local flower seller. His father, the original Mr Marvellous, featured in a *National Geographic* photo shoot in 1958, & the son has carried on the family business, selling fragrant blooms to decorate the houseboats & charm the guests.

Mr Mehboob Nagin Lake; m 990 671 3870. Yet another floating emporium, Mr Mehboob sells the fine papier mâché that Srinagar is famous for. Though his prices are slightly higher than elsewhere in the city, the quality is high & he'll lay out a carefully chosen selection of wares on the veranda of your boat. Prices start from Rs100 for papier mâché boxes, & he also stocks baubles, trays & coaster sets.

NCE Carpets & Pashminas [194 B2] Behind WelcomHeritage Houseboats, Nagin Lake; 242 5229; e ncegroup@vsnl.com; www.ncerugs. com. Genuine pashminas & Kashmiri carpets are expensive, even in Srinagar, so if you want to ensure you're getting the real deal, you have to go to the experts. Visiting the owner, Saboor, is an educational experience: he can arrange for you to watch the carpets being made, & will explain painstakingly the manufacturing process, as well as how to identify the different materials & levels of quality. Carpets here start from US$500 & go up to more than US$40,000. Many are investment pieces, & all of them are beautiful.

Sona Sultana Saidakadal Rd; 242 0797. Sona Sultana is primarily a woodcarving workshop rather than a shop, but it also sells finished pieces & it's wonderful to watch the artisans intricately carving everything from decorative boxes & elephant figurines to ornate screens & tables.

OTHER PRACTICALITIES

Communications Srinagar is home to what is probably the world's only floating **post office** [198 C2] (⏰ *11.00–20.00 Mon–Sat*), moored on Boulevard Road. It is the only houseboat permanently docked on this side of the water, and the bright red India Post gives it away in any case. The same boat also houses a small and uninspiring **Philately Museum** that is free to enter.

To send anything of value, it is best to use a courier. **DTDC** [194 B4] (*Residency Rd*; 247 3242) is a reputable company.

If you need to get online, **Sky Biz Internet Café** [198 B4] is conveniently situated on Dal Gate.

Medical There are pharmacies all over Srinagar, most of which are well stocked and have at least one English-speaking member of staff. Particularly convenient are the **Abi Zeenath Medical Hall** [198 B3] (*Dal Gate*; m 941 994 4559) and **Dhar Brothers Chemists** [198 B3] (*Dal Gate*), which also benefits from having an attached polyclinic.

TREKKING EQUIPMENT HIRE

If you are planning to trek in the mountains around Srinagar and need to hire equipment locally, the most affordable and convenient option is JKTDC at the tourist reception centre (see *Tourist information*, page 195). It has a variety of trekking and camping items available, and sample prices per day/week are as follows:

Four-person tent	Rs300/1,500	Crampons	Rs40/200
Sleeping bag	Rs60/300	Ropes	Rs300/1,500

Srinagar has a number of medical facilities, the most significant of which is the **SMHS Hospital** (*Karan Nagar;* \245 2013; *www.smhs.info*), which is also part of the Government Medical College. The hospital has a 24-hour emergency department and well-qualified doctors.

Money Most of India's banks have branches in Srinagar, and there are plenty of 24-hour ATMs. The vast majority of these are on Residency Road where you'll find **HDFC Bank** [194 B4] and **J&K Bank** [194 B4], both of which have ATMs, and also **SBI** and **ICICI** ATMs.

If you need to send or receive money, there is a branch of **Western Union** [198 B3] on Boulevard Road, next to Hotel Paradise.

ACTIVITIES
Angling Srinagar's rivers and lakes are rich in fish, in particular the fat brown trout introduced by the British in the 19th century. Fishing is permitted, but you need to get an angling permit from Qazi Riyaz at the **Department of Fisheries** (*Gogribagh;* m *959 609 8882*). When the new tourist reception centre (see page 195) opens, you will be able to get one there too.

Golf Srinagar has a number of golf courses, the most exclusive of which is the 18-hole **Royal Springs Golf Course** [198 E2] (*Cheshma Shahi, Boulevard Rd;* \250 1158; e *bookings@royalspringsgolfcourse.com*). Set among 300 acres of rolling hills and, of course, the four springs that give the club its name, Royal Springs also has a pool, a gym and a restaurant. Green fees for non-members are Rs1,500/US$40 for Indians/foreigners. Hire of golf sets is Rs200 and caddies cost Rs300.

An alternative option, much closer to the centre of town, is the **Kashmir Golf Course** [198 A3] (\247 6677) on MA Road. The oldest course in Srinagar, it has 18 holes and nine fairways. Non-members pay Rs3,000 on weekdays and Rs1,500 at weekends. Golf sets cost Rs150 to hire.

Watersports JKTDC has constructed a brand-new **boat club** [194 B2] (*nr Nagin Lake*) with natural pine interiors and large windows for spectators to enjoy the view. In addition to swimming, which is popular in summer, you can try your hand at sailing, kayaking and windsurfing. Local travel agents can also arrange white-water rafting on some of the rivers around the city.

If you prefer to explore the water in a more leisurely fashion, hire one of the colourful *shikaras* (Rs400/hr) and be paddled at your leisure among the floating gardens with their bright pink and white lotus flowers.

Ballooning On the southern side of Dal Lake you can go up in a **tethered balloon** (*Zabarwan Pk; Rs500*). The balloon rises 106m above the shore, giving panoramic views and an enviable photographic opportunity.

WHAT TO SEE Srinagar and its environs are packed with a bewildering array of incredible sites: you'd have to stay for months to be able to see them all and do them justice. Though your personal tastes (natural landscapes, formal gardens, religious buildings, archaeological sites, etc) will inevitably help shape your choice of itinerary, there are some places that no-one should miss: the floating vegetable market and lotus gardens; views across the city from the Hari Parbat fort; and an afternoon in one or more of the world-famous Mughal Gardens.

Badamwari [194 B2] (*nr Hari Parbat;* ⊕ *09.00–19.00*) Historical but not technically a Mughal Garden, this lovely park at the foot of Hari Parbat takes its name from the almond trees (*badam* meaning almond) with which it was originally planted. Recently restored with support from J&K Bank, the garden is especially attractive in the springtime when the almond trees are covered in fluffy, white blossom: you can survey the site best from the Hari Parbat eco-reserve above (see page 204).

Botanical gardens [198 F2] (*Cheshma Shahi Rd;* m *969 706 9964;* ⊕ *08.00–20.00; entrance ticket Rs10/5 adult/child*) Srinagar's attractive botanical gardens, opened in 1969, complement the Mughal Gardens (see box, pages 203–4) by providing both more informal areas of parkland and, importantly, nurseries for botanical research. In total the garden covers more than 80ha of land, and more than 300 species of plant are represented.

The gardens are family friendly and, in addition to picnicking in the grounds (which is especially popular at weekends), you can also hire a pedalo on the manmade **boating lake**. This costs Rs50 for 30 minutes and each of the pedalos seats four people.

The stunning **Tulip Garden** (⊕ *April only*), built in memory of assassinated prime minister Indira Gandhi, is a riot of colour in the springtime, with different-coloured tulips carefully planted in stripes across the hillside to maximise their visual impact. The blooms don't last very long, however, so get there while you can.

Floating gardens [map, page 198] Though Dal and Nagin lakes look on the map like two separate bodies of water, they are in fact joined with waterways through a labyrinth of floating islands, manmade areas reclaimed from the water where people live but also grow their crops. Like in Venice, water taxis are the only way to travel from A to B, and travelling the back waters you'll see *shikaras* carrying children to school, men to the market and women on their way to visit friends.

Exploring any part of these waterways is a delight, but particular highlights are the **Lotus Gardens** [194 B2] where pink and white water lilies and lotus flowers float upon the surface of the lake. Try to deter your *shikara* man from picking one for you: they look best in their natural setting.

Business at the floating **vegetable market** [198 C2] (⊕ *04.00–06.30*) starts even before the sun comes up. Men in their open *shikaras* haggle enthusiastically for armfuls of knobbly green gourds, white radishes and bundles of spinach. Though this is a photographer's dream, and large numbers of tourists do come to spectate on the scene, this is a real market, the place of choice for local people to buy their vegetables, fruits and fresh flowers.

Hari Parbat Fort [map, page 197] (*Hari Parbat Hill;* ⊕ *09.30–17.30 daily*) Hari Parbat is actually the name of the hill, but it has come to be used for the fort on top of it too. Legend has it that the hill was once a lake and inhabited by the demon Jalobhava. The demon terrorised local people (as demons are wont to do), and so they called out to the goddess Parvati for protection. Taking the shape of a bird, Parvati flew into the sky and dropped a rock on the demon, crushing him to death. The rock continued to grow until eventually it was as large as a hill. There is a **Parvati Temple** on the western slope.

Many people will tell you that the fort is Mughal, built by Emperor Akbar in 1590, but actually this isn't true: the fortified outer wall was built by Akbar in anticipation of him building a new city inside, but this city never materialised. The present fort

It doesn't matter if horticulture isn't your thing: the Mughal Gardens are far more than collections of plants. Built in accordance with traditional Persian garden design, which in turn took its inspiration from the Islamic view of heaven, replete with flowing water, fruit trees and architectural follies, these were the pleasure gardens of the late medieval period. Sensitively restored and lovingly tended by teams of gardeners, they show man's desire and ability, now as when they were first made, to shape the wilderness, to tame aspects of nature to his will.

CHASHMA SHAHI [198 G3] (*Cheshma Shahi Rd;* ⏱ *09.00–19.00; entrance fee Rs10/5 adult/child*) The 'Garden of the Royal Spring' was built in 1632 by Ali Mardan Khan, a noble at the court of Shah Jahan. Steep stone steps flanked with bright flowers lead visitors to the painted, Mughal archway that marks the entrance to the garden. Laid out in the traditional Persian style across three terraces, replete with watercourses that delight the local pigeon population as well as small children, and immaculately maintained, the planting is carefully thought out and complements the fountains, watercourses and other architectural features. Though substantially smaller than some of the other Mughal Gardens, Chashma Shahi is a beautiful, calm place and well worth taking time to visit, especially in the early evening.

Though they speak little English, the gardeners are happy to chat about their work and will eagerly identify the different plants for you if you don't know quite what you're looking at. They'll also sell you a selection of ten different packets of seeds that they've collected from the garden (Rs100).

NISHAT BAGH [194 D2] (*Nishat–Harwan Rd;* ⏱ *09.00–19.00; entrance fee Rs10/5 adult/child*) On the eastern shore of Dal Lake, with views back across the water, the 'Garden of Joy' is thought to have been commissioned by Asaf Khan, brother-in-law of the Mughal emperor Jahangir, in the early 1600s. It is said that Jahangir's son, Shah Jahan, visited the garden in 1633 and, having repeatedly stated how beautiful he found it, he expected it to be given it as a gift. When Asaf Khan demurred (he was, after all, rather fond of his garden himself), Shah Jahan ordered that the garden's water supply, which came from his own Shalimar Garden, be cut off. A servant disobeyed the order, and the garden and its plants were saved.

Nishat Bagh is divided into four equal parts, with a water channel separating each section and leading one's eye to the lake. Originally it had both public areas and a separate, private section for the women of the *zenana* (harem), although this is no longer the case today.

dates in fact from 1808 and was built by the Afghan Shuja shah Durrani, though its red sandstone structure is certainly reminiscent of Mughal forts elsewhere.

Having been closed to the public for years, and partially occupied by the Indian army, the Hari Parbat fort finally reopened for tourists at the end of 2013. Relatively little conservation work has so far been done, and so you need to watch your feet as you explore the higgledy-piggledy courtyards, towers, tanks and terraced gardens. Though no longer roofed, the walls (and, thus, the layout) of internal rooms are still easily visible, and peering out through the archers' slits in the metre-thick walls gives an almost birds'-eye view of Srinagar.

Though you can drive straight up to the gates of the fort, it's far more pleasurable to walk up through the newly designated **eco-reserve**, which is stocked with fruit trees,

The garden has a total of 12 terraces, and it is remarkable how the water flow is manipulated to pass from one to the next: there are successions of pools, chutes, channels and numerous fountains. Equally of note is the wooden *baradari* (pavilion), the octagonal towers flanking what was the *zenana* garden, and the *chadar*, the manmade waterfalls carved from slabs of marble and sometimes elaborately engraved.

PARI MAHAL [198 F3] (*Chashma Shahi Rd; ⊕ 09.00–19.00; entrance fee Rs10/5 adult/child*) Up above the Chashma Shahi is the Pari Mahal, the 'Fairy Palace'. Founded by Dara Shikoh, the eldest son of Mughal emperor Shah Jahan, in 1635, the garden was originally watered by natural springs, though many of these have now run dry. The garden was built across seven terraces, five of which survive, and they lead up to the central building with its numerous archways. Perhaps originally built as a Buddhist monastery, it was converted by Dara Shikoh into an observatory, as he was a keen and able astronomer.

The Pari Mahal is floodlit at night, and indeed the early evening is the best time to come here. The soft light is flattering to both the buildings and the plants, and there can be no more romantic place from which to watch the sun set across the lake.

SHALIMAR GARDENS [194 D1] (*Nishat–Harwan Rd; ⊕ Apr–Oct 08.00–20.30; Nov–Mar 09.00–19.00; entrance fee Rs10/5 adult/child*) The largest and most famous of the Mughal Gardens is Shalimar, 'The Abode of Love'. There has been a structure on the site since the 6th century, but it was Jahangir who built the first garden here in 1619. It was then extended in 1630 on the orders of Shah Jahan, ultimately covering an area of 12.4ha.

The garden is made up of four terraces, the water for which is supplied by a nearby tank and network of canals lined with chinar trees. The different terraces were originally for the use of the public, the emperor, and his *zenana*.

Though the planting is as exquisite as in any of the other Mughal Gardens, it is the buildings that set Shalimar apart. Just above the entrance gate is the **Diwan-i Aam**, the public audience hall where the emperor would sit atop his black marble throne to attend to daily affairs of state. Little save the foundations of the **Diwan-i Khas** (private audience hall) remains, but there are a number of other attractive pavilions, including the **Black Pavilion**, a marble structure in the *zenana* garden, and smaller buildings that would have been used as guardhouses, preventing unwanted visitors from accessing the *zenana*.

aromatic plants and other indigenous species. A **visitor centre** is under construction, and a new footpath will ultimately wind its way from the road (close to Badamwari) up to the fort, with plenty of places along the way to stop and admire the view.

Hazratbal Mosque [194 C2] (*Hazratbal Rd; ⊕ closed during prayers*) On the western shore of Dal Lake is the pearl-like Hazratbal Mosque. The name 'Hazratbal' means holy place and is earned by virtue of the fact that the shrine contains a holy relic, a hair of the Prophet Muhammad. The hair itself is referred to as Moi-e-Muqqadas (the sacred hair).

It is said that the hair was first brought to India by a descendant of the Prophet, Syed Abdullah, in the 1600s. The relic passed into the care of a wealthy Kashmiri merchant, Khwaja Nur-ud-Din Ishbari, but was then seized by the Mughal emperor Aurangzeb, who displayed it at the Chishti shrine in Ajmer, Rajasthan. Realising eventually that such a sacred item should not be taken by force, Aurangzeb repented and sent the hair to Srinagar, along with the body of Ishbari, who was recently deceased. Ishbari's daughter, Inayat Begum, became custodian of the relic, and established the Hazratbal Shrine in which to preserve it in 1700.

The shrine building you see today, as magnificent in its reflection in the lake water as in reality, is the only domed mosque in the city: the others have distinct, pagoda-like roofs. The mosque is relatively modern, and was completed by the Muslim Auqaf Trust in 1979.

Jamia Masjid [map, page 197] (*Ganderbal Rd*; ⊕ *closed during prayers*) Srinagar's main mosque was built in 1398 by Sultan Sikander, and later expanded by his son so that 33,333 worshippers could gather here to pray at any one time. During Friday prayers, the Jamia Masjid is almost full to capacity.

The architecture of the mosque is unique: the 370 pillars surrounding the magnificent courtyard are built from wood as the area around the city was historically thickly forested. Each column is made from a single tree. Though the layout of the mosque is conventional, the pagoda-like design of the minarets shows the regional influence of Tibetan Buddhism. The building has been destroyed by fire three times, most recently during the reign of Maharaja Pratap Singh, but every time it has been rebuilt to the original design, just as elegantly as before.

The entire area around the Jamia Masjid is being renovated to improve its appearance: new façades on the shops mirror the mosque's own architecture, and there is a newly built **visitor centre** over the top of the mosque's ablutions area.

Makhdoom Sahib Shrine [map, page 197] (*Makhdoom Sahib Rd*) Getting to the Makhdoom Sahib Shrine is half the fun; there is a new cable car (⊕ *10.00–17.00 daily; Rs100 rtn*) and the ride up there, though short, is very enjoyable indeed.

Makhdoom Sahib, also known as Hazrat Sultan, was a Sufi saint who lived in Kashmir in the early 16th century. Highly educated, he was a mystic and several miracles are attributed to him: he grew a long, white beard in an instant, and having collected together in his hand the bones of a bird he had just eaten, the bones rejoined, and the bird came back to life and flew away.

The shrine is Makhdoom Sahib's burial place, and it remains an important place of pilgrimage for Sufis, many of whom come here to pray. Men and women are welcome in the shrine (though only men are allowed into the inner sanctum). Shoes must be left at the entrance and women must cover their heads.

Rozabal Shrine [map, page 197] (*Ganderbal Rd*) Small and unassuming, the Rozabal Shrine is also one of the most controversial sites in Kashmir: some people, including Muslims belonging to the Ahmeddiya sect, claim that Jesus did not die on the cross but in fact survived the crucifixion, continued his teachings in Kashmir, and was eventually buried here (see box, page 133).

Rozabal is, in any case, a holy place for Muslims: it is officially the tomb of Saint Yuz Asaf, and as such it is a place of prayer and quiet reflection. There has been some resistance to tourists coming here sightseeing (as opposed to visiting on pilgrimage) in recent years, so you should take advice locally as to whether or not you are welcome to go inside. In any case, you should behave, dress and speak respectfully here, as you would in any other holy place.

Shankacharya Temple [198 C3] (*Shankacharya Hill;* ⊕ *06.00–18.00*) Perched atop the hill, with superb (albeit frequently misty) 360° views down across Srinagar and the lakes, is the Shankacharya Temple. Thought to be the oldest Shiva temple in Kashmir, though previously dedicated to Jyeshthesvara, the current structure dates from the 9th century, though it is likely that it is on the site of an older building. This earlier building probably pre-dates the current temple by 200–300 years. The temple is set on an octagonal plinth (traditionally ascribed to King Gopaditya) and the inner sanctum contains a *lingam*, above which is a decorative ceiling built on the instruction of the Mughal emperor Shah Jahan in 1644.

Note that security around the temple is tight. There is a security check at the bottom of the hill and all vehicle passengers must disembark, rejoining their car on the other side of the checkpoint. In the parking area at the top of the hill, 200 stone steps beneath the temple itself, there is another police checkpoint and you have to pass through a metal detector. Rules for those entering the temple are strict: you may not carry about your person any tobacco or meat products, mobile phones or other electronics.

AROUND SRINAGAR Dedicated to Lord Shiva, the **Pandrethan Temple** is 6km east of Srinagar. It was built between 913 and 921 and is situated at the centre of a pond or tank fed by a natural spring. It is the draining of this pool over the past millennium that has caused the structure to shift: it now tilts by approximately five degrees. The temple is relatively small, square and is built of stone. Its stone ceiling, carved with geometric patterns is, remarkably, original and intact, and the temple attracted the attentions of numerous 19th-century visitors.

Pandrethan is situated inside an army cantonment, so you'll need to get permission from the officers on duty before going inside.

The village of **Harwan**, 3km north of the Shalimar Gardens (and so 21km from central Srinagar), looks unremarkable enough from the road. It is, however, the site at which the earliest archaeological discoveries around Srinagar were made, and hence is certainly worth a visit.

A J&K Tourism board points you in the direction of the ancient **stupa**, evidence of the area's Buddhist past. The Kushan emperor Kanishka is said to have convened the Great Council nearby, so it is likely that the stupa dates from this period.

Neighbouring the stupa site is **Harwan Garden** (⊕ *07.30–19.30; entrance fee Rs10/5 adult/child*), another formal garden that appears to take its inspiration from the Mughal Gardens, with its lake, canals and chinar trees.

Harwan is also the preferred access point for **Dachigam National Park** (⊕ *Mon–Fri*), which covers some 141km². The park has been a protected area since 1910 and it takes its name from the ten villages that had to be relocated when it was made: Dachigam means '10 villages'. The park sprawls across the Zabarwan Hills and includes a substantially sized lake, the Sarband. Habitats in the park range from grassland and scrub to coniferous forest, and the mammal population includes otters, marmots and weasels, Himalayan black and brown bears, leopards and leopard cats, musk deer and jackals. The birdlife is similarly diverse, with regular sightings of black bulbuls, golden orioles, pygmy owlets, the Kashmir flycatcher, streaked laughingthrushes and bearded and Himalayan griffon vultures among others.

Note that to gain access to the park you will need to get a **permit** from the chief wildlife warden (*Wildlife Dept, nr Lalit Grand Hotel, Srinagar;* ☏ *246 2327; Rs25*) beforehand. It is issued while you wait, though allow two hours to be on the safe side.

Some 50km northeast of Srinagar is **Naranag**, a village set in a scenic valley. Though the flower-filled meadows have their own charm in springtime, the principal attraction here is the group of **Naranag Temples**, one of which is very similar in style and age to the Pandrethan Temple (see page 207). Dedicated to Shiva by King Laladitya in the 8th century, the temples are built of stone, and the main complex (which includes seven different temple structures) is really quite impressive indeed. Look out for the elaborate architectural details such as the trefoil arches, Graeco Roman-style pediments, and a vast gateway like the one at Avantipora (see page 216).

From Naranag village it is a nine-hour trek to the high-altitude **Gangabal Lake**. This is a sacred site, considered by some Hindus to be as holy as Haridar, and in September each year a number of Kashmiri pandits still take a three-day *yatra* to the shore. Stunningly beautiful, unspoilt and a prime spot for camping, it is understandably popular with tourists too, many of whom trek up here and then spend a few days among the shepherds, fishing for the fat brown trout that thrive in the waters of the lake.

Northwest of Srinagar, some 60km away, is **Wular Lake** (*www.wularlake.org*), one of the largest freshwater lakes in Asia. Fed by the Jhelum River, Wular appears in a number of ancient texts, including the writings of the Persian traveller and writer Al Biruni (930–1031).

Wular is recognised as a wetland of international importance: it supports a large number of species of birds (including kites, sparrowhawks and eagles), and also vast numbers of fish. Fishing is a major local business, and more than 8,000 fishermen are thought to make their living from Wular's waters.

Since 2011, J&K Tourism has been developing various opportunities for **watersports** on the lake, including boat hire and waterskiing.

GULMARG *Telephone code: 01954*

In the 1500s, Gaurimarg ('the fair one') was renamed Gulmarg ('meadow of flowers') by Sultan Yusuf Shah. Both names are equally apt. Set among rolling hills and thickly carpeted with flowers throughout spring and into summer, it's an idyllic place to walk and picnic when the weather is warm.

It's in winter, however, that Gulmarg comes into its own: it's India's winter sports capital. The gondola is open year-round and from November to March transports skiers and snowboarders 5km up the mountainside to a height of 4,267m, and you can ski all the way down to Tangmarg. There are some excellent accommodation options (albeit all at the more expensive end of the spectrum) to choose from, and a lively crowd of youthful skiers (both Indians and foreigners) means you'll have plenty of playmates with whom you can enjoy the après ski.

HISTORY Easily accessible from Srinagar, Gulmarg has been a popular tourist spot ever since the medieval period. The Mughal emperor Jahangir came here to collect flowers for his garden, and the British found it a cool and pleasant playground where they could escape both the city and the heat of the plains. The British built the golf course and the Anglican church (see *What to see*, page 211), and Gulmarg soon became a centre for golf competitions and general fun and frolics until its links with the outside world were severed by the militancy in 1989. Now on the road to recovery, its gondola was installed in two stages in 1998 and 2005, and the town hosted India's National Winter Games in 1998, 2004 and 2008.

GETTING THERE AND AWAY Gulmarg lies 56km to the west of Srinagar, and is easily accessible by road. **Tourist buses** depart from the TRC Stand in Srinagar, take 2½ hours and cost Rs360 return. The much cheaper **standard bus** goes from Srinagar to Tangmarg (the neighbouring village to Gulmarg) and costs Rs24 one way. **Taxis** will charge you from Rs1,790/1,990 one-way for a non-air-conditioned/air-conditioned car.

GETTING AROUND Gulmarg town is best explored on foot, and indeed there was no road here at all until 50 years ago. If you plan to ski or otherwise go up into the hills, however, you'll need to take the **gondola**. From the base station you ascend the 400m to Kongdori (Rs400), then the second phase takes you up to Aparwath (Rs600). There is also a **chair lift** (Rs300) from Kongdori to Marry Shoulder. In winter, however, it is more cost-effective to get a ski pass (see *Winter sport*, page 210).

TOURIST INFORMATION Information about skiing in Gulmarg, and also use of the gondolas and chair lift, is available online from **Gulmarg Gondola** (*www. gulmarggondola.com*). You can also call on the customer care line (**m** 965 022 6555).

Courses for all levels and information for advanced skiers are available from the **Indian Institute of Skiing and Mountaineering** (*nr Gulmarg Golf Course;* 193 403; **e** *skitigers@gmail.com; www.iismgulmarg.com*). For more general information about what to see and do in Gulmarg, you have to contact the Tourist Reception Centre in Srinagar (see page 195).

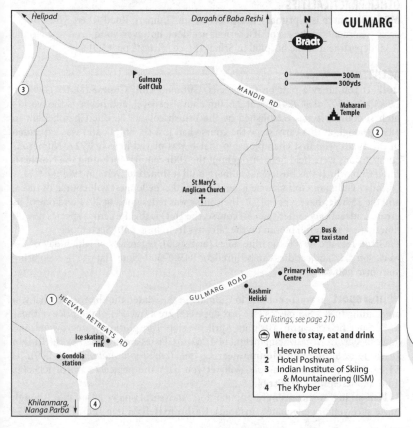

GULMARG

For listings, see page 210

🍴 **Where to stay, eat and drink**
1 Heevan Retreat
2 Hotel Poshwan
3 Indian Institute of Skiing
   & Mountaineering (IISM)
4 The Khyber

9

🏠 WHERE TO STAY AND EAT

Though Gulmarg does have some excellent accommodation options, they are quite expensive by local standards. If you are travelling on a budget, you will find it cheaper (though not as convenient) to stay in Srinagar and take the bus up here for the day. All listings are shown on the map on page 209.

🏠 **Heevan Retreat** (35 rooms) ✆0194 250 1323; e info@ahadhotelsandresorts.com; www.ahadhotelsandresorts.com. Crisp, white linens in wood-panelled rooms welcome you to the restful Heevan Retreat. Staff are friendly, food in the restaurant is good, & there's a games room with snooker tables to enjoy in the evenings. $$$$$

🏠 **The Khyber** (80 rooms, 4 cottages) ✆254 666; e info@khyberhotels.com; www.khyberhotels.com. Gulmarg's finest hotel is this stunning resort & spa. Built like an alpine chalet, the large rooms have teak floors & have Kashmiri carpets. Meals are served in 1 of the 4 restaurants & cafés. It is, quite simply, perfect. $$$$$

🏠 **Hotel Poshwan** (43 rooms) ✆254 506; manager@hotelposhwan.com; www.hotelposhwan.com. Substantially cheaper than many of Gulmarg's hotels, Poshwan is centrally located & warm, if a bit scruffy around the edges. $$$$

🏠 **Indian Institute of Skiing and Mountaineering (IISM)** Nr Gulmarg Golf Course; ✆254 480; e skitigers@gmail.com; www.iismgulmarg.com. If you're a ski fanatic, the obvious place to stay is at the IISM. Rooms are large, comfortable & warm, bathrooms are clean & there's a restaurant on site. $$$$

OTHER PRACTICALITIES

Medical   There is a primary health centre on Gulmarg Road where you can get basic treatment. In the event of a serious accident, however, you'd need to go to the A&E department at the hospital in Srinagar (see *Medical*, page 201).

ACTIVITIES

Golf   If you fancy a putt on the greens, **Gulmarg Golf Course** (*Outer Gulmarg Link*; ✆ *254 507, 254 424*) lies at 2,650m above sea level, and hence is the world's highest course. It was established by the British colonel Neville Chamberlain in 1890 (though at this early stage the course had just six holes), and was expanded in the 1920s. The first championship match was played here in 1922. Numerous competitions were held here throughout the 20th century, including the Northern India Cup, which was hosted at Gulmarg until it shifted to Delhi in 1989.

Today Gulmarg Golf Course is, at 7,505 yards, the longest golf course in India, and the 18 holes have a par of 72. The course was redesigned in 2011 and one of its greatest attractions (other than, of course, the golf) is the numerous species of wild flowers that are in full bloom on the fairways from June until September.

Green fees are Rs800 (or nine holes for Rs600), regardless of which day of the week you play, and caddies can be hired for Rs300–500. Note that you need to bring your own golf balls.

Winter sport   If you're coming to Gulmarg in the winter, the chances are that you are coming to ski. Ski passes (see box opposite) are a fraction of the price of those in Europe, the ski season lasts until April, the slopes are gloriously uncrowded, and you can start from a dizzying height of 4,267m. Classes are provided by the **Indian Institute of Skiing and Mountaineering** (see *Tourist information*, page 209). Its 14-day ski school, for example, will set you back the princely sum of Rs5,000. Tuition, therefore, is irresistible.

Heli-skiing is increasingly popular too, and surprisingly affordable (though make sure you are adequately insured). **Kashmir Heliski** (*c/o Hotel Global*; ✆ *254*

Ski passes in Gulmarg are issued by Gulmarg Gondola or, to give the company its official, rather more unwieldy name, the J&K State Cable Car Corporation. Prepaid ski passes can be purchased online (*www.gulmarggondola.com*), and they're also available from the tourist reception centre in Srinagar (see page 195) and at the gondola base station. You pay separately for phases 1 and 2 of the gondola and for the chairlift, unless you buy a season pass.

The prices below are given in rupees.

Indians

	Phase 1	Phase 2	Chairlift	All Lifts
One-time	200	300	200	
Day pass	600	1,000	700	
Week pass	2,600	6,000	3,000	
Season pass				30,000

Foreigners

	Phase 1	Phase 2	Chairlift	All Lifts
One-time	200	300	200	
Day pass	1,000	1,600	1,200	
Week pass	4,500	8,000	5,000	
Season pass				30,000

519; e *billa@kashmirheliski.in*) arranges both heli-skiing and heli-boarding, as well as guided backcountry skiing. It offers a flexible helicopter charter package for US$250 per day, which includes up to ten runs.

There is an **ice-skating rink** on the corner of Gulmarg Road and Heevan Retreat Road. It is also possible to try **tobogganing** and **snow scooters**.

WHAT TO SEE If skiing's not your thing, or you fancy a few days off, Gulmarg has a number of interesting sites to keep you entertained. **St Mary's Anglican Church** stands proudly in the midst of the golf course. Dating from 1902, it certainly wouldn't look out of place in an English village.

A little older is the **Maharani Temple** (also known as the Mohineshwar Shivalaya), a curious, cone-shaped shrine that was used by the Dogra rulers. The temple shot to fame in the Bollywood film *Aap ki Kasam*, as one of the main songs was recorded here.

AROUND GULMARG A 6km trek from Gulmarg brings you to gorgeous **Khilanmarg**, by turns a snow- and flower-carpeted meadow from where it is possible to see the impressive mountain peak that is Nanga Parba (7,100m).

A similarly easy walk (8km), leads to the **Dargah of Baba Reshi**. The saint was a noble at the court of King Zain-ul-Abidin in the mid 15th century, but he renounced all worldly ties to follow the spiritual leader Sheikh Nur-ud-Din Noorani. When Baba Reshi died in 1480, he was buried here, and his tomb became a place of pilgrimage for Kashmiri Muslims.

10

The Kashmir Valley

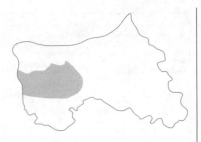

The Kashmir Valley lies between the Karakoram and Pir Panjal mountain ranges, stretching out along the Jhelum River. Though it includes areas to the north and west of Srinagar too, such places are covered in *Chapter 9: Srinagar and Gulmarg*. This chapter examines the central and southern sections of the valley, from the vibrant saffron fields of Pampore, to the Mughal tank and garden at Verinag.

PAMPORE *Telephone code: 01933*

Pampore lies just 14km (9 miles) to the south of Srinagar, a small and unremarkable ribbon development along the main highway. It is famed for its saffron production, and indeed this is the main reason for its existence, though inevitably the saffron crocuses are grown in the surrounding fields and not in the town itself.

GETTING THERE AND AWAY Given the proximity to Srinagar, all of the buses heading south from the city pass through Pampore. Start from Srinagar's **Panthchowk bus station** on the southern outskirts of the city. The bus takes half an hour and tickets, regardless of which bus you take, should cost not more than Rs10.

WHAT TO SEE In Pampore you will find the **Khanqah-i-Khawaja Masood Wali**, the last surviving wooden *khanqah* (shrine) in Kashmir. Khawaja Masood was a prominent trader in the late 1500s, but he gave up his worldly wealth to move closer to God. His *khanqah* is built over two floors, and though many hideous additions have been made to the structure, its original beauty is still just about discernible.

On the edge of Pampore at Namblabal is the 15th-century **Shrine of Mir Syed Ali Hamdani**. A Persian Sufi and poet, Hamdani was influential in spreading Islam in Kashmir, and he is credited with shaping much of the culture that we associate with Kashmir today. Built by Hamdani's son between 1393 and 1405, this shrine too has been very badly damaged by vandals over recent years, but there is surviving woodwork beneath the roof that is of great architectural significance.

AROUND PAMPORE The principal attraction of Pampore is the **fields of saffron** surrounding the town. Though there's little to see for much of the year, in the autumn it looks as though a carpet of violet and mauve has been thrown across the land.

One of the largest local growers is **Kashmir Kissan Kasser** (*Chandhar Pampora*; m 941 900 8750), whose packaging is recognisable by the emblem of a man driving two oxen, and then a crocus bulb. The owner speaks some English and is happy to talk about his crocuses, his factory and the process of making saffron.

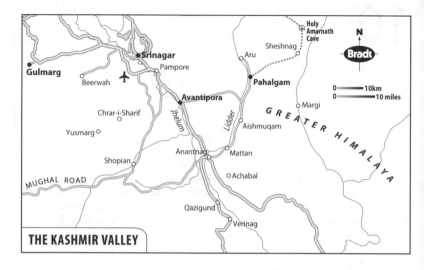

THE KASHMIR VALLEY

 Telephone code: 01951

Yusmarg is 'the meadow of Jesus,' a glorious, alpine valley where local people believe Jesus came and stayed a while (see box, page 133). The grassy pastures give way slowly to dense pine forest, framed by a mountainous backdrop. Exceptionally photogenic and a prime spot for short walks and picnics, it is also significantly quieter than the likes of Sonamarg and Gulmarg.

GETTING THERE AND AWAY Yusmarg is 47km southwest of Srinagar, towards the end of a main road. The easiest and cheapest way to get here is by bus. The ordinary, **J&K State Road Transport Corporation (JKSRTC) bus** costs Rs146 each way and takes two hours, and in summertime **J&K Tourism Development Corporation (JKTDC)** also runs its own daily bus service, costing Rs360 return.

In winter, the road is only open as far as Chrar-i-Sharif. After this point you would have to proceed on foot.

WHERE TO STAY AND EAT
As relatively few visitors come to Yusmarg, the only accommodation option is the **JKTDC Tourist Bungalows and Hutments ($$–$$$)**. It provides double rooms and whole huts but, if your budget won't stretch that far, also dorm beds for a very affordable Rs150.

JKTDC also runs a **restaurant ($$)** nearby serving basic Indian and continental dishes.

WHAT TO SEE AND DO It is a gorgeous, 10km **trek** from Yusmarg to the frozen lake at **Sang e safed**, and easily doable in a day by someone of moderate fitness. The lake remains frozen for much of the year, and it is possible to camp on the shore. The weather at this altitude can change unpredictably, so carry plenty of warm clothing with you.

Rather less popular, but no less scenic, is the trek to **Tosa Maidan**, a vast meadow where Gujjar nomads graze their livestock. Used as an army firing ground since 1964, it has only recently become re-accessible to tourists. Getting to the meadow requires you to cross the **Basmai Gali Pass** (3,962m), which was the traditional route from Kashmir into the Punjab.

Saffron is the colour of Greek mythical passion, the scent of amorous queens, and the taste of the finest Indian and Persian dishes. From the fabric dye of the early Buddhist monks, to an anti-depressant tea of the modern era, saffron has been widely prized, traded, used and abused.

The humble *Crocus sativus* corm (not bulb) from which saffron is derived originated in Turkey and through the usual twists and turns of history found its way into the hands of an *arhat* (Buddhist missionary), Madhyantika, who is credited with introducing saffron to Kashmir in the 5th century BC. Where he got the corms from is unrecorded, but once in Kashmir they flourished in the light soils surrounding Pampore, and from there saffron spread to the rest of India. The Buddha loved the saffron dye so much that on his death those monks close to him decreed saffron to be the official colour for Buddhist mantles and robes, and so it has been since.

Each purple crocus blossom contains three stigmas, which are painstakingly hand-plucked from the flower in the early morning during harvesting. In October, the warm and gentle wind destined for the Himalayas makes the myriad of mauve flower heads rock as though they are a violet sea. The scent is heavenly, as is the setting before a mountain backdrop. The harvest lasts for two to three weeks, ending in mid-November, after which the fields look quite bare.

Each one of the plucked stigmas forms a delicate, red saffron thread. It takes more than 85,000 stigmas to produce a kilo of raw saffron and, once dried and ready for packaging, this represents just 200g of marketable product. It is a labour of love indeed. Known locally as *kesar*, the stalls lining the road at Pampore sell tiny, plastic boxes of the precious spice for a fraction of what you would pay at home, and it's an easily transportable souvenir that will bring pleasure for months to come.

Around Yusmarg Just before you reach Yusmarg you come to the bowl-shaped valley of **Dudhpathri**, a place first described to us as the merger between the crystal-clear waters of Pahalgam and the mountains and meadows of Gulmarg. This is virgin territory, yet to be discovered by most tourists, so if you like your wilderness tranquil (but still accessible by bus), this is the place to come.

At Dudhpathri too you will find the **shrine of Hazrat Sheikh Nur-ud-Din Wali**, which is surrounded by seven springs. A mystic and Sufi saint, he stayed and prayed at Dudhpathri for 12 years, teaching Islam to the local people. Legend has it that when he struck the ground, water and milk burst forth, and this could be the source of Dudhpathri's name, *dudh* being the word for milk.

The town of **Chrar-i-Sharif** is around 20km from Yusmarg, and in winter it's as close as you can get to Yusmarg by road. The town has grown up around the sacred, 600-year-old **shrine of Sheikh Noor-ud-din Noorani**, a poet who espoused the teachings of Islam through his verse.

Sheikh Noor-ud-din Noorani, also known as Alamdar-e-Kashmir (the flag bearer of Kashmir), was a Sufi saint born in India in 1377. Legend has it that he refused to drink milk for the first three days of his life, at which point the Yogini Lal Arifa fed him from her own breast. While he was still in the cradle, she named him her spiritual heir.

The sheikh's teachings spoke to both Hindus and Muslims in the valley: he preached non-violence, tolerance of other faiths, and vegetarianism. When he died,

900,000 people came to his shrine (already erected by a disciple on the site where he would come to pray). The shrine has twice been destroyed (most recently by fire in 1995), but each time it has been rebuilt, and people have lost none of their reverence for it. To this day Chrar-i-Sharif is considered among the holiest shrines in India.

AVANTIPORA   *Telephone code: 01933*

Avantipora is a small and unassuming town spread out along the highway. The reason you should visit, is that it was the capital of King Awanti Varman (855–83), from whose name Avantipora (Avanti's city) is derived, and two of the magnificent stone temples he built here survive.

GETTING THERE AND AWAY   Avantipora lies roughly halfway between Srinagar and Anantnag, right on the national highway. All of the buses between these two cities drive through here, so taking one of them and jumping off early is the best way to reach the town. On the cheapest **bus**, expect to pay Rs20.

The temples are both on the left-hand side of the road (as you are **driving** south) and are both easy to spot. There is a **car park** opposite the Avanti Sawami Temple; outside the Avanti Shovra Temple you have to park on the road.

OTHER PRACTICALITIES   Should you need to stop for cash, **J&K Bank** has an ATM on the main street in Avantipora, not far from the temples.

SHOPPING   If you missed the opportunity to buy saffron in Pampore and are having regrets, there's a stall selling dried fruits and saffron immediately opposite the Avanti Shovra Temple.

WHAT TO SEE   The twin **Avanti Shovra** and **Avanti Sawami temples** (⊕ *07.30– 19.30; combined entrance fee Rs100; camera fee Rs25*) lie 500m apart from each other in the centre of Avantipora, surrounded by modern development. Dedicated to Shiva and Vishnu respectively, they both date from the mid 9th century and, having been severely damaged by earthquakes at some time in their history, were only rediscovered during excavations by British archaeologists in the early 1900s.

The temples have been well restored, and you get a good sense of both the scale and the grandeur of the original structures. The majority of the pillars (or at least their bases) have been stood back upright, enabling you to appreciate just how tall the inner sanctums would have been. Many of the stone construction blocks are richly carved, including with scenes of dancing girls and *afsaras* (angel-like figures).

Of the two temples, Avanti Shovra is generally quieter, and the curator may well spot you across the site and come over to show you things you'd otherwise be likely to miss. Avanti Sawami is, on balance, more impressive, but you might have to share it with a crowd.

While driving through the town, you will also see Avantipora's attractive, **tiered mosque**, which is painted in white and green, the traditional colours of Islam.

SHOPIAN   *Telephone code: 01933*

Shopian is a district headquarters, and has been since the 1870s. The attraction for visitors is that it marks the northern end of the historic Mughal Road (see box opposite), which has recently been restored and is now the location for the annual Mughal Rally.

THE MUGHAL ROAD

The 84km/52-mile Mughal Road stretches from Bafliaz in Poonch district, to Shopian and was first used by the Mughal emperor Akbar during his conquest of Kashmir in 1586. The ties with the Mughals continued beyond this point, however, as it was returning along this same road in 1627 that his son, the Emperor Jahangir, died. His entrails were buried at Chingus Saria, and the rest of his body was carried on to Lahore.

For much of its history, the road would have been little more than a track, the high-altitude stretches in particular (it reaches a height of 350m) making it impassable by vehicles for much of the year. From the 1950s onwards the possibility of metalling the road was mooted, but though construction did begin in the late 1970s, it halted when the militancy began and the bridge at Bafliaz was targeted. When security improved in the mid-2000s, construction started again, and by 2013 the entire route was open with dual carriageways.

In addition to its Mughal links, numerous other historical sites lie along the way, including several caravanserais, a Sufi shrine at Pir Ki Gali, and the Noori Chamb Waterfall, where Jahangir's favourite queen used to take her baths. The route is spectacularly beautiful. It cuts through the meadows, valleys and passes of the Pir Panjal range, and also through a section of the remote Hirpora Wildlife Sanctuary where a variety of rare species, including the Markhoor goat, roam free.

GETTING THERE AND AWAY Shopian is almost due south of Srinagar, but lies to the west of the National Highway. There are regular buses here from Srinagar, and the cost of the ticket is Rs30.

WHAT TO SEE AND DO History buffs like ourselves will get a thrill out of just driving along the Mughal Road (see box above), knowing that they are following in the footsteps (or, more likely, hoofprints) of the Mughal emperors as they wound their way north to Kashmir.

For adrenaline junkies, however, the road offers an annual dose of excitement: the two-day **Mughal Rally** (*www.xplorearth.com/program.htm*). The rally is open to vehicles of any make or model, and two competitions run in parallel, the Xtreme and Enduro rallies. A maximum team of 40 cars can compete in each race, and teams of two are preferred. The entrance fee is Rs20,000 and first prize in each competition is Rs200,000.

ANANTNAG   *Telephone code: 01932*

Anantnag is a sprawling, ugly place with few redeeming qualities save its transport links to other destinations, and its proximity to the remarkable Martand Sun Temple near Mattan.

GETTING THERE AND AWAY Anantnag is a major transport hub in the Kashmir Valley, so the chances are that you'll have to pass through here, and possibly stop a while to change vehicles. Minibuses and taxis all stop at the **taxi stand**, which is near to the Government Degree College.

Intercity **buses** go from Anantnag across J&K but also further afield. The ordinary bus to or from Srinagar costs Rs30, it's Rs199 to Jammu, and Rs346 if you're going all the way to Amritsar.

Though you might see signs in Anantnag for the **railway station**, this is, as yet, not actually connected to the Indian railway network.

If you are travelling in a private vehicle, note that there is a **tollbooth** approaching the town. The fee for a car is Rs20.

OTHER PRACTICALITIES Almost everything you'll need in Anantnag is situated on the main road through town, KP Road. This includes a **post office**, medical facilities (the **Al Raheem Polyclinic** and **Jan Medical Care** pharmacy), a branch of **HDFC Bank**, and **ATMs** belonging to J&K Bank, SBI and PNB.

AROUND ANANTNAG
Mattan 24km east of Anantnag is the town of Mattan, famed for its temples. There are in fact two temples at Mattan, a **modern temple** (⊕ 04.00–21.00) made of white marble in the centre of town, and the far more impressive **Martand Sun Temple**, which is a twisty 4km/2½-mile climb away, near the District Jail in Kehrbal village.

Built by King Lalitaditya (r 724–60), the latter temple comprises a central, oblong sanctum, around which are arranged various small shrines. Substantial parts of the structure are still standing, many of the columns are still upright, and the carvings are well preserved. Attractive flower beds are laid out in the shape of a sun and rays, and the site looks particularly fine in the early evening light.

PAHALGAM   *Telephone code: 01936*

The most charming of the hill resorts in the valley is Pahalgam, where you'll find some excellent accommodation options set among incredible natural beauty. It's a prime place to relax for a few days, reading a book in a pine forest grove or sat gazing into the rushing waters of the Lidder River.

GETTING THERE AND AWAY Pahalgam is a popular tourist destination, and so transport links are reasonable. The ordinary **bus** from Srinagar costs Rs61, and in the summertime JKTDC also operates a **tourist bus**, with tickets costing Rs380 return. The bus journey takes 3½ hours each way.

During the Amarnath *yatra* (pilgrimage) (see box, page 190), JKSRTC runs additional buses to Pahalgam with tickets from Srinagar (starting at Rs160 each way) and Jammu (from Rs220). Buses pick up and drop off passengers on the main road, on the eastern bank of the river.

Taxis will charge from Rs1,800 from Srinagar to Pahalgam; the price is usually the same whether you go one way or return.

If you are travelling in a private vehicle, note that there is a **tollbooth** 6km (3¾ miles) before Pahalgam. The toll for a car is Rs50.

GETTING AROUND Most of the sites in and around Pahalgam are accessible on foot, and indeed the majority of visitors coming here do so in order to trek. If you do need to take a car, however, you will have to hire a taxi locally, as outside vehicles are not permitted to transport guests around the town. Signboards by the taxi stands give the current rate to each local destination: it is usually not more than Rs50.

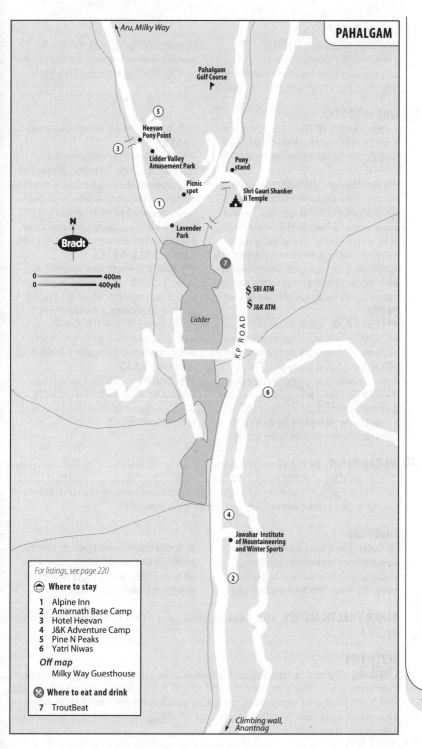

Aru, Milky Way

Pahalgam
Golf Course

⑤

Heevan
Pony Point

③

Lidder Valley
Amusement Park

Pony
stand

Picnic
spot

①

Shri Gauri Shanker
Ji Temple

Lavender
Park

⑦

N

Bradt

0 _____ 400m
0 _____ 400yds

$ SBI ATM

$ J&K ATM

Lidder

KP ROAD

⑥

④

Jawahar Institute
of Mountaineering
and Winter Sports

②

For listings, see page 220

⌂ **Where to stay**

1   Alpine Inn
2   Amarnath Base Camp
3   Hotel Heevan
4   J&K Adventure Camp
5   Pine N Peaks
6   Yatri Niwas

Off map
    Milky Way Guesthouse

✖ **Where to eat and drink**

7   TroutBeat

Climbing wall,
Anantnag

10

TRAVEL AGENTS

Milky Way Aru Valley; 📞 210 899; 📧 milkyway1987@yahoo.com; www.milkywaykashmir.com. Local guesthouse owner Fayaz also acts as a travel agent. He is exceptionally knowledgeable, speaks excellent English &, unusually, is also able to make recommendations & bookings for visitors with reduced mobility.

 ## WHERE TO STAY

See map, page 219. **JKTDC** has a large number of rooms & huts in Pahalgam (**$$$–$$$$**), most of which are at the **J&K Adventure Camp** (*KP Rd*).

 Hotel Heevan (40 rooms) Heevan Link Rd; 📞 243 219; 📧 info@ahadhotelsandresorts.com; www.ahadhotelsandresorts.com. The sister property to Pine N Peaks, Hotel Heevan is set right on the water's edge, the river rushing by almost underneath your nose. Rooms are well appointed & comfortable, & the whole place is kept pleasantly warm. Monkeys play in the trees outside, providing hours of interest for lazy spectators like ourselves. **$$$$$**

 Pine N Peaks (80 rooms) Aru Rd; 📞 243 304; 📧 info@ahadhotelsandresorts.com; www.ahadhotelsandresorts.com. Nestled on the hillside among a grove of pine trees, Pine N Peaks & its immaculate gardens are little slices of heaven. The hotel is quite rightly the recipient of numerous awards & the attention to detail is evident in everything from the design of the rooms to the service provided by the waiting staff. The grilled trout in the restaurant is superb. **$$$$$**

 Alpine Inn (5 rooms) Heevan Link Rd; 📞 243 065; 📧 bookings@alpineinnpahalgam.com; www.alpineinnpahalgam.com. Close to the golf course, the Alpine Inn is a chalet-type building (as one might expect from the name) & feels as if it is caught in a time warp: there's a lot of net curtains & chintz. Staff are pleasant enough but no English is spoken. **$$$$–$$$$$**

 Milky Way Guesthouse (8 rooms) Aru Valley; 📞 210 899; 📧 milkyway1987@yahoo.com; www.milkywaykashmir.com. Set in a delightful garden in the Aru Valley, a short distance from Pahalgam town. The beds at Milky Way are as warm as the welcome. 4 more rooms are under construction to meet the constant demand. Highly recommended. **$$$**

 Yatri Niwas Off KP Rd. A godsend for budget travellers, with dorm beds just Rs250. In Jul & Aug your room-mates will be pilgrims heading to the Amarnath Cave. **$**

 WHERE TO EAT In Pahalgam, room service always scores over a meal in town. But if you can drag yourself away from your window by the river, **TroutBeat** on the main thoroughfare is where you ought to go. Prices can be steep, but we didn't mind paying Rs500 for the buttery, lemony whole trout meunière.

SHOPPING

Crafts Pine N Peaks, Aru Rd; 📞 243 088; www.mandmcottageindustries.com. This small boutique has a selection of high-quality handicrafts, some of which are very fairly priced. We bought beautifully hand-painted papier mâché baubles (Rs100), and also delicate papier mâché gift boxes (Rs400). Staff are happy to help, or to leave you to browse.

OTHER PRACTICALITIES **J&K Bank** and **SBI** have ATMs next door to each other on KP Road.

ACTIVITIES

Climbing There is a training wall for would-be climbers just to the south of Pahalgam town. You can turn up and climb if you know what you're doing and have your own equipment, or get in touch with the Jawahar Institute of Mountaineering and Winter Sports (see *Trekking*, opposite) for instruction, helmet and harness hire.

Fishing The Lidder River that runs through Pahalgam is very well stocked with trout, as attested by the menus in the hotel restaurants and at TroutBeat (see opposite). The best season for angling runs from April to September, and you will need to obtain an angling permit from the Department of Fisheries in Srinagar (see page 202) before you come.

Golf The 18-hole **Pahalgam Golf Course** (m *941 904 9402*) is located in the centre of Pahalgam and, as it both lies at an altitude and is built on a series of steep slopes, offers quite the challenge to golfers. Green fees are Rs1,200, hire of a golf cart is Rs500 (book ahead as only a small number are available) and hire of a caddy Rs180.

Note that you will need to bring your own equipment with you, as golf sets are not available to rent from the club.

Trekking Almost any path that you take out of Pahalgam, be it along the river or up into the hills, will lead to a photogenic location.

If you have several days available, consider trekking to **Aru** (11km) and then via the **Lidderwat** to the hanging glacier of **Kolahoi** (35km), from where there are spectacular views across to **Kolahoi Peak** (5,370m).

Shorter trails from Pahalgam lead to the lush **Baisaram Meadow** (6km), which is surrounded by pine forests; and to the mostly frozen **Tuliyan Lake** (11km) with its ring of snow-capped mountains.

Guides, advice and equipment hire are available from the **Jawahar Institute of Mountaineering and Winter Sports** (*243 002;* e *principal@ jawaharinstitutepahalgam.com*; *www.jawaharinstitutepahalgam.com*) and ponies can be hired from the **Heevan Pony Point** by Hotel Heevan and a second **pony stand** near Shri Gauri Shanker Ji Temple.

WHAT TO SEE Although it is the natural beauty of Pahalgam that is the real attraction, there are a few pleasant enough manmade sites in the town itself. **Lavender Park**, on the shore of the river, is well kept and a popular spot for picnics, and families with small children to entertain frequently find themselves dragged to the neighbouring **Lidder Valley Amusement Park**.

Next door to the Tourist Taxi Stand is the **Shri Gauri Shanker Ji Temple**, which seems to be of interest for Hindu *yatris* passing through *en route* to Amarnath Cave, but is probably less of a draw for general visitors.

Around Pahalgam For many domestic tourists, Pahalgam is just the starting point of their pilgrimage to the **Amarnath Cave** (see box, page 190). The town can become very busy during the pilgrimage, so bear this in mind and book your accommodation ahead if you're planning to come at the same time.

From Pahalgam there is a motorable road to Chandanwari, 16km away, which is where the trek actually starts. The highlight of the trek is the vast and sparkling blue **Sheshnag Lake**, where devotees take an auspicious dip in spite of the bitter cold.

Back on NH1, **Qazigund** is the 'Kashmir Gateway', the border between Jammu and Kashmir. Taxis congregate in the large, central square, on which a J&K Tourism Centre is under construction. It deserves mention here, as shortly past the town, at Lower Munda, is a major **customs post** with a tollbooth. Cars pay a toll of Rs70, and when you stop you're swarmed (fortunately fairly good naturedly) by vendors selling shawls, cricket bats, nuts and dried fruits.

The ancient spring at Verinag is the source of the Jhelum River. Legend has it that the goddess of the river, Vitasta, wanted to burst out from the rock here, but when she did so she found Shiva standing on the spot and was forced to choose another spring a short distance away.

The spring is surrounded by a huge, octagonal tank built by the Mughal emperor Jahangir, and the town was once the site of another Mughal Garden, the ruins of which survive.

GETTING THERE AND AWAY Verinag is 80km (50 miles) south of Srinagar on the main highway. The main road either side of the town is prone to avalanches and is frequently blocked by rock falls. Though the authorities are efficient when it comes to clearing such blockages, you should factor in the possibility of delays nonetheless.

If you don't have your own vehicle, the cheapest way to get here is by **bus** from Srinagar: the regular bus costs Rs42.

WHERE TO STAY AND EAT Cheap but fairly cheerless rooms are offered by **JKTDC** in Verinag for **$–$$** depending on the season.

WHAT TO SEE The central site in Verinag is the **natural spring** from which the Jhelum River flows. Dissatisfied with the way it looked, the Mughal emperor Jahangir constructed a vast, **octagonal tank** around the spring in 1620, and he envisaged it as the centrepiece of huge pleasure gardens and a palace. During his lifetime Jahangir expressed his desire to be buried by the spring when he died, but his wishes were never honoured and he was interred instead in Lahore.

The turquoise waters in the tank are striking, but it is the surrounding structure that we love. Each of the 24 surrounding arcade arches is perfectly proportioned and built from a creamy stone. In one of the arches you will find a **Shiva** *lingam*, and into the walls elsewhere are set two **stone slabs** inscribed with Persian prose, the most important of which reads:

> The king of seven kingdoms, the administrator
> of justice, the father of victory, Nur-ud-din, Jahangir
> son of Akbar, the martyr king, halted at this spring
> of God's grace in the 15th year of his reign. This
> construction was made by order of His Majesty.
> By Jahangir, son of King Akbar,
> This construction was raised to the skies.
> The architect of intelligence got its date –
> 'May the mansion last for ever together with the spring Vernag!'

Downstream from the tank lies the **garden**, with its crumbling pavilions and *hammams* (bathhouses). The traditional *char bagh* design has been altered slightly to accommodate the steep topography of the site, but the rectangular shape, the tank at the top, and the division of the different garden areas with water channels is certainly in keeping with the style.

Immediately outside the Mughal complex is the **Nilanag shrine**, which is dedicated to Shiva. *Naga* means deity of the spring, and Nilanag is the chief of spring deities, so this site is also known colloquially as Nilakunda, or the spring of Nila.

11

Jammu

Though it gives its name to J&K state, the region of Jammu is often overlooked by those rushing to see the remarkable sites of Kashmir and Ladakh. The lands around the holy Tawi River, situated in the south-western corner of J&K, are however no less rich in history and culture than other parts of the state, and indeed their Hindu identity gives an interesting cultural dimension to your visit that though commonplace elsewhere in India, is less evident in this particular state.

Jammu city (often called Jammu Tawi to differentiate it from the surrounding areas) is a large, lively affair with good transport connections, some excellent hotels and so many religious sites that it has become known as the City of Temples. It is also the transit hub for pilgrims making their way to the Vaishno Devi and Shiv Khori shrines around Katra, and for the domestic tourism hot-spot of Patnitop. Elsewhere in the area you'll find picturesque lakes, some attractive forts and palaces, and opportunities for adventure sports.

PATNITOP   *Telephone code: 01992*

Patnitop has the potential to be a most charming hill resort: the natural environment with its majestic peaks, thick pine forests and springs is sublime. Its beauty is, unfortunately, also its downfall as mass tourism has brought with it large and frequently ugly hotels, package tourists and their litter. We found it a convenient place to stay while driving south to Jammu but, unlike the domestic tourists who stay here for a week or more at a time, wouldn't recommend it as the central component of a holiday.

GETTING THERE AND AWAY   Patnitop is 110km north of Jammu city along NH1, and it's a slow, slow road once you get into the mountains: the way twists and turns, the road surfaces are variable, and not infrequently you get stuck behind trucks and men herding their sheep and goats, especially at twilight. In winter, the road is frequently closed due to snowfall, and though an 11km tunnel is under construction from Kud, which will ultimately reduce the journey by 50km, this will only benefit those bypassing Patnitop. Those visiting the resort will still have to resign themselves to the climb.

The closest city to Patnitop is Jammu, and there are various transport options to get between the two. By **taxi** the journey takes just over three hours each way and costs Rs3,500 return, spending the night in Patnitop. One-way, you'll pay Rs1,800–2,000. The **bus** takes significantly longer at around five hours, but can be cheaper. Bus fares start from Rs150 and go up to Rs1,000 for the de luxe coaches.

Coming from Srinagar, the best option is to take the **luxury bus** to Jammu, getting off *en route* at Patnitop, about six hours into the journey. The bus runs in summer only, departing from Srinagar's main bus station at 07.30. Arrive half an hour early to buy your ticket, which costs Rs500.

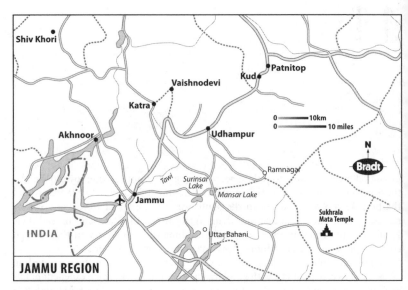

JAMMU REGION

WHERE TO STAY

Vardaan Resort (44 rooms) 287 585; e vardaanresorts@gmail.com; www.patnitop.net. Vardaan is a sprawling resort hotel catering primarily to domestic tourists. Rooms are large & comfortable, & those in the new wing have superb views. Wi-Fi & on-site restaurant. Heating provided on request. Our 1 criticism is that the hotel is employing young boys as porters. This is to be strongly discouraged. **$$$$**

JKTDC Tourist Complex www.jktdchotels online.com/hotel-patnitop.html. JKTDC operates a large tourist complex with a range of options including bungalows (**$$$$**) & rooms at Hotel Alpine (**$$$**) and Hotel Maple (**$$**). Full details and booking instructions are available online.

Substantial discounts are available in low season (1 Aug–15 Dec & 16 Jan–31 Mar).

Hotel Surya (7 rooms) 287 518. The building may look a little haphazard, but the hillside drops away immediately behind Hotel Surya, offering some of the most dramatic views in Patnitop. Best avoided by those with a fear of heights, however. Some rooms are a little dark but it's clean. **$$$**

Youth Hostel (42 rooms) 287 540; m 941 916 2799; e aftabshah_16@yahoo.com. Located close to the Forestry Dept's Awareness Centre, Patnitop's youth hostel offers sgl, dbl & dorm rooms, all with AC. **$$**

WHERE TO EAT
The majority of resort hotels in Patnitop offer meal packages, and these are generally the best option if you are staying for a few days. If you are just driving through, however, the following restaurants will serve you something reasonable. Outside the now-defunct Hot and Chilly Restaurant you'll find a row of snack and fast-food stalls (**$–$$**).

Hotel Patnitop Bar & Restaurant Nr Hotel Subash Palace; ⏰ 10.00–21.00 daily. The upstairs restaurant is cheap & bland but fine for a quick meal. The downstairs bar is well stocked with domestic alcohol & no doubt busy in the evenings. **$$**

Krishna Cottage Nr Jai Shree Hotel; ⏰ all day. The food here is unimaginative but quickly served & the surroundings are clean enough. **$$**

SHOPPING
There are several small shops selling blankets and shawls opposite the Jai Shree Hotel. A few souvenir sellers tout their wares alongside the food stalls outside the now-defunct Hot and Chilly Restaurant.

WHAT TO SEE AND DO The majority of visitors come to Patnitop in summer to escape the heat of the plains, to walk in the mountains and to picnic with their families. There's a laid-back feel to the place and plenty of pleasant paths to follow: the 8km route downhill to the apple orchards at **Batote** is particularly attractive and in places offers panoramic views of both the mountains and the Chenab River.

If you come to Patnitop in January and February, it is possible to **ski**. Though the resort is far less developed than the one at Gulmarg, there are several beginners' slopes, classes are available, and the possibility of constructing a ski lift is under discussion.

Local devotees also visit the 600-year-old **Naag Temple** close to the centre of Patnitop, but unless you have a particular love of snakes (cobras, specifically), you'll probably want to give this a miss.

Around Patnitop Situated 17km from Patnitop, J&K Tourism is developing **Sanasar** as a centre for adventure sports, and, in particular, aerial sports.

Deriving its name from the two local lakes, Sana and Sar, activities here are year-round. A nine-hole **golf course** is under construction, with a lake at its centre, you can **paraglide** either across the lakes or all of the way to Kud, and it is also possible to try **hot-air ballooning**. All equipment and instruction is available from the **JKTDC Tourist Complex** (*www.jktdc.co.in*), which can also provide accommodation, either in double rooms (**$$**) or for Rs500 per person in ten-bed dormitories.

For those looking for something more cultural, the 400-year-old **Shank Pal Temple** overlooks Sanasar. Dedicated to Nag Shank Pal, it is about three hours' walk above the lakes and is notable for the fact that no mortar was used in its construction and yet the stones still stand solid.

A little further away, 42km to the southeast of Patnitop, is the **Sudh Mahadev Temple**. This holy site is believed by some to be as much as 2,800 years old (though the modern structure is far more recent); the inner sanctum contains a natural black marble *lingam* (representative of Shiva), Shiva's trident, and a mace said to belong to Bhim (see page 188). The temple is busiest during the Sudh Mahadev Festival (which takes place during the full moon in June–July), when pilgrims come to pray and also enjoy the song and dance.

Before entering the temple, devotees typically wash themselves in the **Pap Nashni Baoli**, a natural spring that has been developed into a step well. JKTDC provides a small amount of **tented accommodation ($)** here if you wish to stay the night, and devotees sometimes donate money for meals for travellers, served from various hot food and snack stalls.

UDHAMPUR

The fourth-largest city in J&K, Udhampur is the Northern Command Headquarters of the Indian army. Though subtropical in climate and set among eucalyptus forest, the army dominates all areas of life and it feels overwhelmingly like a garrison town. There's no real reason for tourists to visit, though the town does have most amenities you could need.

GETTING THERE AND AWAY
By road Udhampur lies 70km north of Jammu on NH1. The road is wide and well maintained, and doesn't suffer from the rock and snowfall that plagues it further north. By **bus** the standard single fare is Rs46; by **taxi** expect to pay Rs900–1,000.

By rail The railway extension north of Jammu city, which will ultimately go as far as Srinagar, already connects Udhampur to the rest of the Indian railway network. Though several trains do pass through the station each day, the most useful is the Jammu Mail, which departs from Udhampur daily at 14.45, reaches Jammu at 16.00 and then continues through a variety of stops, finally reaching Delhi at 05.45. Prices on this train to or from Jammu start from Rs225 and Rs395 one-way from Delhi. In both cases the cheapest tickets are travelling sleeper class.

 ## WHERE TO STAY AND EAT

 Hotel Singh Axis (32 rooms) NH1A, Raghunathpura. Udhampur's accommodation options are really nothing to write home about, but Hotel Singh Axis is the pleasant exception.

Rooms are clean & many have mountain views. Staff are friendly & food in the on-site restaurant is tasty & affordable. Wi-Fi & parking is free. B/fast included. **$$$**

OTHER PRACTICALITIES If you need a pharmacy, **Shiva Medical Store** and several other chemists are situated near to Chibber Enclave.

All the main banks are represented in the town: **J&K Bank** and **Punjab National Bank** have branches along NH1, and both they and **SBI** have ATMs.

WHAT TO SEE The first time we drove past Udhampur's **rock garden** we saw it only out of the corner of our eyes, and it appeared to be regular park enjoyed by a dozen or so unusually ugly children. On closer inspection, the children are in fact rock sculptures decorated with coloured tiles, and they depict different members of the community in miniature. The uniform-clad soldier clasping the hands of two schoolchildren is especially menacing.

Elsewhere in the town, several **decommissioned tanks** and also a small **military aircraft** decorate public spaces.

KATRA *Telephone code: 01991*

The town of Katra lies at the foothills of the Trikuta range and is frequently known as Katra Vaishno Devi on account of it being the access point for treks to the Vaishno Devi Shrine. It is a thriving place that attracts around nine million Hindu pilgrims each year, as well as a number of non-Hindu tourists curious to see what all the fuss is about.

GETTING THERE AND AWAY You can get to Katra by either train or road. The fastest **train** service, the New Delhi–Katra AC Express (train number 22461), departs from Delhi at 17.30 every day except Thursday. It stops in Jammu at 03.30 and then reaches its final destination, Katra, at 05.30. This is a new railway line: the extension to Katra was officially opened by Prime Minister Manmohan Singh only in February 2014.

Standard **buses** leave from Jammu's train station and cost Rs38 per person. If you prefer to travel to Katra from Jammu by **taxi**, expect to pay from Rs1,000 one-way, or Rs1,300 if you need a taxi with air conditioning.

WHERE TO STAY AND EAT Due to the volume of pilgrims passing through, JKTDC has opened various options in Katra, all of which should be booked in advance at www.jktdc.co.in. You can also turn up at the **JKTDC Tourist Retiring Centre** (*nr bus stand;* 232 309). The smartest of these options is **Hotel Saraswati** (*off Ban Ganga Rd;* 254 9065; **$$$**), with both AC and non-AC rooms, followed by **Hotel City Residency** near the shrine (**$$$**). The latter also has very cheap beds in vast dormitories, as does **Yatri Niwas** (both **$**).

🏠 **KC Residency** (57 rooms) Reasi Rd; 📞 234 622; e kcresidency@kcresidency@katra.com; www.kcresidencykatra.com. Large, modern hotel with AC rooms, many of which overlook the Trikuta Hills. We had particular fun with the table tennis table in the games room. **$$$$$**

🏠 **The Atrium on the Green** (61 rooms) Nr railway station; 📞 211 178; e theatriumkatra@ gmail.com; www.theatriumkatra.com. Head & shoulders above other hotels in Katra. Set among well-kept lawns & with a holistic spa on site, this is the place to relax. Staff are attentive & service is personal. Food in the restaurant is organic & the ice cream in the coffee shop is welcome. Be sure to book ahead in summer. **$$$$$**

WHAT TO SEE AND DO It is a 26km trek from Katra to the **Vaishno Devi Shrine** and back, but each year between nine and ten million pilgrims still make the journey to what is one of Hinduism's holiest shrines. The shrine is accessible year-round, and while the majority of pilgrims travel on foot, it is also possible to travel by pony or take a seat in a helicopter (Rs699).

The way to the shrine is paved, and along the route are stalls selling snacks and souvenirs. *En route* devotees stop at **Ardhkunwari** to climb through a small cave where a goddess is thought to have meditated, and then again just short of the main shrine to bathe and offer prayers.

Inside the shrine, which is accessed via a long corridor, are three important idols, the goddesses Mahakali, Mahalakshmi and Mahasaraswati. Each one is represented by a natural rock structure, heavily decorated with gold jewellery and flowers. The final part of the *yatra* involves visiting the **Bhairav Temple**, 2km beyond the main shrine.

If you wish to participate in the pilgrimage, you must register in advance with the **Mata Vaishno Devi Shrine Board** (*www.maavaishnodevi.org*). Registration is free and can be done online, or in person at the Yatra Registration Counter near Katra's bus stand.

Katra is also the starting point for another pilgrimage route, that to **Shiv Khori**. Those who worship here believe it is the site where Shiva appeared to the demon Bhasmasura as a beautiful woman, tricking Bhasmasura into turning himself to ash. Using his trident Shiva was also able to cut a tunnel through the mountain, which is said to lead all the way to Amarnath.

Devotees must travel 78km from Katra to the village of Ransoo, and thence proceed on foot to the holy cave, which is 150m long and has inside it a tapered Shiva *lingam*, 1.2m high. Similar shapes in the cave are associated with Parvati, Ganesh and Nandi.

Full information about the pilgrimage to Shiv Khori is available from the **Shiv Khori Shrine Board** (*www.shivkhori.org*).

On the way from Katra to Ransoo, look out also for the **Aghar Jitto**, a cute, landscaped garden in which are displayed statues of the folk hero and saint Baba Jitto and his daughter. Baba Jitto gained renown 500 years ago as a revolutionary figure who stood up against feudal exploitation and was killed, and a week-long festival, the Jhiri Mela, is held in his honour each year.

JAMMU   *Telephone code: 0191*

The winter capital of J&K, Jammu city lies out along the banks of the Tawi River, and indeed the name Jammu Tawi is also used for the city to differentiate between it and the Jammu region as a whole when the need arises. Colloquially, however, Jammu is known as the City of Temples due to the vast number of Hindu temples and shrines that are found here, and, of course, the fact that the city is packed with

Hindu pilgrims passing through on their way to the Vaishno Devi Shrine (see page 229 and box below). This gives Jammu a very different feel from other places in J&K, and it is well worth planning to spend a few days here, soaking up the atmosphere.

HISTORY Archaeological evidence suggests that the area around Jammu has been inhabited for more than 4,000 years. There was certainly a town on the banks of the Tawi River in the early centuries AD, and the area was occupied in turn by the Hephthalites, Kushans, Guptas and Ghaznavids.

The history of modern Jammu begins, however, in the 17th century with Jamboo Lohan, the brother of the local chieftain credited with building the Bahu Fort (see page 236). It is said that Jamboo was out hunting one day when he saw a lion and a lamb stood side by side, both drinking from the Tawi River. Amazed, he decided to build a city on the site, and the foundation stones of Jamboo Nagar (literally Jamboo's place, and later corrupted to Jammu) were laid.

The Dogra dynasty ruled Jammu and Kashmir princely state from 1846 until 1947, and they made Jammu their capital. The Dogras introduced to Jammu many modern inventions, including the railway and the telegraph service, and patronised the construction of many of the city's temples.

GETTING THERE AND AWAY

By air Jammu airport (also known as Satwari airport) is in the southwest of the city on RS Pura Road. There is just one terminal, and it services domestic flights. The airport code is IXJ.

You can fly to Jammu airport from Delhi, Chennai and Mumbai, and there are also occasional connections from Jammu to Leh and Srinagar. Flights from Delhi cost around Rs5,000 each way, and all of the options leave Delhi early in the morning. The flight takes 80 minutes. Flights from Leh to Jammu also take 80 minutes and cost Rs5,000.

By train Jammu Tawi is a vast, sprawling station on the imaginatively named Railway Road in the centre of Jammu, a few blocks south of the river. Large numbers of porters in red shirts are on hand to help with your luggage (information boards suggest appropriate rates of remuneration) and the staff at the information desk are helpful if you don't know where to go. Note that you will need a ticket to pass through security in order to get on to the platform.

VAISHNO DEVI AND THE SHRINE

The origins of the Vaishno Devi Shrine are cloaked in legend. It is said that Bhairavnath, a famous Hindu Tantric, saw the young Vaishno Devi at an agricultural fair and fell madly in love with her. When she fled into the Trikuta Hills to escape his amorous advances, he followed in hot pursuit, and for nine months she hid and meditated in the Ardhkunwari Cave.

Bhairavnath eventually located Vaishno Devi and she fled once again, this time to the site of the main shrine. Here she assumed the form of the goddess Mahakali and struck out at Bhairavnath, cutting off his head with her sword. Bhairavnath's head hit the floor and bounced but still he was able to beg for forgiveness. Though she could not save his life, Vaishno Devi decided that a temple should be built in his honour, and that here too devotees would offer up prayers.

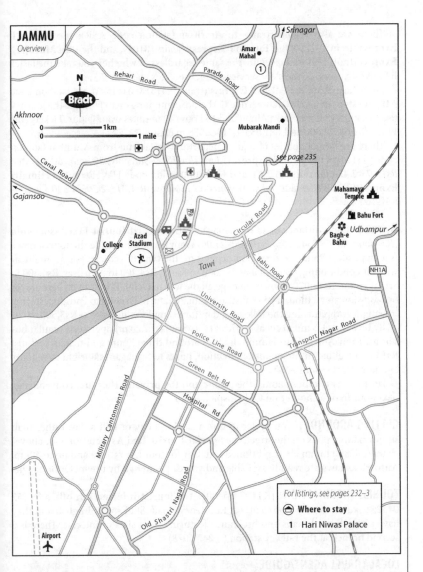

see page 235

JAMMU
Overview

N

Akhnoor

Gajansoo

0   1km

0   1 mile

Rehari   Road

Parade Road

Amar Mahal

Srinagar

Mubarak Mandi

Canal Road

Circular Road

Mahamaya Temple

Bahu Fort

Udhampur

Bagh-e Bahu

Azad Stadium

College

Tawi

Bahu Road

NH1A

University Road

Transport Nagar Road

Police Line Road

Green Belt Rd

Military Cantonment Road

Hospital Rd

Old Shastri Nagar Road

Airport

For listings, see pages 232–3

Where to stay

1   Hari Niwas Palace

The rail link to Jammu was completed in 1897 and functioned well throughout the first half of the 20th century. The line connected Jammu to Sialkot, however, and so when independence came in 1947 the line was severed, and it would be more than 20 years until Jammu was reconnected to the Indian railway network.

Getting to Jammu by train is exceptionally easy and inexpensive. Nine trains run daily from **Delhi to Jammu Tawi** (station code JAT). Delhi has several railway stations, so make sure you know which one you're leaving from. The **Malwa Express** (train 12919) leaves New Delhi railway station (station code NDLS) at 05.30 and arrives in Jammu at 16.05. Tickets cost Rs810/1,145 for class 3A/2A. There is no 1A class on this train. If you prefer to travel overnight, the **Jammu Mail** (train 14033) leaves Delhi Junction (station code DLI) at 20.10 and arrives the following morning at 09.15. Tickets cost Rs775/1,110/1,865 for class 1A/2A/3A.

There are also regular trains to Amritsar (station code ASR): the **BTI JAT Express** (train 19225); the **Tata JAT Express** (train 18101); and the **Rou Muri JAT Express** (train 18109). Prices are the same regardless of whether you take the faster BTI JAT Express, or the slow services: Rs470/665 for class 3A/2A.

From Rajasthan, the **All JAT Express** (train 12413) starts in Ajmer (station code AII) and stops in Jaipur (station code JP) before continuing on to Jammu. The journey takes around 18 hours from Ajmer and 15 hours 40 minutes from Jaipur. Tickets cost Rs1,150/1,645/2,800 and Rs1,055/1,510/2,555 in classes 3A/2A/1A respectively.

There are longer and less frequent departures to Jammu from Mumbai (station code BDTS) on the **Swaraj Express** (*Mon, Thu, Fri & Sun only; 30 hours 50 minutes; Rs1,695/2,470 for class 3A/2A*), and Kolkata (station code HWH) on the **Himgiri Express** (*Tue, Fri & Sat only; 36 hours 35 minutes; Rs1,715/2,505/4,320 for class 3A/2A/1A*).

By road   Long-distance **taxis** are managed by the **Special Tourist Taxi Association** (*Residency Rd;* 🞖 *254 6266;* ⊕ *06.00–21.00*) from it's office outside the tourist office (see opposite). Rates are fixed and depend on the type of vehicle. For an Indi Car with air conditioning you will pay Rs1,300 to Katra, Rs4,200 to Amritsar, Rs4,500 to Srinagar, and Rs12,000 if you want to go all the way to Delhi. Prices given here are for one-way journeys, though you can also arrange a return. Driving to Patnitop, staying overnight and returning the following day, for example, will cost you Rs3,500.

By **bus**, travel is much cheaper. JKSRTC (*www.jksrtc.co.in*) operates a regular bus service from Amritsar to Jammu. It takes around three hours and tickets cost just Rs135. Travelling in the opposite direction, buses to Srinagar take eight–ten hours and fares start from Rs230.

Jammu has two bus stands, the **public** and the **private**. They are, conveniently, next door to one another on Old Hospital Road.

GETTING AROUND   If you prefer to hire a car for a day or half a day, rather than simply hailing taxis on the street, the **Special Tourist Taxi Association** (see above) charges Rs800 for an air-conditioned Indi Car for four hours' hire and up to 40km. **Auto-rickshaws** are readily available and you can either go by the meter or haggle.

TOURIST INFORMATION   JKTDC operates the **tourist information office** (🞖 *252 0432;* e *jkdtourism@yahoo.co.in*) on Residency Road. Staff speak English and they have a selection of maps and brochures featuring local sites of interest. There is a second branch at the railway station (🞖 *247 6078*).

LOCAL TRAVEL AGENT/GUIDE
Sahib Travel Solutions   71 Residency Rd; 🞖 256 0643; e ssaravjit@yahoo.com. Efficient ticketing agent also able to arrange local tours.
Chandan Kumar   m 946 954 5962; e chandu. kumar671@gmail.com. For a reliable local guide, try this former teacher. He has a good command of English & now splits his time between Zanskar (Jun–Sep) and his home city of Jammu, where he works the rest of the year.

 WHERE TO STAY   Hotels are shown on the map on page 235 unless otherwise stated.

Fortune Riviera   (See ad, page 224) (29 rooms) 9 Gulab Singh Marg; 🞖 256 1415; e innriviera@fortunehotels.in; www. fortunehotels.in. Centrally located, Fortune's hotel is a haven of calm & good service. Rooms have all mod cons, there are 3 good restaurants & a coffee shop, & all the staff speak excellent English. **$$$$$**

Hari Niwas Palace Hotel [map, page 231] (40 rooms) Palace Rd; ☏ 254 3303; e hnp@hariniwaspalace.in; www. hariniwaspalace.in. We stayed just a night at Hari Niwas but adored the whole experience. The rooms are immaculate, while the management & front-desk staff are delightful. As you sit on manicured lawns drinking tea (or a G&T) you really do feel like a royal guest. Some rooms have river-facing balconies, & room 311 has a 4-poster bed. It is historically interesting, too: the treaty between Lord Mountbatten & Maharaja Hari Singh was signed in 1948 in room 318. **$$$$–$$$$$**

Jammu Residency (148 rooms) Behind Tourist Office, Residency Rd; ☏ 247 9554. Large, colonial-era hotel run by the govt & in need of love. There's a beautiful, painted ceiling in reception. Rooms have fans but no AC. **$$$–$$$$**

Parkash Yatri Bhawan (34 rooms) Opp Tourist Office, Residency Rd; m 979 622 2647. The very central location & low price are the 2 redeeming features of a building that desperately needs renovating. All rooms have attached bathroom with geyser. 4 rooms have AC. Rooms are let to tourists in May–Oct only as the govt rents the whole building in winter. **$**

WHERE TO EAT There are numerous places to eat in Jammu, and most types of cuisine are represented. All of the following establishments are marked on the map on page 235. At the upper end of the market, the Fortune Riviera hotel (see opposite) has three excellent restaurants that are open to both guests and non-guests: a multi-cuisine buffet is served in **The Orchid**; there is a delicious Chinese menu and views across Jammu towards the river at the **Oriental Pavilion**; and in **Earthen Oven** you'll find traditional north Indian cuisine, including dishes cooked in the *tandoor*. These three restaurants all fall within the **$$$$** price bracket.

If you've been craving American-style pizza, there's a **Domino's Pizza** (**$$$–$$**) in City Square Mall. A large number of the pizzas are vegetarian. **Café Coffee Day**, India's answer to Starbucks, is located on Residency Road and is open until late. For fresh juices, try the **Juice Bar** on Old Hospital Road, where a cup of freshly squeezed juice will set you back just Rs30.

ENTERTAINMENT AND NIGHTLIFE As a major city, there are actually opportunities for evening entertainment in Jammu. **Hari Cinema** (*Old Hospital Rd; tickets Rs70*) shows Bollywood flicks in slightly run-down surroundings but in a convenient location.

For an evening drink, the **Polo Bar** at Hari Niwas hotel (see above) oozes old-world charm: you can slide back in time with a cocktail in hand. More centrally located and contemporary in style, **Neptune** and **Metel** (both at the Fortune Riviera hotel, see opposite) have a good selection of spirits and attract mostly travelling businessmen, as well as a few well-heeled locals. All three bars open around 19.00 but don't get busy until after 21.00.

SHOPPING Jammu lacks the higher-end craft and souvenir shops of Srinagar and Leh, but wandering in the Main Bazaar still provides an hour or so's entertainment. There's an underwhelming but fixed-price selection of handicrafts on sale at the **Kashmir Government Arts Emporium** [235 B2] (*Residency Rd; ⏰ 10.00–18.00 daily*) and the rather more rewarding **Jay Kay Book House** [235 B2] (*Residency Rd; ⏰ 10.00–20.00 Mon–Sat*) a few doors along.

For photo printing and camera and phone accessories (including memory cards and chargers), try **Clifton Studios** [235 B1] (*Residency Rd; ⏰ 10.00–18.00 daily*). You may also find what you need among the general selection of upmarket retail outlets at **City Square Mall** [235 A3] (*Exhibition Ground Rd*).

OTHER PRACTICALITIES

Communications There are plenty of **internet cafés** around Jewel Chowk offering cheap but not terribly fast access. You may need to show your passport or other photo ID to get online. The **post office** [235 A3] is next door to City Square Mall.

Medical Jammu's main hospital, **SMHS Hospital** [235 A1] (⟨ *245 2013*), is centrally located on Shalimar Road. It is the city's teaching hospital and all main areas of practice, including A&E, are covered.

If you are simply in need of a pharmacy, **Medical Shop** [235 B1] (m *941 919 1128*) is on Old Hospital Road.

Money All of the major Indian banks are well represented in Jammu, and ATMs are commonplace. Most conveniently located are the **J&K Bank** and **PNB** ATMs at the railway station [235 D6]; the **Axis Bank** [235 A3] and ATM next door to City Square Mall; the **SBI** ATM [235 A2] on Old Hospital Road; and the **Oriental Bank of Commerce** and **UCO Bank** ATMs [235 B2] on Residency Road. The ATMs are accessible 24 hours.

WHAT TO SEE Jammu is home to a vast number of sites of interest to both leisure tourists and pilgrims. Though none of the individual attractions will hold your attention for very long, the sheer variety of things to see means you can easily fill several days of your itinerary soaking up all that the city has to offer.

Amar Mahal [map, page 231] (*Palace Rd;* ⊕ *Apr–Sep 09.00–13.00 & 14.00–18.00 Tue–Sat; Oct–Mar 09.00–13.00 & 14.00–17.00; entrance fee Rs10/20 child/adult; Rs50 camera*) Set in an imposing position above the River Tawi, the Amar Mahal is the former royal palace of the 19th-century Dogra king Raja Amar Singh. Designed by a French architect and inhabited by the family until 1967, it now houses the Amar Mahal Museum, an eclectic collection of family heirlooms, artworks and photographs.

The wood-panelled **hall** contains family photos and an informative biography of Dr Karan Singh, prince, singer, environmentalist, cabinet minister, diplomat and state governor. From here you move into the **Nala Damyanti Gallery** with its full-length oil portraits of the royal family and a large and well-presented collection of 18th-century Pahari miniatures. There are also two fascinating models: a 1:633,600 scale (1 inch = 10 miles) topographical model of J&K, and a finely made wooden model of the Brihadishwara Temple in Tanjore.

The museum also contains a **contemporary art gallery** with three works by M F Husain; a throne room that is permanently locked but you can look at the throne through the window; and the **Dash Avatar Gallery**, a display space containing a dozen unremarkable modern oils and a rather more attractive fibreglass Buddha in an antechamber.

Opposite the palace entrance is the impressive **statue of Maharaja Gulab Singh,** founder of J&K state, commissioned by Dr Karan Singh and unveiled by the vice president of India in 2000.

Aquarium [235 D2] (*Nr Bahu Fort;* ⟨ *243 5596;* ⊕ *Apr–Sep 09.00–21.00 daily; Oct–Mar 09.00–20.00; entrance fee Rs10/20 child/adult*) The architects really had fun designing Jammu's aquarium: the building is in the shape of a giant, silver fish. Run by the Department of Fisheries, most of the aquarium is actually underground, making it rather dark. The aquarium's principal function is to educate local school children. Foreigners who have already seen the sea may wish simply to photograph the outside of the building and, while standing in the driveway, take a look up at the fort.

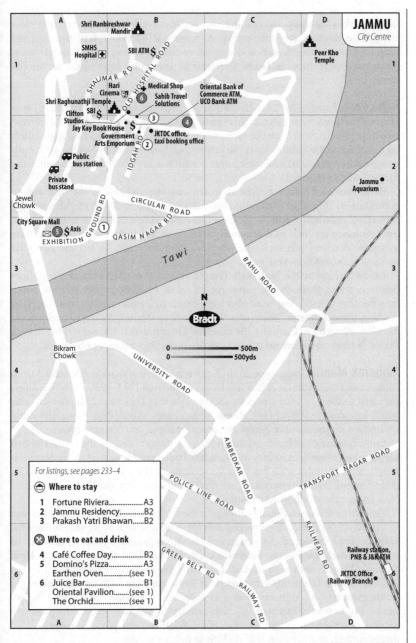

JAMMU
City Centre

Shri Ranbireshwar Mandir

SMHS Hospital

SBI ATM $

Peer Kho Temple

SHALIMAR RD

OLD HOSPITAL ROAD

Hari Cinema

Medical Shop

Oriental Bank of Commerce ATM, UCO Bank ATM

Shri Raghunathji Temple

Sahib Travel Solutions

Clifton Studios

SBI $

3

4

Jay Kay Book House

Government Arts Emporium

JKTDC office, taxi booking office

2

IDGAH RD

Public bus station

Private bus stand

Jammu Aquarium

Jewel Chowk

CIRCULAR ROAD

City Square Mall

5 $ Axis

1

EXHIBITION

GROUND RD

QASIM NAGAR RD

Tawi

BAHU ROAD

N

Bradt

Bikram Chowk

0 ————— 500m
0 ————— 500yds

UNIVERSITY ROAD

AMBEDKAR ROAD

TRANSPORT NAGAR ROAD

For listings, see pages 233–4

⌂ **Where to stay**

1 Fortune Riviera...............A3
2 Jammu Residency...........B2
3 Prakash Yatri Bhawan.....B2

✖ **Where to eat and drink**

4 Café Coffee Day..............B2
5 Domino's Pizza................A3
Earthen Oven.............(see 1)
6 Juice Bar........................B1
Oriental Pavilion........(see 1)
The Orchid.................(see 1)

POLICE LINE ROAD

GREEN BELT RD

RAILWAY RD

RAILHEAD RD

Railway station, PNB & J&K ATM

JKTDC Office (Railway Branch)

Bagh-e Bahu [map, page 231] (*Bahu Rd;* ⊕ *Apr–Sep 08.00–22.00 daily; Oct–Mar 09.00–21.00; entrance fee Rs5/10 child/adult; car parking Rs20*) Probably the most delightful public space in Jammu; if you stand in the Bagh-e Bahu (Bahu Garden) you look down on the river and up at the fort. Families picnic in shady patches beneath the trees, and tiny chipmunk-squirrels chase each other across the lawns.

The park is carefully laid out and well maintained. Paved pathways and water channels demarcate the different areas, manmade waterfalls lead the eye, and dark pink and purple flowers add a splash of colour. Sitting in the rose garden is particularly peaceful. The **JKDC Cafeteria** in the centre of the park serves soft drinks and ice creams.

Bahu Fort [map, page 231] (*Bahu Rd; No entrance fee; car parking Rs20*) It is claimed there has been a fort on this site for around 3,000 years, though the current structure mostly dates from the 1800s when it was rebuilt by Jammu's Dogra rulers on top of an earlier (16th century) structure. A substantial section of the fort's walls collapsed in August 2013 following heavy rains; it is as yet unknown if or when the damage will be repaired.

Bahu Fort looks quite a sight from the outside, and this is the best way to appreciate it. If you are determined to get inside you must first fight your way through a parking lot and an arcade of souvenir shops selling all manner of tat for devotees: very little of it is actually sold, so expect to be pursued aggressively by stallholders and beggars if you show the slightest interest. This is also a popular hangout for street dogs and goats.

Inside the fort is the **Mahakali Temple** and so you must remove your shoes before entering through the gates, regardless of whether or not you are going into the shrine itself. You must also leave cameras, mobile phones and any other electronic items outside. There is nothing to see in the fort courtyard and you are not allowed up on to the walls: the monkeys are apparently too aggressive, though the live wires and numerous trip hazards are probably a more serious threat.

Mubarak Mandi [map, page 231] (*Panjthirthi;* ✎ *256 3084*) The Mubarak Mandi complex was the royal seat of Jammu's Dogra rulers from 1824–1925 when Hari Singh relocated to the new Hari Niwas Palace (see *Where to stay*, page 233). The vast site, which includes the Darbar Hall, Sheesh Mahal, Hawa Mahal, Pink Palace and Royal Courts, is a smorgasbord of European Baroque, Mughal and Mewari styles.

Sadly, however, the buildings are in extreme danger, already the victims of two earthquakes, more than 30 fires and decades of unforgivable neglect. A conservation programme is under way, but as large sections of the palace have already been gutted or collapsed, conservators are limited in what they can do. The monkeys have taken over, along with the birds.

One of the few operational buildings in the complex is the **Dogra Art Museum** (🕐 *10.00–17.00 Tue–Sun; entrance fee Rs10/50 local/foreigner; Rs100/200 camera/ video camera*), though that too is in need of damp-proofing, a clean and a lick of paint. The highlights of the museum's collection are displayed in the **Main Hall**, a double-height room with internal balconies. We were particularly taken by the beautiful mural fragments removed from Reasi Fort, four 4th-century terracotta heads excavated at Ambaran near Akhnoor, and the large Kushan coin hoard. Look out also for the hoard of 107 12th-century coins found recently by prisoners gardening within the confines of Kot Bhalwal Jail.The rest of the museum is a bit disappointing, and the dour staff do little to bring it to life.

The **Long Gallery** on the first floor has an attractive, carved wooden ceiling that is original to the building and a glass cabinet containing what is apparently a piece of elephant fossil, though you'll have to use your imagination. The adjoining room has a display of 19th-century paintings, unremarkable individually but pleasant enough as a group, and two sets of colourful doors salvaged from somewhere else in the Mubarak Mandi complex.

The **contemporary art gallery** is best avoided unless you like your art either banal or hideous. A dozen or so pieces of sculpture on plinths are arranged around a sunken bath alongside two truly monstrous larger works and a few unremarkable paintings.

Other temples Jammu is, of course, famed for its **Hindu temples** and though you're unlikely to want to visit all of them (there are, by some estimates, more than 300), visiting a few of them will give you valuable insight into the city, its people and their beliefs. If you are going to the Bahu Fort, continue on to the neighbouring **Mahamaya Temple** [map, page 231] in the forest on the facing ridge. This 19th-century temple contains a *pindi*, said to be the manifestation of the goddess, and offers superb views across both the city and the forest.

Peer Kho Temple [235 D1] (*Circular Rd*) dates back far earlier than Jammu's other temples, having been a place of prayer since the late 1400s. The holy man Jogi Guru Garib Nath lived and meditated in this cave (*kho* meaning cave) as it contains a Shiva *lingam*. The cave is also thought to have been visited by Jamwant, the bear figure in the *Ramayana* epic. This temple is particularly busy during the Shivratri festival (February/March).

The most famous of Jammu's temples is the **Shri Raghunathji Temple** [235 B1] (*Old Hospital Rd*), the largest temple complex in northern India. Built by Maharaja Ranbir Singh in 1857, the main temple's interior walls are covered with sheets of gold, and there are large statues of Rama, Sita and Lakshman. Bibliophiles may also want to check out the **Sanskrit library**, which contains a number of rare manuscripts.

Also built by Maharaja Ranbir Singh, but several years later, is the temple that bears his name: the **Shri Ranbireshwar Mandir** [235 B1] (*Shalimar Rd*). It took 15 years to complete and is the largest Shiva temple in northern India. Inside you'll see a large Shiva *lingam* surrounded by nearly a dozen smaller crystal *lingams*, and 125,000 tiny *lingams* brought from the Narmada River in central India.

For details on a far wider selection of Jammu's temples, as well as its *gurudwaras* and churches, pick up the free *Jammu: City of Temples* brochure from the tourist office (see page 232).

AROUND JAMMU

AKHNOOR On the banks of the River Chenab, 20km northwest of Jammu is the town Akhnoor, over which the impressive **Akhnoor Fort** presides. Though construction of the present buildings began only in 1762 (and was not completed until 1802), archaeological evidence suggests there have been a succession of structures on this site since Harappan times, and some of the finest exhibits in the Dogra Art Museum (see opposite) were excavated here. Conservation of the fort is ongoing, so do heed the advice of local caretakers about where it is safe to go.

Another archaeological site here of great historical importance is **Ambran** (⊕ *dawn to dusk*), a series of 2,000-year-old structures including a Buddhist stupa. The Archaeological Survey of India is slowly excavating the site, and has already unearthed decorative terracotta figurines, copper objects, beads made from semi-precious stones, pottery and caskets containing human relics.

Elsewhere in Akhnoor it is possible to visit the **Pandava Gufa**, an ancient cave hidden behind the pink façade of a modern building, which somewhat spoils the atmosphere. It is believed that the five Pandava brothers, heroes of the *Mahabharata*, took refuge here and so pilgrims still come to pray.

Jammu JAMMU

11

237

SURINSAR-MANSAR LAKES The lakes lie 42km outside of Jammu to the east. Declared a wildlife sanctuary in 1981, these wetlands are a prime habitat for birdlife and it is possible to see both local and migratory species, including various types of cranes and ducks.

The twin lakes are of great religious importance too, and for this reason it is not permitted to swim in the water or attempt to catch the fish. Legend has it that Arjuna, hero of the *Mahabharata*, shot an arrow into the ground at Mansar, and it exited at Surinsar, creating the two lakes. Mansar is also considered to be the home of Sheshnag, a mythical (one would hope) six-headed snake god who is lord of all serpents. The **Sheshnag Shrine** is on the eastern bank of the lake, and it is visited by newly-wed couples seeking his blessings.

Should you wish to stay overnight at the lakes, JKTDC operates a **guesthouse complex** (*www.jktdc.co.in;* **$$**) with rooms and bungalows on the shore of Lake Mansar.

SnowLion Expeditions Pvt. Ltd

Pangong Lake, Ladakh

www.snowlion-india.com

Appendix 1

LANGUAGE

Although English is widely spoken, especially in the state's urban areas and places with a high footfall of tourists, the official language of J&K is Urdu, an Indo-European language closely related in its grammar and vocabulary to Hindi, but that is written from right to left in the Perso-Arabic script. As a spoken language it is relatively straightforward and you will be able to pick up common phrases quickly; learning to read and write it will take more time and, in any case, it is unlikely to be necessary on a short visit as most signage is written in English.

While in Ladakh, you may want to try speaking a few words of Ladakhi too. Ladakhi is rather more difficult: it is a Tibetic language (though not mutually intelligible with Standard Tibetan). Some dialects of Ladakhi are tonal.

See also *Language*, page 248, for books on learning Urdu and Ladakhi.

URDU
Alphabet

ا	as in **a**pple	ذ	as in **th**at	ق	a **k** in the throat
ب	as in **b**ook	ر	trilled **r**	ک	as in **k**ilo
پ	as in **p**ool	ڑ	as in **r**abbit	گ	as in **g**uest
ت	t as in **t**ime	ز,ظ	as in **z**en	ل	as in **l**eaf
ٹ	as in **a**rt	ژ	as in plea**s**ure	م	as in **m**uch
ث	as in **th**ank	س	as in **s**mall	ن	as in **n**ot
ج	as in he**dge**	ش	as in wor**sh**ip	و	varies between
چ	as in ca**tch**	ص	as in **s**ue		**w** and **v**
ح	as in **h**ead	ض	as in **th**ose	ه	as in **h**ouse
خ	as in Ba**ch**	ط	as in s**t**able	ی	as in **y**ak
د	as in **d**ove	غ	similar to a French r	ے	as in **w**a**y** and **y**ell
ڈ	as in **dr**ink	ف	as in **f**ood		

Useful phrases

Hello	*salaam aleikum*
How are you?	*aap kaise hain?*
I am fine	*main thik hun*
Where do you come from?	*kahan se aap?*
I come from…	*mai… se hun*
What is your name?	*aapka naam kya hai?*
My name is…	*mera naam… hài*
Goodbye	*khuda haafiz*
Yes	*haan*
No	*nahin*
Thank you	*shukriya*

I understand	*main samajhta/ti hun*
I don't understand	*main nahin samajhta/t*
Do you have…?	*kya aap ke paas…?*
How much is this?	*yah kitna hai?*
May I have…?	*mujhe de dijie…* (lit. Please give me…)
I am hot	*mujhe garam lagta/ti hai*
I am cold	*mujhe thanda lagta/ti hai*
I am tired	*mujhe thaki hui hai*
I am ill	*mujhe bimaar hai*

Urdu numbers

1	*ek*	11	*gyrah*	30	*tees*
2	*do*	12	*baarah*	40	*chalees*
3	*teen*	13	*taraah*	50	*pechchas*
4	*char*	14	*chaudah*	60	*sath*
5	*panch*	15	*pendrah*	70	*sattar*
6	*cheh*	16	*solah*	80	*aasi*
7	*saath*	17	*setrah*	90	*navway*
8	*aath*	18	*aatraah*	100	*ek sau*
9	*noh*	19	*unees*	1,000	*hazaar*
10	*das*	20	*bees*		

LADAKHI
Alphabet

ཀ	ka	ད	da	ཞ	zha
ཁ	kha	ན	na	ཟ	za
ག	ga	པ	pa	འ	'a
ང	nga	ཕ	pha	ཡ	ya
ཅ	ca	བ	ba	ར	ra
ཆ	cha	མ	ma	ལ	la
ཇ	ja	ཙ	tsa	ཤ	sha
ཉ	nya	ཚ	tsha	ས	sa
ཏ	ta	ཛ	dza	ཧ	ha
ཐ	tha	ཝ	wa	ཨ	a

Useful phrases

Hello	*juley*
How are you?	*rdemo ina?*
I am fine	*kasa dju*
Where do you come from?	*nyerang kane in le?*
I come from…	*nga… ne in le*
What is your name?	*nay rangi ming la chi yin?*
My name is…	*nay ming la… yin lay*
Goodbye	*juley*
Yes	*yot*
No	*met*
Thank you	*juley*
I understand	*gnya hago*
I don't understand	*gnya hamago*
Do you have…?	*… yo ta lay?*
How much is this?	*eebowa zrin sam in lay?*

May I have…?	thobina le…?
I am hot	tsante rak
I am cold	tangmo mi rak
I am tired	ngalte rak
I am ill	zumo rak

Ladakhi numbers

1 chik	11 chug-tzik	30 somtchu
2 nyis	12 chug-nis	40 jiptchu
3 sum	13 chug-sum	50 ngaptchu
4 jzhe	14 chug-jzhe	60 tuktchu
5 nghra	15 chug-nghra	70 rduntchu
6 tuk	16 chu-ruk	80 rgyet tchu
7 dun	17 chub-dun	90 rgup tchu
8 gyat	18 chob-gyat	100 rgya
9 gyu	19 chur-gu	1,000 stong
10 chu	20 nyi-shu	

Appendix 2

afsaras	angel-like figures
amchi	medicine man
arhat	Buddhist missionary
auto	motorised rickshaw
avatar	incarnation of a deity or other holy figure
azad	free
azan	call to prayer
bagh	garden
baksheesh	donation or bribe
bandh	strike
baradari	pavilion
Bharat	India
BJP	Bharatiya Janata Party
BSNL	Bharat Sanchar Nigam Limited, a state-owned telecommunications company
Bodhisattva	one who has obtained enlightenment but remains on earth to show others the way
Bollywood	nickname for the Mumbai (formerly Bombay) film industry
Buddha	Prince Gautama Buddha, the first mortal to obtain 'Enlightenment'
caste system	Hindu social and religious hierarchy
chadar	blanket
chai	tea
chana dal	chickpeas
chang	homemade barley beer
char bagh	Persian garden
charpoy	rope bed
choli	sari blouse
chorten	*see* Stupa
chowk	crossroads or marketplace
Congress	Congress Party of India
crore	ten million
curd	yoghurt
dagoba	*see* stupa
dal	lentils
dargah	burial place or shrine of a Muslim saint

Devi	goddess
dhaba	roadside café
dharma	moral or natural code
dhobi	washerman
dosa	rice flour pancake
dudh	milk
dukhang	Tibetan prayer hall
dum aloo	spiced potato curry
dzo	offspring of a yak and a cow
gabba	Kashmiri rug with appliqué
galoti kebab	minced meat with chickpeas and spices
ghee	clarified butter
gompa	Buddhist monastery
guru	teacher or religious leader
Gurudwara	Sikh temple
Guru Granth Sahib	Sikhism's holy book
gushtaba	minced lamb meatballs with yoghurt gravy
Gypsy	popular 4x4 manufactured by Maruti
haaq saag	local variety of spinach
harissa	stew of slow-cooked mutton, rice and spices
hijab	headscarf worn by Muslim women
jijra	eunuch or transvestite
Hindustan	India
HPTDC	Himachal Pradesh Transport Development Corporation
imam	Muslim religious leader
idli	South Indian snack made from rice flour
J&K	Jammu and Kashmir state
Jama Masjid	Friday mosque
jataka	story from the life of the Buddha
Jeep	any 4x4 vehicle regardless of make
jalebi	deep-fried sweet dipped in sugar syrup while hot
ji	honorific suffix
Jihad	Holy war
Jimdak	Korean dish
JKLF	Jammu and Kashmir Liberation Front
JKSRTC	J&K State Road Transport Corporation
juley	Ladakhi greeting
kahwah	green tea prepared with saffron and almonds
Kanger	pot filled with hot embers
karma	justice for past deeds (good or bad)
kesar	saffron
khadi	homespun cloth
khalsa	Sikh brotherhood
khanqah	shrine
Kiang	wild ass
Koran	Islam's holy book

lakh	100,000
lama	Buddhist monk
lassi	yoghurt-based drink flavoured with sugar or salt
lingam/linga	phallus symbolic of Hindu god Shiva
LoC/LOC	Line of Control
Losar	Tibetan New Year
LTOCL	Ladakh Taxi Operators Cooperative Limited
lyodoor tschaman	paneer cooked in turmeric gravy
madrassa	Islamic school
Mahabharata	famous Hindu epic poem
mahal	palace
maharani	queen
maharaja	king
malai kofta	vegetable dumplings in a creamy sauce
mandal	shrine
mandala	circular artwork symbolising the universe
mandir	temple
mani	stone wall with religious inscriptions
masala	spice
masala chai	sweet tea with cardamom, cinnamon and other spices
masjid	mosque
mehndi	henna tattoos painted on the hands and feet
methi chaman	paneer with fenugreek leaves and spinach
mihrab	prayer niche in a mosque
minaret	tower on a mosque
mirch	chilli pepper
momos	steamed dumplings filled with vegetables or minced meat or cheese
mudra	ritual hand gesture
muezzin	man who sings the call to prayer
nadru	lotus roots
nadru yakhni	lotus roots cooked with yoghurt and spices
nag	snake, specifically a cobra
namaste	Hindi greeting
namaz	Muslim prayers
nawab	Muslim prince or major landowner
neophyte	trainee monk
NH	National Highway
nirvana	release from the cycle of reincarnation
noon chai	salted green tea served with bread
om	sacred symbol
paan	mild narcotic made from betel nut
pagoda	*see* stupa
paisa	money; there are 100 paise (pl) in a rupee
Pali	ancient script in which the Buddhist scriptures were first recorded

paneer	soft, white cheese often used as an ingredient in curries
paratha	flat bread, sometimes stuffed with potato or cheese
Partition	division of British India into the countries of India and Pakistan
pashmina	fine woollen shawl made with wool from a pashmina goat
phiren	traditional woollen tunic
photang	place for buddhist teaching
pindi	stone manifestation of the goddess Shakti
pir	Muslim saint
POK	Pakistan Occupied Kashmir
prasad	offering of food to the gods
puja	prayers or session of religious teaching
pulao	rice-based disk akin to biryani
qawwali	Muslim devotional singing
qila	fort
Raj	period of British rule
Ramadan	Islamic holy month of fasting that ends with the festival of Eid ul Fitr
rasgulla	Indian sweet dipped in sugar syrup
Rigveda	important Hindu religious text written in Sanskrit
rista	mutton meatballs in gravy
rogan josh	slow-cooked lamb in spicy gravy
sadhu	Hindu ascetic
samosa	deep-fried pastry triangle stuffed with minced lamb or vegetables
sangha	Buddhist community
Sanskrit	classical language in which Hindu religious texts were written
shahi paneer	cheese curry
shalwar kameez	woman's outfit of tunic and baggy trousers
Sharia	Islamic law
sheer chai	salted green tea served with bread
shikara	punt-like boat used on the backwaters and lakes of Kashmir
shivling	*see* lingam
shri	Lord, or Mr
shrimati	Mrs
stupa	domed structure covering sacred relics
Sufism	mystical Islam
synoon pulaav	meat pulao
tank	reservoir
tarami	large serving dish with a copper dome to keep food warm
thali	large, round dish on which rice and multiple curries are served
thangka	Tibetan cloth painting
thukpa	soup with noodles
tilak	a red mark on the forehead that denotes a blessing
tso	lake

uttapam	South Indian snack akin to a thick pancake
vasta waaza	head chef
waazwaan	traditional banquet served on special occasions
yakhni	lamb cooked in yoghurt gravy
yatra	pilgrimage
yatri	pilgrim
zenana	harem

Appendix 3

FURTHER INFORMATION

BOOKS
History and archaeology

Boulnois, Luce *Silk Road: Monks, Warriors and Merchants on the Silk Road* Odyssey Guides, 2012. Detailed history of the people and ideas that spread along the Silk Road. Also available in French.

Dewan, Parvez *A History of Ladakh, Gilgit, Baltistan* Manas Publications, 2007. The founder of the Ladakh Festival brings alive the region's past from pre-history to the present day.

Fewkes, Jacqueline *Trade and Contemporary Society along the Silk Road: An Ethnohistory of Ladakh* Routledge, 2011. Fewkes combines archaeology, history and anthropology in this book on Ladakh and its trading links.

Fouq, Muhammad *A Complete History of Kashmir* Gulshaan, 2009. Translation and reprint of a wordy, 19th-century history written in Urdu. Covers more than 5,000 years of history.

Rai, Mridu *Hindu Rulers, Muslim Subjects: Islam, Community and the History of Kashmir* C Hurst & Co Publishers Ltd, 2004. Rai looks back to the British policies of the 19th century for the underlying causes of Kashmir's 20th century problems.

Rizvi, Janet *Ladakh: Crossroads of High Asia* OUP India, 1999. Himalayan specialist Rizvi takes a multi-disciplinary approach to the history of Ladakh, including recent economic and social change.

Kashmir post-1947

Ali, Tariq *Kashmir: The Case for Freedom* Verso, 2011. Collected writings from Tariq Ali, Arundhati Roy, Hilal Bhatt and others.

Noorani, A G *Article 370: A Constitutional History of Jammu and Kashmir* OUP India, 2011. Collection of White Papers, letters, memorandums and other documents that goes some way to explaining the complex constitutional status of J&K, and the impact of that status since independence.

Quraishi, Humra *Kashmir: The Untold Story* Penguin Books India, 2004. A look behind the statistics & propaganda at the human tragedy of the Kashmir conflict.

Schofield, Victoria *Kashmir in Conflict: India, Pakistan and the Unending War* IB Tauris Publishers, 2010. Expert Schofield explores the roots of the modern conflict and how it developed into a possible nuclear war. Schofield is both highly articulate and well informed.

Whitehead, Andrew *A Mission in Kashmir* Penguin Books, 2007. The story of how conflict started in 1947, drawn from oral history, contemporary media and archive materials.

Memoirs and travellers' accounts

Boyden, Mark *Travels in Zanskar* Liffey Press, 2013. In 1981 Boyden set out on horseback to explore Ladakh and Zanskar, in doing so becoming one of the first foreigners to visit the Zanskar Valley. Foreword by Dervla Murphy.

Hardy, Justine *In the Valley of Mist: Kashmir's Long War* Rider, 2010. Beautifully written, personal account of Hardy's own travels in Kashmir, and the lives of those she's met. Poignant and accomplished.

Harvey, Andrew *A Journey in Ladakh* Rider, 2003. A travel writer and academic, Harvey explores Ladakh's Buddhist culture in a captivating way.

Keenan, Brigid *Travels in Kashmir* Hachette India, 2013. Formerly fashion editor at the *Sunday Times*, Keenan vividly explores the colours and textures of Kashmir, and in particular its cultural heritage.

Omrani, Bijan *Asia Overland: Tales of Travel on the Trans-Siberian and Silk Road* Odyssey Guides, 2010. Beautifully written and heavily illustrated historical travelogue drawing on accounts from Fa Xian to Marco Polo to Francis Younghusband. Full of humour, it is an entertaining and informative read for armchair travellers and modern-day explorers alike.

Peer, Basharat *Curfewed Night: A Frontline Memoir of Life, Love and War in Kashmir* Harper Press, 2011. Passionate account from a Kashmiri journalist. Winner of the Crossroad Prize for non-fiction.

Culture and traditions

Ames, Frank *The Kashmir Shawl and its Indo-French Influence* Antique Collectors' Club Ltd, 1999. Vast coffee-table book exploring the history and influences of Kashmiri shawls, written by a renowned textile dealer.

Isaac, John *The Vale of Kashmir* W W Norton & Company, 2008. Photographic tribute to the people and places of the Kashmir Valley. Coffee-table format.

Jaitly, Jaya *Crafts of Jammu, Kashmir and Ladakh* Grantha Corporation, 1999. General introduction to the regions' crafts, with photos from contemporary artisans.

Koch, Ebba *Mughal Architecture* Prestel, 1991. Still the definitive book on the Mughal emperors' mosques, palaces, pleasure gardens and shrines.

Michell, George *Mughal Architecture and Gardens* Antique Collectors' Club Ltd, 2011. Authoritative book with superb photos.

Rizvi, Janet *Pashmina: The Kashmir Shawl and Beyond* Marg Publications, 2009. Sumptuous photographic book. A fitting tribute to the most beautiful of products.

Van Ham, Peter *Heavenly Himalayas: The Murals of Mangyu and Other Discoveries in Ladakh* Prestel, 2011. Focusing principally on the Mangyu Monastery, Van Ham explores Mayahana Buddhism in India and its impact on the visual arts.

Walker, Daniel *Flowers Underfoot: Indian Carpets of the Mughal Era* Thames & Hudson, 1998. Published to coincide with an exhibition at the Metropolitan Museum in New York, this is the definitive history of Mughal carpets and their motifs.

Language

Delay, Richard *Read and Write Urdu Script* Teach Yourself, 2010. Helpful book for those simply wanting to understand the Urdu script. Ideal for readers with a prior knowledge of Hindi.

Koshal, Sanyukta *Conversational Ladakhi* Hanish & Co, 2005. Weighty hardback tome for those keen to gain a greater understanding of the Ladakhi language.

Koshal, Sanyukta *Guide to Learn Ladakhi Language* Hanish & Co, 2006. A smaller, lighter and generally more accessible version of Koshal's earlier textbook. Includes helpful tips on pronunciation and numerous useful phrases arranged by scenario.

Matthews, David *Complete Urdu* Teach Yourself, 2010. Well-written introduction to the script, vocabulary and grammar of the Urdu language.

Norman, Rebecca *Getting Started in Ladakhi* Melong Publications, 2012. Beginners language guide with clearly explained sections on grammar and pronunciation. Pocket sized.

The website www.koshur.org offers a good introduction to the Kashmiri language, with downloadable texts, vocabulary and lessons for beginners.

Literature

Chandra, Vikram *The Srinagar Conspiracy* Penguin India, 2000. Described as 'Great Game meets Bollywood', this modern thriller revolves around two childhood friends, one Muslim and the other Hindu, whose lives are torn apart by war.

Ded, Lal *I, Lalla: The Poems of Lal Ded* Penguin Classics, 2013. Collected poems of the 14th-century Kashmiri mystic Lal Ded. New translation into English.

Ghani, Tahir *The Captured Gazelle: The Poems of Ghani Kashmiri* Penguin Classics, 2013. Translated poems of the 17th-century Persian poet Mulla Tahir Ghani.

Raina, Trilokinath *A History of Kashmiri Literature* Sahitya Akademi, 2002. Very few overviews of Kashmiri literature exist. This title is likely to be available only in India.

Singh, Jaspreet *Chef: A Novel* Bloomsbury USA, 2010. Tragic novel about the Kashmir conflict, as seen through the eyes of a young Sikh chef in the Indian army.

Thomas, Rosie *The Kashmir Shawl* Overlook Press, 2013. Evocative novel transporting readers from colonial-era houseboats to modern Wales.

Waheed, Mirza *The Collaborator* Penguin, 2012. Gripping debut novel that paints a devastating picture of Kashmir and the brutality of the conflict.

NEWSPAPERS Major Indian newspapers are published in English as well as vernacular languages, and their content is usually available online even if the distribution of paper copies does not reach as far as the town you are in. This is frequently the case in J&K, and especially in the remoter areas.

Of the large, English-language newspapers, only the *Indian Express* (*www.indianexpress.com*) is available in Jammu. Smaller, more regionally focused newspapers available in J&K include *Greater Kashmir* (Srinagar only) and *Kashmir Times* (*www.kashmirtimes.in*), Jammu only.

MAPS Though it may not be easily to get maps of J&K abroad, once you arrive they are plentiful, though not always of the highest quality, which is an issue if you are planning to trek. Note that some maps published in India do not demarcate the LoC, which would bring you into difficulty if you inadvertently were to cross into areas under the control of Pakistan.

India North & West 1:1,900,000 ITMB International Travel Maps. Large, folding map of northern India that includes the entirety of J&K.

Jammu & Kashmir 1:1,000,000 TTK Maps. Road map of J&K with larger-scale insets of Anantnag, Kargil, Leh and Srinagar. Note that the LoC is not shown on this map.

Ladakh 1:500,000 Hanish & Co, 2013. Widely available in Leh, this trekking map covers Ladakh, Zanskar and Manali and includes information on the most important monasteries.

Ladakh & Zanskar 1:150,000 Editions Olizane, 2008. The most detailed trekking map available is published in three parts (north, central and south). It is printed on non-tear paper and includes a short glossary.

Ladakh & Zanskar 1:175,000 Milestone Books, 2013. Detailed topographical map. Fairly accurate and, due to its scale, of most use to trekkers.

Ladakh Trekking & Road Map HPC Publications, 2012. Small folding map (A4) with laminated surface. Not to scale.

Trekking Map of Ladakh Sonam Tsetan, 2007. Locally published trekking map, now in its fifth edition. Not to scale.

WEBSITES
Travel advice
www.fco.gov.uk/travel Foreign and Commonwealth Office travel advice.
www.fitfortravel.nhs.uk NHS travel health advice
www.travel.state.gov US State Department travel advice.
www.ukinindia.fco.gov.uk Website of the British High Commission in New Delhi.

Tourist information
www.jksrtc.co.in J&K State Road Transport Corporation.
www.jktdc.in J&K Tourism Development Corporation: accommodation booking.

Government sites
www.jammu.nic.in Jammu district.
www.leh.nic.in Leh district.
www.srinagar.nic.in Srinagar district.

News and political analysis
www.bbc.co.uk/news/world/asia/india BBC news coverage from India, including J&K.
www.greaterkashmir.com E-paper and online video content.
www.kashmirtimes.com The oldest, English-language paper in J&K.
www.knskashmir.com The first online news service for J&K.
www.risingkashmir.com Local news published from Delhi, Jammu and Srinagar.

Culture
http://whc.unesco.org/en/tentativelists/5580 The Mughal Gardens on UNESCO's Tentative List of World Heritage Sites.
www.heritageofkashmir.org Articles on culture and conservation.
www.ladakhstudies.org The International Association for Ladakh Studies (IALS).

Index

Entries in **bold** indicate main entries; those in *italic* indicate maps

INDEX OF ADVERTISERS

THE AUSTRALIAN
Women's Weekly
100 classic cakes

Contents

We've all grown up with the idea of 'a cup of tea and nice piece of cake' – even if our lives today don't easily afford us the opportunity to sit down for a few minutes. I hope that you find a few reminders in this book of just how easy it is to make that nice piece of cake! From traditional dundee cakes to perfect little butterfly cakes… So kick off your shoes and get the kettle on!

Pamela Clark

CLASSIC
Butter cakes

Most of the cakes we know and love are butter
cakes of some sort. We use butter in our recipes
because it will hold the flavour of the cake,
it will keep the texture moist, and the cake will
cut and keep well, but, best of all, it makes
the cakes taste just wonderful.

basic butter cake

prep + cook time 1 hour 30 minutes **serves** 12

250g butter, softened
1 teaspoon vanilla extract
1¼ cups (275g) caster sugar
3 eggs
2¼ cups (335g) self-raising flour
¼ cup (180ml) milk

1 Preheat oven to 180°C/160°C fan-assisted. Grease
deep 22cm-round or 19cm-square cake tin; line base
with baking parchment.
2 Beat butter, extract and sugar in medium bowl with
electric mixer until light and fluffy. Beat in eggs, one at
a time. Stir in sifted flour and milk, in two batches.
3 Spread mixture into tin; bake about 1 hour. Stand
cake in tin 5 minutes before turning, top-side up, onto
wire rack to cool.

marble cake

prep + cook time 1 hour 40 minutes serves 12

250g butter, softened
1 teaspoon vanilla extract
1¼ cups (275g) caster sugar
3 eggs
2¼ cups (335g) self-raising flour
¾ cup (180ml) milk
pink food colouring
2 tablespoons cocoa powder
2 tablespoons milk, extra
butter frosting
90g butter, softened
1 cup (160g) icing sugar
1 tablespoon milk

1 Preheat oven to 180°C/160°C fan-assisted. Grease deep 22cm-round or 19cm-square cake tin; line base with baking parchment.
2 Beat butter, extract and sugar in medium bowl with electric mixer until light and fluffy. Beat in eggs, one at a time. Stir in sifted flour and milk, in two batches.
3 Divide mixture among three bowls; tint one mixture pink. Blend sifted cocoa with extra milk in a cup; stir into second mixture; leave remaining mixture plain. Drop alternate spoonfuls of mixtures into tin. Pull a skewer backwards and forwards through cake mixture.
4 Bake cake about 1 hour. Stand cake in tin 5 minutes before turning, top-side up, onto wire rack to cool.
5 Make butter frosting. Spread over top of cake.
butter frosting Beat butter in small bowl with electric mixer until light and fluffy; beat in sifted icing sugar and milk, in two batches.

lemon sour cream cake

prep + cook time 1 hour 15 minutes **serves** 16

250g butter, softened
1 tablespoon finely grated lemon rind
2 cups (440g) caster sugar
6 eggs
¾ cup (180g) soured cream
2 cups (300g) plain flour
¼ cup (35g) self-raising flour
½ cup (80g) pine nuts
1 tablespoon demerara sugar
¼ cup (90g) honey

1 Preheat oven to 180°C/160°C fan-assisted. Grease deep 23cm-square cake tin; line base and two opposite sides with baking parchment, extending paper 5cm over edges.
2 Beat butter, rind and caster sugar in medium bowl with electric mixer until light and fluffy. Beat in eggs, one at a time. Stir in soured cream and sifted flours, in two batches. Spread mixture into tin; bake 15 minutes.
3 Meanwhile, combine pine nuts and demerara sugar in small bowl.
4 Remove cake from oven; working quickly, sprinkle nut mixture evenly over cake, press gently into top. Return cake to oven; bake a further 45 minutes. Stand cake in tin 5 minutes before turning, top-side up, onto wire rack.
5 Meanwhile, heat honey in small saucepan. Drizzle hot cake evenly with hot honey; cool before serving.

orange cake

prep + cook time 50 minutes **serves** 12

150g butter, softened
1 tablespoon finely grated orange rind
⅔ cup (150g) caster sugar
3 eggs
1½ cups (225g) self-raising flour
¼ cup (60ml) milk
¾ cup (120g) icing sugar
1½ tablespoons orange juice

1   Preheat oven to 180°C/160°C fan-assisted.
Grease deep 20cm-round cake tin; line base with
baking parchment.
2   Beat butter, rind, caster sugar, eggs, flour and milk
in medium bowl on low speed with electric mixer until
just combined. Increase speed to medium; beat about
3 minutes or until mixture is smooth and pale in colour.
3   Spread mixture into tin; bake about 40 minutes.
Stand cake in tin 5 minutes before turning, top-side up,
onto wire rack to cool.
4   Meanwhile, combine sifted icing sugar and orange
juice in small bowl; stir until smooth. Spread icing over
top of cake.

cut & keep butter cake

prep + cook time 1 hour 30 minutes **serves** 10

125g butter, softened
1 teaspoon vanilla extract
1¼ cups (275g) caster sugar
3 eggs
1 cup (150g) plain flour
½ cup (75g) self-raising flour
¼ teaspoon bicarbonate of soda
½ cup (125ml) milk

1 Preheat oven to 180°C/160°C fan-assisted. Grease deep 20cm-round cake tin; line base of tin with baking parchment.
2 Beat ingredients in medium bowl on low speed with electric mixer until just combined. Increase speed to medium; beat about 3 minutes or until mixture is smooth and pale in colour.
3 Spread mixture into tin; bake about 1¼ hours. Stand cake in tin 5 minutes before turning, top-side up, onto wire rack to cool. Dust cake with sifted icing sugar, if desired.

madeira cake

prep + cook time 1 hour 15 minutes **serves** 12

180g butter, softened
2 teaspoons finely grated lemon rind
⅔ cup (150g) caster sugar
3 eggs
¾ cup (110g) plain flour
¾ cup (110g) self-raising flour
⅓ cup (55g) mixed peel
¼ cup (35g) slivered almonds

1 Preheat oven to 160°C/140°C fan-assisted. Grease deep 20cm-round cake tin; line base with baking parchment.
2 Beat butter, rind and sugar in small bowl with electric mixer until light and fluffy; beat in eggs, one at a time. Transfer mixture to large bowl, stir in sifted flours.
3 Spread mixture into tin; bake 20 minutes. Remove cake from oven; sprinkle with mixed peel and almonds. Return to oven; bake about 40 minutes. Stand cake in tin 5 minutes before turning, top-side up, onto wire rack to cool.

cinnamon teacake

prep + cook time 50 minutes **serves** 10

60g butter, softened
1 teaspoon vanilla extract
⅔ cup (150g) caster sugar
1 egg
1 cup (150g) self-raising flour
⅓ cup (80ml) milk
10g butter, extra, melted
1 teaspoon ground cinnamon
1 tablespoon caster sugar, extra

1 Preheat oven to 180°C/160°C fan-assisted. Grease deep 20cm-round cake tin; line base with baking parchment.
2 Beat butter, vanilla extract, sugar and egg in small bowl with electric mixer until light and fluffy. Stir in sifted flour and milk.
3 Spread mixture into tin; bake about 30 minutes. Stand cake in tin 5 minutes before turning, top-side up, onto wire rack. Brush top of cake with melted butter; sprinkle with combined cinnamon and extra sugar. Serve warm with whipped cream or butter.

malt loaf

prep + cook time 2 hours **serves** 10

4 cups (640g) wholemeal plain flour
½ cup (110g) firmly packed brown sugar
1½ cups (250g) sultanas
1 teaspoon bicarbonate of soda
1 tablespoon hot water
1¼ cups (310ml) milk
1 cup (250ml) liquid malt
½ cup (125ml) treacle

1 Preheat oven to 160°C/140°C fan-assisted. Grease 15cm x 25cm loaf tin; line base with baking parchment.
2 Sift flour into large heatproof bowl; stir in sugar and sultanas.
3 Add soda to the water in medium jug; stir in milk.
4 Place malt and treacle in medium saucepan; stir over low heat until mixture begins to bubble; stir in milk mixture. Stir foaming milk mixture into flour mixture.
5 Spread mixture into prepared tin; bake about 1¾ hours. Stand cake in tin 5 minutes before turning, top-side up, onto wire rack to cool.

tip Liquid malt is a malt extract available from brewing shops and some health-food stores.

cherry almond cake

prep + cook time 1 hour 50 minutes (plus cooling time) **serves** 22

185g butter, softened
1 cup (220g) caster sugar
1 teaspoon almond essence
3 eggs
⅔ cup (140g) red glacé cherries, quartered
1 cup (160g) sultanas
⅔ cup (90g) slivered almonds
1 cup (150g) plain flour
½ cup (75g) self-raising flour
⅓ cup (80ml) milk

1 Preheat oven to 160°C/140°C fan-assisted. Line base and side of deep 20cm-round cake tin with three thicknesses of baking parchment, extending paper 5cm above edge.
2 Beat butter, sugar and essence in small bowl with electric mixer until light and fluffy. Beat in eggs, one at a time. Combine cherries, sultanas and nuts in large bowl; stir in butter mixture, sifted flours and milk.
3 Spread mixture into tin; bake about 1½ hours. Cover tin tightly with foil; cool cake in tin.

tip Cover cake loosely with foil during baking if it starts to overbrown. Give the cake quarter turns several times during baking to help uneven browning.

almond butter cake

prep + cook time 1 hour 20 minutes **serves** 10

250g butter, softened
1 teaspoon almond essence
1 cup (220g) caster sugar
4 eggs
1 cup (150g) self-raising flour
½ cup (75g) plain flour
¾ cup (90g) ground almonds

1   Preheat oven to 180°C/160°C fan-assisted. Grease deep 19cm-square cake tin; line base and two opposite sides with baking parchment, extending paper 5cm over edges.
2   Beat butter, essence and sugar in medium bowl with electric mixer until light and fluffy. Beat in eggs, one at a time. Fold in sifted flours and ground almonds in two batches.
3   Spread mixture into tin; bake for 30 minutes. Reduce oven temperature to 160°C/140°C fan-assisted; bake a further 30 minutes. Stand cake in tin 5 minutes before turning, top-side up, onto wire rack to cool. Serve dusted with icing sugar and toasted flaked almonds, if you like.

greek yogurt cake

prep + cook time 1 hour serves 12

125g butter, softened
1 cup (220g) caster sugar
3 eggs, separated
2 cups (300g) self-raising flour
½ teaspoon bicarbonate of soda
¼ cup (40g) finely chopped blanched almonds
1 cup (280g) plain yogurt

1 Preheat oven to 180°C/160°C fan-assisted. Grease 20cm x 30cm traybake tin; line base and long sides with baking parchment, extending paper 5cm over edges.
2 Beat butter and sugar in small bowl with electric mixer until light and fluffy. Add egg yolks, beat well. Transfer mixture to large bowl; stir in sifted flour and soda in two batches, then nuts and yogurt.
3 Beat egg whites in small bowl with electric mixer until soft peaks form. Gently fold egg whites into yogurt mixture in two batches.
4 Spread mixture into tin; bake about 35 minutes. Stand cake in tin 5 minutes before turning, top-side up, onto wire rack to cool. Dust cake with sifted icing sugar, if desired.

quick-mix cupcakes

prep + cook time 40 minutes **makes** 24

125g butter, softened
½ teaspoon vanilla extract
¾ cup (165g) caster sugar
3 eggs
2 cups (300g) self-raising flour
¼ cup (60ml) milk

1   Preheat oven to 180°C/160°C fan-assisted. Line two 12-hole (2 tablespoon/ 40ml) deep flat-based bun tins with paper cases.
2   Beat ingredients in medium bowl on low speed with electric mixer until ingredients are just combined. Increase speed to medium; beat about 3 minutes or until mixture is smooth and pale in colour.
3   Drop rounded tablespoons of mixture into paper cases; bake about 20 minutes. Stand cakes in tins 5 minutes before turning, top-sides up, onto wire racks to cool.
4   Top cakes with icing of your choice.

variations

chocolate & orange
Stir in 1 teaspoon finely grated orange rind and ½ cup (95g) dark chocolate chips at the end of step 2.

passionfruit & lime
Stir in 1 teaspoon finely grated lime rind and ¼ cup (60ml) passionfruit pulp at the end of step 2.

banana & white chocolate chip
Stir in ½ cup overripe mashed banana and ½ cup (95g) white chocolate chips at the end of step 2.

mocha
Blend 1 tablespoon sifted cocoa powder with 1 tablespoon strong black coffee; stir in at the end of step 2.

glacé icing

2 cups (320g) icing sugar
20g butter, melted
2 tablespoons hot water, approximately

1   Place sifted icing sugar in small bowl; stir in butter and enough of the hot water to make a firm paste. Stir over small saucepan of simmering water until icing is spreadable.

variations

chocolate
Stir in 1 teaspoon sifted cocoa powder.

coffee
Dissolve 1 teaspoon instant coffee granules in the hot water.

passionfruit
Stir in 1 tablespoon passionfruit pulp.

butterfly cakes

prep + cook time 50 minutes **makes** 24

125g butter, softened
1 teaspoon vanilla extract
⅔ cup (150g) caster sugar
3 eggs
1½ cups (225g) self-raising flour
¼ cup (60ml) milk
½ cup (160g) jam
300ml whipping cream, whipped

1 Preheat oven to 180°C/160°C fan-assisted. Line two 12-hole (2 tablespoon/40ml) deep flat-based bun tins with paper cases.
2 Beat butter, extract, sugar, eggs, sifted flour and milk in small bowl on low speed with electric mixer until ingredients are just combined. Increase speed to medium; beat about 3 minutes or until mixture is smooth and pale in colour.
3 Drop rounded tablespoons of mixture into cases. Bake about 20 minutes. Stand cakes in tins 5 minutes before turning, top-sides up, onto wire racks to cool.
4 Using sharp pointed vegetable knife, cut a circle from the top of each cake; cut circle in half to make two 'wings'. Fill cavities with jam and whipped cream. Place wings in position on top of cakes. Dust with a little sifted icing sugar before serving, if you like.

upside-down cashew & maple syrup loaf

prep + cook time 1 hour 20 minutes **serves** 10

125g butter
¾ cup (150g) firmly packed brown sugar
2 eggs
1 cup (150g) self-raising flour
½ cup (75g) plain flour
½ teaspoon mixed spice
½ cup (120ml) soured cream
2 tablespoons pure maple syrup
90g butter, extra
½ cup (110g) firmly packed brown sugar, extra
2 tablespoons pure maple syrup, extra
1 cup (150g) unsalted roasted cashews, chopped
coarsely

1 Preheat oven to 180°C/160°C fan-assisted.
Grease 15cm x 25cm loaf tin; line base and long sides
with baking parchment, extending paper 5cm above
the edges.
2 Beat butter, sugar, eggs, sifted flours and spice,
cream and syrup in medium bowl on low speed
with electric mixer until combined. Increase speed
to medium; beat about 3 minutes or until mixture is
smooth and pale in colour.
3 Beat extra butter, sugar and syrup in small bowl
with wooden spoon until smooth; spread over base of
tin. Sprinkle with cashews; spread with cake mixture.
Bake about 1 hour. Stand cake in tin 5 minutes before
turning out onto wire rack to cool.

ginger cake

prep + cook time 1 hour 45 minutes **serves** 24

1½ cups (330g) firmly packed brown sugar
1½ cups (225g) plain flour
1½ cups (225g) self-raising flour
½ teaspoon bicarbonate of soda
1 tablespoon ground ginger
2 teaspoons ground cinnamon
1 teaspoon ground nutmeg
250g butter, softened
2 eggs
1 cup (250ml) buttermilk
½ cup (175g) golden syrup
lemon frosting
60g butter, softened
2 teaspoons finely grated lemon rind
2 tablespoons lemon juice
2 cups (320g) icing sugar

1   Preheat oven to 160°C / 140°C fan-assisted. Grease deep 23cm-square cake tin; line base with baking parchment.
2   Sift dry ingredients into large bowl; add remaining ingredients. Beat mixture on low speed with electric mixer until ingredients are combined. Increase speed to medium; beat mixture about 3 minutes or until mixture is smooth and pale in colour.
3   Spread mixture into tin; bake about 1½ hours. Stand cake in tin 10 minutes before turning, top-side up, onto wire rack to cool.
4   Meanwhile, make lemon frosting. Spread cold cake with frosting.
lemon frosting Using a wooden spoon, beat butter and rind in small bowl; gradually beat in juice and sifted icing sugar.

coconut cake

prep + cook time 1 hour 5 minutes **serves** 20

125g butter, softened
½ teaspoon coconut essence
1 cup (220g) caster sugar
2 eggs
½ cup (40g) desiccated coconut
1½ cups (225g) self-raising flour
1¼ cups (300g) soured cream
⅓ cup (80ml) milk
coconut ice frosting
2 cups (320g) icing sugar
1⅓ cups (100g) desiccated coconut
2 egg whites, beaten lightly
pink food colouring

1 Preheat oven to 180°C/160°C fan-assisted. Grease deep 23cm-square cake tin; line base with baking parchment.
2 Beat butter, essence and sugar in small bowl with electric mixer until light and fluffy. Beat in eggs, one at a time. Transfer mixture to large bowl; stir in coconut, sifted flour, soured cream and milk, in two batches.
3 Spread mixture into tin; bake about 40 minutes. Stand cake in tin 5 minutes before turning, top-side up, onto wire rack to cool.
4 Meanwhile, make coconut ice frosting. Drop alternate spoonfuls of white and pink frosting onto cake; marble over top of cake.
coconut ice frosting Sift icing sugar into medium bowl; stir in desiccated coconut and egg white. Place half the mixture in small bowl; tint with pink colouring.

kisses

prep + cook time 40 minutes **makes about** 40

125g butter, softened
½ cup (110g) caster sugar
1 egg
⅓ cup (50g) plain flour
¼ cup (35g) self-raising flour
⅔ cup (100g) cornflour
¼ cup (30g) custard powder
vienna cream
60g butter, softened
¾ cup (120g) icing sugar
2 teaspoons milk

1   Preheat oven to 180°C/160°C fan-assisted. Grease two baking trays.
2   Beat butter and sugar in small bowl with electric mixer until smooth and creamy; beat in egg. Stir in sifted dry ingredients in two batches.
3   Spoon mixture into piping bag fitted with 1cm tube. Pipe 3cm-diameter rounds of mixture, about 3cm apart, onto trays. Bake about 10 minutes or until browned lightly. Loosen cakes; cool on trays.
4   Meanwhile, make vienna cream. Sandwich cold cakes with vienna cream; dust with a little extra sifted icing sugar, if desired.
vienna cream Beat butter until as white as possible. Gradually beat in half the sifted icing sugar; beat in milk. Gradually beat in remaining icing sugar.

cream cheese lemon cake

prep + cook time 1 hour 15 minutes **serves** 10

125g butter, chopped
125g cream cheese, chopped
3 teaspoons finely grated lemon rind
1 cup (220g) caster sugar
2 eggs
¾ cup (110g) self-raising flour
½ cup (75g) plain flour
lemon glacé icing
1 cup (160g) icing sugar
10g butter, melted
2 tablespoons hot water approximately
½ teaspoon finely grated lemon rind

1   Preheat oven to 180°C/160°C fan-assisted. Grease 20cm savarin tin (or grease deep 20cm-round cake tin and line base and side with baking parchment).
2   Beat ingredients in medium bowl on low speed with electric mixer until combined. Increase speed to medium; beat about 3 minutes or until mixture is smooth and pale in colour.
3   Spread mixture into tin; bake about 55 minutes. Stand cake in tin 5 minutes before turning onto wire rack to cool. Spoon icing over cold cake.
lemon glacé icing Sift icing sugar into small heatproof bowl; stir in butter and enough of the water to make a firm paste. Stir over small saucepan of simmering water until icing is spreadable. Stir in rind.

pound cake

prep + cook time 1 hour 20 minutes **serves** 12

250g butter, softened
1 cup (220g) caster sugar
1 teaspoon vanilla extract
4 eggs
½ cup (75g) self-raising flour
1 cup (150g) plain flour

1   Preheat oven to 180°C/160°C fan-assisted.
Grease deep 20cm-round cake tin; line base with
baking parchment.
2   Beat butter, sugar and extract in small bowl with
electric mixer until light and fluffy. Beat in eggs, one
at a time. Transfer mixture to large bowl; fold in sifted
flours in two batches.
3   Spread mixture into tin; bake about 1 hour. Stand
cake in tin 5 minutes before turning, top-side up, onto
wire rack to cool.
4   If you like, serve the cake with whipped cream and
strawberries, and dust with sifted icing sugar.

coffee walnut streusel cake

prep + cook time 1 hour **serves** 12

1 tablespoon instant coffee granules
¼ cup (60ml) boiling water
125g butter, softened
1cup (220g) caster sugar
1 teaspoon vanilla extract
2 eggs
⅔ cup (160g) soured cream
1¼ cups (185g) plain flour
¼ cup (35g) self-raising flour
¼ teaspoon bicarbonate of soda
walnut streusel
⅔ cup (100g) self-raising flour
⅔ cup (150g) firmly packed brown sugar
100g cold butter, chopped
1 cup (110g) coarsely chopped walnuts, roasted

1 Preheat oven to 180°C/160°C fan-assisted. Grease 20cm x 30cm traybake tin; line base and long sides with baking parchment, extending paper 5cm over edges.
2 Combine coffee and the water in small bowl; stir until coffee dissolves. Cool 5 minutes.
3 Make walnut streusel.
4 Beat butter, sugar and extract in medium bowl with electric mixer until light and fluffy; beat in eggs, one at a time. Stir in soured cream and sifted flours and soda, in two batches. Stir in coffee mixture.
5 Spread mixture into tin; sprinkle walnut streusel over top of mixture. Sprinkle over remaining walnuts. Bake about 30 minutes.
walnut streusel Combine flour and sugar in medium bowl; rub in butter, using fingertips, until mixture resembles coarse breadcrumbs. Stir in half the walnuts.

CLASSIC
Sponge cakes

❧

Eggs are the star ingredients in sponge cakes,
they are responsible for the light airy textures
and the melt-in-the mouth appeal. A quick light
touch is needed when the other ingredients
are combined with the beaten egg mixture.
These cakes can be challenging to make,
but are worth the effort.

best-ever sponge cake

prep + cook time 50 minutes serves 8

4 eggs
¾ cup (165g) caster sugar
1 cup (150g) self-raising flour
1 tablespoon cornflour
10g butter, softened
⅓ cup (80ml) hot water
⅓ cup (115g) lemon curd
⅓ cup (180ml) whipping cream, whipped
1 tablespoon icing sugar

1 Preheat oven to 180°C/160°C fan-assisted.
Grease two deep 20cm-round cake tins; line base
with baking parchment.
2 Beat eggs in small bowl with electric mixer about
10 minutes or until thick and creamy. Gradually add
sugar, beating until dissolved between additions.
Triple-sift flours; fold into egg mixture. Pour combined
butter and the water down side of bowl; using one
clean hand, fold through egg mixture.
3 Pour mixture evenly into pans; bake about
25 minutes. Immediately turn sponges, top-side up,
onto baking-parchment-covered wire rack to cool.
4 Sandwich sponges with lemon curd and cream.
Serve dusted with sifted icing sugar.

génoise sponge

prep + cook time 1 hour **serves** 8

4 eggs
½ cup (110g) caster sugar
⅔ cup (100g) plain flour
60g butter, melted, cooled
300ml whipping cream
1 tablespoon icing sugar
¼ cup (80g) strawberry jam, warmed
500g strawberries, sliced thinly
1 tablespoon icing sugar, extra

1 Preheat oven to 180°C/160°C fan-assisted. Grease deep 20cm-round cake tin; line base with baking parchment.
2 Combine eggs and sugar in large heatproof bowl, place over saucepan of simmering water (do not allow water to touch base of bowl); beat with electric mixer about 10 minutes or until mixture is thick and creamy. Remove bowl from saucepan; beat mixture until it returns to room temperature.
3 Sift half the flour over egg mixture; carefully fold in flour. Sift remaining flour into bowl, fold into mixture. Working quickly, fold in melted butter.
4 Pour mixture into tin; bake about 20 minutes. Turn immediately, top-side up, onto baking-parchment-covered wire rack to cool.
5 Beat cream and sifted icing sugar in small bowl with electric mixer until soft peaks form. Split sponge in half; place one half, cut-side up, on serving plate. Spread with jam and cream; top with the strawberries, then remaining sponge. Decorate cake with extra sifted icing sugar, and strawberries, if you like.

jam roll

prep + cook time 30 minutes **serves** 10

3 eggs, separated
½ cup (110g) caster sugar
2 tablespoons hot milk
¾ cup (110g) self-raising flour
¼ cup (55g) caster sugar, extra
½ cup (160g) jam, warmed

1 Preheat oven to 200°C / 180°C fan-assisted. Grease 25cm x 30cm swiss roll tin; line base and long sides with baking parchment, extending paper 5cm over sides.
2 Beat egg whites in small bowl with electric mixer until soft peaks form; gradually add sugar, 1 tablespoon at a time, beating until sugar is dissolved between additions. With motor operating, add egg yolks, one at a time, beating about 10 minutes or until mixture is thick and creamy.
3 Pour hot milk down side of bowl; add triple-sifted flour. Working quickly, use plastic spatula to fold milk and flour through egg mixture. Spread mixture into tin; bake about 8 minutes.
4 Meanwhile, place a piece of baking parchment cut the same size as the tin on worktop; sprinkle with extra sugar. Turn hot sponge onto parchment; peel away lining paper. Cool; trim all sides of sponge.
5 Roll sponge from short side; unroll, spread evenly with jam. Re-roll cake, from same short side, by lifting parchment and using it as a guide. Serve jam roll with whipped cream, if desired.

honey spice sponge cake

prep + cook time 30 minutes **serves** 6

2 eggs
½ cup (110g) caster sugar
⅓ cup (50g) cornflour
1½ tablespoons custard powder
1 teaspoon mixed spice
½ teaspoon cream of tartar
¼ teaspoon bicarbonate of soda
300ml whipping cream
2 tablespoons honey
1 tablespoon icing sugar

1   Preheat oven to 180°C/160°C fan-assisted. Grease 25cm x 30cm swiss roll tin; line base and long sides with baking parchment, extending paper 5cm over sides.
2   Beat eggs and ⅓ cup of the sugar in small bowl with electric mixer about 10 minutes or until thick and creamy.
3   Meanwhile, triple-sift dry ingredients; fold into egg mixture. Spread mixture into tin; bake 10 minutes.
4   Place a piece of baking parchment cut the same size as the tin on worktop; sprinkle evenly with remaining sugar. Turn hot sponge onto parchment; peel away lining paper. Cool; trim all sides of sponge.
5   Beat cream and honey in small bowl with electric mixer until firm peaks form.
6   Cut sponge widthways into three equal-sized rectangles. Place one piece of sponge on serving plate; spread with half the cream mixture. Top with second piece of sponge and remaining cream. Finish with remaining sponge piece then dust with sifted icing sugar.

featherlight sponge cake

prep + cook time 40 minutes serves 10

4 eggs
¾ cup (165g) caster sugar
⅔ cup (100g) cornflour
¼ cup (30g) custard powder
1 teaspoon cream of tartar
½ teaspoon bicarbonate of soda
⅓ cup (110g) apricot jam
300ml whipping cream, whipped

1 Preheat oven to 180°C/160°C fan-assisted. Grease and flour two deep 22cm-round cake tins; shake away excess flour.
2 Beat eggs and sugar in small bowl with electric mixer until mixture is thick and creamy and sugar is dissolved; transfer to large bowl.
3 Triple-sift dry ingredients; fold gently into egg mixture. Divide sponge mixture between prepared tins; bake about 20 minutes. Turn sponges, top-side up, onto baking-parchment-covered wire rack to cool.
4 Sandwich sponges with jam and whipped cream.

strawberry powder puffs

prep + cook time 40 minutes makes 36

2 eggs
⅓ cup (75g) caster sugar
2 tablespoons cornflour
2 tablespoons plain flour
2 tablespoons self-raising flour
½ cup (125ml) whipped cream
2 tablespoons icing sugar
½ cup (65g) finely chopped strawberries

1 Preheat oven to 180°C/160°C fan-assisted. Grease and flour three 12-hole shallow (1-tablespoon/20ml) round-based bun tins; shake away excess flour.
2 Beat eggs and sugar in small bowl with electric mixer about 4 minutes or until thick and creamy. Triple-sift flours; fold into egg mixture.
3 Drop 1 teaspoon of mixture into bun tray holes. Bake about 7 minutes; turn immediately onto wire racks to cool.
4 Beat cream and half the sifted icing sugar in small bowl with electric mixer until firm peaks form; fold in strawberries. Sandwich puffs with strawberry cream just before serving. Dust with remaining sifted icing sugar.

tip If you don't have three bun trays, just wash, grease and flour the tray again, and continue using until all the mixture is baked.

32

victoria sponge sandwich

prep + cook time 50 minutes serves 10

250g butter
1 teaspoon vanilla extract
1 cup (220g) caster sugar
4 eggs
⅓ cup (80ml) milk
2 cups (300g) self-raising flour
⅓ cup (110g) raspberry jam, warmed

1   Preheat oven to 180°C/160°C fan-assisted. Grease two deep 20cm-round cake tins; line bases with baking parchment.
2   Beat butter, extract and sugar in small bowl with electric mixer until light and fluffy. Beat in eggs, one at a time. Add milk and beat well. Transfer mixture to large bowl. Stir in half the sifted flour, then remaining sifted flour; stir until mixture is smooth.
3   Divide mixture evenly between tins; bake about 30 minutes.
4   Turn cakes, top-sides up, onto baking-parchment-covered wire rack to cool. Sandwich cakes together with jam; dust with sifted icing sugar, if you like.

strawberry jelly cakes

prep + cook time 50 minutes (plus refrigeration time) **makes** 15

6 eggs
⅔ cup (150g) caster sugar
⅓ cup (50g) cornflour
½ cup (75g) plain flour
⅓ cup (50g) self-raising flour
80g packet strawberry jelly crystals
2 cups (160g) desiccated coconut
300ml whipping cream, whipped

1   Preheat oven to 180°C/160°C fan-assisted. Grease 20cm x 30cm traybake tin; line base and long sides with baking parchment, extending paper 5cm over sides.
2   Beat eggs in large bowl with electric mixer about 10 minutes or until thick and creamy; gradually add sugar, beating until dissolved between additions. Triple-sift flours; fold into egg mixture.
3   Spread mixture into baking tin; bake about 35 minutes. Turn cake immediately onto baking-parchment-covered wire rack to cool.
4   Meanwhile, make jelly as per packet instructions; refrigerate until set to the consistency of unbeaten egg white.
5   Trim all sides of cake. Cut cake into 15 squares; dip squares into jelly, drain off excess. Place coconut into medium bowl; toss squares in coconut. Refrigerate 30 minutes. Halve cakes horizontally; sandwich cakes with whipped cream.

chocolate coconut squares

prep + cook time 50 minutes **makes** 16

6 eggs
⅔ cup (150g) caster sugar
⅓ cup (50g) cornflour
½ cup (75g) plain flour
⅓ cup (50g) self-raising flour
2 cups (160g) desiccated coconut
chocolate icing
4 cups (640g) icing sugar
½ cup (50g) cocoa powder
15g butter, melted
1 cup (250ml) milk

1 Preheat oven to 180°C/160°C fan-assisted. Grease 20cm x 30cm traybake tin; line base and long sides with baking parchment, extending paper 5cm over sides.
2 Beat eggs in large bowl with electric mixer about 10 minutes or until thick and creamy; gradually add sugar, beating until dissolved between additions. Triple-sift flours; fold into egg mixture.
3 Spread mixture into tin; bake about 35 minutes. Turn cake immediately onto baking-parchment-covered wire rack to cool.
4 Meanwhile, make chocolate icing.
5 Cut cake into 16 squares; dip each square into icing, drain off excess. Place coconut into medium bowl; toss squares in coconut. Place on wire rack to set.
chocolate icing Sift icing sugar and cocoa into medium heatproof bowl; stir in butter and milk. Set bowl over medium saucepan of simmering water; stir until icing is of a coating consistency.

chocolate sponge

prep + cook time 40 minutes (plus standing time) serves 10

3 eggs
½ cup (110g) caster sugar
¼ cup (35g) cornflour
¼ cup (35g) plain flour
¼ cup (35g) self-raising flour
2 tablespoons cocoa powder
300ml whipping cream, whipped
coffee icing
3 teaspoons instant coffee granules
2 tablespoons milk
1½ cups (240g) icing sugar
1 teaspoon softened butter

1   Preheat oven to 180°C/160°C fan-assisted.
Grease deep 22cm-round cake tin; line base with
baking parchment.
2   Beat eggs in small bowl with electric mixer about
10 minutes or until thick and creamy; gradually add
sugar, beating until dissolved between additions;
transfer mixture to large bowl. Triple-sift dry
ingredients; fold into egg mixture.
3   Spread mixture into tin; bake about 25 minutes.
Turn sponge immediately onto baking-parchment-
covered wire rack to cool.
4   Make coffee icing.
5   Split sponge in half; sandwich with cream. Spread
top with coffee icing; stand until set before cutting.
coffee icing Combine coffee and milk in small bowl;
stir until dissolved. Sift icing sugar into small bowl;
stir in butter and enough of the coffee mixture to give a
firm paste. Stir over hot water until icing is spreadable;
do not over-heat. Use immediately.

passionfruit curd sponge cakes

prep + cook time 40 minutes (plus refrigeration time) **serves** 12

3 eggs
½ cup (110g) caster sugar
¾ cup (110g) self-raising flour
20g butter
¼ cup (60ml) boiling water
passionfruit curd
⅓ cup (80ml) passionfruit pulp
½ cup (110g) caster sugar
2 eggs, beaten lightly
125g unsalted butter, chopped coarsely

1   Make passionfruit curd.
2   Preheat oven to 180°C/160°C fan-assisted. Grease 12-hole (½-cup/125ml) mini muffin tin; dust lightly with flour.
3   Beat eggs in small bowl with electric mixer about 10 minutes or until thick and creamy. Gradually add sugar, beating until dissolved between additions. Transfer mixture to a large bowl. Fold in sifted flour then combined butter and the boiling water.
4   Divide mixture among flan tin holes; bake about 12 minutes. Working quickly, loosen edges of cakes from tin using a small knife; turn immediately onto baking-parchment-covered wire racks to cool.
5   Split cooled cakes in half. Spread cut-sides with curd; replace tops. Dust lightly with sifted icing sugar before serving, if you like.
passionfruit curd Combine ingredients in medium heatproof bowl; stir over pan of simmering water about 10 minutes or until mixture coats the back of a wooden spoon (do not allow the water to touch base of bowl). Cover; refrigerate for 3 hours.

chocolate coconut roll

prep + cook time 45 minutes (plus refrigeration time) **serves** 10

3 eggs
½ cup (110g) caster sugar
¾ cup (110g) self-raising flour
2 tablespoons hot milk
¾ cup (60g) desiccated coconut
butter cream filling
90g unsalted butter, softened
1 teaspoon vanilla extract
1 cup (160g) icing sugar
1 tablespoon milk
chocolate icing
1 cup (160g) icing sugar
¼ cup (25g) cocoa powder
1 teaspoon softened butter
2 tablespoons milk

1 Preheat oven to 180°C/160°C fan-assisted.
Grease 26cm x 32cm swiss roll tin; line base and
long sides with baking parchment, extending paper
5cm over sides.
2 Beat eggs in small bowl with electric mixer about
10 minutes or until thick and creamy; gradually add
sugar, beating until dissolved between additions.
Fold in sifted flour and milk, in two batches; pour into
tin. Bake about 12 minutes.
3 Place a piece of baking parchment cut the same size
as the tin on worktop; sprinkle evenly with a third of
the coconut. Turn hot sponge onto parchment; peel
away lining paper. Using parchment as a guide, loosely
roll sponge from long side. Stand 2 minutes; unroll.
Cool; trim all sides of sponge.
4 Make butter cream filling. Make chocolate icing.
5 Spread filling over sponge. Using parchment as a
guide, roll sponge from long side. Place on wire rack set
over tray; pour icing over roll. Press remaining coconut
onto roll; refrigerate 30 minutes or until set.
butter cream filling Beat butter and extract in small
bowl with electric mixer until pale and creamy.
Gradually beat in sifted icing sugar and milk until light
and fluffy.
chocolate icing Sift icing sugar and cocoa into small
heatproof bowl; stir in butter and milk. Place bowl over
small pan of simmering water; stir until icing reaches a
pouring consistency.

ginger sponge

prep + cook time 40 minutes **serves** 10

5 eggs, separated
¾ cup (165g) caster sugar
1 tablespoon golden syrup
⅓ cup (50g) self-raising flour
⅓ cup (50g) cornflour
3 teaspoons ground ginger
1 teaspoon ground cinnamon
2 teaspoons cocoa powder
300ml whipping cream, whipped

1 Preheat oven to 180°C/160°C fan-assisted. Grease two deep 20cm-round cake tins; line bases with baking parchment.
2 Beat egg whites in medium bowl with electric mixer until soft peaks form; gradually add sugar, beating until sugar is dissolved between additions. Beat in egg yolks and golden syrup. Triple-sift dry ingredients; fold into egg mixture.
3 Pour mixture into tins; bake about 18 minutes. Immediately turn sponges, top-side up, onto baking-parchment-covered wire rack to cool.
4 Sandwich sponges with whipped cream. Serve dusted with sifted icing sugar.

angel food cake

prep + cook time 50 minutes (plus standing time) **serves** 10

½ cup (75g) plain flour
½ cup (75g) cornflour
1¼ cups (275g) caster sugar
¼ teaspoon salt
12 egg whites
1 teaspoon cream of tartar
1 teaspoon vanilla extract

1   Preheat oven to 180°C/160°C fan-assisted.
2   Sift flours, ¼ cup of the sugar and the salt together six times.
3   Beat egg whites in large bowl with electric mixer until foamy; beat in cream of tartar. Gradually add remaining sugar to egg mixture, beating until completely dissolved between additions. Add extract; beat until firm peaks form. Transfer egg mixture to a larger bowl; use a whisk to gently fold in flour mixture.
4   Spread mixture into ungreased 25cm tube tin; bake about 30 minutes.
5   Place a piece of baking parchment cut larger than the tin on worktop; turn tin upside down onto bench over baking parchment (the tin should rest on its 'feet', or the tube, above the paper) – do not move tin until cake is cold (the cake will drop from the tin when cold). If necessary, use a metal spatula to release the cold cake from the dome and base. Decorate with fresh berries, if you like.

note It is essential to use the correct tin for this recipe. A tube tin is a round cake tin with tall, smooth sides and a hollow metal tube in the centre. The tube (which may be higher than the outside of the tin) helps give a more even baking in the centre of the cake. If you cannot locate a suitable tin in your high-street cook shop, there are many specialist bakeware suppliers on the Internet.

CLASSIC
Chocolate cakes

—◦◦◦—

When in doubt about what kind of cake to make,
make it chocolate, you won't go wrong.
Chocolate cakes range in density from extremely
rich and moist like mud cakes, flourless cakes and
brownies through to light, fluffy, spongy chiffon
cakes and everything in between.

one-bowl chocolate cake

—◦◦◦—

prep + cook time 1 hour 20 minutes **serves** 20

125g butter, softened
1 teaspoon vanilla extract
1¼ cups (275g) caster sugar
2 eggs
1⅓ cups (200g) self-raising flour
½ cup (50g) cocoa powder
⅔ cup (160ml) water
chocolate icing
90g dark eating chocolate, chopped coarsely
30g butter, softened
1 cup (160g) icing sugar
2 tablespoons hot water

1   Preheat oven to 180°C/160°C fan-assisted. Grease deep 20cm-round cake tin; line with baking parchment.
2   Beat butter, extract, sugar, eggs, sifted flour and cocoa, and the water in large bowl with electric mixer on low speed until ingredients are combined. Increase speed to medium; beat about 3 minutes or until mixture is smooth and pale in colour.
3   Spread mixture into tin; bake about 1 hour. Stand cake in tin 5 minutes before turning, top-side up, onto wire rack to cool.
4   Make chocolate icing. Spread cold cake with icing.
chocolate icing Melt chocolate and butter in small heatproof bowl over small saucepan of simmering water (do not allow water to touch base of bowl); gradually stir in sifted icing sugar and the water, stirring until icing is spreadable.

mississippi mud cake

prep + cook time 1 hour 45 minutes (plus cooling & standing time) **serves** 16

250g butter, chopped
150g dark eating chocolate, chopped
2 cups (440g) caster sugar
1 cup (250ml) hot water
⅓ cup (80ml) coffee liqueur
1 tablespoon instant coffee granules
1½ cups (225g) plain flour
¼ cup (35g) self-raising flour
¼ cup (25g) cocoa powder
dark chocolate ganache
½ cup (125ml) double cream
200g dark eating chocolate, chopped coarsely

1   Preheat oven to 160°C/140°C fan-assisted. Grease deep 20cm-round cake tin; line base and side with baking parchment.
2   Combine butter, chocolate, sugar, the water, liqueur and coffee granules in medium saucepan. Using wooden spoon, stir over low heat until chocolate melts.
3   Transfer mixture to large bowl; cool 15 minutes. Whisk in combined sifted flours and cocoa, then egg. Pour mixture into prepared tin.
4   Bake cake about 1½ hours. Stand cake in tin 30 minutes before turning, top-side up, onto wire rack to cool.
5   Meanwhile, make dark chocolate ganache; spread over top of cake before serving.
dark chocolate ganache Bring cream to the boil in small saucepan. Pour hot cream over chocolate in medium heatproof bowl; stir until smooth. Stand at room temperature until spreadable.

devil's food cake

prep + cook time 1 hour **serves** 10

180g butter, softened
1¾ cups (385g) caster sugar
3 eggs
1½ cups (225g) self-raising flour
½ cup (75g) plain flour
½ teaspoon bicarbonate of soda
⅔ cup (70g) cocoa powder
3 teaspoons instant coffee granules
½ cup (125ml) water
½ cup (125ml) milk
½ teaspoon red food colouring
300ml whipping cream, whipped
rich chocolate frosting
60g dark eating chocolate, chopped
60g butter, chopped

1   Preheat oven to 180°C/160°C fan-assisted.
Grease two deep 20cm-round cake tins; line bases
with baking parchment.
2   Beat butter and sugar in small bowl with electric
mixer until light and fluffy; beat in eggs, one at a time.
3   Transfer mixture to large bowl; fold in sifted flours,
soda and cocoa powder with combined coffee, the
water, milk and colouring, in two batches.
4   Pour mixture into tins; bake about 45 minutes.
Stand cakes in tins 5 minutes before turning, top-side
up, onto wire racks to cool.
5   Make rich chocolate frosting.
6   Sandwich cold cakes with whipped cream; top
with frosting.
rich chocolate frosting Combine chocolate and
butter in small heatproof bowl over small saucepan of
simmering water (do not allow water to touch the base
of the bowl); stir until smooth. Remove from heat. Cool
at room temperature, stirring occasionally, until frosting
is spreadable.

sacher torte

prep + cook time 1 hour 10 minutes (plus cooling & standing time) **serves** 10

150g dark eating chocolate, chopped
1 tablespoon water
150g butter, softened
½ cup (110g) caster sugar
3 eggs, separated
1 cup (150g) plain flour
2 tablespoons caster sugar, extra
1 cup (320g) apricot jam, warmed, strained
chocolate icing
125g dark eating chocolate, chopped
125g butter, softened

chocolate icing Melt chocolate and butter in small heatproof bowl over small saucepan of simmering water (do not allow water to touch base of bowl). Cool at room temperature until spreadable, stirring occasionally; this can take up to 2 hours.

1 Preheat oven to 180°C/160°C fan-assisted. Grease 22cm-round cake tin; line base with baking parchment.
2 Melt chocolate in small heatproof bowl over pan of simmering water (do not allow water to touch base of bowl); stir in the water; cool to room temperature.
3 Cream butter and sugar with electric mixer until light and fluffy. Add yolks one at a time, beating until combined. Stir in chocolate mixture, then sifted flour.
4 Beat egg whites in small bowl until soft peaks form, gradually beat in extra sugar, beating until dissolved between each addition; fold into chocolate mixture.
5 Spread mixture into tin. Bake about 30 minutes. Stand cake in tin 5 minutes before turning onto wire rack to cool; leave cake upside down.
6 Meanwhile, make chocolate icing.
7 Split cake in half; place one half, cut-side up, on serving plate. Brush with warmed jam, top with other cake half. Brush all over with remaining jam. Stand about 1 hour at room temperature or until jam has set. Spread icing over cake; leave to set.

lemon & lime white chocolate mud cake

prep + cook time 2 hours 10 minutes (plus cooling and refrigeration time) **serves** 12

250g butter, chopped
2 teaspoons finely grated lemon rind
2 teaspoons finely grated lime rind
180g white eating chocolate, chopped coarsely
1½ cups (330g) caster sugar
¾ cup (180ml) milk
1½ cups (225g) plain flour
½ cup (75g) self-raising flour
2 eggs
coconut ganache
140ml can coconut cream
360g white eating chocolate, chopped finely
1 teaspoon finely grated lemon rind
1 teaspoon finely grated lime rind

1 Preheat oven to 170°C/150°C fan-assisted. Grease deep 20cm-round cake tin; line base with baking parchment.
2 Stir butter, rinds, chocolate, sugar and milk in medium saucepan over low heat until smooth. Transfer mixture to large bowl; cool 15 minutes.
3 Stir sifted flours and eggs into mixture; pour into tin.
4 Bake about 1 hour 40 minutes. Cool cake in tin.
5 Meanwhile, make coconut ganache.
6 Turn cake, top-side up, onto serving plate; spread ganache over cake.
coconut ganache Bring coconut cream to the boil in small saucepan. Place chocolate and rinds in medium bowl, add hot cream; stir until smooth. Cover; refrigerate, stirring occasionally, about 30 minutes or until ganache is spreadable.

chocolate buttermilk cake

prep + cook time 1 hour 20 minutes (plus refrigeration time) serves 10

180g butter, softened
1 teaspoon vanilla extract
1½ cups (330g) caster sugar
4 eggs, separated
¾ cup (110g) self-raising flour
⅓ cup (35g) cocoa powder
¾ cup (180ml) buttermilk
chocolate filling
400g dark eating chocolate, melted
250g butter, melted
½ cup (80g) icing sugar

1   Preheat oven to 180°C/160°C fan-assisted. Grease deep 20cm-round cake tin; line base with baking parchment.
2   Beat butter, extract and sugar in small bowl with electric mixer until light and fluffy; beat in egg yolks, one at a time, until just combined. Transfer mixture to large bowl; stir in sifted dry ingredients and buttermilk.
3   Beat egg whites in clean small bowl with electric mixer until soft peaks form; fold into cake mixture in two batches. Pour mixture into tin. Bake about 1 hour. Cool cake in tin.
4   Meanwhile, make chocolate filling. Reserve about 1 cup of filling.
5   Split cake into three layers; place one layer on serving plate, spread thinly with some of the chocolate filling. Repeat layering with remaining cake layers and filling. Spread reserved filling all over cake. Refrigerate cake 3 hours before serving.
chocolate filling Combine chocolate and butter in medium bowl; stir in sifted icing sugar. Cool filling to room temperature; beat with wooden spoon until thick and spreadable.

chocolate fudge cake

prep + cook time 50 minutes **serves** 12

250g dark eating chocolate, chopped
125g butter, chopped
⅔ cup (150g) caster sugar
⅔ cup (100g) self-raising flour
4 eggs, lightly beaten

1 Preheat oven to 180°C/160°C fan-assisted. Grease 19cm x 29cm traybake tin; line base and long sides with baking parchment, extending paper 5cm above sides.
2 Stir chocolate and butter in medium heatproof bowl over medium saucepan of simmering water (do not allow the water to touch base of bowl); cool.
3 Combine chocolate mixture and remaining ingredients in medium bowl; beat on low speed with electric mixer until ingredients are combined. Increase speed to medium; beat about 3 minutes or until mixture is changed in colour and smooth.
4 Pour mixture into tin; bake about 30 minutes. Stand cake 5 minutes before turning, top-side up, onto wire rack to cool. Serve dusted with sifted icing sugar, if desired.

flourless chocolate hazelnut cake

prep + cook time 1 hour 30 minutes **serves** 8

⅓ cup (35g) cocoa powder
⅓ cup (80ml) hot water
150g dark eating chocolate, melted
150g butter, melted
1⅓ cups (295g) firmly packed brown sugar
1 cup (100g) ground hazelnuts
4 eggs, separated
1 tablespoon cocoa powder, extra

1 Preheat oven to 180°C/160°C fan-assisted. Grease deep 20cm-round cake tin; line base and side with baking parchment.
2 Blend cocoa with the water in large bowl until smooth. Add chocolate, butter, sugar, ground hazelnuts and egg yolks; stir until combined.
3 Beat egg whites in small bowl with electric mixer until soft peaks form; fold into chocolate mixture in two batches.
4 Pour mixture into tin; bake about 1 hour. Stand cake in tin 15 minutes before turning, top-side up, onto wire rack to cool. Dust with sifted extra cocoa before serving.

chocolate fudge brownies

prep + cook time 1 hour 20 minutes **makes** 16

150g butter, chopped
300g dark eating chocolate, chopped
1½ cups (330g) firmly packed brown sugar
3 eggs
1 teaspoon vanilla extract
¾ cup (110g) plain flour
¾ cup (140g) dark chocolate chips
½ cup (120g) soured cream
¾ cup (110g) roasted macadamias, chopped coarsely

1 Preheat oven to 180°C/160°C fan-assisted. Grease 19cm x 29cm traybake tin; line base and sides with baking parchment, extending paper 5cm above long sides.
2 Combine butter and chocolate in medium saucepan; stir over low heat until smooth. Cool 10 minutes.
3 Stir in sugar, eggs and extract, then sifted flour, chocolate chips, soured cream and nuts. Spread mixture into prepared tin; bake 40 minutes. Cover tin with foil; bake a further 20 minutes. Cool in tin before cutting into 16 pieces.
4 Dust brownies with sifted cocoa powder, if desired.

chocolate chiffon cake

prep + cook time 1 hour 30 minutes **serves** 16

½ cup (50g) cocoa powder
¾ cup (180ml) boiling water
2 cups (300g) self-raising flour
1½ cups (330g) caster sugar
7 eggs, separated
½ cup (125ml) vegetable oil
1 teaspoon vanilla extract
walnut praline
1 cup (220g) caster sugar
½ cup (50g) walnuts
60g dark eating chocolate, chopped
brandied butter cream
190g butter, softened
3 cups (480g) icing sugar
¼ cup (25g) cocoa powder
¼ cup (60ml) brandy

1   Preheat oven to 180°C/160°C fan-assisted. Grease deep 22cm-round cake tin; cover base and side with baking parchment.
2   Blend cocoa with the water in small bowl; cool. Sift flour and sugar into large bowl; add cocoa mixture, egg yolks, oil and extract. Beat with electric mixer until smooth and mixture is changed in colour.
3   Beat egg whites in large bowl with electric mixer until soft peaks form; fold into cocoa mixture in four batches.
4   Pour mixture into tin; bake about 1 hour or until firm. Stand cake 5 minutes before turning, top-side up, onto wire rack to cool.
5   Make walnut praline; make brandied butter cream.
6   Split cold cake into three layers; join layers with some of the butter cream. Spread cake evenly with remaining butter cream. Decorate with walnut praline.
walnut praline Place sugar in heavy-based frying pan; cook over heat, without stirring, until sugar is melted and golden brown. Add nuts; pour onto greased oven tray; cool. Blend or process praline with chocolate until finely chopped.
brandied butter cream Cream butter in small bowl with electric mixer until as white as possible; beat in sifted icing sugar and cocoa, then brandy.

chocoholic's chocolate cake

prep + cook time 2 hours 35 minutes (plus standing and refrigeration time) **serves** 16

250g butter, chopped
1 tablespoon instant coffee granules
1½ cups (375ml) water
2 cups (440g) caster sugar
1 teaspoon vanilla extract
100g dark eating chocolate, chopped coarsely
2 eggs
1½ cups (225g) self-raising flour
1 cup (150g) plain flour
¼ cup (25g) cocoa powder
180g white eating chocolate, melted
2 x 45g packets Maltesers™
chocolate ganache
100g dark eating chocolate, chopped coarsely
⅓ cup (80ml) double cream

1 Preheat oven to 150°C/130°C fan-assisted. Grease deep 19cm-square cake tin; line base and sides with baking parchment.
2 Heat butter, coffee, the water, sugar, extract and dark chocolate in large saucepan, stirring until smooth. Transfer mixture to large bowl; cool 20 minutes. Stir in eggs and sifted dry ingredients, in two batches. Pour mixture into tin.
3 Bake cake about 1 hour 50 minutes. Stand cake in tin 15 minutes; turn, top-side up, onto wire rack to cool.
4 Meanwhile, make chocolate ganache.
5 Spread white chocolate into 15cm x 20cm rectangle onto baking parchment; stand until just set. Using 3cm- and 5cm-star cutter, cut as many stars as possible from chocolate. Stand about 30 minutes or until firm.
6 Spread cake with ganache; decorate with stars and Maltesers™.
chocolate ganache Stir ingredients in small saucepan over low heat until smooth. Cover; refrigerate 1 hour or until spreadable.

fudge-frosted chocolate cupcakes

prep + cook time 1 hour 10 minutes **makes** 24

2 cups (500ml) hot water
¼ cup (75g) cocoa powder, sifted
250g butter, softened
2 cups (440g) caster sugar
2 teaspoons vanilla extract
3 eggs
1½ cups (225g) plain flour
1 cup (150g) self-raising flour
½ teaspoon bicarbonate of soda
silver cachous
fudge frosting
50g butter, softened
¼ cup (60ml) milk
1 teaspoon vanilla extract
¼ cup (25g) cocoa powder
2 cups (320g) icing sugar

1   Preheat oven to 180°C/160°C fan-assisted. Line two
12-hole (⅓-cup/80ml) muffin tins with paper cases.
2   Whisk the water and cocoa together in a medium
size bowl.
3   Beat butter, sugar and vanilla in large bowl with
electric mixer until light and fluffy. Beat in eggs, one at
a time. Fold in half of the combined sifted flours and
soda then half of the cocoa mixture; stir in remaining
flour mixture and cocoa mixture until just combined.
4   Divide mixture among paper cases; bake about
25 minutes. Cool cakes in tins 5 minutes before turning
onto wire racks to cool.
5   Meanwhile, make fudge frosting. Spread frosting
over cakes; decorate with cachous.
fudge frosting Beat butter in medium bowl with
electric mixer until light and fluffy. Add milk, extract,
sifted cocoa and half the sifted icing sugar; beat about
5 minutes or until light and fluffy. Add remaining sifted
icing sugar; beat a further 5 minutes.

CLASSIC
Fruit cakes

⊷⊶

Fruit – dried, fresh, frozen or canned, along
with some vegetables like carrot and courgette,
all go to make up ever-popular fruit cakes.
The more fruit-packed the cakes are, the better
they will keep. Store them airtight in a cool
dark cupboard, or, if the weather is steamy,
in the refrigerator.

one-bowl sultana loaf

⊷⊶

prep + cook time 1 hour 45 minutes **serves** 8

125g butter, melted
750g sultanas
½ cup (110g) firmly packed brown sugar
2 tablespoons marmalade
2 eggs, lightly beaten
¼ cup (60ml) sweet sherry
¾ cup (110g) plain flour
¼ cup (35g) self-raising flour
30g blanched almonds
2 tablespoons apricot jam

1 Preheat oven to 150°C/130°C fan-assisted. Grease
15cm x 25cm loaf tin; line base with baking parchment.
2 Beat butter, sultanas, sugar, marmalade, egg, sherry
and flours in large bowl using a wooden spoon until
combined.
3 Spread mixture into tin; decorate top with blanched
almonds. Bake about 1½ hours. Cover cake with foil;
cool in tin. Brush top of cold cake with warmed sieved
apricot jam.

banana cake

prep + cook time 1 hour 15 minutes **serves** 10

You will need 2 large (460g) overripe bananas to get the amount of mashed banana needed for this recipe.

125g butter, softened
¾ cup (165g) caster sugar
2 eggs
1 cup mashed banana
1 teaspoon bicarbonate of soda
2 tablespoons hot milk
1 cup (150g) plain flour
⅔ cup (100g) self-raising flour
icing sugar, to dust

1 Preheat oven to 180°C/160°C. Grease deep 20cm-round cake tin; line base and side with baking parchment.
2 Beat butter and sugar in small bowl with electric mixer until light and fluffy. Beat in eggs, one at a time. Transfer to large bowl; stir in banana. Combine soda and milk in small jug; stir into banana mixture then stir in sifted flours.
3 Spread mixture into tin; bake about 50 minutes. Stand cake in tin 5 minutes before turning, top-side up, onto wire rack to cool. Dust with sifted icing sugar to serve.

hummingbird cake

prep + cook time 1 hour 10 minutes **serves** 12

You need two large overripe (460g) bananas for this recipe.

450g can crushed pineapple in syrup
1 cup (150g) plain flour
½ cup (75g) self-raising flour
½ teaspoon bicarbonate of soda
½ teaspoon ground cinnamon
½ teaspoon ground ginger
1 cup (220g) firmly packed brown sugar
½ cup (40g) desiccated coconut
1 cup mashed banana
2 eggs, beaten lightly
¾ cup (180ml) vegetable oil
cream cheese frosting
30g butter, softened
60g cream cheese, softened
1 teaspoon vanilla extract
1½ cups (240g) icing sugar

1 Preheat oven to 180°C/160°C fan-assisted.
Grease deep 23cm-square cake tin; line base with
baking parchment.
2 Drain pineapple over medium bowl, pressing with
spoon to extract as much syrup as possible. Reserve
¼ cup (60ml) of the syrup.
3 Sift flours, soda, spices and sugar into large bowl.
Using wooden spoon, stir in the drained pineapple,
reserved syrup, coconut, banana, egg and oil.
4 Pour mixture into tin; bake about 40 minutes.
Stand cake in tin 5 minutes before turning, top-side up,
onto wire rack to cool.
5 Meanwhile, make cream cheese frosting; spread
cake with frosting.
cream cheese frosting Beat butter, cream cheese and
vanilla extract in small bowl with electric mixer until
light and fluffy; gradually beat in sifted icing sugar.

boiled whisky fruit cake

prep + cook time 3 hours 35 minutes (plus standing and cooling time) **serves** 16

1½ cups (220g) raisins, chopped
1½ cups (210g) dried pitted dates, chopped
1½ cups (250g) pitted prunes, chopped
1½ cups (250g) sultanas
⅓ cup (70g) red glacé cherries, quartered
⅓ cup (55g) mixed peel
2 tablespoons caster sugar
30g butter
½ cup (125ml) whisky
250g butter, chopped, extra
1 cup (220g) firmly packed dark brown sugar
½ teaspoon bicarbonate of soda
½ cup (70g) slivered almonds
2 cups (300g) plain flour
2 teaspoons mixed spice
5 eggs
¼ cup (60ml) whisky, extra

1   Combine raisins, dates, prunes, sultanas, cherries and mixed peel in large bowl.

2   Place caster sugar in large heavy-based saucepan over medium heat; move pan occasionally until sugar is melted. Add butter and whisky to pan; stir over low heat until smooth.

3   Add extra butter, brown sugar and fruit to pan. Stir over heat until butter melts; bring to the boil. Remove from heat; stir in soda. Transfer to large bowl, cover; stand overnight at room temperature.

4   Preheat oven to 150°C/130°C fan-assisted. Grease deep 19cm-square cake tin; line base and sides with two layers of brown paper then baking parchment, extending paper 5cm over edges.

5   Add nuts, sifted flour and spice, and eggs to fruit mixture; stir until combined.

6   Spoon mixture into corners of tin then spread remaining mixture into tin. Drop tin from a height of about 15cm onto worktop to settle mixture into tin and to break any large air bubbles; level surface of cake with wet spatula. Bake about 3 hours.

7   Brush hot cake with extra whisky. Cover hot cake tightly with foil; cool in tin.

sticky date cake with butterscotch sauce

prep + cook time 1 hour 10 minutes **serves** 20

3¾ cups (525g) dried pitted dates
3 cups (750ml) hot water
2 teaspoons bicarbonate of soda
185g butter, softened
2¼ cups (500g) firmly packed brown sugar
6 eggs
3 cups (450g) self-raising flour
½ cup (60g) coarsely chopped walnuts
½ cup (60g) coarsely chopped pecans
butterscotch sauce
2 cups (440g) firmly packed brown sugar
500ml whipping cream
250g butter, chopped

1 Preheat oven to 180°C/160°C fan-assisted. Grease 26cm x 36cm baking tin; line base and long sides of dish with two layers baking parchment, extending paper 5cm above edges.
2 Combine dates and the water in medium saucepan; bring to the boil. Remove from heat; stir in soda. Stand 5 minutes then blend or process date mixture until smooth.
3 Beat butter and sugar in large bowl with electric mixer until light and fluffy. Beat in eggs, one at a time. Stir date mixture and sifted flour into egg mixture; spread mixture into tin. Sprinkle with nuts; bake about 50 minutes. Stand cake in tin 10 minutes before turning, top-side up, onto wire rack to cool.
4 Meanwhile, make butterscotch sauce.
5 Brush surface of hot cake with ⅓ cup of the hot butterscotch sauce. Serve with remaining sauce.
butterscotch sauce Stir ingredients in medium saucepan over heat, without boiling, until sugar dissolves; bring to the boil. Reduce heat; simmer 3 minutes.

apple streusel cake

prep + cook time 1 hour 15 minutes (plus freezing time) **serves** 16

200g butter, softened + 25g butter, extra
2 teaspoons finely grated lemon rind
⅔ cup (150g) caster sugar
3 eggs
1 cup (150g) self-raising flour
½ cup (75g) plain flour
⅓ cup (80ml) milk
5 medium apples (750g)
⅓ cup (75g) firmly packed brown sugar
streusel
½ cup (75g) plain flour
¼ cup (35g) self-raising flour
⅓ cup (75g) firmly packed brown sugar
½ teaspoon ground cinnamon
80g cold butter, chopped finely

streusel Process flours, sugar and cinnamon until combined. Add butter; process until ingredients come together. Wrap in cling film; freeze 1 hour or until firm.

1   Preheat oven to 180°C/160°C fan-assisted. Grease deep 23cm-round cake tin; line base with baking parchment.
2   Make streusel.
3   Beat butter, rind and caster sugar in small bowl with electric mixer until light and fluffy. Beat in eggs, one at a time. Transfer to large bowl; stir in sifted flours and milk, in two batches. Spread into tin; bake 25 minutes.
4   Meanwhile, peel, core and quarter apples; slice thinly. Melt extra butter in large frying pan, add apple; cook, stirring, about 5 minutes or until browned lightly. Add brown sugar; cook, stirring, about 5 minutes or until mixture thickens slightly. Set aside.
5   Remove cake from oven. Working quickly, top cake with apple mixture then coarsely grate streusel over apple. Return cake to oven; bake about 25 minutes. Stand cake in tin 10 minutes before turning, top-side up, onto wire rack to cool. Serve cake warm or cold.

pecan & raisin loaf

prep + cook time 45 minutes (plus cooling time) **serves** 8

⅓ cup (50g) raisins
90g butter, chopped
½ cup (110g) firmly packed brown sugar
⅓ cup (80ml) water
½ teaspoon bicarbonate of soda
2 eggs, beaten lightly
½ cup (60g) coarsely chopped pecans
½ cup (75g) plain flour
½ cup (75g) self-raising flour

1   Combine raisins, butter, sugar and the water in medium saucepan; bring to the boil. Remove from heat; stir in soda. Transfer mixture to medium bowl; cool 15 minutes.
2   Preheat oven to 150°C/130°C fan-assisted. Grease 8cm x 25cm cake tin; line base of tin with baking parchment.
3   Stir egg and nuts into raisin mixture; stir in sifted flours. Pour mixture into tin; bake about 35 minutes. Stand cake in tin 5 minutes before turning, top-side up, onto wire rack to cool.

lumberjack cake

prep + cook time 1 hour 40 minutes serves 12

2 large apples (400g), peeled, cored, chopped finely
1 cup (150g) finely chopped pitted dried dates
1 teaspoon bicarbonate of soda
1 cup (250ml) boiling water
125g butter, softened
1 teaspoon vanilla extract
1 cup (220g) caster sugar
1 egg
1½ cups (225g) plain flour
coconut topping
60g butter, chopped
½ cup (110g) firmly packed brown sugar
½ cup (125ml) milk
⅔ cup (50g) shredded coconut

1   Preheat oven to 180°C/160°C fan-assisted. Grease deep 23cm-square cake tin; line base and sides with baking parchment.
2   Combine apple, dates and soda in large bowl, stir in the water; cover bowl with cling film, stand 10 minutes.
3   Meanwhile, beat butter, extract, sugar and egg in small bowl with electric mixer until light and fluffy. Add butter mixture to apple mixture; stir to combine. Add sifted flour; stir to combine. Pour mixture into tin; bake about 50 minutes.
4   Meanwhile, make coconut topping.
5   Remove cake carefully from oven to worktop. Using metal spatula, carefully spread warm topping evenly over cake; return to oven, bake about 20 minutes or until topping is browned.
6   Stand cake in tin 5 minutes before turning, top-side up, onto wire rack to cool.
coconut topping Combine ingredients in medium saucepan; using wooden spoon, stir mixture over low heat until butter melts and sugar dissolves.

date & walnut rolls

prep + cook time 1 hour 10 minutes **serves** 20

60g butter, chopped
1 cup (250ml) boiling water
1 cup (150g) finely chopped pitted dried dates
½ teaspoon bicarbonate of soda
1 cup (220g) firmly packed brown sugar
2 cups (300g) self-raising flour
½ cup (60g) coarsely chopped walnuts
1 egg, beaten lightly

note It is essential to use the correct tin for this recipe.
A nut roll tin is a cylindrical cake tin with removable
ends top and bottom. If you cannot locate a suitable tin
in your high-street cook shop, there are many specialist
bakeware suppliers on the Internet.

1   Adjust oven shelves to fit upright tins.
2   Preheat oven to 180°C/160°C fan-assisted. Grease
two 8cm x 19cm nut roll tins; line bases of tins with
baking parchment. Place tins upright on oven tray.
3   Combine butter and the water in medium saucepan;
stir over low heat until butter melts.
4   Transfer mixture to large bowl; stir in dates and
soda, then sugar, sifted flour, nuts and egg.
5   Spoon mixture into tins; replace lids. Bake rolls, tins
standing upright, about 50 minutes.
6   Stand rolls 5 minutes, remove ends (top and
bottom); shake tins gently to release nut rolls onto wire
rack to cool.

yogurt fruit loaf

prep + cook time 2 hours **serves** 10

100g butter, softened
2 teaspoons finely grated orange rind
¾ cup (165g) caster sugar
2 eggs
2 cups (320g) wholemeal self-raising flour
1 cup (280g) plain yogurt
⅓ cup (80ml) orange juice
1 cup (200g) finely chopped dried figs
1 cup (160g) coarsely chopped raisins

1 Preheat oven to 180°C/160°C fan-assisted. Grease 14cm x 21cm loaf tin.
2 Beat butter, rind, sugar, eggs, sifted flour, yogurt and juice in medium bowl with electric mixer, on low speed, until just combined. Stir in figs and raisins.
3 Pour mixture into tin; cover with foil. Bake 1¼ hours; remove foil, bake about 15 minutes. Stand loaf in tin 10 minutes before turning, top-side up, onto wire rack to cool. Serve at room temperature, or toasted, with butter.

apple custard tea cakes

prep + cook time 50 minutes (plus cooling time) **makes** 12

90g butter, softened
½ teaspoon vanilla extract
½ cup (110g) caster sugar
2 eggs
¾ cup (110g) self-raising flour
¼ cup (30g) custard powder
2 tablespoons milk
1 unpeeled large apple (200g), cored, sliced finely
30g butter, extra, melted
1 tablespoon caster sugar, extra
½ teaspoon ground cinnamon
custard filling
1 tablespoon custard powder
1 tablespoon caster sugar
½ cup (125ml) milk
¼ teaspoon vanilla extract

1   Make custard filling.
2   Preheat oven to 180°C/160°C fan-assisted. Line 12-hole (⅓ cup/80ml) muffin tin with paper cases.
3   Beat butter, extract, sugar, eggs, sifted flour and custard powder, and milk in small bowl with electric mixer, on low speed, until ingredients are just combined. Increase speed to medium, beat until mixture is pale in colour.
4   Divide half the mixture among paper cases; top with custard, then add remaining cake mixture, spread mixture to cover custard. Top with apple, pressing slightly into cakes. Bake about 30 minutes.
5   Turn cakes, top-side up, onto wire rack. Brush hot cakes with extra butter, then sprinkle with combined extra sugar and cinnamon. Serve warm or cold.
custard filling Blend custard powder and sugar with milk and extract in small saucepan; stir over heat until mixture boils and thickens. Remove from heat; cover surface with cling film, cool to room temperature.

raspberry coconut slice

prep + cook time 1 hour **makes** 16

90g butter, softened
½ cup (110g) caster sugar
1 egg
¼ cup (35g) self-raising flour
⅔ cup (100g) plain flour
1 tablespoon custard powder
⅔ cup (220g) raspberry jam
coconut topping
2 cups (160g) desiccated coconut
¼ cup (55g) caster sugar
2 eggs, beaten lightly

1 Preheat oven to 180°C/160°C fan-assisted. Grease 20cm x 30cm traybake tin; line base and long sides with baking parchment, extending paper 5cm above sides.
2 Beat butter, sugar and egg in small bowl with electric mixer until light and fluffy. Transfer to medium bowl; stir in sifted flours and custard powder. Spread dough evenly into tin; spread with jam.
3 Make coconut topping; sprinkle topping over jam.
4 Bake about 40 minutes; allow slice to cool in tin before cutting.
coconut topping Combine ingredients in small bowl.

dutch ginger & almond slice

prep + cook time 50 minutes **makes** 20

1¾ cups (260g) plain flour
1 cup (220g) caster sugar
⅔ cup (150g) coarsely chopped glacé ginger
½ cup (80g) blanched almonds, chopped coarsely
1 egg
185g butter, melted
2 teaspoons icing sugar

1   Preheat oven to 180°C/160°C fan-assisted. Grease 20cm x 30cm traybake tin; line base and long sides with baking parchment, extending paper 5cm above sides.
2   Combine sifted flour, sugar, ginger, nuts and egg in medium bowl; stir in butter.
3   Press mixture into tin; bake about 35 minutes. Stand slice in tin 10 minutes before lifting onto wire rack to cool. Dust slice with a little sifted icing sugar before cutting.

citrus poppy seed friands

prep + cook time 45 minutes makes 12

6 egg whites
185g butter, melted
1 cup (120g) ground almonds
1½ cups (240g) icing sugar
½ cup (75g) plain flour
1 tablespoon poppy seeds
2 teaspoons finely grated orange rind
1 teaspoon finely grated lemon rind

1   Preheat oven to 200°C/180°C fan-assisted. Grease 12 x ½-cup (125ml) friand or muffin tins; place on oven tray.
2   Place egg whites in medium bowl; whisk lightly with fork until combined. Stir in remaining ingredients.
3   Divide mixture among tins; bake about 25 minutes. Stand cakes in tins 5 minutes before turning, top-side up, onto wire rack to cool. Serve cakes dusted with a little extra sifted icing sugar, if desired.

note A friand is a small densely-textured sponge cake, popular in Australia and New Zealand and similar to a French Financier. Traditionally baked in oval shapes, they are made with butter, ground almonds and a variety of flavourings. If you can't get hold of the traditional oval tins, then deep muffin tins work just as well.

berry muffins

prep + cook time 30 minutes makes 12

2½ cups (375g) self-raising flour
90g cold butter, chopped
1 cup (220g) caster sugar
1¼ cups (310ml) buttermilk
1 egg, beaten lightly
200g fresh or frozen mixed berries

1   Preheat oven to 180°C/160°C fan-assisted. Grease 12-hole (⅓-cup/80ml) muffin tin.
2   Sift flour into large bowl; rub in butter. Stir in sugar, buttermilk and egg. Do not overmix – the mixture should be lumpy. Add the berries and stir gently through the mixture.
3   Spoon mixture into tin holes; bake about 20 minutes. Stand muffins in tin 5 minutes before turning, top-side up, onto wire rack to cool.

celebration fruit cake

prep + cook time 3 hours 50 minutes (plus standing & cooling time) **serves** 24

3 cups (500g) sultanas
1¾ cups (300g) raisins, halved
1¾ cups (300g) dried dates, chopped finely
1 cup (150g) currants
⅔ cup (110g) mixed peel
⅔ cup (150g) glacé cherries, halved
¼ cup (50g) coarsely chopped glacé pineapple
¼ cup (60g) coarsely chopped glacé apricots
½ cup (125ml) dark rum
250g butter, softened
1 cup (220g) firmly packed brown sugar
5 eggs
1½ cups (225g) plain flour
⅓ cup (50g) self-raising flour
1 teaspoon mixed spice
2 tablespoons dark rum, extra

1 Combine fruit and rum in large bowl, mix well; cover tightly with cling film. Store mixture in a cool, dark place overnight, or for up to a week, stirring every day.
2 Preheat oven to 150°C/130°C fan-assisted. Line deep 22cm-round cake tin with three layers of baking parchment, extending paper 5cm above the edge.
3 Beat butter and sugar in small bowl with electric mixer until just combined. Beat in eggs, one at a time.
4 Add butter mixture to fruit mixture; mix well. Mix in sifted dry ingredients; spread mixture evenly into prepared tin. Bake about 3½ hours.
5 Brush cake with extra rum. Cover hot cake tightly with foil; cool in tin.

tip If cake starts to brown too much during baking, cover loosely with foil.

last-minute fruit cake

prep + cook time 2 hours 20 minutes (plus cooling time) **serves** 20

1½ cups (250g) sultanas
1 cup (150g) raisins, chopped coarsely
1 cup (150g) currants
½ cup (85g) mixed peel
⅓ cup (70g) glacé cherries, halved
2 tablespoons coarsely chopped glacé pineapple
2 tablespoons coarsely chopped glacé apricots
185g butter, chopped
¾ cup (165g) firmly packed brown sugar
⅓ cup (80ml) brandy
⅓ cup (80ml) water
2 teaspoons finely grated orange rind
1 teaspoon finely grated lemon rind
1 tablespoon treacle
3 eggs, beaten lightly
1¼ cups (185g) plain flour
¼ cup (35g) self-raising flour
½ teaspoon bicarbonate of soda
½ cup (80g) blanched almonds

1 Combine fruit, butter, sugar, brandy and the water in medium saucepan, stir over medium heat until butter is melted and sugar is dissolved; bring to the boil. Remove from heat; transfer to large bowl. Cool to room temperature.
2 Preheat oven to 150°C/130°C fan-assisted. Line base and side of deep 20cm-round cake tin with three thicknesses of baking parchment, extending paper 5cm above edge.
3 Stir rinds, treacle and egg into fruit mixture then stir in sifted dry ingredients. Spread mixture into tin; decorate with nuts. Bake about 2 hours.
4 Cover hot cake tightly with foil; allow to cool in tin overnight.

rich sherried fruit cake

prep + cook time 3 hours 45 minutes (plus cooling and standing time) **serves** 20

250g butter, softened
2 tablespoons plum jam
2 teaspoons finely grated orange rind
1¼ cups (275g) firmly packed brown sugar
5 eggs
¾ cup (180ml) sweet sherry
1½ cups (225g) plain flour
½ cup (75g) self-raising flour
2 teaspoons mixed spice
1kg (5 cups) mixed dried fruit
½ cup (125ml) sweet sherry, extra, warmed

1   Preheat oven to 150°C/130°C fan-assisted. Line base and side of deep 22cm-round cake tin with four thicknesses of baking parchment, extending paper 5cm above edge.

2   Beat butter, jam, rind and sugar in medium bowl with electric mixer until just combined. Beat in eggs, one at a time.

3   Stir in ½ cup of the sherry, sifted dry ingredients and fruit; mix well.

4   Spread mixture into tin. Bake about 3¼ hours.

5   Brush top of hot cake with remaining ¼ cup of sherry, cover hot cake with foil; cool in tin overnight.

6   Remove cake from tin, peel paper away from cake. Brush cake all over with 2 tablespoons of the warmed extra sherry each week for 3 weeks.

boiled pineapple rum cake

prep + cook time 2 hours 20 minutes (plus cooling time) serves 20

450g can crushed pineapple in syrup
1kg (5 cups) mixed dried fruit
250g butter, chopped coarsely
1 cup (220g) firmly packed brown sugar
2 tablespoons orange marmalade
2 tablespoons dark rum
4 eggs, beaten lightly
1⅔ cups (250g) plain flour
⅓ cup (50g) self-raising flour
½ teaspoon bicarbonate of soda
1 tablespoon dark rum, extra

1   Drain pineapple over large jug; discard ½ cup of the syrup.
2   Combine pineapple, remaining syrup, fruit, butter, sugar, marmalade and rum in large saucepan. Using wooden spoon, stir over heat until butter melts and sugar dissolves; bring to the boil. Reduce heat; simmer, covered, 10 minutes. Cool to room temperature.
3   Preheat oven to 150°C/130°C fan-assisted. Line base and side of deep 20cm-round cake tin with three thicknesses baking parchment, extending paper 5cm above edges.
4   Using wooden spoon, stir egg and sifted dry ingredients into fruit mixture. Pour mixture into tin; bake about 2 hours.
5   Brush hot cake with extra rum. Cover tin tightly with foil; cool cake in tin.

rock cakes

prep + cook time 30 minutes **makes** 18

2 cups (300g) self-raising flour
¼ teaspoon ground cinnamon
⅓ cup (75g) caster sugar
90g cold butter, chopped
1 cup (160g) sultanas
1 egg, beaten lightly
½ cup (125ml) milk
1 tablespoon caster sugar, extra

1 Preheat oven to 200°C/180°C fan-assisted. Grease oven trays.
2 Sift flour, cinnamon and sugar into medium bowl; rub in butter. Stir in sultanas, egg and milk. Do not overmix.
3 Drop rounded tablespoons of mixture about 5cm apart onto trays; sprinkle with extra sugar. Bake about 15 minutes; cool cakes on trays.

carrot cake with lemon cream cheese frosting

prep + cook time 1 hour 45 minutes **serves** 12

You need three large carrots (540g) for this recipe.

1 cup (250ml) vegetable oil
1⅓ cups (295g) firmly packed brown sugar
3 eggs
3 cups firmly packed, coarsely grated carrot
1 cup (110g) coarsely chopped walnuts
2½ cups (375g) self-raising flour
½ teaspoon bicarbonate of soda
2 teaspoons mixed spice
lemon cream cheese frosting
30g butter, softened
80g cream cheese, softened
1 teaspoon finely grated lemon rind
1½ cups (240g) icing sugar

1   Preheat oven to 180°C/160°C fan-assisted. Grease deep 22cm-round cake tin; line base with baking parchment.
2   Beat oil, sugar and eggs in small bowl with electric mixer until thick and creamy. Transfer mixture to large bowl; stir in carrot, nuts then sifted dry ingredients.
3   Pour mixture into tin; bake about 1¼ hours. Stand cake in tin 5 minutes before turning, top-side up, onto wire rack to cool.
4   Meanwhile, make lemon cream cheese frosting. Spread cake with frosting.
lemon cream cheese frosting Beat butter, cream cheese and rind in small bowl with electric mixer until light and fluffy; gradually incorporate the sifted icing sugar.

upside-down toffee banana cake

prep + cook time 1 hour 10 minutes **serves** 10

You need four bananas for this recipe; two large overripe bananas weighing about 460g to make 1 cup of mashed banana, and two medium bananas.

1 cup (220g) caster sugar
1 cup (250ml) water
2 medium bananas (400g), sliced thinly
2 eggs, beaten lightly
⅔ cup (160ml) vegetable oil
¾ cup (165g) firmly packed brown sugar
1 teaspoon vanilla extract
⅔ cup (100g) plain flour
⅓ cup (50g) wholemeal self-raising flour
2 teaspoons mixed spice
1 teaspoon bicarbonate of soda
1 cup mashed banana

1 Preheat oven to 180°C/160°C fan-assisted. Grease deep 22cm-round cake tin; line base with baking parchment.
2 Stir caster sugar and the water in medium saucepan over heat, without boiling, until sugar dissolves; bring to the boil. Boil, uncovered, without stirring, about 10 minutes or until caramel in colour. Pour toffee into prepared tin; top with sliced banana.
3 Combine egg, oil, brown sugar and extract in medium bowl. Stir in sifted dry ingredients, then add the mashed banana.
4 Pour mixture into tin; bake about 40 minutes. Turn cake onto serving plate; peel off baking parchment. Serve cake, warm or at room temperature, with thick cream, if desired.

dundee cake

prep + cook time 3 hours 20 minutes (plus cooling time) **serves** 15

180g butter, softened
¾ cup (165g) caster sugar
5 eggs, lightly beaten
1½ cups (225g) plain flour
½ cup (75g) self-raising flour
½ teaspoon mixed spice
⅔ cup (80ml) milk
1¼ cups (200g) raisins, chopped coarsely
1½ cups (250g) currants
1¼ cups (200g) sultanas
⅔ cup (70g) red glacé cherries, chopped coarsely
2 tablespoons mixed peel
½ cup (80g) blanched almonds
1 tablespoon brandy

1   Preheat oven to 150°C/130°C fan-assisted. Line deep 19cm-square cake tin with three layers of baking parchment, extending paper 5cm above edges.
2   Beat butter, sugar, egg, sifted dry ingredients and milk in large bowl with electric mixer on medium speed about 3 minutes or until mixture becomes pale in colour. Stir in the fruit and half the nuts.
3   Spread mixture into tin; decorate top with remaining nuts. Bake about 2 hours. Brush hot cake with brandy; cover tightly with foil, cool in tin.

siena cake

prep + cook time 1 hour 30 minutes (plus cooling and standing time) serves 8

¾ cup (120g) blanched almonds, roasted, chopped coarsely
1 cup (140g) coarsely chopped roasted hazelnuts
¼ cup (80g) finely chopped glacé apricots
¼ cup (55g) finely chopped glacé pineapple
⅓ cup (55g) mixed peel, chopped finely
⅔ cup (100g) plain flour
2 tablespoons cocoa powder
1 teaspoon ground cinnamon
⅓ cup (75g) caster sugar
½ cup (180g) honey
60g dark eating chocolate, melted

1   Preheat oven to 170°C/150°C fan-assisted. Grease deep 20cm-round cake tin; line base and side with baking parchment.
2   Combine nuts, apricots, pineapple, mixed peel, and sifted flour, cocoa and cinnamon in large bowl; mix well.
3   Place sugar and honey in medium saucepan; stir over low heat until sugar dissolves, brushing down side of pan to dissolve any sugar crystals. Bring to the boil; reduce heat, simmer, uncovered, about 5 minutes or until syrup forms a soft ball when a few drops of the syrup are dropped into a glass of cold water.
4   Add syrup and chocolate to fruit and nut mixture; mix well. Spread mixture quickly into tin; bake about 35 minutes. Cool cake in tin. Turn out cake; remove paper. Wrap cake in foil; stand overnight.

courgette walnut loaf

prep + cook time 1 hour 30 minutes **serves** 10

You need 3 medium courgettes (360g), for this recipe.

3 eggs
1½ cups (330g) firmly packed brown sugar
1 cup (250ml) vegetable oil
1½ cups finely grated courgettes
1 cup (110g) coarsely chopped walnuts
1½ cups (225g) self-raising flour
1½ cups (225g) plain flour

1 Preheat oven to 180°C/160°C fan-assisted. Grease 15cm x 25cm loaf tin; line base and long sides with baking parchment, extending paper 5cm above edges.
2 Beat eggs, sugar and oil in large bowl with electric mixer until combined. Stir in courgettes, walnuts and sifted flours in two batches.
3 Spread mixture into tin; bake about 1¼ hours. Stand cake in tin 5 minutes before turning, top-side up, onto wire rack to cool. Serve the cake with butter if you prefer.

CLASSIC
Syrup cakes

Syrup-soaked cakes are at their best served warm,
either just as they are with a good cup of tea or
coffee, or as a dessert with a dollop of cream
and maybe some fresh fruit that ties in with the
flavour of the cake. Slices of cake can be reheated
gently in a microwave oven.

mixed berry cake with vanilla syrup

prep + cook time 1 hour **serves** 8

125g butter, softened
1 cup (220g) caster sugar
3 eggs
½ cup (75g) plain flour
¼ cup (35g) self-raising flour
½ cup (60g) ground almonds
⅓ cup (80g) soured cream
1½ cups (225g) frozen mixed berries
½ cup (100g) drained canned pitted black cherries
vanilla syrup
½ cup (125ml) water
½ cup (110g) caster sugar
2 vanilla pods

1 Preheat oven to 180°C/160°C fan-assisted. Grease 21cm savarin tin thoroughly.
2 Beat butter and sugar in small bowl with electric mixer until light and fluffy. Beat in eggs, one at a time. Transfer mixture to large bowl; stir in sifted flours, ground almonds, soured cream, berries and cherries. Pour mixture into tin; bake about 40 minutes.
3 Meanwhile, make vanilla syrup.
4 Stand cake in tin 5 minutes before turning onto wire rack set over tray. Pour hot syrup over hot cake.
vanilla syrup Combine the water and sugar in small saucepan. Split vanilla pods in half lengthways; scrape seeds into pan then place pods in pan. Stir over heat, without boiling, until sugar dissolves. Simmer, uncovered, without stirring, 5 minutes. Using tongs, remove pods from syrup.

lemon syrup cake

prep + cook time 1 hour 10 minutes **serves** 12

250g butter, softened
1 tablespoon finely grated lemon rind
1 cup (220g) caster sugar
3 eggs
1 cup (250ml) buttermilk
⅓ cup (80ml) lemon juice
2 cups (300g) self-raising flour
lemon syrup
⅓ cup (80ml) lemon juice
¼ cup (60ml) water
¾ cup (165g) caster sugar

1 Preheat oven to 180°C/160°C fan-assisted. Grease 24cm savarin tin (or grease deep 22cm-round cake tin and line base and side with baking parchment).
2 Beat butter, rind and sugar in small bowl with electric mixer until light and fluffy. Beat in eggs, one at a time. Transfer mixture to large bowl; fold in buttermilk, juice and sifted flour, in two batches.
3 Spread mixture into tin; bake about 50 minutes if using savarin tin or bake about 1 hour if using round tin. Cover cake with foil if browning too quickly.
4 Meanwhile, make lemon syrup.
5 Stand cake in tin 5 minutes before turning onto wire rack set over tray. Pour hot syrup over hot cake; serve warm.
lemon syrup Combine ingredients in small saucepan; stir over heat, without boiling, until sugar dissolves. Simmer, uncovered, without stirring, 5 minutes.

orange syrup cake

prep + cook time 1 hour 35 minutes **serves** 12

1 large orange (300g)
2 cups (500ml) water
2 cups (440g) caster sugar
⅔ cup (160ml) brandy
250g unsalted butter, softened
1 cup (220g) caster sugar, extra
4 eggs
1½ cups (225g) self-raising flour
2 tablespoons cornflour

1 Preheat oven to 160°C/140°C fan-assisted. Grease deep 22cm-round cake tin; line base and side with baking parchment.
2 Peel orange. Chop peel and flesh of orange finely; discard pips. Stir orange flesh and peel in medium saucepan with the water, sugar and brandy, over medium heat, until sugar dissolves; bring to the boil. Reduce heat; simmer, uncovered, about 15 minutes or until orange skin is tender. Strain syrup into heatproof jug; reserve orange solids separately.
3 Beat butter and extra sugar in small bowl with electric mixer until light and fluffy. Beat in eggs, one at a time. Transfer mixture to large bowl. Stir in combined sifted flours, and reserved orange solids. Pour mixture into tin; bake about 50 minutes.
4 Meanwhile, simmer reserved syrup over heat in small saucepan until thickened slightly.
5 Stand cake in tin 5 minutes before turning, top-side up, onto wire rack set over tray. Pour hot syrup over hot cake; serve warm.

banana butterscotch syrup cake

prep + cook time 1 hour 15 minutes **serves** 9

You will need 2 large overripe bananas (460g) for this recipe.

125g butter, softened
¾ cup (165g) caster sugar
2 eggs
1 cup mashed banana
¾ cup (110g) self-raising flour
¾ cup (110g) plain flour
½ teaspoon bicarbonate of soda
¾ cup (110g) hazelnuts, roasted, chopped finely
butterscotch syrup
½ cup (110g) firmly packed brown sugar
30g butter, chopped
¾ cup (180ml) water

1 Preheat oven to 180°C / 160°C fan-assisted. Grease deep 19cm-square cake tin; line base with baking parchment.
2 Beat butter and sugar in medium bowl with electric mixer until light and fluffy. Beat in eggs, one at a time. Stir in banana, then combined sifted flours and soda, and nuts. Spread mixture into tin; bake about 1 hour.
3 Meanwhile, make butterscotch syrup.
4 Stand cake in tin 5 minutes before turning, top-side up, onto wire rack set over tray. Drizzle hot syrup over hot cake.
butterscotch syrup Combine sugar and butter in small saucepan; stir over heat until butter melts. Add the water and bring to the boil, stirring; remove from heat.

semolina & yogurt lemon-syrup cake

prep + cook time 1 hour 10 minutes **serves** 8

250g butter, softened
1 tablespoon finely grated lemon rind
1 cup (220g) caster sugar
3 eggs, separated
1 cup (150g) self-raising flour
1 cup (180g) semolina
1 cup (280g) plain yogurt
lemon syrup
1 cup (220g) caster sugar
⅓ cup (80ml) lemon juice

lemon syrup Combine ingredients in small pan; stir over heat, without boiling, until sugar dissolves. Bring to the boil, without stirring, then remove from heat.

1 Preheat oven to 180°C/160°C fan-assisted. Grease 20cm savarin tin (or grease deep 20cm-round cake tin and line base and side with baking parchment).
2 Beat butter, rind and sugar in small bowl with electric mixer until light and fluffy. Beat in egg yolks. Transfer mixture to large bowl; stir in sifted flour, semolina and yogurt.
3 Beat egg whites in small bowl with electric mixer until soft peaks form; fold egg whites into cake mixture, in two batches. Spread mixture into tin; bake about 50 minutes.
4 Meanwhile, make lemon syrup.
5 Stand cake in tin 5 minutes before turning onto wire rack set over tray. Pierce cake all over with skewer; pour hot lemon syrup over hot cake.

espresso syrup cake

prep + cook time 1 hour **serves** 8

3 teaspoons instant espresso coffee granules
1 tablespoon hot water
3 eggs
¾ cup (165g) caster sugar
1 cup (150g) self-raising flour
1 tablespoon cocoa powder
150g butter, melted
espresso syrup
¾ cup (165g) caster sugar
¾ cup (180ml) water
3 teaspoons instant espresso coffee granules

1 Preheat oven to 180°C/160°C fan-assisted. Grease 20cm savarin tin (or grease deep 20cm-round cake tin and line base and side with baking parchment).
2 Combine coffee and the water in small jug; stir until dissolved.
3 Beat eggs in small bowl with electric mixer about 8 minutes or until thick and creamy; gradually add sugar, beating until dissolved between additions. Fold in sifted flour and cocoa, then butter and coffee mixture. Pour mixture into tin; bake about 40 minutes.
4 Meanwhile, make espresso syrup.
5 Stand cake in tin 5 minutes before turning onto wire rack set over tray. Reserve ¼ cup espresso syrup; drizzle remaining hot syrup over hot cake. Serve with reserved syrup.
espresso syrup Combine ingredients in small saucepan; stir over heat, without boiling, until sugar dissolves. Bring to the boil then remove from heat.

cinnamon & walnut syrup cake

prep + cook time 1 hour **serves** 12

3 eggs
¾ cup (165g) caster sugar
¾ cup (110g) self-raising flour
3 teaspoons ground cinnamon
185g butter, melted
¾ cup (80g) coarsely chopped walnuts
sugar syrup
1 cup (220) caster sugar
¾ cup (180ml) water

1   Preheat oven to 180°C/160°C fan-assisted. Grease 23cm-square traybake tin; line base with baking parchment.
2   Beat eggs in small bowl with electric mixer until thick and creamy. Gradually add sugar, beating until dissolved between additions. Beat in sifted flour and cinnamon, in two batches; beat in butter then stir in nuts. Pour mixture into tin; bake about 30 minutes.
3   Meanwhile, make sugar syrup.
4   Stand cake in tin 5 minutes before turning onto wire rack set over tray. Pour hot syrup over hot cake. Serve cake warm or cold.
sugar syrup Combine ingredients in small saucepan; stir constantly over heat without boiling until sugar is dissolved. Bring to the boil; reduce heat, simmer, uncovered, 5 minutes.

lime syrup buttermilk cake

prep + cook time 1 hour 30 minutes **serves** 8

250g butter, softened
1 tablespoon finely grated lime rind
1 cup (220g) caster sugar
3 eggs, separated
2 cups (300g) self-raising flour
1 cup (250ml) buttermilk
lime syrup
⅓ cup (80ml) lime juice
¾ cup (165g) caster sugar
¼ cup (60ml) water

1 Preheat oven to 180°C/160°C fan-assisted. Grease 20cm savarin tin (or grease deep 20cm-round cake tin and line base and side with baking parchment).
2 Beat butter, rind and sugar in small bowl with electric mixer until light and fluffy; beat in egg yolks, one at a time, until combined. Transfer mixture to large bowl; stir in sifted flour, and buttermilk, in two batches.
3 Beat egg whites in small bowl with electric mixer until soft peaks form; fold into flour mixture, in two batches. Spread mixture into tin; bake about 1 hour.
4 Meanwhile, make lime syrup.
5 Stand cake in tin 5 minutes before turning onto serving plate. Gradually pour hot lime syrup evenly over hot cake. Serve cake sprinkled with thinly sliced lime rind, if desired.
lime syrup Combine ingredients in small saucepan; stir over heat, without boiling, until sugar is dissolved. Bring to the boil; remove from heat.

glacé fruit cake

prep + cook time 2 hours 50 minutes (plus cooling time) serves 12

185g butter, softened
½ cup (110g) caster sugar
3 eggs
1 cup (250g) finely chopped glacé apricot
½ cup (80g) finely chopped glacé orange
½ cup (90g) finely chopped glacé ginger
¾ cup (210g) finely chopped glacé fig
1½ cups (225g) plain flour
½ cup (75g) self-raising flour
½ cup (125ml) milk
¼ cup (60ml) ginger wine
ginger syrup
¼ cup (60ml) ginger wine
¼ cup (60ml) water
¼ cup (55g) caster sugar
2 teaspoons lemon juice

1   Preheat oven to 150°C/130°C fan-assisted. Line base and long sides of 14cm x 21cm loaf tin with baking parchment, extending paper 5cm above sides.
2   Beat butter and sugar in small bowl with electric mixer until just combined. Beat in eggs, one at a time. Transfer mixture to large bowl; stir in fruit then combined sifted flours, and combined milk and wine, in two batches. Spread mixture into tin; bake about 2½ hours.
3   Meanwhile, make ginger syrup.
4   Pour hot ginger syrup over hot cake in tin. Cover cake with foil; cool in tin.
ginger syrup Stir ingredients in small saucepan over low heat, without boiling, until sugar dissolves; bring to the boil. Boil, uncovered, without stirring, about 2 minutes or until syrup thickens slightly.

tip Ginger wine, a beverage that is 14% alcohol by volume, has the piquant taste of fresh ginger. You can substitute it with dry (white) vermouth, if you prefer.

almond orange halva cake

prep + cook time 1 hour 15 minutes **serves** 10

125g butter, softened
2 teaspoons finely grated orange rind
½ cup (110g) caster sugar
2 eggs
1 teaspoon baking powder
1 cup (180g) semolina
1 cup (120g) ground almonds
¼ cup (60ml) orange juice
orange & brandy syrup
1 cup (250ml) orange juice
½ cup (110g) caster sugar
1 tablespoon brandy

1   Preheat oven to 180°C/160°C fan-assisted. Grease deep 20cm-round cake tin; line base and side with baking parchment.
2   Cream butter, rind and sugar in small bowl with electric mixer until light and fluffy. Beat in eggs, one at a time, until combined. Transfer mixture to large bowl; stir in dry ingredients and juice in two batches. Spread mixture into tin; bake about 40 minutes.
3 Meanwhile, make orange and brandy syrup.
4   Turn cake, top-side up, onto wire rack set over oven tray; brush half the hot syrup over hot cake. Bake (on wire rack) a further 5 minutes. Remove from oven; brush with remaining hot syrup. Serve cake warm or cold.
orange & brandy syrup Combine juice and sugar in small saucepan; stir constantly over heat, without boiling, until sugar is dissolved. Bring to the boil; reduce heat, simmer, uncovered, without stirring, 5 minutes. Stir in brandy.

whole tangelo cake

prep + cook time 1 hour 5 minutes **serves** 12

2 medium tangelos (420g)
125g butter, softened
1½ cups (330g) caster sugar
2 eggs
1 cup (150g) self-raising flour
½ cup (75g) plain flour
½ cup (45g) desiccated coconut
tangelo syrup
1 cup (220g) caster sugar
rind of 1 tangelo, sliced thinly
⅔ cup (160ml) tangelo juice
⅓ cup (80ml) water

note Tangelos – a citrus fruit that's a cross between a tangerine and grapefruit – have a fairly short season. If you can't get them, use the same weight in either oranges or mandarins.

1   Place tangelos in medium saucepan; cover with cold water. Bring to the boil; drain. Repeat process twice; cool to room temperature.
2   Preheat oven to 180°C/160°C fan-assisted. Grease deep 22cm-round cake tin; line base and side with baking parchment.
3   Halve tangelos; discard seeds. Blend or process tangelo until pulpy; transfer to large bowl.
4   Beat butter, sugar and eggs in small bowl with electric mixer until light and fluffy. Stir butter mixture into tangelo pulp. Stir in sifted flours and coconut. Pour mixture into tin.
5   Bake cake about 45 minutes. Stand cake in tin 5 minutes; turn, top-side up, onto wire rack over tray.
6   Make tangelo syrup; pour hot syrup over hot cake. Serve cake warm.
tangelo syrup Stir ingredients in small saucepan over heat, without boiling, until sugar dissolves; bring to the boil. Reduce heat; simmer, uncovered, without stirring, 2 minutes.

CLASSIC
Dessert cakes

Forget the diet, think luscious indulgence.
Most dessert cakes take a little time and effort to make,
but usually they can be made at least a day ahead of serving.
Leave any assembling, filling and decorating until the
last minute for maximum effect.

black forest cake

prep + cook time 2 hours 25 minutes (plus cooling time) **serves** 12

250g butter, chopped
1 tablespoon instant coffee granules
1½ cups (375ml) hot water
200g dark eating chocolate, chopped
2 cups (440g) caster sugar
1½ cups (225g) self-raising flour
1 cup (150g) plain flour
¼ cup (25g) cocoa powder
2 eggs
2 teaspoons vanilla extract
¼ cup (60ml) kirsch
600ml whipping cream, whipped
2 x 425g cans pitted black cherries, drained, halved
2 teaspoons cocoa powder, extra

1 Preheat oven to 150°C/130°C fan-assisted. Grease deep 22cm-round cake tin, line base and side with baking parchment.
2 Melt butter in medium saucepan; stir in combined coffee and hot water, then chocolate and sugar. Stir over low heat, without boiling, until smooth. Transfer mixture to large bowl, cool to warm.
3 Beat chocolate mixture on low speed with electric mixer; gradually beat in sifted dry ingredients, in three batches. Beat in eggs, one at a time, then extract.
4 Pour mixture into tin; bake about 1¾ hours. Stand cake in tin 5 minutes before turning, top-side up, onto wire rack to cool.
5 Trim top of cake to make it flat. Split cake into three even layers. Place one layer onto serving plate; brush with half of the kirsch, top with half of the whipped cream and half of the cherries. Repeat layering, then top with cake top. Dust with extra sifted cocoa.

apple cake with brandy butterscotch sauce

prep + cook time 1 hour 10 minutes **serves** 8

125g butter, softened
½ cup (110g) caster sugar
2 eggs
⅔ cup (100g) self-raising flour
⅓ cup (50g) plain flour
1 tablespoon milk
3 medium green-skinned apples (450g)
½ cup (160g) apricot jam, warmed
brandy butterscotch sauce
½ cup (100g) firmly packed brown sugar
½ cup (125ml) whipping cream
100g butter, chopped
2 tablespoons brandy

1   Preheat oven to 160°C/140°C fan-assisted. Grease two 8cm x 25cm bar cake tins; line bases and long sides with baking parchment, extending paper 5cm above sides.
2   Beat butter and sugar in small bowl with electric mixer until light and fluffy. Beat in eggs, one at a time. Stir in sifted flours and milk; spread mixture into tins.
3   Peel, core and halve apples; slice each half thinly. Push apple slices gently into surface of cake mixture. Brush apple with jam; bake about 40 minutes.
4   Make brandy butterscotch sauce.
5   Stand cakes in tins 10 minutes before turning out, top-sides up, onto wire racks to cool. Serve pieces of warm apple cake drizzled with the brandy butterscotch sauce.
brandy butterscotch sauce Combine ingredients in small saucepan. Stir over heat, without boiling, until sugar dissolves; bring to the boil. Reduce heat; simmer, uncovered, without stirring, about 3 minutes **or** until mixture thickens slightly.

vanilla pear almond cake

prep + cook time 2 hours 45 minutes (plus cooling time) serves 8

8 firm pears (800g)
2½ cups (625ml) water
1 strip lemon rind
1¾ cups (385g) caster sugar
1 vanilla pod, halved lengthways
125g butter, softened
3 eggs
⅔ cup (160g) soured cream
⅔ cup (100g) plain flour
⅔ cup (100g) self-raising flour
¼ cup (40g) blanched almonds, roasted, chopped coarsely
40g dark eating chocolate, chopped
½ cup (60g) ground almonds

1   Peel pears, leaving stems intact.
2   Combine the water, rind and 1 cup of the sugar in medium pan. Scrape vanilla seeds into pan, then add pod. Stir over heat, without boiling, until sugar dissolves. Add pears; bring to a boil. Reduce heat; simmer, covered, about 30 minutes until pears are just tender. Transfer pears to a bowl; bring syrup to the boil. Boil, uncovered, until syrup reduces by half. Using tongs, remove vanilla pod. Cool syrup completely.
3   Preheat oven to 200°C/180°C fan-assisted. Insert base of 23cm springform tin upside down in tin to give a flat base; grease tin.
4   Beat butter and remaining sugar in medium bowl with electric mixer until light and fluffy. Beat in eggs, one at a time. Add soured cream; beat until just combined. Stir in 2 tablespoons of the syrup, then combined sifted flours, nuts, chocolate and ground almonds.
5   Spread mixture into tin; place pears upright around edge of tin, gently pushing pears to the bottom. Bake about 1 hour 35 minutes. Stand cake 10 minutes before removing from tin.
6   Serve cake warm, brushed with remaining syrup.

plum & almond upside-down cake

prep + cook time 1 hour 15 minutes **serves** 9

50g butter, chopped
½ cup (110g) firmly packed brown sugar
12 small plums (900g), halved, stones removed
125g butter, softened
1 teaspoon vanilla extract
1¼ cups (275g) caster sugar
3 eggs
¾ cup (110g) self-raising flour
¾ cup (110g) plain flour
¾ cup (180ml) milk
1 cup (120g) ground almonds
⅓ cup (25g) flaked almonds, toasted

1 Preheat oven to 180°C/160°C fan-assisted. Grease 19cm-square cake tin; line with baking parchment.
2 Combine butter and brown sugar in a small saucepan, stir over low heat until smooth; pour into base of cake tin. Place plums, cut side down, over caramel mixture.
3 Beat butter, extract and caster sugar in medium bowl with electric mixer until light and fluffy. Beat in eggs, one at a time. Stir in both sifted flours, and milk, in two batches. Stir in ground almonds.
4 Spread mixture into tin; bake about 50 minutes. Stand cake in tin 15 minutes before turning onto wire rack to cool. Serve sprinkled with flaked almonds and a dollop of cream.

banana caramel layer cake

prep + cook time 1 hour 10 minutes **serves** 8

You need two large overripe bananas (460g) for this recipe.

185g butter, softened
1¼ cup (175g) caster sugar
3 eggs
2¼ cups (335g) self-raising flour
½ teaspoon bicarbonate of soda
1¼ cups mashed banana
⅓ cup (80ml) milk
380g dulce de leche (caramel sauce)
¾ cup (180ml) whipping cream, whipped
1 large (230g) banana, sliced thinly

1   Preheat oven to 180°C/160°C fan-assisted. Grease 24cm savarin tin or 24cm patterned silicone tube tin.
2   Beat butter and sugar in small bowl with electric mixer until light and fluffy. Beat in eggs, one at a time. Transfer mixture to large bowl; stir in sifted dry ingredients, mashed banana and milk.
3   Spread mixture into prepared tin; bake about 40 minutes. Stand cake in tin 5 minutes before turning onto wire rack to cool.
4   Split cake into three layers. Spread bottom layer of cake with half the caramel, top with half the cream then half the banana slices. Repeat next layer using remaining caramel, cream and banana slices. Replace top of cake and dust with icing sugar before serving.

chocolate roulade with coffee cream

prep + cook time 30 minutes (plus cooling & refrigeration time) **serves** 8

200g dark eating chocolate, chopped coarsely
¼ cup (60ml) hot water
2 teaspoons instant coffee granules
4 eggs, separated
½ cup (110g) caster sugar
1 tablespoon caster sugar, extra
coffee cream
2 teaspoons instant coffee granules
1 teaspoon hot water
300ml whipping cream
2 tablespoons coffee-flavoured liqueur
1 tablespoon icing sugar

coffee cream Dissolve coffee granules in the hot water in small bowl. Add cream, liqueur and sifted icing sugar; beat with electric mixer until firm peaks form.

1 Preheat oven to 180°C/160°C fan-assisted. Grease 25cm x 30cm swiss roll tin; line base and sides with baking parchment, extending paper 5cm above sides.
2 Combine chocolate, the water and coffee granules in large heatproof bowl. Stir mixture over large saucepan of simmering water until smooth (do not allow water to touch base of bowl); remove from heat.
3 Beat egg yolks and caster sugar in small bowl with electric mixer until thick and creamy; fold egg mixture into warm chocolate mixture.
4 Beat egg whites in small bowl with electric mixer to soft peaks; fold egg whites into chocolate mixture, in two batches. Spread into tin; bake about 10 minutes.
5 Meanwhile, place piece of baking parchment cut the same size as tin on worktop; sprinkle with extra caster sugar. Turn hot cake onto paper; peel lining paper away. Cool, then trim sides of cake. Cover cake with tea-towel.
6 Make coffee cream.
7 Spread cake evenly with coffee cream. Using paper as a guide, roll cake from long side. Cover roll; refrigerate 30 minutes before serving.

soft-centred mocha puddings

prep + cook time 40 minutes **makes** 6

150g dark chocolate, chopped
125g butter, chopped
3 teaspoons instant coffee granules
2 eggs
2 egg yolks
⅓ cup (75g) caster sugar
¼ cup (35g) plain flour
2 teaspoons cocoa powder

1 Preheat oven to 200°C/180°C fan-assisted. Grease six-hole (¾-cup/180ml) large muffin tin well with softened butter.
2 Stir chocolate, butter and coffee in small saucepan, over low heat, until smooth; cool 10 minutes. Transfer mixture to a large bowl.
3 Beat eggs, egg yolks and sugar in small bowl with electric mixer until thick and creamy. Gently fold egg mixture and sifted flour into barely warm chocolate mixture.
4 Divide mixture among tin holes; bake, in oven, 12 minutes. Gently turn puddings, top-side down, onto serving plates. Serve immediately, dusted with sifted cocoa powder.

torta di mamma

prep + cook time 1 hour 50 minutes (plus refrigeration time) **serves** 12

280g packet sponge cake mix
1 cup (250ml) strong black coffee
⅓ cup (80ml) coffee liqueur
⅓ cup (80ml) brandy
1 tablespoon caster sugar
custard filling
½ cup (75g) cornflour
½ cup (60g) custard powder
½ cup (110g) caster sugar
2½ cups (625ml) milk
1½ cups (375ml) double cream
2 teaspoons vanilla extract
30g butter
2 egg yolks
90g dark eating chocolate, melted

1   Preheat oven to 160°C/140°C fan-assisted. Grease deep 22cm-round cake tin; line base with baking parchment.
2   Make sponge cake according to the directions on packet; pour mixture into tin. Bake about 35 minutes. Turn cake onto wire rack to cool.
3   Meanwhile, make custard filling.
4   Combine cold coffee, liqueur, brandy and sugar in small jug; mix well. Split cold cake into four layers. Place first layer on serving plate; brush well with coffee mixture.
5   Spread half the plain custard over cake. Top custard with second layer of cake; brush with coffee mixture. Spread a third of the chocolate custard over cake. Place third layer of cake on top of custard; brush with coffee mixture then spread with remaining plain custard. Top with fourth layer of cake; brush with coffee mixture.
6   Using a large spatula, spread remaining chocolate custard over top and side of cake; refrigerate 3 hours or overnight.
custard filling Combine cornflour, custard powder and sugar in medium saucepan. Gradually add combined milk, cream and extract; stir over low heat until mixture boils and thickens. Add butter; simmer, stirring, 3 minutes. Remove pan from heat; stir in egg yolk. Place custard in large bowl; cover with cling film. Cool. Divide custard mixture between two bowls. Stir melted chocolate into one bowl. Leave remaining custard plain.

flourless chocolate dessert cake

prep + cook time 1 hour (plus refrigeration time) serves 6

100g dark eating chocolate, chopped
100g butter, chopped
½ cup (110g) caster sugar
2 tablespoons marsala
⅔ cup (80g) ground almonds
1 tablespoon instant coffee granules
1 tablespoon hot water
3 eggs, separated
strawberry coulis
250g strawberries
¼ cup (40g) icing sugar

1   Preheat oven to 180°C/160°C fan-assisted. Grease deep 20cm-round cake tin; line base and side with baking parchment.
2   Melt chocolate and butter in small saucepan, over low heat, stirring, until mixture is combined.
3   Combine chocolate mixture with sugar, marsala, ground almonds and combined coffee and the water in a large bowl; beat in egg yolks, one at a time.
4   Beat egg whites in small bowl with electric mixer until soft peaks form; gently fold into chocolate mixture, in two batches.
5   Pour mixture into tin; bake about 45 minutes. Cool cake in tin, cover; refrigerate several hours or overnight.
6   Make strawberry coulis.
7   Carefully turn cake onto board; cut into slices with a hot knife. Serve cake with strawberry coulis. Dust with sifted icing sugar and serve with whipped cream, if you like.
strawberry coulis Blend or process ingredients until mixture is smooth.

rich truffle mud cake

prep + cook time 1 hour 15 minutes (plus cooling and refrigeration time) **serves** 12

6 eggs
½ cup (110g) firmly packed brown sugar
400g dark eating chocolate, melted
1 cup (250ml) thick cream (48% fat content)
⅓ cup (80ml) Cointreau

1   Preheat oven to 180°C/160°C fan-assisted. Grease deep 22cm-round cake tin; line base and side with baking parchment.
2   Beat eggs and sugar in large bowl with electric mixer until thick and creamy. With motor operating, gradually beat in barely warm melted chocolate until combined. Using metal spoon, gently fold in combined cream and liqueur.
3   Pour mixture into tin. Place tin in baking dish; pour enough boiling water into dish to come halfway up side of tin. Bake about 30 minutes. Cover tin loosely with foil; bake about 30 minutes. Discard foil; remove tin from dish, cool cake in tin.
4   Turn cake onto serving plate, cover; refrigerate overnight. Serve dusted with a little sifted cocoa, if desired.

tip Goes well served with a raspberry coulis and fresh raspberries.

opera gateau

prep + cook time 1 hour (plus cooling and refrigeration time) **serves** 24

4 eggs
1¼ cups (150g) ground almonds
1 cup (160g) icing sugar, sifted
⅓ cup (50g) plain flour
25g unsalted butter, melted
4 egg whites
1 tablespoon caster sugar
coffee buttercream
¼ cup (60ml) milk
¼ cup (55g) brown sugar
2 teaspoons instant coffee granules
1 egg yolk
125g unsalted butter, softened
coffee syrup
⅓ cup (80ml) boiling water
2 tablespoons caster sugar
1 tablespoon instant coffee granules
ganache
160g dark eating chocolate, chopped coarsely
⅓ cup (80ml) double cream
glaze
50g unsalted butter, chopped
75g dark eating chocolate

1 Preheat oven to 220°C/200°C fan-assisted. Grease two 25cm x 30cm swiss roll tins; line bases with baking parchment, extending paper 5cm over long sides.
2 Beat eggs, ground almonds and icing sugar in small bowl with electric mixer until creamy; beat in flour. Transfer to large bowl; stir in butter. Beat egg whites in small bowl with electric mixer until soft peaks form; add caster sugar, beating until sugar dissolves. Fold into almond mixture, in two batches. Divide mixture between tins. Bake 7 minutes. Cool.
3 Make coffee buttercream, coffee syrup, and ganache.
4 Place one of the large cake rectangles on baking-parchment-lined tray; brush with half the coffee syrup then spread cake with half the buttercream. Chill 10 minutes. Top buttercream with the two small cake rectangles, side-by-side. Brush tops with the remaining coffee syrup then spread with ganache. Top with remaining cake; chill 10 minutes. Spread remaining buttercream over top of cake; chill 3 hours.
5 Make glaze.
6 Quickly spread glaze evenly over cake. Refrigerate 30 minutes or until set.
coffee buttercream Stir milk, sugar and coffee in small saucepan, over low heat, until sugar dissolves. Whisk yolk in small bowl; gradually whisk in hot milk mixture. Return custard to pan; stir over heat, without boiling, about 5 minutes or until thickened slightly. Cool. Beat butter in small bowl with electric mixer until light and fluffy; beat in custard.
coffee syrup Combine ingredients in small bowl.
ganache Stir ingredients in small heatproof bowl over small saucepan of simmering water until smooth. Refrigerate until spreadable.
glaze Stir ingredients in small heat-proof bowl over small pan of simmering water until smooth. Use while still warm.

rum baba

prep + cook time 40 minutes (plus standing time) **serves** 6

7g sachet dry yeast
¼ cup (35g) plain flour
¼ cup (60ml) warm milk
¾ cup (110g) plain flour, extra
2 tablespoons caster sugar
2 eggs, beaten lightly
60g butter, melted
rum syrup
1½ cups (330g) caster sugar
1 cup (250ml) water
2 tablespoons dark rum

1   Grease six ½-cup (125ml) moulds.
2   Mix yeast with flour and milk in small bowl; cover, stand in warm place about 10 minutes or until mixture is frothy.
3   Sift extra flour and sugar into large bowl; stir in yeast mixture, egg and butter. Beat about 3 minutes with a wooden spoon until batter is smooth. Place batter in large greased bowl, cover; stand in warm place about 40 minutes or until batter has doubled in size.
4   Preheat oven to 200°C/180°C fan-assisted.
5   Beat batter again. Divide batter between moulds; stand, uncovered, until batter rises three-quarters of the way up side of moulds. Place moulds on oven tray; bake about 15 minutes.
6   Meanwhile, make rum syrup.
7   Turn babas onto wire rack set over tray; pour hot rum syrup over hot babas. Place babas on serving plates; pour syrup from tray over babas until all syrup has been absorbed.
rum syrup Combine sugar and the water in small saucepan; stir over heat, without boiling, until sugar is dissolved. Bring to the boil; boil, uncovered, without stirring, 2 minutes. Remove from heat, stir in rum.

brandied apricot chocolate cake

prep + cook time 1 hour 20 minutes (plus refrigeration time) **serves** 10

125g dark eating chocolate, chopped
½ cup (125ml) water
125g butter, softened
1 cup (220g) firmly packed brown sugar
2 eggs
½ cup (125ml) soured cream
1⅓ cups (200g) plain flour
⅓ cup (35g) self-raising flour
¼ cup (80g) apricot jam
1 tablespoon brandy
½ cup (125ml) whipping cream, whipped
chocolate icing
90g dark eating chocolate, chopped
15g butter, chopped

1 Preheat oven to 160°C/140°C fan-assisted. Grease deep 20cm-round cake tin; line base with baking parchment.
2 Stir chocolate and the water in small saucepan, over low heat, until smooth; cool chocolate mixture.
3 Cream butter and sugar in small bowl with electric mixer until light and fluffy. Beat in eggs, one at a time. Transfer mixture to large bowl, stir in chocolate mixture, soured cream and sifted flours in two batches.
4 Spread mixture into tin; bake about 1 hour. Stand cake in tin 5 minutes before turning, top-side up, onto wire rack to cool.
5 Meanwhile make chocolate icing.
6 Split cake in half. Combine jam and brandy. Sandwich cake with jam mixture and cream. Spread cake with icing, refrigerate until set.
chocolate icing Stir chocolate and butter in small bowl set over small saucepan of simmering water until smooth (do not allow water to touch base of bowl); cool.

109

rich mocha gâteau

prep + cook time 1 hour 15 minutes (plus standing & refrigeration time) **serves** 12

½ cup (125ml) Cointreau
2 teaspoons finely grated orange rind
150g milk chocolate, melted
90g unsalted butter, melted
6 eggs, separated
¾ cup (110g) self-raising flour
⅓ cup (75g) caster sugar
rich mocha filling
2 teaspoons instant coffee granules
2 tablespoons hot water
300g dark eating chocolate, melted
6 egg yolks
chocolate butter cream
2 tablespoons instant coffee granules
¼ cup (60ml) hot water
200g dark eating chocolate, melted
4 egg yolks
¼ cup (55g) caster sugar
185g unsalted butter, softened

1   Preheat oven to 180°C/160°C fan-assisted. Grease deep 22cm-round cake tin; line base with baking parchment.
2   Stand liqueur and rind in small bowl for 30 minutes. Strain; reserve rind and liqueur separately.
3   Combine chocolate, butter and rind in large bowl. Stir in 3 teaspoons of the liqueur along with the egg yolks and sifted flour.
4   Beat egg whites in large bowl with electric mixer until soft peaks form; gradually add sugar, beating until dissolved between additions. Fold whites into chocolate mixture, in two batches.
5   Pour mixture into tin; bake about 35 minutes. Stand cake in tin 5 minutes before turning, top-side up, onto wire rack to cool.
6   Meanwhile, make rich mocha filling and chocolate butter cream.
7   Split cake into three layers. Place first layer on serving plate; spread with half the mocha filling. Refrigerate 15 minutes. Top with second layer; spread with remaining mocha filling. Top with third layer; refrigerate 30 minutes. Spread butter cream over top and side of cake; refrigerate 30 minutes.
rich mocha filling Combine coffee and the water in large bowl; stir in melted chocolate, then yolks and ⅓ cup of the remaining liqueur. Refrigerate until set.
chocolate butter cream Combine coffee and the water in large bowl; stir in the chocolate and remaining liqueur. Beat yolks and sugar in small bowl with electric mixer until thick and creamy; beat in butter in several batches until smooth. Gradually beat in chocolate mixture; refrigerate 10 minutes or until spreadable.

italian ricotta cheesecake

prep + cook time 1 hour 40 minutes (plus refrigeration & cooling time) **serves** 16

90g butter, softened
¼ cup (55g) caster sugar
1 egg
1¼ cups (185g) plain flour
¼ cup (35g) self-raising flour
ricotta filling
1kg ricotta cheese
1 tablespoon finely grated lemon rind
¼ cup (60ml) lemon juice
1 cup (220g) caster sugar
5 eggs
¼ cup (40g) sultanas
¼ cup (80g) finely chopped glacé fruit salad

1   Grease 28cm springform cake tin.
2   Beat butter, sugar and egg in small bowl with electric mixer until combined. Stir in half the sifted flours, then work in remaining flours by hand. Lightly knead pastry on floured surface until smooth; wrap in cling film; refrigerate for 30 minutes.
3   Press pastry over base of tin; prick with fork. Place on oven tray; refrigerate 30 minutes.
4   Preheat oven to 200°C/180°C fan-assisted.
5   Cover pastry with baking parchment, fill with beans or rice; bake 10 minutes. Remove parchment and beans; bake 15 minutes or until browned lightly. Cool. Reduce oven temperature to 160°C/140°C fan-assisted.
6   Meanwhile, make ricotta filling.
7   Pour filling into tin; bake about 50 minutes. Cool cheesecake in oven with door ajar.
8   Refrigerate cheesecake 3 hours or overnight. Serve cheesecake dusted with sifted icing sugar, if desired.
ricotta filling Process cheese, rind, juice, sugar and eggs until smooth; stir in fruit.

new york cheesecake

prep + cook time 2 hours (plus refrigeration & cooling time) serves 12

250g plain sweet biscuits
125g butter, melted
cream cheese filling
750g cream cheese, softened
2 teaspoons finely grated orange rind
1 teaspoon finely grated lemon rind
1 cup (220g) caster sugar
3 eggs
¾ cup (180g) soured cream
¼ cup (60ml) lemon juice
soured cream topping
1 cup (240g) soured cream
2 tablespoons caster sugar
2 teaspoons lemon juice

1 Process biscuits until fine. Add butter, process until combined. Press mixture over base and side of 24cm springform cake tin. Place tin on oven tray; chill 30 minutes.
2 Preheat oven to 180°C/160°C fan-assisted.
3 Meanwhile make cream cheese filling.
4 Pour filling into tin; bake 1¼ hours. Remove from oven; cool 15 minutes.
5 Meanwhile make soured cream topping. Spread topping over the cheesecake. Bake 20 minutes. Cool in oven with door ajar.
6 Refrigerate cheesecake 3 hours or overnight.
cream cheese filling Beat cheese, rinds and sugar in medium bowl with electric mixer until smooth. Beat in eggs, one at a time, then soured cream and juice.
soured cream topping Combine ingredients together in small bowl.

chocolate mocha dacquoise terrine

prep + cook time 1 hour 10 minutes (plus cooling & refrigeration time) serves 12

4 egg whites
1 cup (220g) caster sugar
2 tablespoons cocoa powder
200g dark eating chocolate, chopped
¾ cup (180ml) double cream
2 teaspoons cocoa powder, extra
mocha butter cream
1 tablespoon instant coffee granules
2 tablespoons boiling water
100g unsalted butter, softened
2¼ cups (360g) icing sugar

mocha butter cream Dissolve coffee granules in the
boiling water in small bowl; cool 10 minutes. Beat
butter in small bowl with electric mixer until pale in
colour; gradually add sifted icing sugar, beating until
combined. Beat in coffee mixture.

1   Preheat oven to 150°C/130°C fan-assisted. Line
three oven trays with baking parchment; draw a
10cm x 25cm rectangle on each sheet of parchment.
2   Beat egg whites in medium bowl with electric
mixer until soft peaks form. Gradually add sugar,
beating until sugar dissolves between additions; fold
in sifted cocoa.
3   Spread meringue mixture evenly over rectangles;
bake about 45 minutes. Turn off oven; cool meringues
in oven with door ajar.
4   Meanwhile, stir chocolate and cream in small
saucepan, over low heat, until smooth, transfer to
small bowl; refrigerate until firm. Beat chocolate
mixture with electric mixer about 20 seconds or until
just changed in colour.
5   Make mocha butter cream.
6   Place one meringue on serving plate; spread with
half the chocolate mixture, then top with half the
butter cream. Top with another meringue; spread with
remaining chocolate mixture and butter cream. Top with
last meringue layer; cover and chill 3 hours or overnight.
Dust with sifted extra cocoa powder to serve.

chocolate ganache & raspberry cake

prep + cook time 1 hour 50 minutes **serves** 10

⅓ cup (35g) cocoa powder
⅓ cup (80ml) water
150g dark eating chocolate, melted
150g butter, melted
1⅓ cups (300g) firmly packed brown sugar
1 cup (120g) ground almonds
4 eggs, separated
200g dark eating chocolate, chopped coarsely
⅔ cup (160ml) whipping cream
300g raspberries

1　Preheat oven to 160°C/140°C fan-assisted. Grease deep 22cm-round cake tin; line base and side with baking parchment.
2　Blend sifted cocoa with the water in large bowl until smooth. Stir in melted chocolate, butter, sugar, ground almonds and egg yolks.
3　Beat egg whites in small bowl with electric mixer until soft peaks form. Fold egg whites into chocolate mixture, in two batches. Pour mixture into tin. Bake cake about 1¼ hours.
4　Stand cake in pan 15 minutes; turn, top-side up, onto wire rack to cool.
5　Stir chopped chocolate and cream in small saucepan over low heat until smooth.
6　Place raspberries on top of cake; drizzle chocolate mixture over raspberries. Stand cake at room temperature until chocolate sets.

glossary

almonds

ground also known as almond meal; nuts powdered to a coarse flour-like texture.

caramelised toffee-coated almonds available from selected supermarkets, nut stands and gourmet food and specialty confectionery stores.

baking powder a raising agent containing starch, but mostly cream of tartar and bicarbonate of soda in the proportions of 1 teaspoon cream of tartar to ½ teaspoon bicarbonate of soda. This is equal to 2 teaspoons baking powder.

bicarbonate of soda also known as baking soda.

biscuits, plain sweet a crisp sweet biscuit without icing or filling.

butter use salted or unsalted (sweet) butter; 125g is equal to one stick (4 ounces) of butter.

buttermilk originally the term given to the slightly sour liquid left after butter was churned from cream, today it is made in a similar way to yogurt. Sold alongside fresh milk products in supermarkets; despite the implication of its name, it is low in fat. Low-fat yogurt or milk can be substituted.

chocolate

chips also known as chocolate morsels; come in milk, white and dark chocolate varieties. Contain an emulsifier, so hold their shape in baking and are ideal for cake decorating.

dark eating made of cocoa liquor, cocoa butter and sugar.

milk eating most popular eating chocolate, mild and very sweet; similar in make-up to dark eating chocolate, with the difference being the addition of milk solids.

cinnamon dried inner bark of the shoots of the cinnamon tree. Available as a stick or ground.

cocoa powder also known as cocoa; dried, unsweetened, roasted then ground cocoa beans.

coconut

desiccated dried, unsweetened, finely shredded coconut.

essence produced from coconut flavouring, oil and alcohol.

flaked dried, flaked coconut flesh.

shredded strips of dried coconut.

coffee liqueur we use Kahlúa or Tia Maria, but you can use your favourite brand.

Cointreau a citrus-flavoured liqueur based on oranges. You can use your favourite brand.

cornflour also known as cornstarch; used as a thickening agent. Available as 100% maize (corn) and wheaten cornflour.

courgette also known as zucchini; small green, yellow or white vegetable belonging to the squash family.

cream cheese also known as Philadelphia, a soft cow's milk cheese. Also available as spreadable light cream cheese – a blend of cottage and cream cheeses.

cream of tartar the acid ingredient in baking powder; added to confectionery mixtures to help prevent sugar from crystallising. Keeps frostings creamy and improves volume when beating egg whites.

cream

We used fresh cream, unless otherwise stated. Also known as pure cream and pouring cream, it has no additives unlike commercially thickened cream. Minimum fat content 35%.

soured thick commercially-cultured soured cream. Minimum fat content 35%.

thick we used thick cream with 48% fat content.

whipping a cream containing a thickener. Minimum fat content 35%.

currants tiny, almost black raisins named after a grape variety that originated in Corinth, Greece.

custard powder instant mixture used to make pouring custard.

date fruit of the date palm tree, eaten fresh or dried, on their own or in prepared dishes. About 4cm to 6cm in length, oval and plump, thin-skinned, with a honey-sweet flavour and sticky texture.

dulce de leche a caramel sauce made from milk and sugar. Can be used straight from the jar for cheesecakes, slices and tarts. Has similar qualities to sweetened condensed milk, only a thicker, caramel consistency; great to use in caramel desserts.

flour

plain an all-purpose flour made from wheat.

self-raising plain flour sifted with baking powder in the proportion of 1 cup flour to 2 teaspoons baking powder.

wholemeal flours milled from the whole wheat grain (bran, germ and flour). Available in both plain and self-raising varieties.

friand a small densely-textured sponge cake, popular in Australia and New Zealand and similar to a French Financier. Traditionally baked in oval shapes, they are made with butter, ground almonds and a variety of flavourings.

ginger also known as green or root ginger; the thick gnarled root of a tropical plant.

ginger wine (green ginger wine) a beverage that is 14% alcohol by volume and has the taste of fresh ginger. You can substitute it with dry (white) vermouth, if you prefer. The character of the ginger is drawn out by infusing it in spirit for an extended period.

glacé fruit fruit such as cherries, peaches, pineapple, orange and citron cooked in heavy sugar syrup then dried.

golden syrup a by-product of refined sugarcane; pure maple syrup or honey can be substituted.

hazelnuts also known as filberts; plump, grape-sized, rich, sweet nut.

hundreds & thousands tiny sugar-syrup-coated sugar crystals that come in many bright colours. Used to decorate cakes and party foods.

jam also known as preserve or conserve; usually made from fruit.

jelly crystals a powdered mixture of gelatine, sweetener, and artificial fruit flavouring that's used to make a moulded, translucent, quivering dessert.

kirsch cherry-flavoured liqueur.

lemon butter also known as lemon cheese or lemon curd; a smooth spread, usually made from lemons, butter and eggs.

maple syrup a thin syrup distilled from the sap of maple trees found only in Canada and parts of North America. Maple-flavoured syrup is not an adequate substitute for the real thing.

marmalade a preserve, usually based on citrus fruit.

marsala a sweet, fortified wine.

mixed dried fruit a mix of sultanas, raisins, currants, mixed peel and cherries.

mixed peel candied citrus peel.

mixed spice a blend of ground spices usually consisting of cinnamon, allspice and nutmeg.

nutmeg dried nut of an evergreen tree; available in ground form or you can grate your own with a fine grater.

nuts, how to roast place shelled, peeled nuts, in a single layer, on oven tray, roast in moderate oven for 8-10 minutes. Be careful to avoid burning nuts.

pecans Native to the United States; golden-brown, buttery and rich. Good in savoury and sweet dishes; especially good in salads.

poppy seeds tiny black seeds with a pungent flavour; store in an airtight container in a cool place or freezer.

raisins dried sweet grapes.

ricotta cheese a soft, sweet, moist, white, cow's milk cheese with a low fat content (about 8.5 per cent) and a slightly grainy texture. The name roughly translates as 'cooked again' and refers to its manufacture from a whey that is itself a by-product of other cheese making.

semolina made from durum wheat; milled into either fine or coarse granules.

sugar

brown soft, finely granulated sugar retaining molasses for its characteristic colour and flavour.

caster also known as superfine or finely granulated table sugar.

demerara a rich, golden-coloured small-grained crystal sugar having a subtle molasses flavour.

icing sugar also known as confectioners' sugar or powdered sugar; granulated sugar crushed together with a small amount of added cornflour.

raw natural light-brown coloured granulated sugar with a honey-like taste.

white a coarse, granulated table sugar, also known as crystal sugar.

sultanas dried grapes, also known as golden raisins.

sweet sherry fortified wine.

tangelo an orange-coloured loose-skinned, juicy, sweetly-tart citrus fruit with few seeds. Hybrid between a grapefruit and a mandarin.

treacle thick, dark syrup not unlike molasses; a by-product of sugar refining.

vanilla

extract made by pulping chopped vanilla pods with a mixture of alcohol and water. This gives a very strong solution, and only a couple of drops are needed to flavour most dishes.

paste made from vanilla pods and contains real seeds. It is highly concentrated and 1 teaspoon replaces a whole vanilla pod without mess or fuss as you neither have to split or scrape the pod. It is found in the baking aisle of many supermarkets.

pod dried long, thin pod from a tropical golden orchid; the minuscule black seeds inside the pod are used to impart a luscious vanilla flavour in baking and desserts. A whole pod can be placed in the sugar container to make the vanilla sugar often called for in recipes.

yeast a 7g (¼ oz) sachet of dried yeast (2 teaspoons) is equal to 15g (½ oz) compressed yeast if substituting one for the other.

yogurt we used unflavoured plain yogurt unless specified.

index

conversion charts

measures

The cup and spoon measurements used in this book are metric: one measuring cup holds approximately 250ml; one metric tablespoon holds 20ml; one metric teaspoon holds 5ml.

All cup and spoon measurements are level. The most accurate way of measuring dry ingredients is to weigh them. When measuring liquids, use a clear glass or plastic jug with the metric markings.

We use large eggs with an average weight of 60g. This book contains recipes for dishes made with raw or lightly cooked eggs. These should be avoided by vulnerable people such as pregnant and nursing mothers, invalids, the elderly, babies and young children.

dry measures

METRIC	IMPERIAL
15g	½oz
30g	1oz
60g	2oz
90g	3oz
125g	4oz (¼lb)
155g	5oz
185g	6oz
220g	7oz
250g	8oz (½lb)
280g	9oz
315g	10oz
345g	11oz
375g	12oz (¾lb)
410g	13oz
440g	14oz
470g	15oz
500g	16oz (1lb)
750g	24oz (1½lb)
1kg	32oz (2lb)

liquid measures

METRIC	IMPERIAL
30ml	1 fluid oz
60ml	2 fluid oz
100ml	3 fluid oz
125ml	4 fluid oz
150ml	5 fluid oz (¼ pint/1 gill)
190ml	6 fluid oz
250ml	8 fluid oz
300ml	10 fluid oz (½ pint)
500ml	16 fluid oz
600ml	20 fluid oz (1 pint)
1000ml (1 litre)	1¾ pints

length measures

METRIC	IMPERIAL
3mm	⅛ in
6mm	¼in
1cm	½in
2cm	¾in
2.5cm	1in
5cm	2in
6cm	2½in
8cm	3in
10cm	4in
13cm	5in
15cm	6in
18cm	7in
20cm	8in
23cm	9in
25cm	10in
28cm	11in
30cm	12in (1ft)

oven temperatures

These oven temperatures are only a guide for conventional ovens. For fan-assisted ovens, check the manufacturer's manual.

	°C (CELSIUS)	°F (FAHRENHEIT)	GAS MARK
Very low	120	250	½
Low	150	275-300	1-2
Moderately low	160	325	3
Moderate	180	350-375	4-5
Moderately hot	200	400	6
Hot	220	425-450	7-8
Very hot	240	475	9

This book is published in 2012 by Octopus Publishing Group Limited
based on materials licensed to it by ACP Magazines Ltd,
a division of Nine Entertainment Co.
54 Park St, Sydney
GPO Box 4088, Sydney, NSW 2001
phone (02) 9282 8618; fax (02) 9267 9438
acpbooks@acpmagazines.com.au; www.acpbooks.com.au

General Manager – Christine Whiston
Test kitchen and Food Director – Pamela Clark
Editorial director – Susan Tomnay
Creative director – Hieu Chi Nguyen

Published and Distributed in the United Kingdom by Octopus Publishing Group Limited
Endeavour House
189 Shaftesbury Avenue
London WC2H 8JY
United Kingdom
phone + 44 (0) 207 632 5400; fax + 44 (0) 207 632 5405
aww@octopusbooks.co.uk; www.octopusbooks.co.uk
www.australian-womens-weekly.com

Printed and bound in Thailand

International foreign language rights, Brian Cearnes, ACP Books
bcearnes@acpmagazines.com.au

A catalogue record for this book is available from the British Library.
ISBN 978-1-907428-80-7
© ACP Magazines Ltd 2010
First published in 2010, reprinted 2012
This edition published 2012 for Index Books.

This publication is copyright. No part of it may be reproduced or transmitted in any form without the written permission of the Publisher.

To order books:
telephone LBS on 01903 828 503
order online at www.australian-womens-weekly.com
or www.octopusbooks.co.uk